Celebrating Diversity

Celebrating Diversity

A Multicultural Resource

Luther B. Clegg
Etta Miller
William H. Vanderhoof Jr.

Delmar Publishers Inc.™

I(T)P™ *An International Thomson Publishing Company*

New York • London • Bonn • Detroit • Madrid • Melbourne • Mexico City • Paris
Singapore • Tokyo • Toronto • Washington • Albany NY • Belmont CA • Cincinnati OH

Cover Design: Hud Armstrong

Delmar Staff
Associate Editor: Erin J. O'Connor
Project Editor: Colleen A. Corrice
Production Coordinator: James Zayicek
Art and Design Coordinator: Timothy J. Conners

COPYRIGHT © 1995
By Delmar Publishers Inc.
a division of International Thomson Publishing Inc.

 The ITP logo is a trademark under license

Printed in the United States of America

For more information contact:

Delmar Publishers, Inc.
3 Columbia Circle, Box 15015
Albany, New York 12212-5015

International Thomson Publishing
Berkshire House
168–173 High Holborn
London, WC1V7AA
England

Thomas Nelson Australia
102 Dodds Street
South Melbourne 3205
Victoria, Australia

Nelson Canada
1120 Birchmont Road
Scarsborough, Ontario
M1K5G4, Canada

International Thomson Editores
Campos Eliseos 385, Piso 7
Col Polanco
11660 Mexico D F Mexico

International Thomson Publishing GmbH
Konigswinterer Str. 418
53227 Bonn
Germany

International Thomson Publishing Asia
221 Henderson Bldg. #05–10
Singapore 0315

International Thomson Publishing Japan
Kyowa Building, 3F
2–2–1 Hirakawa-cho
Chiyoda-ku, Tokyo 102
Japan

1 2 3 4 5 6 7 8 9 10 XXX 01 00 99 98 97 96 95 94

Library of Congress Cataloging-in-Publication Data

Clegg, Luther B.
    Celebrating diversity: a multicultural resource / Luther B.
Clegg, Etta Miller, William H. Vanderhoof, Jr. — 1st ed.
        p.   cm.
    Includes bibliographical references and index.
    ISBN 0-8273-6209-9
    1. Multicultural education--United States--Handbooks, manuals,
etc.   2. Education, Elementary—United States—Activity programs–
–Handbooks, manuals, etc.   3. Teaching—Aids and devices—Handbooks,
manuals, etc.   I. Miller, Etta.   II. Vanderhoof, William H.
III. Title.
LC1099.3.C54   1994
370.19'6--dc20   94-6814
                                                    CIP

Contents

Preface

Looking forward to a new century with all the challenges that confront our nation, we are increasingly aware that America is a multicultural society—in fact as well as in name. Therefore, it seems appropriate for curricula to reflect and accommodate the diverse needs of this changing population.

Intended Audience. This book is written primarily for those who are preparing to become intermediate or middle-school teachers in the twenty-first century. University faculty of methods and curriculum development classes may use the book as a means for assisting future members of the teaching profession in gaining knowledge about the materials and instructional activities used to promote multicultural concepts. Therefore, it may serve as a text or as a supplement to other texts used in education methods courses. The book is of value to students as they work to develop a solid base of activities and ideas that serve as a foundation for the initial stages of their teaching careers. We address the material contained in the text to teachers, using the second-person "you." We believe that it is also proper to include in our audience those students who have made a serious commitment to prepare themselves for the teaching profession, and who may now be enrolled in professional courses.

Practicing teachers face the true challenge of incorporating multicultural concepts into their classrooms, and thus this book should be of value to them. Although this book was written primarily for professionals in the area of social studies, we deliberately have included materials and suggestions for instructional activities that can be used within a variety of curricular contexts. Teachers of language arts, reading, and other subjects will find this book beneficial.

Organization: The book is organized into chapters which follow the calendar of the traditional school year, beginning with September. It is divided into four major sections by seasons. The seasonal events are from the orientation of our hemisphere. In general, we also describe climatic conditions from the perspective of the Northern Hemisphere. There are references,

however, to the climatic and seasonal differences between the hemispheres.

About the Calendars. Each chapter has a calendar of the month showing selected events and personalities. Following the monthly calendar is a daily listing of people, places, and events. We have included the names of events or the birthdays of individuals that we believe to be noteworthy, and which you might use as a basis for instructional activities. These represent only a selected set of people and events, for we generally have limited our references to items that are of particular relevance to the United States. It is intended that this section serve only as a brief reference or introduction to the topic. For classroom use, you may need to extend this information considerably. By consulting sources, either those included in the bibliographies or others, you can add more information, develop additional materials, or even create your own calendar for the month.

A blank calendar is included in the appendix. You may copy it for use to construct your own calendar of people, places, and events that are unique to your curriculum and local and regional area. There may be many events and individuals that would be more significant for your particular community than those we have suggested. While the contributions of the individuals on your calendar may not be well known outside the local community, the inclusion of such people and events may prove just as significant in accomplishing the goals of multicultural education.

About the Teaching Unit. The teaching unit in each chapter is related to some topic or aspect of multicultural education. The unit forms a major component of each chapter and includes suggested teaching activities and bibliographical data. The teaching units are independent of one another and need not necessarily be used during the month they are presented. It is likely that some will be more meaningful for your students if studied during the month in which they are shown, for example, December's "Winter Holidays around the World" and July's "Striving for Independence: A Continuing Struggle."

The units are suggestions for incorporating new or different perspectives on major historical themes. Therefore, they should be integrated into your regular instructional program rather than viewed as an added curricular segment. This position is seen as consistent with recommendations made by authorities in the field of multicultural education.

About the Potpourri Sections. Within each chapter are several suggested activities which we call "potpourris." They are directly or indirectly related to specific events or people connected to the monthly calendar. Each contains information as well as descriptions of short teaching/learning activities.

Caveat. In order not to mislead the reader, the authors wish to make it clear that this textbook does not contain techniques for teaching students from diverse cultural backgrounds. It does, however, provide you with ways to incorporate multicultural education techniques into your classroom. The teaching activities are constructed so that they can be adapted to different learning styles associated with students from a variety of cultures. The themes or topics of the units and activities were selected with the diversity of American cultural groups in mind. Other texts are available which have as their focus the theory and practice of multicultural education with specific pedagogical and curricular recommendations.

Acknowledgments

The authors and staff at Delmar Publishers wish to express their appreciation to the reviewers of this manuscript, whose thoughtful and constructive suggestions resulted in an improved text.

Sr. Rosemarie Bosler
Trinity College
Washington, DC

J. Perry Carter
Richland College
Dallas, Texas

Colleen Finegan-Stoll
Wright State University
West Chester, Ohio

Susanne P. Kirk
Xavier University
Cincinnati, Ohio

John Ragle
University of Texas
Austin, Texas

Timothy Reagan
University of Connecticut
Storrs, Connecticut

Jill Stanton
University of Wisconsin—Stout
Menomonie, Wisconsin

Theresa Sullivan-Stewart
Sangamon State University
Springfield, Illinois

José Vega
University of Wisconsin
River Falls, Wisconsin

Introduction to Multicultural Education

The stimulus for writing a book called *Celebrating Diversity: A Multicultural Resource* arose from several sources. First, although the United States has always been a society composed of different cultural groups, only recently have we attempted to ensure that the contributions of each group are included in curricular materials. Second, there is more diversity of cultural groups as well as a larger proportion of such students in today's classrooms than in the past. This is likely to result in significant cultural differences between teachers and students. Third, these groups of students, as well as the contributions of their cultures in developing the rich texture of the American experience, need to be recognized and celebrated in the schools.

What Is a Cultural Group? Each of us is a member of a variety of groups, one of which is a cultural group (Banks, 1991). A culture, as defined by some anthropologists, is the way a group of people adapts to its physical, social, and metaphysical environment. An ethnic group, such as Korean-Americans, is a microculture within a broader group or culture. The way an individual defines her microculture is related to the groups with which she associates and the importance those groups bring to her life.

There are many different microcultures within the United States. These groups share some aspects of the larger culture that unite all of the citizens of the country. However, within any microculture, there are other components such as values and traditions unique to it. Therefore, although there is a common history and set of traditions that all Americans share, within particular microcultures there may be some values and interests that differ from those of other groups. For example, however, all groups within the United States may celebrate the Fourth of July as a holiday. The way in which, or even whether, one celebrates a winter holiday depends on the microculture, either ethnic or religious, to which one belongs.

The cultural and ethnic composition of our nation has changed during the past twenty years. The numbers and national origins of new immigrants have dramatically shifted. Between 1951 and 1968, most immigrants to the United States came from Europe. From 1971 through 1980, however, European immigration fell to 18 percent of the total; from 1981 through 1988, Europeans constituted only 10.8 percent of legal immi-

grants. The majority of new immigrants now come from Asia and Latin America (Banks, 1994, p. 28).

Inspection of recent demographic data also reveals significant changes within the school-age population. In 1982, nearly three-fourths of the young people under eighteen were European-American (Pallas, Natriello, & McDill, 1989). Today, in one-fourth of our nation's largest urban school districts, a majority of the students come from diverse cultural and linguistic backgrounds. Projections made from these data suggest that by the year 2000, one of every three residents of the United States will be a person of color (Banks, 1994). By the year 2020, nearly half of the school-age population will be students belonging to ethnic and cultural groups other than European-American (Au, 1993). For example, in one Texas metropolitan school district, students speaking fifty-three different languages currently are enrolled in the English as a Second Language programs.

Heath (1983) points out that the characteristics of ethnic groups have led to conflict between the home and the school. Schools have been slow to adapt their curriculum and pedagogy to make them more compatible with the needs of these students. Instead, most curriculum and teaching and motivation strategies have remained unchanged.

Students of color are disproportionately represented in statistics of low-level achievement, dropout rates, and discipline infractions, leading to tension in many urban school districts. Banks (1994, p. 28) points out that because of this, "The parents blame teachers and administrators; the school blames the home and the student's culture."

To resolve this tension, schools will have to improve the academic achievement of their multicultural students by implementing a curriculum that reflects the cultures, experiences, and perspectives of these groups. One aspect of this change to a more desirable direction began in the 1960s and 1970s, when a variety of courses in ethnic and women's studies were implemented as a result of pressure placed on school administrators by ethnic groups of color to support a philosophy of cultural pluralism.

Diverse school populations, lowered achievement levels, and the need to reflect the experiences of all constituents have caused schools to begin to implement the goals of multicultural education. Multiculturalism is concerned with modifying the total educational environment so that it reflects the ethnic diversity of American society. After the emergence of the ethnic revival movement in the 1960s, curriculum and materials have been designed to respond to the needs of *all* ethnic and immigrant groups.

Banks and Banks (1993) propose multicultural education as an idea, a reform movement, a process, and a way of thinking and teaching. They offer curricular and pedagogical recommendations for reforming schools. This reformed curriculum incorporates the basic ideals of this country: freedom, justice, and equality. These recommendations require schools to create an environment in which all students have an equal opportunity to achieve at their highest levels (Banks, 1994; Grant & Sleeter, 1989; Parekh, 1986). Banks and other proponents of this view (Appleton, 1983; Bennett, 1990) have recommended the following principles related to multicultural education:

Instructional Principles

1. Students of all cultures are curious individuals who are capable of learning complex material and performing at a high skill level.
2. Each student has a unique learning style that may be related to the microculture to which she or he belongs.
3. Teachers should use the conceptual schemes, or background information, that students bring to school.
4. Teachers should have high and realistic expectations for all students.
5. Teachers should foster cooperation among all members of the school.
6. Teachers should treat all young people, regardless of gender, equally.
7. Teachers should help students to develop and foster positive self-concepts.

Curricular Principles

1. The curriculum should present diverse perspectives, experiences, and contributions, particularly by those who traditionally have been underrepresented.
2. The concepts taught should be relevant to diverse cultural groups and both genders.
3. The contributions and perspectives that are selected should depict each group as its members would want to be depicted and as an active and dynamic entity.
4. Curricular materials and displays should include all groups: different cultural and ethnic groups, handicapped individuals, and both genders.
5. Diverse curricular materials should be used to present alternative viewpoints.

6. Schools should create environments which are consistent with cultural diversity and democratic ideals.

However, Banks (1994) conceives of multicultural education as much more than content integration. His paradigm includes five dimensions: (1) content integration, (2) pedagogy of equity, (3) knowledge construction process, (4) prejudice reduction, and (5) an empowered school culture and social structure. *Content integration* refers to the extent to which teachers use examples and content from a variety of cultures. An *equity pedagogy* requires teachers to modify their instruction in a way to facilitate the achievement of all students by incorporating a variety of teaching and learning styles which are consistent with those favored by different cultural and ethnic groups. *Knowledge construction* involves helping students understand and determine implicit cultural assumptions, perspectives, and biases existing within a discipline. Teachers should endeavor to modify students' racial attitudes through pedagogy and teaching materials to *reduce prejudice*. An *empowered* school culture exists when a school empowers students from diverse racial, ethnic, and cultural groups.

Thus far, this introductory chapter has attempted to summarize the current views of major figures in the field of multicultural education. Now it is time to explicate the beliefs which shaped our work Every professional activity should be governed by the shared knowledge of the field and the author's particular perspective. Although we have been guided by the scholarly efforts of researchers in multicultural education, this work also reflects our own set of beliefs and operating assumptions. Our beliefs arose as a result of reflections upon the existing work by individuals who have clarified the idea of multicultural education, and their efforts to promote reform needed to ameliorate American education. The ultimate result desired would be the creation of a more equitable and just society.

These beliefs also reflect and incorporate significant values of the authors with regard to human beings and social groups in general, as well as responsibilities that educators bear for preparing future citizens who will work for the betterment of our society. These beliefs fall into two major categories. First are those that delineate the professional responsibilities of teachers who are committed to the implementation of recommendations for reform advocated by proponents of multicultural education. The second set of statements are generalizations about social phenomena that are relevant to the development of curricular plans and materials consistent with the ideas of multicultural education. It should be noted that this is not a complete set of our beliefs, but includes those that seem most pertinent to our particular task.

Responsibilities of Teachers Related to Multicultural Education

1. *Teachers must engage in **deliberate** educational activities that encourage the understanding and appreciation of the cultures that constitute American society.* Our attempts to assist teachers in satisfying this responsibility is reflected in almost all of the units and instructional activities contained in this work.

2. *Teachers' curricular efforts should take account of their students' cultural identity, yet must avoid precipitous judgments and stereotypes regarding cultural identity.* One should not infer cultural membership from a single factor, such as language or ethnicity. Otherwise, it is far too tempting to fall prey to the numerous existing stereotypes.

3. *Teachers must not assume that if an American family is associated with a particular cultural group it will necessarily maintain all the practices of that culture.* One should not conclude, for example, that individuals of Mexican descent will necessarily have piñatas present during their celebrations at Christmas or other festive occasions. Teachers should keep this in mind when interacting with students and when planning instructional activities for them. The degree of cultural assimilation evident will be a function of several factors, including the number of generations the family is removed from the former culture, the reason for emigrating, the motivation to assimilate one's family into the dominant culture more readily, and so on.

4. *Teachers should work to create a school atmosphere in which aspects of all cultures are included in all subject matter areas and are equally valued. In addition, students should be assisted in developing their own cultural, national, and global identities.* One of the benefits that accrues to those who grow up and live in a richly multicultural society is that while honoring one's own cultural identity, it is also possible to appreciate and value aspects of other cultures. We all gain by being familiar with the wide range of opportunities for enriched cultural experiences available in a multicultural society. The study of works of literature and the discussion of the contributions of individuals from various cultural groups may prove to be a significant factor in developing one's cultural identity. It is also likely to contribute to the improvement of one's self-concept.

No multicultural curriculum should pressure individuals to modify their own cultural identities through accommodating their standards to those of the dominant culture. In the classroom, this dominant culture is often that of the teacher, the person who holds the "balance of power." Instead, the curricular efforts of the teacher should be geared toward promoting a classroom environment in which students from the full range of cultures cooperate to produce a composite school culture.

Generalizations Regarding Social Phenomena

1. *Interaction between different cultures provides the impetus for creative developments in many intellectual and artistic areas.* The impact that peoples in the Near East and Africa had on the thoughts of Greek philosophers, scientists, writers, and artists during the golden age of Greece because of commercial trade and other cultural transactions illustrates this view. The rich and varied culture that we enjoy, and the significant achievements of individuals from each of the cultural groups that make up our nation, provide additional confirmation of this belief.

2. *At present, our society represents a "blending" of the contributions of groups of immigrants from many areas of the world along with those of the Native Americans.* Piaget has used the notions of assimilation and accommodation to explain the process by which individuals make sense of the world. We sometimes assimilate the outside world to our own set of cognitive schema, and other times we must alter our schema to interact more effectively and sensibly with the world at large. This seems to express quite well the reaction of new immigrant groups to the culture that they find when they arrive in the United States.

   All immigrant groups, whether they came to the United States in the recent or more distant past, faced difficulties in this regard. They had to accommodate their own cultural practices and behaviors to existing ones, while attempting to maintain the cultural practices that formed the core elements of social life in their homelands. The process of such interactions of the many immigrant groups within the existing society is a subtle and complex one. In interacting with the existing culture, no group leaves it unchanged, weaving its own threads into the tapestry that represents America. Even so, no group is able to live in such a rich cultural environment without being influenced by it; thus, even if a group does not wish it, its own cultural practices will be changed in some measure.

3. *All humans share in the quest to establish social organizations that will meet their basic needs for food, shelter,*

and security. Although their customs and beliefs may exhibit much diversity throughout the world, we believe that we share much in common with other peoples. Striking similarities exist among groups—for example, in their celebrations of events in the lives of individuals, family groupings, communities, and nations.

Our approach emphasizes both the multicultural and the global aspects of human activities. Although the description of a particular cultural practice may seem to highlight the diversity that exists among cultures, we attempt to show the common elements associated with human beings regardless of the physical environments and the institutional frameworks within which they function as social beings.

Today's classroom, with its diverse populations, gives the teacher the opportunity to celebrate and to use the variety of cultural experiences of the students as important resources. As teachers become aware of the diversity within their classrooms, they should take advantage of this. For, as Herber and Herber (1993) state, "Students become diverse resources for instruction when their minds are engaged and when their prior knowledge and experiences are utilized in instruction." Students who have lived in different parts of the world can share with each other information about the locations and places they know, their real life experiences, and the customs and traditions they practice. This reporting of real experiences makes information from social studies and literature texts come alive. In addition, when students come from a variety of cultural experiences, they offer differing perspectives on issues and interpretations of events and literature. Parents and members of extended families, when included as part of the instructional resources used by the teacher, also provide concrete examples, expertise, perspectives, and information. Thus, the teacher has the power to bring the community into the school and help parents realize how much the school is part of the community (Foerster, 1982).

References and Bibliography

Au, K. (1993). *Literacy instruction in multicultural settings.* Fort Worth: Harcourt Brace Jovanovich College Publishers.

Appleton, N. (1983). *Cultural pluralism in education: Theoretical foundations.* White Plains, NY: Longman.

Banks, J. (1991). *Teaching strategies for ethnic studies.* (5th ed.) Needham Heights, MA: Allyn & Bacon.

Banks, J. A., & Banks, C. (1993). *Multicultural education: Characteristics and goals.* Needham Heights, MA: Allyn & Bacon.

Banks, J. (1994). *Multiethnic education: Theory and practice,* (3rd ed.). Needham Heights, MA: Allyn & Bacon.

Bennett, C. I. (1990). *Comprehensive multicultural education* (2nd ed.). Needham Heights, MA: Allyn & Bacon.

Foerster, L. (1982). Moving from ethnic studies to multicultural education. *The Urban Review,* 14, pp. 121–126.

Gollnick, D. M., & Chinn P. C. (1990). *Multicultural education in a pluralistic society* (3rd ed.). Columbus, OH: Merrill Publishing.

Grant, C. A., & Sleeter, C. E. (1989). *Turning on learning: Five approaches for multicultural teaching plans for race, class, gender and disability.* Columbus, OH: Merrill Publishing.

Heath, S. B. (1983). *Ways with words: Language, life, and work in communities and classrooms.* New York: Oxford University Press.

Herber, H., & Herber J. (1993). *Teaching in content areas with reading, writing, reasoning.* Needham Heights, MA: Allyn & Bacon.

Kruse, G. & Horning, K. (1991). Multicultural literature for children and young adults. In *A selected listing of books 1980–1990 by and about people of color.* Madison, WI: Cooperative Children's Book Center, University of Wisconsin–Madison.

Pallas, A. M., Natriello, G., & McDill, E.L. (1989). Changing nature of the disadvantaged population: Current dimensions and future trends. *Educational Researcher,* 18(5), pp. 16–22. Cited in Au (1993).

Parekh, B. (1986). The concept of multicultural education. In S. Modgil, G. K. Verma, K. Mallick, & C. Modgil (Eds.), *Multicultural education: The interminable debate.* (pp. 19–31). Philadelphia: Falmer Press.

Section One: Autumn

There Is Something in the Autumn

RIPENING CROPS, falling leaves, and thickening coats on animals signal the onset of autumn and colder weather. Autumn or "fall," as it is called by those living in the United States, occurs at the autumnal equinox. This celestial event, on approximately September 21, marks the beginning of shortened daylight hours in the Northern Hemisphere and lengthening days and warmer weather in the Southern Hemisphere.

Countries in all parts of the world celebrate holidays. Holidays mark national, ethnic, religious, or personal events. Within the United States, people observe all of these different types of holidays.

North of the equator, autumn traditionally has been the time of harvest-related holidays, either secular or religious in practice, which have been held during both ancient and modern times. Thanksgiving is the American national holiday observed during this season. Native American Iroquois celebrated the harvesting of their staple foods by singing, dancing, and playing a type of dice game. Many African-Americans are reestablishing a tradition called Harambee. People who trace their heritage from China and India practice customs related to harvest holidays that differ from the traditional American Thanksgiving. For Jewish people, this season is one of the holiest of the year, containing holidays of reflection and atonement as well as an eight-day harvest festival.

Chapter 1

Thirty Days Hath September

For most American children, September symbolizes one thing: the beginning of school, along with school buses, new clothes, school supplies, and homework. For many adults, it also means Labor Day picnics, the end of vacations, the beginning of harvest, and cooler weather with the coming of the autumnal equinox in the northern half of the world. For Jewish people, September is a special month; four important Jewish holidays are observed in September or early October, including the new year, Rosh Hashanah.

People in the Southern Hemisphere view September in a different light. For them, the month marks not the end of summer and the promise of skiing and other cold weather activities, but rather the end of winter and the beginning of spring. School does not begin in September for children in Australia, New Zealand, and many other countries south of the equator. They have been going to school since January or February, so for them September is much like March is to children in America—a time for spring break.

September is derived from the Latin word *septem*, which means seven. September was the seventh month of the year in the old Roman calendar, but became the ninth month when Julius Caesar changed the calendar to make the year begin on January 1 instead of March 1. According to the old nursery rhyme, "Thirty days hath September," and thus it has always had, even in the old Roman calendar.

September

Sunday	Monday	Tuesday	Wednesday	Thursday	Friday	Saturday

SEPTEMBER

SELECTED EVENTS

1. Edgar Rice Burroughs (1875–1950)
2. Christa McAuliffe (1948–1986)
   Lydia Kamekeha Liliuokalani (1838–1917)
3. Prudence Crandall (1803–1890)
   Sarah Orne Jewett (1849–1909)
4. François René de Châteaubriand (1768–1848)
5. Johann Christian Bach (1735–1782)
6. Marquis de Lafayette (1757–1834)
   Jane Addams (1860–1935)
7. Brazil Independence Day
   Elizabeth I (1533–1603)
   Grandma Moses (1860–1961)
8. United Nations International Literacy Day
   Antonín Dvořák (1841–1904)
9. Cardinal Richelieu (1585–1642)
10. José Feliciano (1945–)
11. William Sydney Porter (O. Henry) (1862–1910)
12. USSR launch of first rocket to moon (1959)
13. Walter Reed (1851–1902)
14. Alexander von Humboldt (1769–1859)
    Margaret Sanger (1883–1966)
15. National Hispanic Heritage Month begins
    Agatha Christie (1890–1976)
16. Mexico Independence Day
    Mayflower Day
17. Citizenship and Constitution Day
    Andrew (Rube) Foster (1879–1930)
18. Samuel Johnson (1709–1784)
19. India: Gahesh Chaturthi
20. Ferdinand ("Jelly Roll") Morton (1885–1941)
    Upton Sinclair (1878–1968)
21. Herbert George Wells (1866–1946)
22. First all-woman jury in Colonies (1656)
    Michael Faraday (1791–1867)
23. Augustus (63 B.C.–A.D. 14)
    William McGuffey (1800–1873)
24. F. Scott Fitzgerald (1896–1940)
    Jim Henson (1936–1990)
25. Balboa views the Pacific Ocean (1513)
26. John ("Johnny Appleseed") Chapman (1774–1847)
    George Gershwin (1898–1937)
27. George Cruikshank (1792–1878)
28. Frances E. Willard (1839–1898)
    Kate Douglas Wiggin (1856–1923)
    Confucius (551–479 B.C.)
29. Horatio Nelson (1758–1805)
30. James Meredith enrolls in the University of Mississippi (1962)

People, Places, and Events of September

What's Happening in September:

All-American Breakfast Month
Chile National Month
National Rice Month
Women of Achievement Month

Other September Events:

First Monday: Labor Day
Labor Day weekend: Cherokee Nation Holiday
First week: Brazil Independence Week
Child Accident Prevention Week
Second week: National Hispanic Heritage Week

Events Scheduled According to Non-Gregorian Calendar Usually Occurring in September:

Rosh Hashanah (Jewish New Year)
Yom Kippur

September's Daily Calendar

1

Emma M. Nutt Day. Honoring the first woman telephone operator, who began her career in 1878.

Kanto (Japan) Earthquake Memorial Day. In remembrance of fifty-seven thousand people who died in disaster of 1923.

Korean Air Lines Flight 007 disaster. Commercial aircraft shot down in 1983 by Soviet interceptor plane, killing all 269 people on board.

Libyan Arab Republic Revolution Day. Commemorating revolution of 1969.

Mission San Luis Obispo de Tolosa (California) founded in 1772.

Birth anniversary of:
Edgar Rice Burroughs (1875–1950). Author of *Tarzan* series of books.
Rocky Marciano (1923–). Heavyweight boxing champion.

2

Birth anniversary of:
James Forten (1766–1842). Abolitionist movement leader born of free black parents.

Christa McAuliffe (1948–1986). High school teacher who was to have been first "ordinary citizen" in space.

Lydia Kamekeha Liliuokalani (1838–1917). Queen of Hawaii.

3

Qatar Independence Day. Located on Arabian peninsula; declared independence from Britain in 1971.

San Marino: Anniversary of Founding Day. Located in northern Italy; claims to be oldest state in Europe, formed in fourth century.

Birth anniversary of:

Prudence Crandall (1803–1890). Quaker school teacher who sparked controversy in 1830s with establishment of school for "young ladies and misses of colour."

Sarah Orne Jewett (1849–1909). Author of stories about New England.

Macfarlane Burnet (1899–1985). Australian doctor and expert in viral diseases.

4

Birth anniversary of:

François René de Châteaubriand (1768–1848). French poet, novelist, and historian.

5

Birth anniversary of:

Johann Christian Bach (1735–1782). German composer and organist.

Jesse James (1847–1882). Outlaw in the Old West.

6

Swaziland Independence Day. Located in southern Africa; became independent of British rule in 1968.

Birth anniversary of:

Marquis de Lafayette (1757–1834). French soldier and statesman.

Jane Addams (1860–1935). Worker for peace, social welfare, rights of women, and founder of Hull House in Chicago.

7

Brazil Independence Day. Commemorating break from Portuguese rule in 1822.

Birth anniversary of:

Elizabeth I (1533–1603). Queen of England; daughter of King Henry VIII.

Buddy Holly (1936–1959). Popular music performer and composer.

Grandma Moses (1860–1961). Modern primitive American painter who began painting at the age of seventy-eight.

8

United Nations International Literacy Day

Birth anniversary of:

Patsy Cline (1932–1963). Country and western singer.

Antonín Dvořák (1841–1904). Czech composer.

9

Bulgaria Liberation Day. Commemorating abolishment of monarchy in 1946.

California Admission Day. Became thirty-first state admitted to the Union (1850).

Birth anniversary of:

Cardinal Richelieu (1585–1642). French statesman.

10

Birth anniversary of:

José Feliciano (1945–). Puerto Rican composer and guitarist.

11

Birth anniversary of:

William Sydney Porter (1862–1910). Author who wrote under the pen name of O. Henry.

D. H. Lawrence (1885–1930). English novelist.

Ferdinand Marcos (1917–1989). Former ruler of the Philippines.

12

USSR launch of first rocket to moon (1959)

Birth anniversary of:

Irène Joliot-Curie (1897–1956). French scientist.

Jesse Owens (1913–) African-American athlete and Olympic champion who set twelve world records in track and field events.

13

Birth anniversary of:

Sherwood Anderson (1876–1941). Author and newspaper publisher.

Walter Reed (1851–1902). Army physician who proved that mosquitoes carry yellow fever.

14

Birth anniversary of:

Alexander von Humboldt (1769–1859). German scientist and geographer.

Margaret Sanger (1883–1966). Founder of Planned Parenthood.

15

Miguel Hidalgo y Costilla. Father of Mexican Independence; rang bell in Church of Delores (1810).

National Hispanic Heritage Month (September 15–October 15).

Honduras Independence Day. Gained independence from Spain in 1821.

Guatemala Independence Day. Gained independence from Spain in 1821.

El Salvador Independence Day. Gained independence from Spain in 1821.

Costa Rica Independence Day. Gained independence from Spain in 1821.

Nicaragua Independence Day. Gained independence from Spain in 1821.

First National Convention for Blacks held in Philadelphia (1830).

Birth anniversary of:

Roy Acuff (1903–1992). Country and western singer.

Agatha Christie (1890–1976). English mystery writer.

James Fenimore Cooper (1789–1851). Author of *The Last of the Mohicans.*

William H. Taft (1857–1930). Twenty-seventh president of the United States; born in Ohio.

16

Mexico Independence Day. Gained independence from Spain in 1821.

Malaysia Independence Day. Commemorating break from British rule in 1963.

Papua New Guinea Independence Day. Given independence from Australia in 1975.

Cherokee Strip Day. Parts of Oklahoma opened for settlement in 1893.

Mayflower Day. The *Mayflower* departed from Plymouth, England, in 1620 with 102 passengers and a small crew aboard.

Birth anniversary of:

Marvin Middlemark (1919–1989). Inventor of "rabbit ears" television antenna.

Anthony Panizzi (1797–1879). Italian librarian and political activist. Only librarian ever hanged in effigy.

Francis Parkman (1823–1893). Historian and author of *The Oregon Trail.*

17

Citizenship and Constitution Day.

Birth anniversary of:

Andrew (Rube) Foster (1879–1930). Organized first Negro league in baseball.

Hiram King (Hank) Williams (1923–1953). Country and western singer.

18

Chile Independence Day. Gained independence from Spain in 1818.

U.S. Capitol cornerstone laid by President George Washington in 1793.

Harriet Maxwell Converse. White woman, made chief of the Six Nations Tribe in 1891. Given the name of Ga-si-wa-noh, meaning "The Watcher."

Birth anniversary of:

Samuel Johnson (1709–1784). English lexicographer and author.

John Diefenbaker (1895–1979). Lawyer, statesman, and Canadian prime minister.

19

India: Gahesh Chaturthi. Sand models of Ganesh, the elephant-faced god, worshipped and carried in grand processions and immersed in the sea.

Mexico City earthquake killed ten thousand people (1985).

St. Christopher (St. Kitts) and Nevis National Day. Located in the Carribean; became fully independent of British rule in 1983.

20

Billie Jean King won the "Battle of the Sexes" tennis match (1973).

Birth anniversary of:

Ferdinand ("Jelly Roll") Morton (1885–1941). Jazz pianist, composer, and singer.

Upton Sinclair (1878–1968). Writer and politician.

21

World Gratitude Day to unite all people in a positive emotion of gratitude.

Belize Independence Day. Located in Central America; formerly called British Honduras; became independent in 1981.

Malta Independence Day. Located in Mediterranean Sea; became independent of British rule in 1964.

Birth anniversary of:

Herbert George Wells (1866–1946). English novelist and historian.

22

Republic of Mali Independence Day. Located in the interior of north central Africa; formerly called Sudanese Republic; gained independence in 1960.

First all-woman jury empaneled in Colonies (1656).

Tacy Richardson's Ride (1777). Rode to warn General Washington of the approach of British troops.

Birth anniversary of:

Michael Faraday (1791–1867). English scientist and experimenter with electricity.

23

Birth anniversary of:

Augustus (63 B.C.–A.D. 14). First Roman emperor.

Ray Charles [Robinson] (1930–). Singer, composer, and musician.

Julio Iglesias (1943–). Singer and songwriter born in Madrid, Spain.

William McGuffey (1800–1873). Educator and author of the *McGuffey Reader* series.

Louise Nevelson (1900–1988). Sculptor.

Bruce Springsteen (1949–). Singer and songwriter ("Born in the USA").

Victoria Claflin Woodhull (1838–1927). Feminist, reformer, and first female candidate for the presidency of the United States.

24

Trinidad and Tobago Republic Day. Located in northern South America; became a republic in 1976.

Birth anniversary of:

F. Scott Fitzgerald (1896–1940). Short story writer and novelist.

Jim Henson (1936–1990). Creator of Miss Piggy, Kermit, and the other Muppets.

25

Vasco Núñez de Balboa of Spain became first European to look upon the Pacific Ocean (1513).

Birth anniversary of:

Dmitri Shostakovich (1906–1975). Russian composer.

26

Birth anniversary of:

John ("Johnny Appleseed") Chapman (1774–1847). Planter of orchards and friend of animals.

T. S. Eliot (1888–1965). Writer, poet, and playwright.

George Gershwin (1898–1937). Composer.

27

Birth anniversary of:

George Cruikshank (1792–1878). English illustrator.

Thomas Nast (1840–1902). German-American political cartoonist.

28

Cabrillo Day. Commemorating landing in California by Portuguese navigator Juan Rodríguez Cabrillo in 1542.

Taiwan: Confucius's birthday and teachers' day.

Birth anniversary of:

Frances E. Willard (1839–1898). Educator and reformer.

Kate Douglas Wiggin (1856–1923). Children's writer and organizer of first free kindergarten on the West Coast.

Confucius (551–479 B.C.). Chinese philosopher.

29

Michaelmas. The feast of St. Michael and All Angels in the Greek and Roman Catholic Churches.

Birth anniversary of:

Horatio Nelson (1758–1805). English naval hero.

30

Botswana Independence Day. Located in southern Africa; formerly a British protectorate called Bechuanaland; gained independence in 1966.

First criminal execution in American colonies (1630). John Billington, one of the first pilgrims to land in America, was hanged for murder.

James Meredith became first African-American to enroll in the University of Mississippi (1962).

Birth anniversary of:

Truman Capote (1924–1984). Novelist and literary celebrity.

In the Beginning

Teaching Unit for September

A Word about this Unit. In the Northern Hemisphere, the opening of school in September is the beginning of a new academic year, an appropriate time to explore how many common elements found in all cultures began. This part of the book is a good place to start your study of diversity. Several themes are introduced that reappear throughout the other units. Among them: (1) the language, customs, and holidays that exist in the United States today were influenced by the many international groups that converged here; (2) humans, regardless of their ancestry or where they now live, share common needs that are satisfied in a variety of ways; and (3) understanding cultural differences helps to create a more educated individual. Hence, students are encouraged to collect information about a broad range of topics and human groups. They will organize, synthesize, and analyze the information in order to formulate and understand possible trends and generalizations. Material in this unit will incorporate and build on all of these themes.

Part I: There Was the Land and the Land Bridge

The Beginnings of America

Motivation. Ask the students the following questions and have them write their responses either individually or in groups. As they struggle with the answers, follow with "How do we know?"

Who were the first people to set foot on the land we now call the Americas?
How did the first people come to the Americas?

Immersion. In this part of the unit, students gather information about the topic. You can either read the short excerpts of information included in this text, read from a variety of trade books, or direct students to search for information using appropriate reference sources.

Information. Archaeological evidence, consisting of crude, chipped stone weapons, suggests that humans

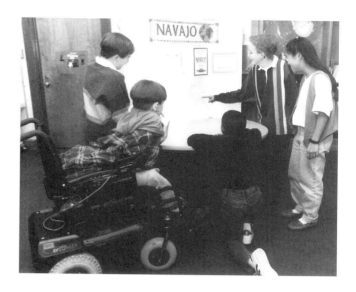

have inhabited the land we call the Americas for thousands of years. Historians generally hold that Stone Age hunters followed woolly mammoths and other animals as they grazed and roamed over the tundra. They eventually crossed over a land bridge from Asia to what is now Alaska. These hunters probably came from northern Siberia. This assertion is based on examination of the teeth of these groups. Indigenous peoples—Native Americans and Inuit (Eskimo)—have the same type of teeth as do people living in northern Asia today. Europeans, on the other hand, have a different tooth structure (Neal, 1981). Therefore, archaeologists have concluded that Native Americans and the people of northern Asia share a common genetic pool.

This immigration lasted for thousands of years before the earth's climate slowly began changing as temperatures grew warmer and the polar ice cap began to melt. The oceans rose, covering the land bridge with water.

One theory holds that these earliest immigrants gradually spread throughout North and South America. However, some scholars believe that the native peoples of Central and South America are descendants of the original inhabitants of the islands in the Pacific Ocean, who sailed to the western shores of South America or Mexico.

During this long period of time, great civilizations arose in the Americas. Three main cultures developed from these earliest migrations. One consisted of big-game hunters, which became the culture found in the Arctic and along the western coast of Canada. A second cultural tradition, called the Old Cordilleran, developed in the northwestern part of North America, from Alaska south to Oregon. The desert tradition was the third, developing and flourishing in the Great Basin, the Southwest, and in northeast Mexico. Some of these civilizations continue to exist and have become part of the many different peoples living in the Americas; others have disappeared, leaving only archaeological remains as evidence of their time on this land.

The first great civilization in southern Mexico was created by the **Olmecs** between 1500 B.C. and A.D. 400. The Olmecs built great stone monolithic heads and temples on mounds of earth. They probably ate cultivated plants as well as small game. This culture became the base for the Mayans, the Zapotecs, and the Teotihuacáns in the Valley of Mexico, northeast of Mexico City.

The ancestors of today's **Mayas** lived in what is now Guatemala, Honduras, and Yucatan, where they built at least sixty cities. This culture may have developed as early as 1500 B.C. and reached its peak about A.D. 880 (Leon, 1989). These early Mayas left structures and records indicating that they were master builders, mathematicians, and skilled astronomers. Their sophisticated mathematics, astronomy, and calendar, made the Mayas the most advanced civilization in the Americas, even outdistancing the Greeks and Romans of that time. However, an invasion of the Toltecs from central Mexico led to a drop in achievement by the time the Spanish arrived in the 1700s. Today, the descendants of the early Mayan people live in parts of Mexico and Central America.

The **Aztecs** lived in the Central Valley of Mexico from A.D. 1160 and flourished until the early sixteenth century, when they were conquered by the Spanish. They, too, had a sophisticated calendar, studied astronomy, developed a picture-based writing system, and built great pyramids. By A.D. 1500 they had built an economic and military empire that stretched from the eastern coast to the western coast of Mexico and extended south to Guatemala. Many crafts, words, foods, and beliefs of the Aztecs are still evident in the culture of their modern Mexican descendants.

Another group of aboriginal people of the Americas, the **Hopewells,** lived in central North America for more than six hundred years (from approximately 200 B.C. to A.D. 400) before disappearing. Archaeological discoveries indicate that they built mound cities in the area from what is now Kansas to Ohio and from Wisconsin to the Gulf of Mexico.

The **Incas** also built a large empire, but one which lasted fewer than one hundred years. Their principal city of Cuzco was built high in the Andes in present-day Peru.

Thousands of years after the first migrations across the great land bridge, others began to navigate the seas and explore the area now known as North and South America. Various types of archaeological evidence, both direct and inferred, indicate that explorers from Africa, China, Japan, Phoenicia, Ireland, and northern Europe probably came to America before Columbus.

Although some people may mark the year of the discovery of North America by the date of Columbus's first expedition, archaeological evidence suggests that many explorers reached American shores before Columbus. Based on pottery remains similar to those found in Europe and Asia, there is speculation that as early as five thousand years ago (Maestro & Maestro, 1991) **Japanese fishermen** may have visited South America. Remains of stone anchors similar to ones found in China suggest that **Chinese sailors** may have reached the west coast of the Americas. For example, evidence seems to indicate that during the fifth century, Hoei-shin, a Chinese Buddhist monk, explored portions of North and Central America. During the sixth century, an **Irish monk** named St. Brendan apparently made a boat trip from his homeland to what is now Newfoundland. A journal circulated in Europe about that time told of a man making a voyage across the Atlantic in a small boat constructed of wood and leather, and Europeans believed that this told of St. Brendan's expedition. Many scholars contend that there is evidence that the **Phoenicians** may have traded with people in the Americas.

The **Vikings**, who were originally from Norway, left evidence that they made voyages to the Americas. Leif Eriksson landed on the North American continent in the year A.D. 1000. However, this voyage and the subsequent establishment of a settlement in Vinland (Greenland) by Eric the Red were not well known in Europe until centuries later.

Mali, a country on the western coast of Africa, was rich and prosperous in the thirteenth century. According to written texts, the ruler of Mali outfitted ships to explore the Atlantic Ocean. Stone statues with facial features similar to people living in Africa have been found on land that contains the remains of the Olmec culture of Central America. Therefore, some conclude that explorers from Mali may have landed in Central America as early as A.D. 1200.

Early Explorers. During the 1400s renewed interest developed in Europe for exploration and trading. Portuguese explorers made voyages to islands in the Atlantic and along the African coast. **Bartholomeu Dias** sailed southward along the coast of western Africa and around the Cape of Good Hope.

Born in Italy in 1451, a young man named Christoforo Colombo, whom English speakers today call

Christopher Columbus, decided that if he sailed west across the Atlantic Ocean he could reach the trade in the Far East more quickly than if he traveled the more traditional eastern overland route. After eight years of trying, Columbus convinced Queen Isabella and King Ferdinand of Spain to finance his expedition. In all, Columbus made four voyages to America. He reached what is now Puerto Rico, Jamaica, Trinidad, the coast of South America, as well as numerous islands in the waters of the Caribbean Sea. Although he was mistaken when he thought he had reached the East Indies of Asia, he did discover the best possible sea routes between Europe and the Americas.

Another European, **John Cabot** of England, also made voyages across the Atlantic to North America. In 1497, he chose a northern route across the ocean, reaching what is now Newfoundland in Canada.

In 1499, **Amerigo Vespucci**, following the routes of Columbus, wrote about his journeys to South America. Unlike Columbus, he believed the lands he discovered were unknown continents. The name "America" comes from the name of this young Italian navigator.

Because the Europeans thought that this continent was unknown and unowned, competition between the various countries became fierce. Ruling monarchies financed expeditions to search for wealth and to explore and claim lands on their behalf.

In 1513, **Vasco Núñez de Balboa** was the first European to view the Southern Sea (Pacific Ocean) from his high lookout post along the central mountain range between the Atlantic and the Pacific oceans. A Spanish explorer, he sailed to Panama and then went overland through jungles and over mountains to reach the west coast of Central America. He is credited with naming the body of water he saw as "Oceano Pacific," meaning "calm ocean."

Jacques Cartier was a French navigator who explored the St. Lawrence River and claimed lands for France in 1534. The French and Spanish had both established trading posts and missions before the Pilgrims landed at Plymouth in 1620. Still, explorers continued to chart the land, which was virtually unknown to the Europeans. **René-Robert Cavelier La Salle** was a French explorer who led expeditions, beginning in 1681, that traced the Mississippi River to its mouth. **Meriwether Lewis** and **William Clark** were commissioned in 1804 by President Thomas Jefferson to explore the Missouri and Columbia river basins. Guided by an Indian woman, Sacagawea, and York, a slave owned by Clark, they explored along a northern route from the Mississippi River to the headwaters of the Missouri and on west to the Pacific Ocean.

Thus, the exploration and charting of North and South America were undertaken by a great many

WHO REALLY DISCOVERED THE AMERICAS?

Group	Time period	Places explored	Evidence offered
Asians	20,000 years ago	Alaska	Similarity of teeth of modern Asians and Native Americans
Phoenicians	1400 B.C.	Gulf of Mexico	Wind/water currents, *Ra* expeditions
Chinese	_____	Gulf of Mexico	Remains of the Olmec culture. Olmecs worked with jadelike stones. The discovery of stone anchors similar to those used by the Chinese.
Mali	1200s	_____	_____
Vikings	_____	_____	_____
Portuguese	_____	_____	_____
Spaniards	_____	_____	_____

THE AGE OF EXPLORATION

Mapping Africa

Person	Country	Place Explored	Date

Mapping the Arctic and Antarctic

Person	Country	Place Explored	Date

Mapping Australia and the Pacific Rim Countries

Person	Country	Place Explored	Date

Mapping the Oceans

Person	Country	Place Explored	Date

Exploring Space, the Last Frontier

Person	Country	Place Explored	Date

people from diverse backgrounds and from many countries of the world.

Instructional Activities

Activity 1.1: Who Really Discovered the Americas?

The unit on early explorers is a place to begin the study of the types of evidence historians use to validate information and to develop theories. Students can read the various sources cited and learn about archaeological evidence. As they collect information, they can complete the chart "Who Really Discovered the Americas?" You may wish, however, to use the chart as a transparency and complete it as a classroom project.

Analyzing Information and Making Generalizations

Based on the evidence you have discovered, which of the different groups do you think reached the Americas before Columbus?

What evidence did you use to make this judgment? What evidence is needed to prove conclusively which groups were among the first to arrive in the Americas?

In the Beginning There Were Other Explorers

This section has included a brief introduction to the exploration of North and South America. However, during the Age of Exploration, major expeditions were undertaken to other continents as well. Your students may be interested in researching these lesser-known explorers and their accomplishments.

Motivation. Begin by asking the class questions such as:

Who was the first European to see the source of the Nile River?

Who was the first person of European descent to explore the Arctic and/or Antarctic lands?

Why do people risk their lives to travel to unknown lands?

Information. Use the following "mini-facts" as a stimulus to interest your students to conduct additional research.

Roald Engebreth Amundsen was a Norwegian polar explorer. He reached the South Pole on December 15, 1911. How did he get there?

Robert Burke was an Irish soldier and police officer who, in 1860, led the first expeditions of Europeans across the Australian continent. Why would he want to do this and what did he expect to find?

Sir Richard Burton explored part of Africa. He may have been the first non-Muslim to enter Mecca when he did so in approximately 1853. What dangers did he face during his explorations?

James Cook may not be considered important to North Americans, but he is very well known in the Pacific Rim countries. He was the first European to explore New Zealand, parts of Australia, Hawaii, and many of the Pacific islands. He was also the first European to venture south of the Antarctic Circle. Trace the voyages of Captain Cook and and his ship, the *Intrepid*.

Mary Kingsley was a British explorer who traveled through West Africa from 1892 to 1899. She wrote books about her travels, helping Europeans to understand more about Africa. How difficult for a young woman was a trip of this nature in the late 1800s?

Francisco de Orellana was a Spanish conquistador who led a group of Europeans on an expedition to navigate the Amazon River in 1541–42. Use an atlas of South America to trace his voyage. How different might the rain forest of Brazil have been during Orellana's time?

Matthew Henson, an African-American called the "Trail Breaker," and **Robert Peary,** an American naval officer, are given credit for being the first nonindigenous persons to set foot on the North Pole. They stood "on top of the world" on April 6, 1909. What is the controversy that surrounds Peary's account of his discovery? Who actually was first to arrive at the North Pole?

Activity 1.2. The Age of Exploration

Directions. Use a variety of sources to find information about important explorers. Complete the chart "The Age of Exploration."

Analyzing Information and Drawing Conclusions

Based on your research, answer the following:

Why did people leave their countries to explore "unknown" territories?

Discuss how technology would have made a difference in the lives of the explorers.

How did these explorations and early settlements affect the lives of indigenous peoples?

References and Bibliography

Berdan, F. (1989). *The Aztecs*. New York: Chelsea House. Provides archaeological evidence of what is known about this culture. Illustrated.

Caso, A. (1958). *The Aztecs: people of the sun*. Norman: University of Oklahoma Press.

Driver, H. (1970). *Indians of North America* (2nd ed., rev.). Chicago: University of Chicago Press.

Haskins, J. (1992). *Against all opposition. Black explorers in America*. New York: Walker.

Irwin, C. (1980). *Strange footprints on the land: Vikings in America*. New York: Harper & Row.

Leon, G. D. (1989). *Explorers of the Americas before Columbus*. New York: Franklin Watts. Short summary of the various groups that lived in and explored the Americas before Columbus. Cites some of the evidence used to support the claims made for the many explorers before Columbus.

Logan, D. (1983). *The Vikings in history*. New York: Barnes & Noble.

Lomask, M. (1988). *Great lives: exploration*. New York: Charles Scribner's Sons. Brief biographical sketches of twenty-five individual geographical explorers.

Maestro, B., & Maestro, G. (1991). *The discovery of the Americas*. New York: Lothrop, Lee & Shepard Books. Presents information about the many hypothetical and documented expeditions of discovery of the Americas.

Neal, H. E. (1981). *Before Columbus: who discovered America?* New York: Julian Messner. Discusses evidence presented to support several theories about who discovered the Americas before Columbus.

Smith, J. H. G. (1987). *Eskimos: The Inuit of the Arctic*. Vero Beach, FL: Rourke Publications. Describes the history of the Inuit for the past eight thousand years.

Whitlock, R. (1976). *Everyday life of the Maya*. New York: G. P. Putnam's Sons.

Part II: Calendars—The Beginning of Recorded Time

Motivation. Ask the students the following questions and have them write their responses either individually or in groups. As they struggle with the answers, follow with questions such as "How do you know?" and "Why do you think this is true?"

How many days are in a week?

How many days are in a month?

When does the next day begin? How was that originally determined?

Where did the months and days get their names?

Immersion. In this part of the unit, students gather information about the topic. You can either read the short excerpts of information included in this text, read from a variety of trade books, or have the students search for information in appropriate books, encyclopedias, almanacs, or other sources.

Information. It is impossible to determine when the first attempt was made to record time and its relationship to the events that occurred in the lives of early peoples. Social scientists know that ancient people observed the earth and the heavens and made note of the special cycles of the sun and the moon. They saw that the sun appeared to rise in one place and then set in another, changing night to day and day to night. They observed that the moon, too, seemed to move across the sky, disappearing and then reappearing in a fuller shape at regular intervals. Early people realized that the sun somehow determined the seasons and that the moon could be used as a measure for recording time.

Early people noticed that the earth's revolution around the sun takes approximately 365 days and that this cycle seemed to be a natural way to mark time. They also noted the changing positions of the stars and sun at different times throughout the year. The first calendar probably had its origin in the observations of individuals who kept records of these occurrences. Eventually, they could predict the seasons and determine the ideal time to plant crops. Because of the need of humans to bring meaning and order into their lives, calendars were developed to measure and record the passage of time. Calendars allowed people to prepare for significant events and to record when those events would occur.

Ancient astronomers were the first to realize that the earth's revolution around the sun takes slightly longer than 365 days (i.e., 365 days and approximately six hours). This meant that, over a long period of time, annual religious holidays, which were originally set by the movement of the stars or the sun's position on the horizon, eventually became farther away from dates set centuries before. The need to adjust the calendar became evident. For example, on the old Roman calendar, Julius Caesar established the system of "leap years" to adjust for the change caused by the extra six hours. Julius Caesar was off by eleven minutes and fourteen seconds. This extra time amounts to about three days every four centuries. By the sixteenth century, using the Julian calendar, the first day of spring occurred on March 11 instead of March 21. Pope Gregory XIII ordered a calendar reform in 1582. The new Gregorian calendar initially added ten days, thereby correcting Julius Caesar's error, and then revised the system of calculating leap years. The Gregorian calendar is used today by many countries of the world, including the United States.

Throughout recorded time, civilizations of the world have developed thirteen different calendars, some of them still in use today. Arranged in alphabetical order, these calendars are: Aztec, Babylonian, Chinese, Egyptian, French Revolutionary, Gregorian, Hebrew, Islamic, Julian, Mayan, Roman, Stonehenge, and World (Fisher, 1987).

The **Aztec calendar** was really two interrelated calendars, one solar and the other ritual. The solar calendar was based on a 365-day year, but consisted of eighteen months—each with four weeks of five days, for a total of twenty days. Five more days were added at the end of the calendar to complete the year. These additional five days were considered to be unlucky. The solar calendar was used for marking the agricultural cycle and for setting major marketing days, which were held by communities once a week.

Within the 365-day year was a special group of 260 days, forming an Aztec religious calendar called the *tonalpohualli*. This calendar contained a sequence of twenty names. Each name was combined with each number to produce 260 days. The calendar began with one alligator and continued with two wind, three house, and so on. After 260 days, one alligator would appear again. This calendar was used by astrologers to predict a person's fate or to select good days for special events (Berdan, 1989, p. 85).

When both calendars were combined, they produced a fifty-two-year cycle. Because the seasons no longer matched, every fifty-two years the Aztecs began another fifty-two-year cycle calendar. It did not matter in which fifty-two-year cycle one lived, because the Aztecs viewed time as forever moving through these cycles.

The **Babylonian calendar** was developed in approximately 3000 B.C. by Sumerian priests/astronomers in order to plan for farming. In 1750 B.C., the Babylonians, who came after the Sumerians, devised a 354-day lunar calendar that alternated months between twenty-nine and thirty days. To make up for the actual time the earth took to rotate around the sun, two "leap" months were added seven times during each nineteen-year-period, once every two and two-thirds years. The Babylonians were among the first civilizations to develop the seven-day week.

Based on a 354-day lunar year with twelve months having twenty-nine or thirty days, the **Chinese calendar** is the oldest continuously used calendar in the world. The calendar is repeated in sixty-year cycles, five cycles of twelve years each. Each of the twelve years is named for an animal: monkey, rooster, dog, pig, rat, ox, tiger, hare, dragon, snake, horse, and sheep. The arrival of a new month is signaled by a new moon. Each new year begins when a new moon is closest to the constellation Aquarius, which comes between January 20 and February 18 on the Gregorian calendar. The ancient lunar calendar is still used to determine the New Year and other special Chinese events. However, except for determining religious and cultural holidays, in most Asian countries the Gregorian calendar is used as the daily unit of measure.

The **Egyptian calendar** was based on the flooding of the Nile River. More than five thousand years ago, farmers found that they could tell when to expect the flood by observing the sky. The flooding began whenever Sirius appeared on the eastern horizon. The Egyptians then developed a lunar calendar, which began the year with the first new moon following the first appearance of Sirius. This lunar calendar had twelve months of twenty-nine and one-half days each. Because this calendar was eleven days short of a 365-day year, the Egyptians occasionally added an extra month in order to keep the calendar consistent with the flooding of the Nile. Later, they were the first to develop a more accurate solar calendar with twelve months of thirty days each, which included the seven-day week. Because the new calendar was short by five days, these days were added to the last month of the year.

During the time of the French Revolution, which began in 1789, the National Convention developed the **French Revolutionary calendar** as a way to demonstrate the complete breaking away from French affairs and the monarchy. The new year began on September 22, the date which established the new republic. Like the Egyptian calendar, this one had twelve months of thirty days each. Five days were added to complete the 365-day calendar. This calendar was based on thirty-six weeks of ten days each. Every tenth day was a day of rest. The calendar was abolished by Napoleon Bonaparte in 1806.

The **Gregorian calendar** was established in 1582, when Pope Gregory XIII ordered the Julian calendar changed to correct the errors that had thrown off the dates of major Catholic holy days. Easter was supposed to be celebrated on the vernal equinox, which was to occur on the first Sunday following the first full moon after March 21. Because of the error of the Julian calendar, however, by the sixteenth century March 21 occurred before the equinox. The calendar was changed when the pope decreed that October 5, 1582, would become October 15, 1582, in order to bring the dates closer into line with the sun's position. Protestant Europe did not accept this calendar for nearly two hundred years. Many countries keep traditional calendars for calculating special festival days, but use the Gregorian calendar for conducting business.

The **Hebrew or Jewish calendar** is based on the lunar month. After being captives in Babylonia, the Hebrews formulated a lunar/solar calendar which used a seven-day week and a twenty-four-hour day, with each day beginning at sunset. In order to compensate for "true" sun time, the Hebrew calendar must be adjusted by adding seven extra months during each nineteen-year cycle. The Hebrew calendar used the same timing as that of the Babylonians, beginning the the new year in autumn.

The **Islamic calendar** was developed by the Muslims a few years after Muhammad's death. Muhammad was a prophet in southwestern Arabia and lived from 570 to 632. This calendar begins the year on the anniversary of the date that Muhammad was forced to flee Mecca and go to Medina. It, too, is a lunar calendar, fixing the Islamic year at 354 days. Each month was set to begin with the sighting of the crescent new moon. Extra days are added periodically to correct any misalignments between the lunar year and the solar year. Like the Hebrews, the Muslims begin and end their day at sundown. The first day of the week, el Jumah, corresponds to Friday on the Gregorian calendar. The Islamic calendar is used as the religious calendar throughout the Muslim world.

The **Julian calendar** had its beginnings in 49 B.C., when Julius Caesar reformed the Roman calendar, which was a 355-day, twelve-month calendar that soon became out of line with the solar year. Holidays that had been celebrated for many years were eventually occurring during the wrong months. Sosigenes, a Greek astronomer, was commissioned by Caesar to develop a 365½-day solar-year calendar. Sosigenes added ninety days to 46 B.C., bringing the months and seasons back to where they belonged according to astrological calculations. The new year was to begin in *Januarius*. Every fourth year, the second month, *Februarius*, would have an extra day. Julius Caesar's successor, Augustus, rearranged the number of days in each month. About three hundred years later, it was discovered that this Julian calendar was in error because leap years were not observed properly (Fisher, 1987).

The **Mayan calendar** was developed three hundred years before the birth of Christ. The Mayan priests/astronomers developed a precise system for measuring the movements of the planets, time, and eclipses. They developed two calendars that worked together: one a 365-day civil calendar and the other a religious calendar having 260 sacred days.

The **Roman calendar** is said to have originated with Romulus, the legendary founder of Rome. This calendar began at the spring equinox and consisted of 305 days divided into 10 months of thirty or thirty-one days each. The calendar was sixty days short, so Romulus interjected sixty extra days throughout the year. This calendar lost one day every four years, which meant that in 120 years it would be a month behind the sun and the seasons would occur in the wrong months. Rome's second king added two more months, Januarius and Februarius. He divided the twelve months into seven months of twenty-nine days, four months of thirty-one days, and one month of twenty-eight days.

He was short by ten and one-half days for a complete solar year and thus inserted days to make up the difference. However, too many days were inserted and the calendar became unreliable.

Stonehenge is still a mystery. No one knows who erected the great stone monuments on the Salisbury Plain in southwestern England. The stones are believed to have been brought from Wales about four thousand years ago. The monument is nearly one hundred feet in diameter and approximately thirty feet high. Two circles of huge stones surround two half-circles. At the center core of the inner half-circle is the Altar Stone. The Heel Stone is beyond the outer circle.

Stonehenge seems to serve as a calendar by the way the stones are placed. Sunrise, on the longest days of the year, is directly over the Heel Stone and casts a long shadow across the Altar Stone. On the shortest day of the year, when viewed from the Altar Stone, the moon rises between the two tall inner-circle stones that frame the Heel Stone.

The **World calendar,** the most recent instrument for recording time, was developed by Elizabeth Achelis in 1930. For this calendar, the year is divided into quarters, each quarter containing ninety-one days or three months. The new year begins on Sunday, January 1. Each of the four quarters also begins on a Sunday. To align this calendar with the 365-day solar year, a "Worldsday" is added following December 30 of each year and a leap-year day is added following June 30 of every fourth year. This calendar repeats itself exactly each year (Fisher, 1987).

Instructional Activities

Activity 1.3. How Time Flies

As an alternative to your presenting information about calendars, students can use books, almanacs, or other sources to research the topic. They may also interview people within the community whose experience includes the use of a variety of calendars, in order to find out the many ways that people mark the passage of time. Provide the students with a list of different calendars from which they can select one they are interested in researching. The chart "Researching the Calendar" can be used for recording and summarizing the information.

After completing the chart, the students should discuss or write the answers to the following questions:

Based on your research, how are all calendars similar and how are they different?

How did the association with other cultures influence the Gregorian calendar?

RESEARCHING THE CALENDAR

Name of Calendar _____

Country of Origin _____

Based on _____

Cycle _____

Names of the Months _____

_____

Unusual Feature _____

_____

Activity 1.4: What Is Your Sign?

As an extension of Activity 1.3, students can research the relationship between the zodiac and the Gregorian calendar. They could make a drawing of the signs of the zodiac and explain the differences between it and our calendar.

References and Bibliography

Adler, I., & Adler, R. (1967). *The calendar.* New York: John Day.

Apfel, N. (1985). *A first book: calendars.* New York: Franklin Watts.

Bendick, J. (1963). *The first book of time.* New York: Franklin Watts.

Berdan, F. (1989). *The Aztecs.* New York: Chelsea House.

Fisher, L. E. (1987). *Calendar art: thirteen days, weeks, months, and years from around the world.* New York: Four Winds Press.

September's Potpourri of Teaching Ideas

The purpose of each month's Potpourri of Teaching Ideas is to provide additional resources from which to build your curriculum. Most, but not all, of the activities listed each month relate directly to that month. It is not intended that you use them all, but rather that you choose those which are appropriate for your program. Although the topics are written for a particular month, many of them would be appropriate for use throughout the year. How you use these activities will depend on your curricular goals. You may wish to use some of the activities as they are presented, and you may need to modify some to meet your needs. Perhaps some of them will give you ideas for entirely different potpourris.

A Bowl of Rice, Please!

September is National Rice Month. Rice is one of the world's principal food crops, with more than half the world's population relying on it almost exclusively for grain and cereal. People in many Asian countries eat an average of more than two hundred pounds of rice annually, but rice consumption for the typical U.S. citizen is less than ten pounds a year.

What determines how much rice a person eats? Is it because persons of rice-eating countries like rice better than wheat or other grains? What determines where rice is grown? Is it because farmers in rice-producing countries enjoy growing rice more than other grains? Why does the average U.S. citizen eat so little rice in comparison to people in many other countries? As an introduction to the foods the world's population eats, students may research these and other questions to help them understand that food is not only a matter of taste, but also of many factors, including climate, location, and economics.

Try These Activities

1. Encourage students to research the leading rice-producing countries, as well as the states that are the leading rice growers in the U.S. Graphs depicting the production of these areas can be constructed.
2. A world atlas showing annual rainfall, weather patterns, and average yearly temperatures will help to explain rice production in certain locales. Find a map that illustrates topographical features of rice-producing areas and ask students to form hypotheses about why rice is more important to people in some countries than it is to others.
3. Rice cakes, puffed rice cereal, and cooked rice (served as a grain without sugar) may be prepared and sampled by students who have limited experience with rice as a principal food source.

Suggested Reading

Kenworthy, L. S. (1979). *The story of rice.* New York: Julian Messner.

Petersham, M., & Petersham, M. (1948). *The story book of rice.* Philadelphia: Winston.

Addams and Moses: Two Women, Two Achievers

Jane Addams and Grandma Moses, two women born in September 1860, one day apart, believed strongly in women's right to vote. Jane Addams was born on the sixth of September in Cedarville, Illinois, and is honored as a social worker, humanitarian, and founder of Hull House. Anna Mary Robertson, born in New York the next day, is remembered as "Grandma Moses," a primitive-style artist who first began painting after the age of seventy.

As a young woman, Jane Addams established a settlement house or neighborhood center for the immigrants of Chicago. There she operated a variety of programs—from day care for children to college courses. She welcomed every nationality and ethnic group. Addams was involved in many social issues, including fighting poverty and crime, training social workers, and organizing civic groups to bring pressure for change on elected officials. Some of her achievements include the first eight-hour law for working women, the first state child-labor law, housing reform, and the first juvenile court. She was also active in women's suffrage issues. Jane Addams died in 1935 at the age of seventy-five.

Grandma Moses lived a productive life for nearly seventy years before beginning a career as an artist. Although she was a farm woman with no responsibilities outside her home, like Jane Addams, she believed strongly in women's suffrage. In her autobiography she wrote, "I think women should vote. They have to make a living just the same as the men do, so why should they not have a say-so? Some women are more capable of holding office than some men are." After the death of her husband, faced with painful arthritis that kept her from needlework, she began to paint "for pleasure and to pass the time away."

At the age of eighty-one, Grandma Moses was awarded the New York State Prize for her painting *The Old Oaken Bucket*. Soon thereafter, her paintings were reproduced on Christmas cards, and she was on her way to becoming a national celebrity. When she was ninety years old, she received the Achievement Award from the Women's National Press Club, and at ninety-five she was interviewed by Edward R. Murrow, a noted TV journalist. Her last painting, *Rainbow*, was finished only a few months before her death in 1961. She died one week after her 101st birthday.

Try These Activities

1. Ask your students to compare and contrast the lives of these two contemporaries — an artist and a social worker—different but alike in many ways. The students can research the women's suffrage movement. When did voting become possible for women? Who were other leaders in the movement? What were some of the reasons given for not allowing women to vote?
2. Grandma Moses's paintings are exhibited in many museums. Locate reproductions of some of her

works in art books and ask students to study and discuss the style and techniques used.

3. Encourage students to seek examples of other people who accomplished unusual feats after the typical "retirement age" of sixty-five. The biography of Laura Ingalls Wilder reveals that she was born in 1867, a contemporary of Addams and Moses, and that she began writing her *Little House* books in her later years. She was in her sixties when her first book was published. Find examples of other men and women who made a difference during their "senior years."

Suggested Reading

Biracree, T. (1989). *Grandma Moses: painter.* New York: Chelsea House.

Judson, C. I. (1951). *City neighbor: the story of Jane Addams.* New York: Charles Scribner's Sons.

Meigs, C. (1970). *Jane Addams, pioneer of social justice.* Boston: Little, Brown.

Oneal, Z. (1986). *Grandma Moses: painter of rural America.* New York: Viking Kestrel.

Peterson, H. S. (1965). *Jane Addams, pioneer of Hull House.* Champaign, IL: Garrard Publishing.

Why Don't We Labor on Labor Day?

For many young people, the term Labor Day and the holiday festivities associated with it seem contradictory. It is difficult to relate "a day of labor" to an end-of-summer picnic. Labor Day is not a day of labor, as many children might perceive, but is intended to commemorate the work ethic and to honor the achievements of those who helped improve working conditions for the men and women who toil for their livelihood.

Labor Day falls on the first Monday in September, but it has not always been a national holiday. Some sources credit Peter McGuire, president of the United Brotherhood of Carpenters and Joiners of America, as the originator of the first Labor Day celebration. Other accounts indicate that the organizer was Matthew Macguire, a machinist from New Jersey. Regardless of who was first responsible, records show that members of the Central Labor Union voted to hold a "monster labor festival." In September 1882, a grand parade with thousands of men marched through the streets of New York City to celebrate and honor the value and dignity of work.

September was chosen as the best time for such a celebration because of the still-warm weather and the fact that it falls midway between the Fourth of July and Thanksgiving. In October 1884, at a labor meeting in Chicago, members voted to make Labor Day a national holiday. By 1889, more than four hundred cities were holding Labor Day parades and festivities. Oregon was the first state to legalize the holiday, soon followed by Colorado, Massachusetts, New Jersey, and New York. By September 3, 1934, all states had voted to make Labor Day a legal holiday.

Try These Discussion Questions

1. In 1848, Pennsylvania became the first state to pass laws that prevented children under the age of twelve from working. It was not until 1917 that Congress enacted national child-labor laws. What laws today relate to minors? Discuss whether students think the laws are too restrictive or whether they are too ineffective and need to be more strictly controlled.

2. In the last fifty years Congress has passed many laws that relate to the worker, including the Fair Labor Standards Act. What effect did this Act have on workers? Why was the law enacted in 1938 rather than ten years earlier?

3. One of the most pervasive labor laws passed by Congress regulates the minimum wage an employer must pay a worker. Discuss the benefits and shortcomings of such a law. Should minimum-wage restrictions apply to youth who are not supporting a family but want to work after school for extra spending money? Why?

Suggested Reading

Grigoli, V. (1985). *Patriotic holidays and celebrations.* New York: Franklin Watts.

Marnell, J. (1966). *Labor Day.* New York: Thomas Y. Crowell.

Scott, G. (1982). *Labor Day.* Minneapolis: Carolrhoda Books.

The Earth Quakes! The Earth Quakes!

In recorded history, at least three major earthquakes have occurred during the month of September. In 1923, an earthquake in Japan left one-third of Tokyo and most of Yokohama devastated, killing more than 140,000 people. In 1978, a killer quake hit Tabas, Iran, leaving twenty-five thousand dead. Seven years later, Mexico City was struck by an earthquake that registered 8.1 on the Richter scale. Thousands of buildings were destroyed, and an estimated twenty-five thousand people were killed.

Try These Activities

1. Locate Japan, Mexico, and Iran on a map. Where are they in comparison to one another. Discuss their locations and hypothesize as to why these distant areas have been hit by major earthquakes.

2. Use a recent world almanac as a reference to determine the following:

When and where was the earliest recorded earthquake? How destructive was it? Had there been other earthquakes before this one? How do scientists know?

When and where was the world's most destructive earthquake? How many people were killed? How much property damage resulted?

The *1990 Information Please Almanac* lists only twelve earthquakes from the birth of Christ to 1950. However, since 1950 another twelve have been recorded. What may be the reason for this spate of earthquake reports in the last forty years?

3. Use an atlas or wall map to locate where most earthquakes and volcanoes have occurred. Does there appear to be a correlation between the two? What is meant by "the circle of fire" and why do you think scientists have given it this name?

Celebrate Hispanic Week with Children's Literature

To spotlight Hispanic Week, discuss all of the Latin American independence days that occur during September and why Spain had so many colonies in this part of the world. It is also a good time to share some examples of children's literature that focus on this culture (see the Suggested Reading list).

When choosing books for this week, use these criteria:

(1) settings and plot should go beyond the superficial mindset of the tourist, and (2) Hispanic children should be presented as realistic protagonists. Make available a variety of books so that students can appreciate the diversity of this heritage. While reading, you may wish to serve Mexican or Hispanic food.

- -

Mexican Quesadillas

INGREDIENTS:
Flour or corn tortillas
Shredded mozzarella cheese
Mexican hot sauce

DIRECTIONS:
Heat tortillas. Spread generously with cheese. Fold in half and place on ungreased grill. Allow cheese to melt and brown to taste. Serve with hot sauce.

- -

Suggested Reading

Aardema, V. (1991). *Borreguita and the coyote: a tale from Ayutla, Mexico.* New York: Alfred A. Knopf. Folk story in which a sheep continuously outwits the coyote that is trying to catch it.

Beatty, P. (1981). *Lupita manana.* New York: William Morrow. Story about a thirteen-year-old girl who travels to the U.S. as an undocumented worker. The fear of deportation is a major part of her life.

Beherns, J. (1978). *Fiesta: Cinco de Mayo.* Chicago: Childrens Press. Explains activities for the celebration of this holiday, Mexico's day of independence from French occupation.

Garza, C. L. (1990). *Family pictures/cuadros de familia.* San Francisco: Children's Book Press. Memoirs of a Hispanic childhood celebrating family.

Hayes, J. (1987). *La llorona: the weeping woman.* El Paso: Cinco Puntos Press. Classic folktale of the Spanish-speaking people of North America.

Martinez, C. (1991). *The woman who outshone the sun/la mujer que brillaba aun mas que el sol* (Adapted by R. Zubizarreta, H. Rohmer, and D. Schecter). San Francisco: Children's Book Press. Ancient legend told by the Zapotec Indians of Oaxaca about a mysterious lady who walks with an iguana and carries butterflies and flowers on her skirt. Some villagers believe her to have mysterious powers; other villagers believe that she is evil.

Munson, S. (1989). *Our Tejano heroes: outstanding Mexican-Americans in Texas.* Austin: Eakin Press. Profiles of thirty-three significant Mexican-Americans.

Soto, G. (1991). *Neighborhood odes.* New York: Harcourt Brace Jovanovich. Collection of twenty-one poems honoring simplicity and the enjoyment of everyday life.

Soto, G. (1992). *Taking sides.* New York: Harcourt Brace Jovanovich. Story of a Latino youth in a bicultural society. The hero, Lincoln Mendoza, has just moved to the suburbs from the barrios of San Francisco. Conflict arises when Lincoln must face his old team in a basketball game.

Harris, V., et al. (1993, March). Bookalogues: multicultural literature. *Language Arts,* 215–224.

Ramirez, G., & Ramirez, J. L. (1994). *Multiethnic children's literature.* Albany: Delmar Publishers.

Begin a New Tradition

The beginning of the new school year may be the time to try some new traditions. The one suggested here is a tradition that is practiced by Jewish people during the holiday of Rosh Hashanah, or New Year. This holiday occurs in September or early October. (Because Jewish festivals are determined by a lunar calendar, the exact date on the Gregorian calendar varies.) During Rosh Hashanah it is the custom to eat a fruit, usually a slice of apple, dipped in honey to ensure a "sweet year." Although a prayer would be recited by Jews over this food, the custom is not a religious ritual but rather a folkway. You and your students may want to begin your year together by dipping fruit in some honey in anticipation of a "sweet year." No prayers are necessary.

Chapter 2

The Colors of October

October is derived from the Latin word *octo,* which means eight (think of an octopus with eight tentacles), but when the calendar was changed by Pope Gregory XIII in 1582, October became the tenth month of the year.

October is a month that has varying significance for different groups. It is a time when people living in the less temperate parts of the Northern Hemisphere harvest their crops and prepare for the rigors of the coming winter months. In the Southern Hemisphere, however, people look forward to the warmth of summer. October is also a time for celebration and commemoration of important events. In Nigeria, this is the month in which Nigerians celebrate their independence; Polish-Americans and others in the United States commemorate the role of a Polish nobleman, Casimir Pulaski, who was one of a number of individuals who left their homelands to help establish America.

Such commemorations also reveal the disagreements that often arise as different individuals are credited for significant discoveries. For example, during October, Leif Eriksson is celebrated, for there are those who believe that the Vikings were the first Europeans to set foot on American soil. Columbus Day also is celebrated in October, and many give him credit for his explorations. Teachers have become more sensitive to the fact that neither of these individuals—nor, for that matter, any other European—really "discovered" the Americas; entire societies had been here for millennia before the arrival of other groups.

October is also a month of special significance for many religious groups. We may think of it as the tenth month of the year, but for many of the Hindu faith, Diwali, or the Festival of Lights, which falls within the month of October or November, is the first day of the year.

October

Sunday	Monday	Tuesday	Wednesday	Thursday	Friday	Saturday

OCTOBER

People, Places, and Events of October

What's Happening in October:

Brazil: Festival of Penha Month
Family History Month
National AIDS Awareness Month
Polish-American Heritage Month

Other October Events:

First week: Universal Children's Week
Minority Enterprise Development Week
First or second week: Fire Prevention Week
First Sunday: Germany: Erntedankfest (Harvest Thanksgiving Festival)
Grandparents' Day
First Monday: Child Health Day
Second Sunday: Brazil: Beginning of Cirio de Nazare (greatest festival of northern Brazil)
American and Western Samoa: White Sunday (Most important day of the year for children, as traditional roles are reversed. Children, dressed in white, lead church services, are served special foods, and receive gifts.)
Second Monday: Canadian Thanksgiving Day

Events Scheduled According to Non-Gregorian Calendar Usually Occurring in October:

Sukkoth

October's Daily Calendar

1

Nigeria Independence Day. This West African nation became independent of British rule in 1960 and a republic on this date in 1963.
National Book It Day (largest reading incentive program in America).
Korea: Armed Forces Day.
Tuvalu National Holiday. Commemorating independence from Britain in 1978; group of nine islands located in the southwest Pacific Ocean.
United Nations International Day for the Elderly.
Birth anniversary of:
  Jimmy Carter (1924–). Thirty-ninth president of the United States; born in Georgia.
  Vladimir Horowitz (1904–1989). One of the world's greatest pianists.

2

Thurgood Marshall. First African-American to serve as associate justice of U.S. Supreme Court, sworn into office (1967).

Charlie Brown and Snoopy cartoon characters first drawn by Charles M. Schulz (1950).

Birth anniversary of:
Mohandas Karamchand (Mahatma) Gandhi (1869–1948). Indian political and spiritual leader.

3

German Reunification. East and West Germany reunited (1990).

Honduras: Francisco Morazan Holiday. National hero born in 1799.

Korea National Foundation Day. (Also called Tangun Day to commemorate the day when the legendary founder of the Korean nation, Tangun, established his kingdom of Chosun in 2333 B.C.)

First woman U.S. senator, Mrs. W. H. Felton of Georgia, appointed (1922).

Netherlands: Relief of Leiden Day. Celebrating the liberation of Leiden in 1574.

4

Gregorian Calendar Adjustment Anniversary. Pope Gregory XIII decreed that the day following Tuesday, October 4, 1582, should be Friday, October 15, 1582, thus correcting the Julian calendar (then ten days out of date).

Lesotho Independence Day. Located in southern Africa; became independent of British rule in 1966.

Birth anniversary of:
Rutherford Birchard Hayes (1822–1893). Nineteenth president of the United States; born in Ohio.
Edward L. Stratemeyer (1862–1930). Creator of *The Bobbsey Twins*, *The Hardy Boys*, and *Nancy Drew* book series.

5

Chief Joseph surrenders. (Chief Joseph made his famous speech, "From where the sun now stands, I will fight no more forever," in 1877.)

Death of Tecumseh (1813). Regarded as one of the greatest Native Americans.

Birth anniversary of:
Chester Alan Arthur (1830–1886). Twenty-first president of the United States; born in Vermont.
Robert Hutchings Goddard (1882–1945). "Father of the Space Age."

6

Founding of the American Library Association (1876).

Birth anniversary of:
Jenny Lind (1820–1887). Swedish opera singer.
Karol Szymanowski (1882–1937). Polish composer.
George Westinghouse (1846–1914). Inventor.

7

Birth anniversary of:
Heinrich Himmler (1900–1945). Notorious German Nazi leader and chief of the secret police.
James Whitcomb Riley (1849–1916). American "Hoosier" poet.

8

Alvin C. York Day. World War I hero who, on this day, killed 20 enemy soldiers and captured 132 enemy troops.

Great Fire of Chicago began (1871). Destroyed much of the city and killed 250 people.

Birth anniversary of:
Jesse Jackson (1941–) African-American civil rights leader and politician.

9

Iceland: Leif Eriksson Day. Celebrating the landing on North American soil in the year 1000 by this Norse explorer.

Korea: Alphabet Day (Hangul). Celebrating the anniversary of promulgation of the twenty-four-letter phonetic alphabet by King Sejong in 1446.

Founding of Mission Dolores (1776). Oldest building in San Francisco.

Uganda Independence Day. Gained independence from Britain in 1962.

Birth anniversary of:
John Lennon (1940–1980). English composer, musician, and member of The Beatles.

10

Double Tenth Day. Tenth day of the tenth month is observed by many Chinese to commemorate the revolution against the Manchu dynasty in 1911.

Fiji Independence Day. Became independent of British rule in 1970.

Birth anniversary of:
Paul Kruger (1825–1904). Former president of the Republic of South Africa and leader of the Boers.
Guiseppe Verdi (1813–1901). Italian composer of opera, including *La Traviata* and *Aïda*.

11

Birth anniversary of:

Mason Locke Weems (1759–1825). Writer of fictitious stories presented as historical fact, including the story of George Washington and the cherry tree.

Anna Eleanor Roosevelt (1884–1962). Wife of President Franklin Roosevelt and the first wife of a president to hold a news conference in the White House.

12

Columbus Day. (Observed in Chile, Costa Rica, Guatemala, Mexico, Spain; observed in the United States on the second Monday in October.)

Mexico: Dia de la Raza. Commemorating the discovery of America, as well as the cultural heritage of Native American, Spanish, and Hispanic peoples.

Equatorial Guinea Independence Day. West African nation, first ruled by Portugal and later by Spain; gained independence in 1968.

Birth anniversary of:

Ronald E. McNair (1950–1986). Second African-American astronaut in space; killed in the explosion of the space shuttle *Challenger*.

13

Birth anniversary of:

Jesse Leroy Brown (1926–1950). First African-American naval aviator.

Molly Pitcher (1754–1832). Heroine of the American Revolution.

Margaret Thatcher (1925–). First woman elected as prime minister of Britain.

14

Establishment of Peace Corps in 1960. Created by John F. Kennedy; has since drawn more than one hundred thousand volunteers into service.

Birth anniversary of:

Dwight David Eisenhower (1890–1969). Thirty-fourth president of the United States; born in Texas.

William Penn (1644–1718). Founder of Pennsylvania.

15

Crow Reservation opened for settlement. The Crow nation was paid fifty cents an acre for 1.8 million acres of land opened to white settlers in 1892.

Birth anniversary of:

Lee A. Iacocca (1924–). Son of Italian immigrant parents; became chairman of Chrysler Corporation.

Friedrich Wilhelm Nietzsche (1844–1900). German philosopher.

16

John Brown's raid (1859). Abolitionist John Brown and a band of about twenty men seized the U.S. arsenal at Harper's Ferry, West Virginia.

Execution of Marie Antoinette (1793). Accused of extravagance and beheaded during the French Revolution.

United Nations World Food Day. Established to create awareness of world food problems.

Birth anniversary of:

David Ben-Gurion (1886–1973). First prime minister of Israel.

Noah Webster (1758–1843). Compiler of the earliest American dictionary of the English language.

Oscar Wilde (1854–1900). Irish poet and playwright.

17

Black Poetry Day. Established to recognize the contributions of African-American poets and to honor Jupiter Hammon.

Birth anniversary of:

Jupiter Hammon (ca. 1720–1800). First African-American poet published in the United States.

18

Alaska Day. Commemorating the transfer of ownership of Alaska from Russia to the United States in 1867.

Canada: Persons Day. Established to commemorate the 1929 ruling that declared women to be persons (in matters of rights and privileges) in Canada.

Birth anniversary of:

Salomon Auguste Andree (1854–1897). Swedish balloonist and explorer of the North Pole.

19

Evaluate Your Life Day. Established to encourage people to check where they are headed and to determine where they want to be.

Yorktown Day. Last major battle of the American Revolution (1781). Called by some "America's Real Independence Day."

20

Birth of the Bab (1819). Observance of the anniversary of the birth of Siyyid Ali Muhammad, "the Bab," in Persia (now Iran). The Bab was a prophet of the Baha'i faith.

Birth anniversary of:

John Dewey (1859–1952). Psychologist, philosopher, and educational reformer.

Christopher Wren (1632–1723). English architect, astronomer, and mathematician.

21

First incandescent lamp demonstration by Thomas A. Edison (1879).

India: Dussehra/Durga Puja. Important Hindu festival celebrating the triumph of good over evil in the victory of Lord Ramachandra over Ravana.

Somalia National Day. Commemorating the Supreme Revolutionary Council's seizure of power in 1969.

Birth anniversary of:

Samuel Taylor Coleridge (1772–1834). English poet and essayist.

22

Cuban missile crisis (1962). President Kennedy demanded that Soviet missiles be removed from Cuba.

Birth anniversary of:

Franz Liszt (1811–1886). Hungarian composer.

23

Hungary Declaration of Independence from USSR (1989).

Singapore: Festival of the Nine Emperor Gods.

Swallows depart from San Juan Capistrano. Traditional day that swallows leave for the winter before returning the following spring on March 19.

Thailand: Chulalongkorn Day. Commemorating the death of King Chulalongkorn the Great, who, after a reign of forty-two years, died in 1910.

Birth anniversary of:

Nicolas Appert (1752–1841). French chef, inventor, and author, known as the "Father of Canning" for developing a method to preserve foods.

Gertrude Ederle (1906–). Swimming champion; first woman to swim the English Channel.

24

United Nations Day. Commemorating the founding of the United Nations in 1945.

Zambia Independence Day. Instruments of Independence signed in 1964, removing the nation from British rule.

25

Death of Geoffrey Chaucer (1400). English author of *The Canterbury Tales*.

First Female FBI Agents Anniversary (1972).

Taiwan: Retrocession Day. Commemorating the return of Taiwan to Chinese rule in 1945 after fifty years of Japanese occupation.

Birth anniversary of:

Pablo Ruiz Picasso (1881–1973). Spanish artist regarded by many as the greatest artist of the twentieth century.

26

Erie Canal opened to provide a waterway from Lake Erie to the Hudson River (1825).

Mule Day. Anniversary of the importation of Spanish burro jacks (males) to the United States from Spain in 1785. George Washington is said to have bred the first mules in America.

27

Navy Day (observed since 1922).

New York City subway began operation as the first underground and underwater rail system in the world (1904).

Saint Vincent and the Grenadines Independence Day. Gained independence from Britian in 1979.

Birth anniversary of:

Niccolò Paganini (1782–1840). Italian violin virtuoso.

Theodore Roosevelt (1858–1919). Twenty-sixth president of the United States; born in New York. First president to ride in an automobile (1902) and in an airplane (1910).

Dylan Thomas (1914–1953). Welsh poet and playwright.

28

Czechoslovakia Foundation of the Republic Day. Commemorating the historic uniting of the Czechs and Slovaks to form Czechoslovakia (1918).

Anniversary of appointment of first woman U.S. Ambassador (1949).

Greece: Ohi Day. Commemorating Greek resistance to attack by Mussolini's troops in 1940. (*Ohi* means no!).

Founding of Harvard University (1636). First American university.

Hungary: Anniversary of the 1956 Revolution.

St. Jude's Day. Saint of hopeless causes; popular with those who attempt the impossible and with students who ask for help on exams.

Statue of Liberty dedication (1886).

Birth anniversary of:

James Cook (1728–1779). English sea captain and explorer.

Anna Elizabeth Dickinson (1842–1932). Advocate of abstinence, abolition, and women's suffrage who earned the title of "American Joan of Arc."

Desiderius Erasmus (1467–1536). Dutch author and scholar.

Jonas Salk (1914–). Developer of the Salk polio vaccine.

29

Collapse of the U.S. stock market (1929). This particular Tuesday, following the panic of "Black Thursday," saw the collapse of the New York Stock Exchange and marked the beginning of the Great Depression.

Turkey Republic Day. Republic founded in 1923.

Birth anniversary of:

James Boswell (1740–1795). Scottish biographer.

30

"War of the Worlds" broadcast (1938). Orson Welles created panic when he broadcast H. G. Wells's *War of the Worlds*, which described a "realistic" Martian invasion of New Jersey.

Birth anniversary of:

John Adams (1735–1826). Second president of the United States; born in Massachusetts. (Adams wrote in a letter to Thomas Jefferson, "You and I ought not to die before we have explained ourselves to each other." They both died on the same day, July 4, 1826.)

Charles Atlas [Angelo Siciliano] (1894–1972). Bodybuilder and "ex-ninety-seven-pound weakling," born in Italy.

Ezra Loomis Pound (1885–1972). American poet.

31

Halloween or All Hallow's Eve. Occurs before the Feast of All Saints Day on November 1. Based on ancient celebrations combining autumn festivals and Christmas celebrations.

Mount Rushmore completion. After fourteen years of work, sculptures of the heads of Washington, Jefferson, Lincoln, and Theodore Roosevelt were completed in 1941.

National Magic Day. Commemorating the death of Harry Houdini in 1926.

Nevada Admission Day. Became the thirty-sixth state admitted to the Union (1864).

Birth anniversary of:

Chiang Kai-shek (1887–1975). Chinese soldier and statesman.

John Keats (1795–1821). English poet.

Michael Landon (1936–1991). Television actor who played the role of Charles Ingalls on *Little House on the Prairie*.

Juliette Gordon Low (1860–1927). Founded the Girl Scouts of the USA (1912).

Ethel Waters (1896–1977). African-American singer and actress.

Native Americans—The First Nations of the Western Hemisphere

Teaching Unit for October

A Word about This Unit. This unit illustrates the concepts of **power** and **social control** in terms of the discipline of social studies. Banks (1990, p. 349) defines power as "the ability of one individual or group to influence, change, modify, or in some other way affect the behavior of others." Social control refers to the regulation of the behavior of individuals or groups, usually by laws and rules that emerge from a society. The status of present-day Native Americans basically can be attributed to these concepts. European settlers held power over Native Americans—first with guns, eventually with technology (i.e., steel plows, railroads, and cities), and finally by sheer force of numbers. Over the course of time, federal laws were created to regulate and thus exert social control over the lives of Native Americans. The Native American was powerless to determine his own destiny and to counter the forces of "progress" that moved from the East Coast, across the Great Plains, and eventually to the shores of the Pacific Ocean. This unit contains other concepts and generalizations on which you may wish to focus. However, those of power and social control will predominate in the presentation of this unit.

This unit shows how one group of individuals has used power to exert social control over another group. In addition, it attempts to counteract myths, stereotypes, and misinformation about America's first peoples. The image of the Native American held by many has been shaped largely by movies and television programs. For many years "cowboy and Indian" stories were played out on television and movie screens every Saturday across the United States, and they usually involved one basic plot: white settlers on the frontier—farmers, ranchers, merchants, "good, God-fearing, law-abiding citizens"—were constantly engaged in a battle to protect their homes and their lives from brutally savage "redskins" in war paint who routinely scalped fair-haired women and innocent children.

This portrayal was especially evident in films produced before 1960. Jamake Highwater (1975, p. xv), a Native American writer of juvenile and adult literature, was so affected as a child by this image that, years later, he wrote of his childhood, "I remember the faces in the western films I watched as a child. . . . John Wayne was leading a cavalry charge against the 'savages': godless, cruel animals sneaking through the tall grass." It was not until years later that Highwater became aware that the "Indians" were really white men in Max Factor makeup, grimacing under phony war bonnets. Highwater continues, "I am six years old and I'm convinced that Indians are horrible people. At night I have nightmares about them. And in the morning when I brush my teeth, I see in the mirror the face which terrified me in my dream. Sometimes I cry."

Many Americans also had these stereotypes reinforced in elementary school when "The Indian Unit" was taught. Models of teepees and head feathers were constructed. "Indian talk" using phrases such as *How, Ugh*, and *Me Heap Big Chief!* were part of the curriculum. Culminating activities included dressing as Indians and "war whooping" up and down the hallway in a noisy display for children in the other grades.

Fortunately, movies have improved in quality, and in some cases a fairer depiction of Native Americans has emerged. Unfortunately, however, many of the old westerns are still shown on television, and far too many teachers still present the stereotypical "Indian Unit." With the information in this unit, you will be able to dispel some of the myths surrounding Native Americans and eliminate some of the stereotypes and prejudices that have developed since 1492.

Motivation. Begin this unit by discussing what students already know about Native Americans. A good way to collect this information is for students, either individually or in groups, to create a list of "Things I Know about Native Americans." This activity will help you to discover the attitudes that prevail in your classroom. When the lists are completed, record the "knowledge" on the chalkboard. Discussion should follow. Notice especially statements that are stereotypical in nature or that are untrue. If statements are open to debate, you should guide the discussion with questions such as: "Where did you get that information?" "Do you believe the statement?" "Why do you believe it?"

At some point, either now or later in the unit, you will want to introduce the concept of stereotyping. When you do this, students can make a list of true statements, false statements, and those that are based on stereotypes.

Immersion. In this part of the unit, students gather information about the topic. You can either read the short excerpts of information included in this text, select readings from a variety of trade books, or direct students to seek information in appropriate reference books. Hundreds of books, both adult and juvenile, deal with the subject of Native Americans. Some of these books are well written, culturally sensitive, and appropriate for today's classroom. Others are outdated, inaccurate, inappropriate, and often treat the subject in a simplistic, condescending manner.

You will be teaching some important concepts and generalizations in this unit. At its conclusion, students should have some knowledge and understanding of the following:

1. Native Americans are not all alike. They vary from group to group, as do Europeans and Asians.
2. All Native Americans do not have red skin, painted faces, or wear feathers in their hair.
3. The languages spoken by Native Americans number in the hundreds, and unlike the simple, monosyllabic utterances associated with "Indian talk," these languages are complex, involving complicated grammars.
4. In the United States, there is no single definition of an "Indian." Each group of Native Americans has its own criteria for determining who is and who is not a member of its Nation.
5. Before Columbus came to America, native peoples referred to themselves not as Indians but by their tribal names—for example, Cherokee, Iroquois, or Apache.
6. Eskimos refer to themselves as Inuit, meaning "the people."
7. Only about one-half of the Native American population lives on reservations. The remainder live in towns and cities, performing tasks and holding jobs as any other citizen might.
8. Native Americans were not granted U.S. citizenship until 1924.
9. Six years before citizenship was granted to them, Native American men fought in World War I.
10. Western movies are not true depictions of who Native Americans are, how they live, what they believe, or even how they look.

Note to the teacher: In this unit, care should be taken to avoid replacing one set of stereotypes with another. You should stress the positive aspects of Native Americans and depict with honesty and openness the evils that they often faced at the hands of many European settlers. On the other hand, there are always two sides to an issue. Some government officials broke promises, as did some Native Americans. Misunder-standings and irrational fears were common to both groups. It is important to help students understand that it is easy to see the wrongs of an event after it has happened, but it is more difficult to overcome prejudice and bias occurring in the present.

Information. This section should be considered an outline for more advanced study. The information is brief, presenting highlights from each category. In general, the unit is designed to give a broad overview of the history of native peoples in the United States, from pre-Columbian days to the present. It also attempts to focus briefly on native peoples in Canada, Mexico, and Central America.

It should be noted that in this unit the terms **Indian** and **Native American** sometimes are used interchangeably. Generally, however, the term Native American has been chosen as more appropriate. There is some disagreement as to the appropriate term for groups of aboriginal people living in the Americas before the coming of the Europeans. Most recent writers prefer the term "Native American" or a group's national name to "Indian." However, in almost all of the literature, including recently published materials and even those written by persons of Native American ancestry, the term "Indian" is still used. Recently, especially in Canada, Native American groups sometimes are referred to as **First Nations.** As a teacher, you should be sensitive to your audience and choose the term that is judged most appropriate among your constituents. Also, spellings of national or group names vary in many sources. In most cases, the spellings chosen for this text are those in common use.

Columbus Was a Newcomer. Evidence exists that groups of aboriginal peoples were scattered from the northern parts of Alaska to the southern tip of South America thousands of years before the *Niña*, the *Pinta*, and the *Santa Maria* sailed into the clear green waters of the Caribbean. These millennia are referred to as the pre-Columbian era of American history. Large groups of peoples, representing many cultures, shared the two American continents for centuries. They had much in common with one another, and yet they were very different, much like the diverse groups who dwelt in European regions during the same era. The native peoples were divided into nations (sometimes called tribes), each with its own territorial homeland, history, folklore, traditions, and language. These nations were scattered across the vast expanse of both North and South America. However, just as in Europe and other parts of the world, these groups did not always live together peacefully. They fought one another for hunting rights and territorial bounds. The stronger groups were often victorious, capturing individuals for slaves and claiming their property.

Most of what we know about the era before Europeans came to America is not based on written records, but rather on what is called prehistory: legends, oral stories and songs, and archaeological studies. During prehistoric times, hundreds of languages existed in the Americas, but only a few groups in Mexico and Guatemala had created written languages. As a result, historians have attempted to recreate the past through art, such as pictures painted on animal hides or carvings on stone and totems; through music, including songs, chants, and dances; and through oral recollections and accounts of tribal history handed down from one generation to another.

Historians lack answers to many questions about the lives of Native Americans before the arrival of Columbus. Records do not exist regarding how people lived, what they did, why they moved from one location to another, or the myriad other aspects of life in pre-Columbian times. We do know the following: (1) for at least ten thousand years humans have lived on the land now known as America; (2) early people most likely came to this continent thousands of years ago from Asia via a land bridge that existed between Siberia and Alaska; (3) communities, villages, and even large cities were developed over generations, allowing people to live and work productively together and to create complex societies and civilizations; (4) Although originally there may have been a common language, isolation over time led to the development of two to three hundred different languages; and (5) *prehistory* does not mean *no history*, but rather *unknown history*. Historians must work harder to gather evidence about the lives of Native Americans before 1492. Nevertheless, important contributions to today's knowledge base have been made by the people we call Indians or Native Americans.

In 1492, Native Americans Were Everywhere. When early European explorers and settlers arrived in the Americas in the fourteenth and fifteenth centuries, they found large groups of people living across the continents. These people were called *Indians* by Columbus, because by his calculations, he thought he had arrived in India. It is not difficult to see the reasoning behind his error. The people he encountered in the Bahamas had dark complexions, the Caribbean climate like that of India was hot and humid, and Columbus believed that the world was much smaller than it actually is.

Native Americans at that time lived in hundreds of distinct groups—some very large, held together by a common language and culture, and some relatively small and isolated. As has been noted, hundreds of languages were spoken by the various tribes. The way each group lived was determined to a great extent by its location. For example, the Plains Indians sustained

their society and performed their daily tasks quite differently than did the natives of the Pacific Northwest or of the Southeast. However, there were common elements among all groups regardless of their locales.

For the purposes of this unit, discussion of Native Americans will be limited to the United States and Canada. This model can be used to research the diverse and interesting groups of Native Americans who lived in (and are still present in) Central and South America. For simplification, categories have been created around six broad geographic regions: (1) the Northeast and Great Lakes, (2) the Southeast, (3) the Great Plains, (4) the Southwest and Great Basin, (5) California and the Pacific Northwest, and (6) the northern lands of the Arctic and Subarctic.

Native Americans of Canada and the United States

The Northeast and Great Lakes. In the early seventeenth century, during the time of the English settlements, Native Americans were spread across the vast northeastern regions of what was to become the United States. Generally, this area, classified as the Northeast and Great Lakes, stretches westward from New England and the Middle Atlantic shore to the upper Mississippi River Valley and includes the lands from southern Canada to the Ohio River Valley.

Scores of native groups inhabited this territory, living mostly by gathering, fishing, and hunting. The two major language groups were Algonquian and Iroquoian. Only the Winnebagos spoke a different language. They were in many ways very much like their neighbors, but spoke a Siouan language.

Like civilizations throughout history, these native peoples engaged in all types of social conduct. Some were peace loving and friendly; others were warlike, waging battles, often unprovoked, for territory or dominance. The Iroquois Confederacy, consisting of the Mohawk, Oneida, Onondaga, Cayuga, and Seneca, was an especially formidable foe to neighboring groups. Fortunately for the settlers who arrived on the *Mayflower*, friendly Algonquians lived in the Cape Cod area rather than the more hostile groups in upstate New York. Algonquians in the area included Massachusett, Mahican, Nauset, Nipmuc, Pennacook, Pocumtuc, and Wampanoag groups.

Major groups of Native Americans living around the Great Lakes region in early colonial times included the Ojibwa or Chippewa, Sauk, Fox, Kickapoo, Winnebago, Huron, Erie, Menominee, Ottawa, Tobacco, and Potawatomi. Native nations to the south of the Great Lakes in the present states of Illinois, Indiana,

California and Pacific Northwest

Arctic
and
Subarctic

Great
Basin
and
South
West

Great
Plains

Northeast and
Great Lakes

Southeast

Ohio, and Kentucky included the Miami, Peoria, Illinois, and Shawnee.

Although groups in the Northeast were different in a number of important ways, they often functioned in a very similar fashion. Because of the region's abundance of timber, wooden longhouses were constructed by most groups. These dwellings were sometimes one hundred feet long, allowing space for a dozen or more families. The temperate climate, abundant rainfall, and fertile soil supported a variety of vegetation that was consumed both by the human population and by the wide array of wildlife in the area. Thus, the groups were able to provide quite adequately for their communal needs.

The Delaware, Susquehanna, Nanticoke, and Powhatan lived in the southern sections of the Northeast, principally in what is now Virginia, Maryland, New Jersey, Delaware, and Pennsylvania. The Delaware called themselves *Lenni Lenape*, meaning "the people." They lived in a variety of dwellings—from round, domed wigwams to rectangular longhouses with pitched roofs. The Delaware were fond of vermilion paint made from berry juice and minerals mixed with fat. This red concoction was smeared over their bodies, and some historians believe that this led to white settlers first calling Indians "red men" (Maxwell, 1978, p. 118).

When a Delaware boy reached puberty, he was expected to engage in the rite of "Youth's Vigil." He was sent into the forest without food or water for many days to test his ability to survive. Several years later the youth was allowed to marry, but usually there was no ceremony. The couple simply set up a wigwam together or their parents made arrangements for their union. If a couple divorced, the woman always kept both the house and the children. Inheritance was passed through the woman, from mother to daughter; if there were no daughters, a woman's belongings went to her sister's daughters. When a Delaware chief died or was too old to rule, his son did not succeed him. Instead, a close male relative of the same bloodline as the chief's mother became the new leader.

With the westward migration of European immigrants, Native Americans became a stumbling block to settlement. Unfortunately for Native Americans in the Northeast, most who did not die from disease or war were displaced, or "removed," to lands farther west. Many died in the move to new homes; others lost their identity. Today, except for reservations in a few scattered areas, most Native Americans who remain in the Northeast live in cities and towns.

The Southeast. When early European settlers arrived, Native Americans living in the southern part of the United States—from the Atlantic coast to East Texas and from Virginia to Florida—constituted a strong and growing population. The mild climate and abundant rainfall provided an ideal location for large, diverse nations. Creeks, Yamasees, Choctaws, Chickasaws, and Houmas spoke the Muskogean language. Yuchis and Catawbas spoke Siouan. Cherokees were Iroquoian speakers, and the Shawnees spoke Algonquian. The groups living in the Southeast were said to be more advanced than most Native Americans, hence the designation by some as the "Five Civilized Tribes" Cherokee, Creek, Choctaw, Chickasaw, and Seminole.

The lives of the Southeastern tribes were similar in many ways to Indians of the Northeast. Food and timber were plentiful. However, the climate was more agreeable in the Southeast, so the winters were easier on the groups, allowing more time for activities beyond those necessary for survival.

The Southeastern people, like all groups of Native Americans, developed many myths and legends to help them make sense of their environment. They believed the world to be composed of the Upper World, the Lower World, and This World. The Upper World was orderly and stable, pure and unpolluted. The Lower World was the opposite. It was the source of pollution and madness, changeability rather than stability, but it also represented fertility and invention. This World was inhabited by humans, plants, and animals, some friendly and some enemies of mankind.

Southeastern groups were advanced in their knowledge of herbs and medicinal plants. They knew about the pain-relieving properties of salicylic acid, an ingredient found in aspirin, and they used caffeine as a stimulant. Historians are not certain as to what other plants they used, but it is believed that scores of effective medicines were made from dozens of plants. Some medical authorities believe that the Native American's knowledge of herbal cures may have surpassed the expertise of today's medical community with regard to natural drugs (Maxwell, 1978, pp. 89-90).

In the early 1800s, frontiersmen were pushing farther and farther west, desiring to settle on the lands belonging to the Southeastern nations. This situation led to passage of the Indian Removal Act in 1830 (Josephy, 1961, p. 222). This bill gave President Andrew Jackson power to initiate land exchanges with Indian nations living within states or territories. The bill did not authorize forced removal, but since most of the Indians did not want to leave their homelands, force eventually became necessary.

The unsettled land that was to become the state of Oklahoma was chosen for the exchange or removal. In time, Creek and Cherokee from Georgia and Alabama and Choctaw and Chickasaw from Mississippi were forced west to land provided for them. The Seminoles in Florida, as well as smaller tribes throughout the region, followed a similar fate.

So traumatic was the removal and so great were the hardships endured that the Cherokee called the experience the "Trail of Tears." One man gave this account "We were drove off like wolves . . . and our peoples' feet were bleeding with long marches. . . . We are men . . . we have women and children, and why should we come like wild horses?" (Josephy, 1961, p. 224). More than four thousand of the thirteen thousand Cherokee who began the march died en route. The near destruction of the Southeastern tribes was now complete. They had been removed to "Indian Territory."

The Great Plains. The Great Plains encompass millions of acres, stretching from Canada to Texas and from the Mississippi River basin to the foothills of the Rocky Mountains. For generations prior to the arrival of the Europeans, this region was not the most ideal habitat for Native Americans. The groups living on the eastern or western edges of the Great Plains were considerably better off than those living in its flat, grassy center. The eastern section, encompassing the rolling hills of the present states of Arkansas, Missouri, Iowa, and Minnesota, abounded with enough vegetation and game to sustain villages and permanent communities. The same was true, but to a lesser degree, of the western edge of the Great Plains. However, the vast interior of the region was quite different. It lacked sufficient rainfall to support forests, and repeated and prolonged droughts often left the land parched and barren. Permanent settlements were few; most groups here were nomadic gatherers and hunters, surviving on whatever plants they could forage and on whatever small animals, plus an occasional buffalo, they could kill. Although buffalo, or bison, were in great supply throughout the Great Plains, they were difficult to kill without the aid of a horse. It was not often that a group had all the buffalo meat they wanted.

All this changed in 1598, when Spaniards settled in New Mexico along with their sheep, goats, and horses. The horse—mystery dogs, the Indians called them—brought a new way of life, making the tribes of the Great Plains wealthy. Wealth was measured not in terms of money but in terms of food, and with horses, the great herds of bison became easy prey for the native hunters. Food was now plentiful, as were the valuable by-products of the great animals. Buffalo meat was a rich source of protein. It could be sun-dried as jerky and kept for months. When pounded fine and mixed with fat and dried berries, it became the staple called "pemmican." The skins made sturdy coverings for portable tepees. With the fur left on, the hides provided warm bedding and fine articles of clothing. Sinew was used for thread, the bones for tools, and the horns for cups. No part of the buffalo was wasted. Even the stomach was used as a container for cooking and for transporting water (Underhill, 1971, p. 153).

Before long, the less prosperous groups living to the east of the Great Plains began to feel the pressure of the settlers' westward movement. Envious of the wealth and good life of the Plains groups, they soon began migrating into the broad, flat, grassy regions in search of the great bison herds. There they found plenty of space and buffalo for everyone.

There was little need for fighting among the groups for survival or territory, but conflict nevertheless arose. Battles were usually fought to give the young men opportunity for advancement in the group—a prerequisite for marriage. Fathers and sisters urged the young men to join war parties and to take vows of bravery, even in the face of death. The two most important things to many Plains Indians were youth and physical courage. A song of the Blackfoot society illustrates this vividly:

> *It is bad to live to be old*
> *Better to die young*
> *Fighting bravely in battle*
> (Underhill, 1971, p. 160)

The advent of the horse contributed to the stereotypical image of Native Americans many people still hold: the great buffalo hunter of the Plains, barechested with beaded vest and leggings, galloping bareback on his mustang, aiming his iron-pointed lance straight at the buffalo's heart (Underhill, 1971, p. 144). The warriors of the Cheyenne and Dakota Sioux are most often associated with this image, for their societies, more than most groups, were centered around the nomadic lifestyle of buffalo hunting.

Principal nations associated with the northern Great Plains were the Blackfoot, Crow, Mandan, Dakota (Sioux), Omaha, Ponca, and Cheyenne. Central Plains groups included the Pawnee, Arapaho, Kansa, Osage, and Wichita. Further south, extending into Texas, were the Kiowa, Kiowa Apache, Caddo, and Comanche. As in other regions, while there were similarities between groups, there were also differences. The Native Americans of the Great Plains belonged to six major language groups: Siouan, Kiowan, Caddoan, Algonquian, Shoshonean, and Athabascan.

Many factors led to the decline of the Native American on the Great Plains, but basically the issue was simple. Indians had what European settlers wanted: land for farming, hills that held precious metals, and miles and miles of grassland for raising cattle and sheep. Because the typical white man viewed the Indian as savage, ignorant, and lacking the ability to put his domain to good use, he felt he had the right to take the land and used his power to do so. The Native

American, on the other hand, saw the white settlers as a deadly threat to his way of life (Maxwell, 1978, p. 195).

During the last half of the nineteenth century, wars were fought between tribes and U.S. soldiers. Black Kettle, Red Cloud, Crazy Horse, Sitting Bull, and Chief Joseph played important roles in the rich history of the Great Plains. They struggled valiantly to protect their land and people from the advancing forces of "progress." Ultimately, the demise of the Plains Indians is said to have been brought about by the disappearance of the buffalo. In 1800, an estimated sixty million buffalo roamed the Great Plains; a century later, only a thousand or so remained. This was the result of deliberate action on the part of government officials in Washington. Their land gone and their source of food and raw materials eliminated, the native peoples of the Great Plains were given only one alternative: the reservation.

The Southwest, Great Basin, and Plateau. Native Americans of the Southwest, Great Basin, and Plateau are made up of a number of diverse groups. The groups associated with the Great Basin and Plateau extended from the present states of Washington, Idaho, and Montana in the north to southern Utah and Nevada. Principal nations in the Plateau were the Flathead, Kalispel, Cayuse, Yakima, Colville, and Kutenai. In the Great Basin were the Klamath, Modoc, Shoshone, Paiute, and Ute.

The dwellers of the Plateau generally lived in small, permanent winter villages situated along rivers and streams. Groups of forty or fifty—usually members of an extended family, that is, related to one another by blood—lived in each village. Fish was an important staple for these groups. The Plateau people were able to supply most of their basic needs by following a yearly routine. During the spawning season, a year's supply of salmon and trout were caught and preserved. In spring and summer, the families collected tubers and roots and gathered the wild berries and fruits that grew abundantly along the mountain slopes. In the autumn, game was killed and preserved for the difficult winter that lay ahead. With the approach of cold and snow, the groups moved back into their winter villages, awaiting the coming of a new spring.

The Basin people spoke Shoshonean languages—the same language group to which the Aztecs in Mexico belonged. Some historians believe this to be an indication that the early Aztecs passed through the Great Basin on their way south into the highlands of Mexico.

The Great Basin is a much drier, harsher land than the Plateau. Food was more difficult to obtain, so most of the day was devoted to the struggle for survival. The family groups were much smaller in the Basin, usually comprising a father, a mother, children, and perhaps grandparents (Jones, 1973, p. 53). In the spring, the family band searched for green shoots and small game, including insects and reptiles. As summer approached, they moved up the slopes looking for roots, berries, and fish. When autumn arrived, large crops of piñon nuts and acorns were harvested for the winter, along with rabbit and other small game.

Farther south in Arizona and New Mexico, and even into the deserts of northern Mexico, lived the native groups of the Southwest: the Pueblo cultures of the Rio Grande and western pueblos; the non-pueblo dwellers, including the Navajo and Apache; and smaller groups scattered throughout the region, such as the Pima, Papago, Yavapai, Walapai and Havasupai. Different languages were spoken by the groups. Pueblo dwellers spoke languages belonging to the Keresan and Tanoan families, except for the Zuni, whose language belonged to the Uto-Aztecan family.

The Pueblo people were industrious, cooperative, and peace loving. Their large, multistoried stone and mud dwellings contained many rooms for a great number of families—similar to modern apartment complexes, but with one major exception. Apartments in our cities are built compactly to house many tenants, but the inhabitants, although in very close proximity, live separately and apart from one another. Next-door neighbors often do not know each other. Pueblo dwellers, on the other hand, had a bond of community, of family and kinship, not only living side by side but also sharing chores, resources, and food.

Pueblos were constructed of adobe and stone, reflecting the types of building materials in the region. They were usually situated along rivers and streams, near planting fields, and at locations that provided good defense from invading forces. Members of a pueblo wished to live peacefully and harmoniously with one another and with their universe. They believed that only with peace and contentment would rains come, crops be plentiful, and people and animals be healthy and fertile (Jones, 1973, p. 56).

A number of Pueblos exist today, with residents practicing many of the rituals and traditions of their ancestors. Notable pueblo villages with populations of a thousand or more located in New Mexico and Arizona include: Acoma, Isleta, Jemez, Laguna, San Felipe, San Juan, Santa Clara, Santo Domingo, and Zuni.

The Navajos and Hopis, non-pueblo dwellers, continue to share a large section of eastern Arizona and western New Mexico. Although they generally live peacefully together, traditionally they have been enemies. Hopis live mostly on three mesas, each consisting of several villages. They have a reputation for surviving quite well in a harsh land with little rainfall, where modern farmers might fail. The growing season in their area is approximately four and a half months, with an annual rainfall of twelve inches. Yet these dry-land farmers grow corn, squash, beans, and cotton with uncanny regularity.

Navajos call themselves *Dine,* meaning "the people" in the Athabascan language. They or their ancestors have lived in the Southwest for about one thousand years. Navajos have prospered while other Native American groups have dwindled or disappeared. Today their population totals more than one hundred thousand and their lands comprise more than fifteen million acres. Navajos have increased the size of their reservation four times since 1868. More than 97 percent of their people speak the Navajo language, and most can also speak English (Highwater, 1975, p. 268).

Many Navajos still live in traditional dwellings rather than in modern houses. This home, called a hogan or *hooghan,* is constructed of a framework of poles and covered with earth except for the entry and smokehole. The entry always faces east to catch the "first light of dawn" (Highwater, 1975, p. 271). Several superstitious practices are associated with the hogan. When a person dies in a hogan, he or she may be buried in the hogan or the body may be removed for burial through an opening at the back. Then the hogan is boarded up or burned to prevent further use.

Two books of juvenile literature that provide insights into the Navajo culture are Scott O'Dell's (1970) *Sing Down the Moon* and *Annie and the Old One* by Miska Miles (1971). O'Dell's book is a fictional account of two young persons caught in the events of the tragic "Long Walk," which occurred in 1863. This infamous march, overseen by Kit Carson, began when the Navajo were removed from their homeland in the Canyon de Chelly area and forced to walk three hundred miles east to Fort Sumner, New Mexico. Four years later they were allowed to return to eastern Arizona. *Annie and the Old One* has a modern setting and tells a poignant story of a girl's concern for her elderly grandmother. The illustrations may help the reader to visualize the topography of eastern Arizona.

California and the Pacific Northwest. The regions inhabited by the natives of California and the Pacific Northwest were located between the sea and the coastal mountain ranges, within a few miles of the Pacific Ocean. Like all groups of Native Americans, these people were diverse and yet had many similarities. The *way* they lived was directly influenced by *where* they lived. The language groups to which they belonged were in many instances tribal names: Nootka, Chinook, Salish, Haida, Tsimshian, and Tlingit.

Northern California and the Pacific Northwest were ideal for creating a rich, successful, and productive life. Salmon were abundant in streams; seals, sea otters, and whales were plentiful in the coastal waters; and a vast array of useful plants grew on the western slopes of nearby mountains. Easy access to large cedar, redwood, and spruce trees provided building materials for dwellings, canoes, and other utilitarian items.

With this abundance of wealth at hand, it is not surprising that these people had time for pursuits other than survival. Huge quantities of dried fish were displayed at public ceremonies of feasting and gift-giving called *potlach*. Large houses and boats were built, and craftsmen constructed tall totems with elaborate artistic designs depicting symbolic family histories.

A number of Northwest groups practiced the traditions of the maternal society, as did many other Native Americans. The Tlingit people, for example, were very strict in this tradition. The children had their mother's clan affiliation. A father might feel affection for his own children, but his ties to his sisters' children often were stronger, for it would be his sisters' children, not his own, who would inherit his wealth. When his sisters' sons were about ten years old, they would come to live with him, and his own sons, at that age, would go to live with his wife's brothers (Maxwell, 1978, p. 302).

Today, many Native American groups live along the coast of the Pacific Northwest in northern California, Oregon, Washington, Alaska, and British Columbia. Large totems created by ancient and modern artisans are on view in villages and cities throughout the area, and many museums rich in Native American history are located in major cities in the region.

The North Lands of the Arctic and Subarctic. The native peoples who inhabit the arctic regions of North America survive in one of the harshest environments populated by humans. Those living in the subarctic regions experience a climate similar to that of the upper northern United States and southern Canada, with long winter nights and cold chilling winds as a regular part of their existence. Those groups living in the Arctic, however, face even harsher conditions, struggling daily to survive. The bleakness of such an existence has caused many historians to ask how these people came to be and why they remained in such an inhospitable place. Initially it was believed that the Eskimo were driven north by more warlike groups in the south. Scholars now hypothesize that they came more recently from eastern Asia. The reasons given are that these people have features, customs, and languages quite different from other Native American groups. Unlike the original native groups who arrived on the continent about ten thousand years ago, it appears that these Arctic dwellers may have migrated into the area as recently as 3000 B.C.

The most common term used for the Native Americans of the northlands is **Eskimo,** which is an Algonquian word meaning "eaters of raw meat." However, this name has never been accepted by those to whom it was given. They refer to themselves as **Inuit,** meaning "the people" or "the real people." An Inuit myth describes how the earth was begun. Initially, so the legend goes, there was no light, no animals, and no people. The world was emptiness. Soon, two men grew up from the earth, fully grown. In time, they wished to have children, and a magic song changed one of them into a woman. Together, the man and woman had children, and these are the earliest ancestors of the Inuit (Billard, 1974, p. 84).

In order to provide for their families in subzero weather, the Inuit developed amazing survival techniques. Winter clothing was made of caribou skins: two pairs of boots, two suits of trousers, a hooded jacket, and a pair of mittens, which altogether weighed about ten pounds. The inner suit was worn with the fur next to the body, the outer one with the fur outside. These two layers of fur provided insulation, keeping warm air next to the body.

The development of the kayak also helped the Inuit to obtain food. A driftwood frame was tied together with strings of animal hide, then covered with tightly stretched sealskins. This resulted in a swift-moving craft for hunting the seals and caribou near the many lakes and rivers.

The nomadic Inuit could not have survived long without some type of shelter from the freezing winds. They observed how animals buried themselves in snow during the winter, keeping the warmth of the earth and their bodies inside and the cold winds outside. A snowhouse was devised by placing blocks of packed snow in an inward-leaning spiral dome. We call this type of home an igloo, which comes from the Inuit word *iglu,* meaning house or dwelling. The Inuit use the term for any type of house, including a two-story frame construction. This type of dwelling was necessary on the tundra, where there are no trees to furnish lumber. Not all Inuit lived in snowhouses. For many, the snowhouse served as a temporary shelter while hunting and fishing. Usually a more permanent structure was built of sod and stone for winter use, and animal-skin tents were constructed for summer living.

The Inuit lived undisturbed lives for many generations. However, drastic changes began to occur in the arctic regions about fifty years ago. First, a line of radar stations known as the Distant Early Warning (DEW) Line was built in the 1950s. Many Inuit left their traditional ways to work on the construction of these stations. When the jobs were completed, it was difficult for the men to return to their old lives of fishing and hunting. In 1968, oil discoveries on the north slope of Alaska created a new challenge. While this brought employment and money, many Inuit feared that drilling and pipeline construction would cause wildlife to disappear and the land and sea to become polluted. There seemed to be no retreat. "Progress" had overtaken the Inuit.

The stereotypes of yesterday concerning the "Eskimo" were probably not true then, but are certainly less true today. Now the typical Inuit family lives in a permanent wooden house with central heating, a bathroom, and a built-in kitchen with stove and refrigerator. They probably own a television and possibly a videocassette recorder. Snowmobiles rather than dogsleds are the accepted mode of transportation, and airplanes regularly carry Inuit between the remote villages of the north.

This rapid change has not been appreciated and accepted by all. Two juvenile books may help students understand the conflicts that often develop between cultures, and even within a culture between youth and their elders. Jean Craighead George (1972) has written such a story in *Julie of the Wolves*. Julie wishes to retain her heritage, but finds it increasingly difficult in her world of change. Another story of conflict is Ann Turner's (1980) *A Hunter Comes Home*. Jonas, a fifteen-year-old Inuit, is caught in a conflict between his mother, who wants him to go away to high school to prepare for the changing ways of their people, and his grandfather, who wants him to stay in the village and learn the old ways.

The Inuit are a proud, ingenious, fun-loving people. It is said that they have many words for snow but none for war. Their history is steeped in ritual and tradition, but they are a people caught in the middle of a modern world of progress and technology. Like other Native American groups, the elders are trying desperately to retain and teach the traditional ways to their young. According to Smith (1987, p. 45), "The Inuit have made great advances in the past few years, and are generally optimistic about their future. But they know that the fight to preserve their culture and the northern environment upon which it depends is far from over."

Instructional Activities

Activity 2.1: Native American Words We Use Today

The English language developed over hundreds of years and is still evolving. New words have been added when warranted (television and compact disc); some words have been shortened or changed (car from carriage, bus from autobus, perm from permanent wave); and still others have taken on additional, totally different meanings (rock [music], crack, and gay). English speakers are noted for borrowing words from other cultures. When early settlers encountered unfamiliar objects or animals, they borrowed the language of native peoples. Use the boxed list to begin discussion and research of word origins. You many wish to find not only the definitions, but also the language group from which each word is derived. Add other words to this list or instruct your students to locate additional words of Native American origin.

cayuse	opossum	succotash
chipmunk	papoose	tomahawk
hickory	powwow	wampum
hominy	raccoon	wigwam
moccasin	skunk	woodchuck
moose	squash	
muskrat	squaw	

Activity 2.2: How Did Your State Get Its Name?

The names of almost half of the U.S. states are of Native American origin. Some of the names were taken directly from tribal names. Massachusetts, for instance, is named for the Massachusett Indians. Other names are from words that are descriptive of a location or topographical feature of the area. Ohio is a Seneca word for beautiful river, and Nebraska is from the Omaha word *nibdhathka*, which means flat river. Ask your students to complete the following chart. In some instances, it may be impossible to locate the information. References given in this unit may help, as well as almanacs and travel brochures from the various states.

Activity 2.3: The Stories They Told

Many high-quality, authentically told, and beautifully and accurately illustrated juvenile books that deal with Native American and Inuit folk literature have been published in recent years. Included in the Suggested Reading list is a sampling. Your students may enjoy searching the library for others. Fortunately, many new books dealing with this subject are published each year by major presses.

Suggested Reading

Ahenakaw, F. (1988). *How the birch tree got its stripes: a Cree story for children.* Illus. by G. Littlechild. Saskatoon, SK, Canada: Fifth House.

Ahenakaw, F. (1988). *How the mouse got brown teeth: a Cree story for children.* Illus. by G. Littlechild. Saskatoon, SK, Canada: Fifth House.

Baker, B. (1990). *And me, coyote!* Illus. by M. Horvath. New York: Macmillan.

Begay, S. (1992). *Ma'ii and cousin horned toad: a traditional Navajo story.* Illus. by author. New York: Scholastic.

STATE NAMES WITH NATIVE AMERICAN ORIGINS

State	Native Group	Original Word	Meaning
Alabama	Muskogean	Alibamu	Here we rest
Alaska	Aleut	Alakhskhakh	Name of peninsula
Arizona	Papago	_____	_____
Arkansas	_____	Akansea	_____
Connecticut	_____	_____	long river
Illinois	_____	_____	_____
Iowa	_____	_____	_____
Kansas	_____	_____	_____
Kentucky	_____	_____	planted field
Massachusetts	Massachusett	Massachusett	big hill
Michigan	Ottawa	_____	_____
Minnesota	_____	Mnisota	cloudy water
Mississippi	_____	_____	_____
Missouri	_____	_____	_____
Nebraska	_____	_____	_____
New Mexico	_____	_____	_____
North Dakota	_____	_____	_____
Ohio	_____	_____	_____
Oklahoma	Choctaw	_____	_____
South Dakota	_____	_____	_____
Tennessee	_____	_____	_____
Texas	_____	_____	friend or ally
Utah	_____	_____	_____
Wisconsin	_____	_____	_____
Wyoming	_____	_____	_____

Belting, N. M. (1992). *Moon was tired of walking on air.* Illus. by W. Hillenbrand. Boston: Houghton Mifflin.

Bierhorst, J. (1985). *The mythology of North America.* New York: William Morrow.

Bierhorst, J. (1987). *Doctor coyote: a Native American Aesop's fables.* Illus. by W. Watson. New York: Macmillan.

Bierhorst, J. (1987). *The naked bear: folktales of the Iroquois.* New York: William Morrow.

Carey, V. S. (1990). *Quail song: a Pueblo Indian folktale.* Illus. by I. Barnett. New York: G. P. Putnam's Sons.

Coatsworth, E. & Coatsworth, D. (1980). *The adventures of Nanabush: Ojibway Indian stories.* Illus. by F. Kagige. New York: Atheneum.

Cohen, C. L. (1988). *The mud pony: a traditional Skidi Pawnee tale.* Illus. by S. Begay. New York: Scholastic.

Courlander, H. (1970). *People of the short blue corn: tales and legends of the Hopi Indians.* Illus. by E. Arno. Orlando, FL: Harcourt Brace Jovanovich.

DeArmond, D. (1990). *The boy who found the light.* San Francisco: Sierra Club Books.

DePaola, T. (1983). *The Legend of the bluebonnet: an old tale of Texas.* Illus. by the author. New York: G. P. Putnam's Sons.

deWit, D. (1979). *The talking stone: an anthology of Native American tales and legends.* New York: Greenwillow Books.

Elston, G. (Ed.). (1985). *Giving: Ojibwa stories and legends from the children of Curve Lake.* Lakefield, ON, Canada: Waapoone Publishing.

Gillham, C. E. (1943). *Beyond the Clapping Mountains: Eskimo stories from Alaska.* New York: Macmillan.

Grinnell, G. B. (1982). *The whistling skeleton: American Indian tales of the supernatural.* Ed. by J. Bierhorst. Illus. by R. A. Parker. New York: Four Winds Press.

Goble, P. (1984). *Buffalo woman.* Illus. by the author. New York: Bradbury Press.

Goble, P. (1989). *Iktomi and the berries.* Illus. by the author. New York: Orchard Books.

Goble, P. (1990). *Dream wolf.* Illus. by the author. New York: Bradbury Press.

Goble, P. (1990). *Iktomi and the ducks: a Plains Indian Story.* Illus. by the author. New York: Orchard Books.

Goble, P. (1991). *Iktomi and the buffalo skull.* Illus. by the author. New York: Orchard Books.

Goble, P. (1992). *Love flute.* Illus by the author. New York: Bradbury Press.

Harris, C. (1980). *The trouble with princesses.* illus. by D. Tait. New York: Atheneum.

Hayes, J., (Adapt.) (1990). *Coyote and Native American folk tales.* Illus. by L. Jelinek. Santa Fe, NM: Mariposa.

Highwater, J. (1977). *Anpao: an American Indian odyssey.* Philadelphia: J. B. Lippincott.

Hinton, L. (Trans.). (1992). *Ishi's Tale of lizard.* Illus. by S. L. Roth. New York: Farrar, Straus & Giroux.

Kerven, R. (1991). *Earth magic, sky magic: North American Indian stories.* New York: Cambridge University Press.

Lacapa, M. (1992). *Antelope woman: an Apache folktale.* Illus. by the author. Flagstaff, AZ: Northland.

Mayo, G. W. (1989). *Earthmaker's tales: North American Indian stories about earth happenings.* New York: Walker.

Mayo, G. W. (1987). *Star tales: North American Indian stories about stars.* New York: Walker.

McDermott, G. (Adapt.) (1974). *Arrow to the sun: a Pueblo Indian tale.* Illus. by the adapter. New York: Viking.

McDermott, G. (1992). *Papagayo the mischief maker.* Illus. by the author. Orlando, FL: Harcourt Brace Jovanovich.

McDermott, G. (1993). *Raven: a trickster tale from the Pacific Northwest.* Illus. by the author. Orlando, FL: Harcourt Brace Jovanovich.

Monroe, J. G., & Williamson, R. A. (1987). *They dance in the sky: Native American star myths.* Illus. by E. Stewart. Boston: Houghton Mifflin.

Munsch, R., & Kusugak, M. (1988). *A promise is a promise.* Illus. by V. Krykorka. Willowdale, ON, Canada: Annick Press.

Roth, S. (1990). *The story of light.* New York: William Morrow.

Rucki, A. (1992). *Turkey's gift to the people.* Illus. by the author. Flagstaff, AZ: Northland.

Schecter, E. (1992). *The warrior maiden: a Hopi legend.* Illus. by L. Kelly. New York: Bantam Little Rooster.

Scheer, G. F. (1966). *Cherokee animal tales.* New York: Holiday House.

Shetterly, S. H. (1991). *Raven's light: a myth from the people of the northwest coast.* Illus. by R. Shetterly. New York: Atheneum.

Steptoe, J. (Adapt.) (1984). *The story of the jumping mouse: a Native American legend.* Illus. by the adapter. New York: Lothrop, Lee & Shepard Books.

Tanaka, B. (1991). *The chase: a Kutenai Indian tale.* Illus. by M. Gay. New York: Crown.

Taylor, C. J. (1990). *How Two-Feather was saved from loneliness: an Abenaki legend.* Montreal, PQ, Canada: Tundra Books.

Te A. (1989). *Baby rattlesnake.* Adapt. by L. Moroney. Illus. by V. Reisberg. San Francisco: Children's Book Press.

Troughton, J. (1992). *How the seasons came: a North American Indian folk tale.* Illus. by the author. New York: Peter Bedrick Books.

Van Laan, N. (Reteller). (1989). *Rainbow crow.* Illus. by B. Vidal. New York: Alfred A. Knopf.

Wood, M. (1992). *Spirits, heroes, and hunters from North American Indian mythology.* Illus. by J. Sibbick & B. Donohoe. New York: Peter Bedrick Books.

Yolen, J. (1991). *Sky dogs.* Illus. by B. Moser. Orlando: FL, Harcourt Brace Jovanovich.

Activity 2.4: Learning about Individual Nations

Today's libraries have many recently published books dealing with Native Americans. Several publishing companies have developed series that provide detailed descriptions and accounts of individual native groups. A sampling follows:

Rourke Publications, Inc.: Vero Beach, FL. Titles include *Eskimos—The Inuit of the Arctic; Plains Indians of North America;* and *Indians of the Andes.*

Childrens Press: Chicago. The series *A New True Book* includes titles such as *The Chippewa; The Apache; and The Seneca.*

Chelsea House Publishers: New York. Frank W. Porter III is the general editor of an extensive series (more than fifty volumes and still growing) entitled *Indians of North America.* Titles range from the lesser known groups (e.g., *The Abenaki; The Cahuilla; The Hidatsa;* and *The Tunica-Biloxi*) to those more familiar (e.g., *The Cherokee; The Eskimo; The Navajo;* and *The Seminole*). Several books in this series are of a general nature: *American Indian Literature; The Archaeology of North America; Federal Indian Policy;* and *Women in American Indian Society.*

Activity 2.5: Surveying the Area

Every part of the United States was home to groups of Native Americans long before houses, schools, roads, and shopping malls were built. Have your students conduct research to determine evidence of Indian cultures and influence in your immediate locale. Local museums, newspaper offices, and historical groups are good starting places. Look for clues such as the names of nearby rivers, valleys, and mountains. You do not need to live near a reservation to have Native Americans as neighbors. If such a population exists, invite one of the leaders to your school as a guest speaker. Many Native Americans are eager for the opportunity to help students understand the difference between the "Hollywood Indian" and the real Native American.

Activity 2.6: Checking Out the Story

There is so much folklore and misinformation about Native Americans that it is difficult to discern what is real and what is false. As has been noted, stereotypes related to Native Americans abound. It is your responsibility to help students recognize and reject those "facts" that at best are slanted and at worst are downright false.

However, in an attempt to reject all negative aspects related to Native Americans, it may be easy to overlook the fact that some of the "positive" stories actually are not true. Such is the case with *Brother Eagle, Sister Sky: A Message from Chief Seattle*, illustrated by artist Susan Jeffers. Although the environmental message is timely and important to our society, evidence presented in a recent New York *Times* article indicates that the "speech" was not spoken by Chief Seattle but actually was written in 1971 by Ted Perry, a professor of film at the University of Texas (Murray, 1993, p. 100).

Have your students read *Brother Eagle, Sister Sky*. Discuss the meaning of Chief Seattle's "speech" and the implications it has for our world today. Ask them to look for inconsistencies in the text. Seattle's speech, supposedly made in 1854, contains references to railroads and telegraph lines. Would this have been likely? Students may debate the issues surrounding the notion of a writer quoting *actual statements* made by a speaker versus reconstructing *the spirit* of a presentation, even if it contains inaccuracies.

References and Bibliography

Avery, S., & Skinner, L. (1992). *Extraordinary American Indians.* Chicago: Childrens Press.

Banks, J. A. (1990). *Teaching strategies for the social studies: inquiry, valuing, and decision-making (4th ed.).* White Plains, NY: Longman.

Billard, J. B. (Ed.). (1974). *The world of the American Indian.* Washington, DC: National Geographic Society.

Capps, B. (1973). *The Indians.* New York: Time-Life Books.

Capps, B. (1975). *The great chiefs.* New York: Time-Life Books.

Claiborne, R. (1973). *The first Americans.* New York: Time-Life Books.

Driver, H. E. (1969). *Indians of North America (2nd ed.).* Chicago: University of Chicago Press.

Freedman, R. (1987). *Indian chiefs.* New York: Holiday House.

George, J. C. (1972). *Julie of the wolves.* New York: Harper.

Hawke, S. D. & Davis, J. E. (1992). *Seeds of change: the story of cultural exchange after 1492.* Menlo Park, CA: Addison-Wesley.

Highwater, J. (1975). *Fodor's Indian America.* New York: David McKay.

Highwater, J. (1978). *Many smokes, many moons: a chronology of American Indian history through Indian art.* Philadelphia: J. B. Lippincott.

Hirsch, S. C. (1973). *Famous American Indians of the plains.* Chicago: Rand McNally.

Hirschfelder, A. (1986). *Happily may I walk: American Indians and Alaska natives today.* New York: Charles Scribner's Sons.

Jeffers, S. (1991). *Brother eagle, sister sky: a message from Chief Seattle.* New York: Dial.

Jones, J. C. (1973). *The American Indian in America: Vol. I. Prehistory to the end of the 18th century.* Minneapolis: Lerner Publications.

Jones, J. C. (1973). *The American Indians in America. Vol. II. Early 19th century to the present.* Minneapolis: Lerner Publications.

Josephy, A. M., Jr. (Ed.). (1961). *The American Heritage book of Indians.* New York: American Heritage.

Maxwell, J. A. (Ed.). (1978). *America's fascinating Indian heritage. The first Americans: their customs, art, history, and how they lived.* Pleasantville, NY: Reader's Digest Association.

Miles, M. (1971). *Annie and the old one.* Illus. by P. Parnall. Boston: Little, Brown.

Murray, M. (1993, July). The little green lie, *Reader's Digest,* 100–104.

O'Dell, S. (1970). *Sing down the moon.* Boston: Houghton Mifflin.

Smith, C. (Ed.). (1992). *Native Americans of the west.* Brookfield, CT: Millbrook Press.

Smith, J. H. G. (1987). *Eskimos: the Inuit of the Arctic.* Vero Beach, FL: Rourke Publications.

Turner, A. (1980). *A hunter comes home.* New York: Crown.

Underhill, R. M. (1971). *Red man's America: a history of Indians in the United States.* Chicago: University of Chicago Press.

White, J. M. (1979). *Everyday life of the North American Indian.* New York: Holmes & Meier.

Wolfson, E. (1988). *From Abenaki to Zuni: a dictionary of Native American tribes.* New York: Walker.

Yue, C., & Yue, D. (1988). *The igloo.* Boston: Houghton Mifflin.

October's Potpourri of Teaching Ideas

The purpose of each month's Potpourri of Teaching Ideas is to provide additional resources from which to build your curriculum. Most, but not all, of the activities listed each month relate directly to that month. It is not intended that you use them all, but rather that you choose those which are appropriate for your program. Although the topics are written for a particular month, many of them would be appropriate for use throughout the year. How you use these activities will depend on your curricular goals. You may wish to use some of the activities as they are presented, and you may need to modify some to meet your needs. Perhaps some of them will give you ideas for entirely different potpourris.

Let's Play Kickball

Thousands of years ago, the Tarahumara Indians of Mexico played a game called kickball. The Tarahumara still play the game today, as do other Native American groups in the United States. This game of kickball is different from soccer in several respects. First, there is no formal playing field, only a starting and finishing line—which may be from a few miles to thirty or more miles apart. Second, unlike soccer, two balls are used, one for each team. The third difference is that each player is allowed to kick the ball only once in succession. After another teammate has kicked the ball, the original player can kick it again. Finally, the ball cannot be moved by any means other than the feet. No touching of the ball with the head, hip, or other body parts is allowed.

The name Tarahumara means *foot runners*, and even today these people love this game of endurance and skill. Celebrations, attended by thousands, are held annually. Two teams of three to six runners begin at a designated point. The small balls are carved from wood. All players run together, kicking only their own team ball. The object of the game is for one team to reach the finish line first.

Your students can play a modified version of the game. You will need two teams of three to six players. Select two balls that are identical in size and shape. To avoid confusion, the balls should be of different colors. They should be small and not easily bounced. A soft ball or a homemade ball about the size of a grapefruit will be adequate. Do not use a volleyball or soccer ball, for it tends to go too far with each kick.

Establish a running course of about two to three hundred yards. Make sure each team knows the rules and the location of the finish line. Begin the game with one member of each team kicking the team ball. Each team runs together after their ball. The kickers need not observe any kicking order except to be certain that no one kicks the ball twice in a row. The first team kicking the ball across the finish line wins.

Make Your Own Ball. Before the advent of Toys "R" Us, K-Mart, and Sears, children had to make their own toys. Playing-balls were usually made of string, strips of cloth, or coarse materials rolled together into a sphere. An easy way to make balls is to begin with a bag of old rags. Cotton, wool, or synthetics will work quite well. Tear the rags into one-inch strips and roll the strips tightly into a ball of the desired size. Be sure the strips are wound evenly to produce a smooth, firm sphere. When you have a ball of the desired size, fasten the last strip with thread or glue to prevent it from unrolling. Place a cotton or nylon stocking over the ball and create a permanent cover by cutting the stocking to a desired length and tucking the top inside itself. Try

to keep the ball smooth and evenly rounded. It can then be sewed with strong thread to prevent it from unraveling.

Suggested Reading

Whitney, A. (1977). *Sports and games the Indians gave us.* New York: David McKay.
Wiswell, P. (1897). *Kids' games.* New York: Doubleday.

AIDS Awareness: A Worldwide Concern

As part of your school's AIDS awareness campaign, students can write letters to obtain information about the worldwide distribution of this disease. Students may also want to inquire about the change in that distribution over the past ten years. After they receive this information, they can synthesize it by making a graph, chart, or distribution map.

If you students write for information:

1. Include on the letter the address of the official or organization to which you are writing, as well as a return address.
2. State the purpose of the letter in the first sentence.
3. Don't make the official guess about the type of information that you are requesting. Pose clear questions and be specific. If you are interested in the number of reported cases by year, specifically request that data.

Sources for Information Relating to AIDS

Public Health Service
Public Affairs
Hubert H. Humphrey Building
200 Independence Ave., S.W.
Room 725-H
Washington, DC 20201

AIDS Hotline: 800-342-AIDS (provides free teaching packet)

Suggested Reading

Lewis, B. (1991). *The kids guide to social action.* Minneapolis: Free Spirit Publishing.

Football: What's in a Name?

October brings the rustle of leaves and afternoons of football. For many of your students, football means eleven people on each of two teams throwing an oval ball and running toward goal posts. However, for most of the world, football means *soccer*. Soccer is the world's most popular sport and is the national sport of many European and Latin American countries. The World Cup Championship, held every four years, is the sport's major international tournament.

Although modern soccer developed in England during the 1800s, some suggest that a similar game was played by the early Mayans. A game similar to soccer may have been played by the Chinese in 400 B.C. and by the Romans in A.D. 200.

Try This: Your students may want to become experts on this major world sport by:

Tracing the history of soccer
Explaining the positions or rules
Collecting newspaper accounts of World Cup matches
Writing about famous players
Writing papers comparing soccer and American football.

The following general sources of information can be used:

Encyclopedias
Guinness Book of World Records
Guinness Sports Record Book
Information Please Almanac
People's Almanac
World Almanac and Book of Facts

Selected Reading

Rote, K., & Basil, K. (1978). *Kyle Rote, Jr.'s complete book of soccer.* New York: Simon & Schuster.
Yannis, A. (1980). *Inside soccer: the complete book of soccer for spectators, players, and coaches.* New York: McGraw-Hill.

National Dessert Month: International Desserts

What a delicious way for students to share some of their families' special treats! Included here are two dessert recipes for you to send home with your students. In exchange for these desserts, encourage your students to bring in family recipes or recipes from international cookbooks. The class can collect these and make a scrapbook. As students read throughout the year, they can add more recipes.

Patacones from Panama

This dessert is similar to potato chips.

INGREDIENTS:
Green plantains
Oil for frying
Salt

DIRECTIONS:
Slice plantains into coin-shape pieces and salt the slices. Fry in oil until lightly browned and then drain.

Orange Candy from Mexico

INGREDIENTS:
3 cups sugar
¼ cup water
1 cup *undiluted* evaporated milk
1 pinch salt
2 tsp. grated orange peel
1 cup chopped nuts

You will also need an eight-inch square pan and a candy thermometer.

DIRECTIONS:
Pour *1 cup* of sugar into a heavy pan and cook over medium heat until it melts and turns a golden brown. Stir constantly with a wooden spoon. Carefully pour the water into the caramelized sugar and stir until the sugar is dissolved. Add the remaining 2 cups of sugar, evaporated milk, and salt. Place over low heat and stir until the mixture bubbles.

Continue cooking, stirring frequently, until the mixture reaches the soft-ball stage on a candy thermometer. Remove from heat and cool slightly without stirring. Add orange peel and nuts, beating until the candy loses its gloss and holds its shape when dropped from a spoon. Pour into lightly buttered pan. Cool until set and then cut into pieces before candy becomes too firm.

Adapted from: Piper, M. (Ed.). (1975). *Sunset Mexican cookbook.* Menlo Park, CA: Lane Books.

Polish-American Observances

Many Polish-American families celebrate holidays in honor of heroes or commemorative holidays related to important dates in history. One of the most important of these holidays is observed on May 3, the date commemorating the adoption of the first Polish constitution in 1791.

An important Polish hero can be the focus for increased cultural awareness. Count Casimir Pulaski left Poland to fight in the colonial army during the American Revolution. Because he had been a member of the cavalry in the Polish army, he helped to train the colonial cavalry. Count Pulaski led an attack on Savannah, Georgia. He was wounded when the attack failed and died two days later on October 11, 1779.

Try This: Ask your students to locate and read accounts of other Polish-Americans who have made contributions to the United States. They may present their research either orally or in a written report.

Chapter 3

The Cold Winds of November

The Gregorian calendar places November as the eleventh month of the year. However, November was named by the Romans, whose calendar began the new year on March 1. Hence, their November was the ninth month and was named *Novem*, the Latin word for nine. The Roman senate offered to name this month in honor of Tiberius Caesar, for two other months had already been named for ruling monarchs: July for Julius Caesar and August for Augustus Caesar. However, Tiberius Caesar refused the honor. He is reported to have said, "What if you have thirteen emperors?"

In most of the countries in the Northern Hemisphere, November begins a bleak and barren period. The early part of the month may be mild, displaying hazy landscapes filled with ripened fruits and vegetables. During this time in the United States, football is still popular in the cool afternoons on high school and college campuses. Soon, however, the leaves turn brown and fall, leaving only bare tree branches exposed to the coming cold winds and heavy snows.

Several important events occur in November. For Americans, the first is Election Day. Each year, this day is important to citizens across the nation, but every four years there is an unusual air of excitement and anticipation when a national election is held to elect the president of the United States.

In the United States, November also marks the celebration of Thanksgiving. A day of thanksgiving and prayer was first proclaimed by the survivors of the Plymouth colony after their first difficult and deadly winter.

November

Sunday	Monday	Tuesday	Wednesday	Thursday	Friday	Saturday

NOVEMBER

SELECTED EVENTS

1 All Saints Day
   Mexico: Day of the Dead
2 Daniel Boone (1734–1820)
3 John Montague (1718–1792)
4 Will Rogers (1879–1935)
5 England: Guy Fawkes Day
6 John Philip Sousa (1854–1932)
7 Marie Curie (1867–1934)
8 Edmund Halley (1656–1742)
9 Kristallnacht Anniversary (1938)
   Leonard Andrew Grimes (1815–1874)
10 Martin Luther (1483–1546)
11 Canada: Remembrance Day
   France: Armistice Day
12 Singapore: Deepavali Festival of Lights
   Elizabeth Cady Stanton (1815–1902)
13 India: Deepavali (Diwali) Festival of Lights
   Robert Louis Stevenson (1850–1894)
14 Jawaharlal Nehru (1889–1964)
15 Georgia O'Keeffe (1887–1986)
16 William Christopher Handy (1873–1958)
17 National Young Readers Day
18 Mickey Mouse Anniversary (1928)
19 Belize: Garifuna Day
   Gettysburg Address (1863)
20 Mexico Revolution Day
   Robert Francis Kennedy (1925–1968)
21 World Hello Day
   Henrietta Howland (Hetty) Green (1835–1916)
22 John F. Kennedy assassinated (1963)
   Charles de Gaulle (1890–1970)
23 Japan Labor Thanksgiving Day
   Emmett Littleton Ashford (1914–1980)
24 Scott Joplin (1868–1917)
25 Andrew Carnegie (1835–1919)
26 Mary Edwards Walker (1832–1919)
   Death of Sojourner Truth (1883)
27 Fanny Kemble (1809–1893)
28 Panama Independence Day
   John Bunyan (1628–1688)
29 Louisa May Alcott (1832–1888)
30 Philippines: Bonifacio Day
   Scotland: St. Andrews Day

People, Places, and Events of November

What's Happening in November:

Child Safety and Protection Month
Jewish Book Month

Other November Events:

First Monday: Australian Recreation Day in northern Tasmania.
First Tuesday after the first Monday: General Election Day.
First Friday: World Community Day.
First Saturday: Sadie Hawkins Day. (Originated by Al Capp in "Li'l Abner" comic strip in the 1930s. A day when women and girls are encouraged to take the initiative in asking men and boys for dates.)
November 1–7: World Communications Week.
First full week preceding the fourth Thursday: American Education Week.
Fourth Thursday: American Thanksgiving.
Last full week: Latin America Week.

November's Daily Calendar

1

All-Hallomas or All Saints Day. Catholics commemorate the blessed who have no special feast days; set by Pope Gregory IV in 835.
Guatemala: Kite Festival of Santiago Sacatepequez. Youths work for weeks making giant kites to fly on All Saints Day. This activity is believed to rid evil spirits from this village.
Boston Female Medical School opened (1848).
Mexico Day of the Dead. Departed souls are remembered with a spirit of good humor and friendliness.
Founding of Mission San Juan Capistrano (1776).
Virgin Islands Liberty Day. Established to honor the first press in the Virgin Islands in 1915.

2

All-Souls Day. Commemorating the faithful who have died.
North Dakota Admission Day. Became the thirty-ninth state admitted to the Union (1889).
South Dakota Admission Day. Became the fortieth state admitted to the Union (1889).
Birth anniversary of:
   Daniel Boone (1734–1820). Early American frontiersman and explorer.

Warren G. Harding (1865–1923). Twenty-ninth president of the United States; born in Ohio.

James Knox Polk (1795–1849). Eleventh president of the United States; born in North Carolina.

3

Panama Independence Day. Declared independence from Colombia in 1903.

Sandwich Day. Celebrating the birthday of John Montague, Fourth Earl of Sandwich; creator of the sandwich.

Singapore: Thimithi Festival. Fire-walking festival honoring the purity of the goddess Duropadai.

Birth anniversary of:

John Montague (1718–1792). Reported to be a rake and a gambler, he is said to have invented the sandwich so that he could continue gambling while eating.

Stephen Fuller Austin (1793–1836). Principal founder and colonizer of Texas.

4

Discovery of King Tut's tomb (1922).

Mischief Night. Observed in England, New Zealand, and Australia; an occasion for bonfires and firecrackers to celebrate the failure of the plot to destroy the Houses of Parliament in 1605.

Birth anniversary of:

Will Rogers (1879–1935). Writer, actor, and humorist born in Indian Territory (Oklahoma).

5

England: Guy Fawkes Day. Anniversary of the failed gunpowder plot to blow up the Houses of Parliament along with King James I in 1605. Proclaimed as a day of public thanksgiving.

Birth anniversary of:

Raymond Loewy (1893–1986). Inventor and engineer; known as the "Father of Streamlining."

6

Sweden: All Saints Day. Honoring the memory of those who have died.

Birth anniversary of:

James Naismith (1861–1939). Inventor of the game of basketball; born in Ontario, Canada.

Ignace Jan Paderewski (1860–1941). Polish composer and pianist.

Adolphe Sax (1814–1894). Belgian musician and inventor of the saxophone.

John Philip Sousa (1854–1932). Composer and band conductor remembered as the "March King."

7

Completion of the Canadian Pacific Transcontinental Railway (1885).

Birth anniversary of:

Marie Sklodowska Curie (1867–1934). Polish chemist and physicist, who along with her husband, Pierre, discovered radium and plutonium.

8

Montana Admission Day. Became the forty-first state to be admitted to the Union (1889).

X-Ray Discovery Day. Physicist William Conrad Roentgen is credited with the discovery of X-rays in 1895.

Birth anniversary of:

Christiaan Neethling Barnard (1922–). South African surgeon and medical pioneer; performed the first human heart transplant in 1967.

Edmund Halley (1656–1742). English astronomer and mathematician.

9

Fall of the Berlin Wall (1989).

Kristallnacht (Crystal Night) Anniversary (1938). Infamous night in Germany when mobs destroyed thousands of Jewish homes and shops.

Birth anniversary of:

Leonard Andrew Grimes (1815–1874). African-American, born to free parents, who was active in assisting fugitive slaves. Became the minister to Twelfth Street Church in Boston.

10

Birth anniversary of:

Oliver Goldsmith (1730–1774). Irish writer.

Martin Luther (1483–1546). Founder and leader of the Reformation and Protestant movement.

11

Canada: Remembrance Day.

France: Armistice Day. Celebrating the signing of the armistice that ended World War I in 1918.

French West Indies: Concordia Day. Commemorating the peaceful coexistence of the Dutch and French on St. Martin Island.

Sweden: St. Martin's Day. Marks end of autumn's work and beginning of winter activities.

Veterans Day. Originally observed as Armistice Day; changed in 1971 to Veterans Day.

Washington Admission Day. Became the forty-second state admitted to the union (1889).

Birth anniversary of:

Fyodor Mikhailovich Dostoyevsky (1821–1881). Russian novelist.

George S. Patton, Jr. (1885–1945). World War II general.

12

Singapore: Deepavali Festival of Lights. Hindu festival celebrating the triumph of light over darkness and good over evil.

Birth anniversary of:
Auguste Rodin (1840–1917). French sculptor.
Elizabeth Cady Stanton (1815–1902). Woman suffragist and reformer.
Sun Yat-sen (1866–1925). Leader of the 1911 revolution in China.

13

India: Deepavali (Diwali) Festival of Lights. Celebrating the return of Lord Ramachandra.

African-American Carl B. Stokes elected mayor of Cleveland, Ohio (1967).

Birth anniversary of:
Robert Louis Stevenson (1850–1894). Scottish author and poet.

14

First blood transfusion. Blood transferred between two dogs in 1666.

Birth anniversary of:
Robert Fulton (1765–1815). Developer of the steamboat.
Jawaharlal Nehru (1889–1964). Indian leader and the first prime minister after independence.

15

American Enterprise Day. Celebrating the free market economy.

Belgium: Dynasty Day. Celebrating the Belgian monarchy.

Brazil Republic Day. Commemorating foundation as a republic in 1889.

Arthur Dorrington signed with the Atlantic City Seagulls to become the first African-American to play professional hockey (1950).

Gypsy Condemnation Order. Approximately half a million Gypsies were put to death in the Holocaust as result of this order in 1943.

Japan: Shichi-Go-San. Annual children's festival honoring all three-year-olds, five-year-old males, and seven-year-old females.

Birth anniversary of:
Georgia O'Keeffe (1887–1986). Artist.

16

Oklahoma Admission Day. Became the forty-sixth state admitted to the Union (1907).

Birth anniversary of:
William Christopher Handy (1873–1958). American composer and "Father of the Blues."

17

National Young Readers Day. Sponsored by the Center for the Book, Library of Congress, to encourage the love of reading.

Suez Canal opened (1869).

18

Haiti: Army Day. Commemorating the Haitians' defeat of the French in 1803.

Mickey Mouse Anniversary. Mickey Mouse first appeared in Walt Disney's cartoon "Steamboat Willie" in 1928.

United States Uniform Time Zone Plan instituted. Four time zones established and placed in operation by U.S. railroads in 1883.

Birth anniversary of:
Louis-Jacques-Mandé Daguerre (1789–1851). French painter and inventor of the daguerreotype photographic process.

19

Belize: Garifuna Day. Celebrating the arrival of Black Caribs to southern Belize.

Lincoln's Gettysburg Address delivered (1863).

Puerto Rico Discovery Day. Columbus landed at Puerto Rico on his second journey (1493).

Birth anniversary of:
James Abram Garfield (1831–1881). Twentieth president of the United States; born in Ohio.

20

Mexico Revolution Day. Commemorating the social revolution of 1910.

Birth anniversary of:
Andrés Bello (1781–1865). Venezuelan author, diplomat, and humanist.
Chester Gould (1900–1985). Creator of the comic strip "Dick Tracy."
Robert Francis Kennedy (1925–1968). Senator and brother of John F. Kennedy; assassinated while campaigning for the presidency.
Selma Lagerlöf (1858–1940). Swedish author; first woman to receive Nobel Prize for literature.

21

North Carolina Ratification Day. Became the twelfth state to ratify the U.S. Constitution (1789).

World Hello Day. Participants greet ten people in an attempt to advance peace through communication.

Birth anniversary of:
  Henrietta Howland Robinson (Hetty) Green (1835–1916). Financier who managed her own money; was reported to have been the richest woman in America with more than one hundred million dollars.
  Voltaire (François Marie Arouet) (1694–1778). French author and philosopher.

22

John F. Kennedy assassinated (1963)
Birth anniversary of:
  Charles de Gaulle (1890–1970). French general and statesman; president of Fifth Republic from 1958 to 1969.
  George Eliot (Mary Ann Evans) (1819–1880). Female English novelist.

23

Japan Labor Thanksgiving Day. National holiday of thanksgiving.
Birth anniversary of:
  Emmett Littleton Ashford (1914–1980). First African-American to officiate at a major league baseball game.
  William H. (Billy the Kid) Bonney (1859–1881). Legendary western outlaw.
  Adolph Arthur (Harpo) Marx (1888–1964). Comedian and member of the Marx Brothers.
  Franklin Pierce (1804–1869). Fourteenth president of the United States; born in New Hampshire.

24

Birth anniversary of:
  Scott Joplin (1868–1917). African–American musician and composer.
  Baruch Spinoza (1632–1677). Dutch philosopher.
  Zachary Taylor (1784–1850). Twelfth president of the United States; born in Virginia.

25

St. Catherine's Day. Patron saint of maidens, mechanics, and philosophers.
Singapore: Hari Raya Puasa. Muslim festival ending the month-long fast of the Ramadan.
Suriname Independence Day. Located in northern South America; gained independence from the Netherlands in 1975.
Birth anniversary of:
  Andrew Carnegie (1835–1919). Financier, philanthropist, and benefactor of libraries; born in Scotland.
  Carry Amelia Moore Nation (1846–1911). Temperance leader and hatchet-wielding smasher of saloons.

26

Birth anniversary of:
  Sarah Moore Grimke (1792–1873). Antislavery worker and advocate of women's rights.
  John Harvard (1607–1638). Founder of Harvard College, later to become Harvard University.
  Death of Sojourner Truth (ca. 1790–1883). African-American former slave and leader in the struggle to abolish slavery; advocate of women's rights.
  Mary Edwards Walker (1832–1919). First female surgeon in the U.S. Army.

27

Birth anniversary of:
  Fanny Kemble (1809–1893). English actress.
  Chaim Weizmann (1874-–1952). Israeli statesman; played an important role in the establishment of the national home for Jews in Palestine.

28

Mauritania Independence Day. Located in western Africa; gained independence from France in 1960.
Panama Independence Day. Celebrating independence from Spain in 1821.
Birth anniversary of:
  William Blake (1757–1827). English poet and artist.
  John Bunyan (1628–1688). English author; remembered for *Pilgrim's Progress*.

29

Czechoslovakia ends Communist rule (1989).
Birth anniversary of:
  Louisa May Alcott (1832–1888). Author of *Little Women* and *Little Men*.

30

Scotland: St. Andrews Day. Patron saint of Scotland; honors Andrew, apostle and martyr, who died about A.D. 60.
Barbados Independence Day. Island nation in Caribbean Sea; gained independence from Britain in 1966.
Philippines: Bonifacio Day. Also known as National Heroes' Day. Honoring Andres Bonifacio, leader of the 1896 revolt against Spain.
Birth anniversary of:
  Winston Churchill (1874–1965). British statesman, minister of defense, and prime minister.
  Jonathan Swift (1667–1745). Irish author and satirist.
  Mark Twain (Samuel Langhorne Clemens) (1835–1910). Author and creator of Tom Sawyer and Huck Finn.

Harvest and Thanksgiving Celebrations Around the World

Teaching Unit for November

A Word about This Unit. This unit relates to thanksgiving and harvest festivals around the world. It describes how people everywhere participate in similar rituals and celebrations where food is gathered and preparations are made for the coming winter. In the United States, Thanksgiving is celebrated in November to remember the early European settlers who left their homes in search of freedom of worship and to make better lives for themselves. It is also a time to remember all people who have struggled for freedom. Besides focusing on traditional Thanksgiving customs, this unit will help students understand and appreciate festivals and celebrations of thanksgiving around the world.

Motivation. Begin this unit by discussing harvest time and rituals that often accompany celebrations of thanksgiving. Students may be aware only of the American Thanksgiving holiday. Lead the discussion to observances of thanksgiving and harvest festivals in other countries, such as Canada. Many schools still hold "fall carnivals" as fund-raising projects. Discuss the similarities between the school carnival and harvest festivals around the world.

Immersion. In this part of the unit, students gather information about the topic. You can either read the short excerpts of information included in this text, read from a variety of trade books, or direct students to seek information in appropriate reference sources.

Information. Obviously, food has been a basic necessity for all people in all cultures throughout history. In earliest times, people were hunters and gatherers. However, because survival depended on a predictable and ample supply of food, by 3000 B.C. people in the Middle East, Mesopotamia, and South America had developed a system for planting seeds.

The first day of thanksgiving probably can be traced back to these times. A harvest ample enough to sustain life throughout the long winter was viewed as a blessing, and people planned and performed rituals of thanksgiving. These early thanksgiving days may have been celebrated as holy days of prayer and fasting. However, such days were not necessarily set aside strictly for prayer and appeasement of gods, but may

also have been celebrations related to an abundance of food. After the major religions were established, many people continued to celebrate religious rituals related to the harvest.

In the twentieth century, people throughout the world continue to set aside special days as observances of thanksgiving. The celebration of thanksgiving holy days in many countries shows how all peoples are connected by the necessity to meet common needs and the desire to plan rituals and celebrations of important events.

Thanksgiving in the United States

In the United States, Thanksgiving is celebrated on the fourth Thursday in November. The first thanksgiving in the English colonies was probably more a festival of celebration of the harvest than a religious holiday for prayer and fasting. After the first harvest in 1621, the Pilgrims invited their Native American neighbors to share their food. The previous severe winter had left half of their citizens dead, but a plentiful harvest was evident the following autumn. Their settlement now had eleven houses and four common buildings. They had become friends with the Native Americans, who had taught them how to grow corn. This corn was stored away, offering the hope that the colony would survive the winter. The future was uncertain, but it appeared brighter than the past.

The next two years were hard for the Pilgrims, but during the year that followed, after a very hot and dry spring and summer, Governor William Bradford set a day for fasting and prayer. To celebrate the rain that came afterward, Governor Bradford declared a three-day celebration beginning on July 30, 1623, for "the purpose of prayer and rejoicing." Women spent weeks preparing for the feast. Men supplied geese, ducks, and fish, and Native Americans came with deer and wild turkeys. The feast, spread outdoors on big tables, included all types of meats and vegetables.

After that celebration, there is no record of an annual day of thanksgiving; however, individual towns or colonies may have set aside special days. The Continental Congress proclaimed several days of thanksgiving during the American Revolution. President George Washington declared November 26, 1789, as a day of thanksgiving after adoption of the Constitution. In the autumn of 1815, President James Madison proclaimed a day of thanksgiving and feasting for peace after the War of 1812. This day was celebrated mostly in the North until the time of the Civil War. It was then that Sarah Hale, editor of the *Godey's Lady's Book*, advocated a national day of thanksgiving as a way to bring the country together. President Abraham Lincoln declared Thanksgiving a national holiday and set the date as the last Thursday in November, for "a day of thanksgiving and praise." In 1939, President Franklin D. Roosevelt set the date one week earlier to give merchants more time between Thanksgiving and Christmas. In 1942, Congress ruled that thereafter Thanksgiving Day would be a federal holiday observed on the fourth Thursday of November.

History of Thanksgiving in the United States. Although we often read about the first thanksgiving in North America as occurring at the time of the Pilgrims, many festivals of thanksgiving were held across this continent before the European settlers arrived at Plymouth Rock.

Corn was brought to the natives of the upper areas of North America through trade with the Mayas and the Aztecs living in Central America. Native Americans learned to grow many different varieties, some even of different colors. Natives in the Southwest particularly liked blue corn. Because of the importance of corn, many Native Americans had three major corn ceremonies: a planting, a harvest, and a green corn ceremony.

The green corn ceremony, the most important of the three, took place when the corn was nearly ripe. The people gave thanks for the current year's food and asked for the blessing of abundant food in the coming year. It was considered a crime against the gods to eat the new corn before this ceremony was performed. For the people of the Creek nation, the green corn festival symbolized the rebirth of the entire world. In Florida, the Seminoles drank the "black drink" the evening before their ceremony. This drink served as a purge to cleanse their bodies. Then they ate new corn and afterward fasted. At the end of the ceremony they ate a meal of berries, beans, pumpkin, and meat.

The Native Americans of the Southwest pueblos performed ritual dances during their green corn festivals. Some of the dancers represented the spirits of the ancestors, carrying poles with long banners attached. People tried to pass under one of the banners at least four times. Weeks later, just before the harvest, the people cleaned their pueblo to honor and welcome the gods and to appease them so that they would be blessed with a good harvest during the coming year. A green corn dance is still held today by the Navajo people.

The Iroquois developed ceremonies to honor the ripening of different berries. Because they best loved the strawberry, it was the subject of the most important festival. In June, after the women collected the ripe strawberries and the chief prayed and sprinkled grains of tobacco over a fire, the people sang, danced, and played games. At the end of the festival, the strawberries were eaten with maple syrup on corn pudding.

The Salish Native Americans loved wild raspberries. Freshly harvested berries were cooked over a new fire while the Salish stood in a circle. The chief called on the spirit of the raspberry plant for a good harvest. Afterward, the cooked berries were eaten from a newly carved wooden dish.

Because salmon was an important food source to the Native Americans of California, the Karok nation held a ceremony to ensure a good catch when the salmon began to move upstream to spawn.

In their harvest festivals, the Plains Indians wore traditional dress decorated with woven or painted designs. Some made headdresses decorated with feathers and beads. The dancers would chant, dance, and shake rattles, evoking the graces of the spirits. Today, many Native American peoples continue to participate in these harvest celebrations.

Mexico had established colonies in California during the eighteenth century. In 1769, of a group of three hundred people who began a journey to form a new settlement in California, only 126 survived. Father Junipero Serra came to the aid of the group, and on July 1 held a mass of thanksgiving for the survivors.

Native Americans in Alaska celebrated their thanksgiving holidays in connection with their search for food, usually after a successful whale hunt. Because the hunt took place when the ice began to break, the thanksgiving celebration was held in the spring.

Ancient Hawaiians celebrated their thanksgiving festival, Makahiki, for four months. From November through February, work and war were forbidden. The people collected gifts for Lono, the Hawaiian god of plenty. A statue of Lono, sprinkled with coconut oil and decorated with plants and feathers, was carried to the different villages by priests. At each village, the priests collected offerings and prayed to Lono. The villagers then danced in the sand and feasted, in addition to taking part in a variety of sports.

The people of the Virgin Islands celebrate two thanksgivings. Besides the traditional November holiday, an earlier holiday is held on October 25 if there were no hurricanes during the year. This October celebration is a time to give thanks and to pray that there will be no hurricanes during the coming year.

Ancient Harvest Celebrations

Greeks. The people of ancient Greece held a harvest festival in the fall after the grain was collected. To celebrate, they hung apples, pears, and plums on trees. Carrying gifts of grain, they visited the shrine of Demeter, the Greek goddess responsible for crops. The myth that surrounds Demeter explains the yearly growing cycle. Demeter's daughter Persephone was reaching to pick a beautiful flower when Hades, the god of the underworld, appeared. He grabbed Persephone and carried her down into the earth to become his bride. From the top of the home of the gods and goddesses, Demeter heard Persephone crying. Demeter searched the earth for nine days and nights looking for her daughter. Helios, the sun god, told Demeter what had happened to Persephone, and as punishment Demeter stopped the crops from growing. Because the people were unable to use the harvest to make offerings to the gods, Zeus commanded Hades to return Persephone to her mother. However, because Persephone had eaten six pomegranate seeds while in the underworld, Hades demanded that she stay with him for six months each year. Persephone was allowed to return to her mother during the other months. During these six months, Demeter was so happy that she allowed the crops to grow. During the autumn, when it was time to plant the seeds for next year's crops, the Greeks held a festival called Thesmosphoria to honor Demeter.

Romans. The ancient Romans, influenced by the Greeks, held a harvest festival each October 4 in honor of Ceres, the goddess of corn. First fruits and a sow were offered to Ceres, and parades, dances, and sporting contests were held in her honor.

Egyptians. An Egyptian harvest festival was held during the spring in honor of Min, the god of vegetation and fertility. A great parade was led by the current pharaoh. He was followed by a white bull, a large statue of Min borne by priests, and finally another group of priests carrying bundles of lettuce, Min's favorite plant.

In contrast to this joyous festival, when it came time for the actual harvest, the ancient Egyptian farmers wept, pretending to be sad in order to deceive a spirit whom they believed lived in the corn. The belief was that this spirit would be angry with them for cutting and grinding the corn.

Hebrews. The Hebrew people celebrated two thanksgiving festivals, Shavuoth and Sukkoth. The Shavuoth occurred when the first fruits and grains were collected and taken to the Temple in the spring or early summer. Sukkoth, held in the fall, was celebrated for eight days during September or October. Sukkoth was first celebrated by Hebrews in the land of Canaan thousands of years ago, and it is still celebrated by many Jews. Today, during the festival, people build small booths or huts called "sukkots" outside their homes, in their yards, or on their balconies. They spend part of each day in the sukkot, visiting with friends, eating, or praying, as a reminder of the huts in which their ancestors lived during the forty years spent wandering in the wilderness following their captivity in Egypt.

Europeans. Traditionally, the people of **Estonia,** in order to deceive the spirit of the grain, pretended to take a bite from a piece of iron before eating bread made from the freshly harvested crops.

In earlier times, after **German** farmers harvested and ground their grains, they threw handfuls from the rooftops and chanted, "There you are, wind! Cook meal for your child!" (Penner, 1986, p. 237).

England celebrated several different harvest rituals. In some parts of England, farmers were afraid that cutting the last grain plant would kill the spirit of the crops. Therefore, all the harvesters stood around the last plant and threw their sickles at it, hoping that the spirit would not know whose tool had taken its life.

In some parts of England, during a celebration known as Harvest Home, the man who cut the last sheaf would be named Lord of the Harvest. After all the grain was piled onto a cart, he would ride home on top, surrounded by the other farmhands, who would laugh, joke, and sing. People hiding in the bushes along the way would jump out and throw buckets of water on the procession. A big feast provided by owners of the farms would be waiting at the ending of the parade.

Another custom practiced in England was called "Crying the Neck." After the last of the grain was cut, it was braided into a neck-shaped object. The field worker who braided the neck held it over his head and lowered it to the ground. The other workers standing around him would bend to the ground and touch the stubble of the newly harvested grain. When they stood up, they lifted their hats in the air and called out, "The Neck! The Neck!," while the neck was lifted into the air. This ritual was repeated three times (Penner, 1986, p. 32).

In some regions of England, the last sheaf of grain was formed into a doll, which then might be decorated with ribbons, yarn, or flowers. It was hung on the farmhouse wall until it was time to plant next year's crops. Then the doll might be cut into pieces and fed to the horses or burned and the ashes plowed into the newly tilled fields.

The **Celts**, who lived in what is now France and the British Isles, held a festival called Samhain around the beginning of November. This day combined a harvest festival with remembrance of the dead. It was believed that on Samhain Eve the dead souls came back to seek warmth and shelter. The Celtic people gave offerings of food to these spirits.

In **Sweden**, a cake shaped like a little girl was formed from the last sheaf of grain, and everyone in the family ate a piece of it.

Polish farmers made the sheaf of wheat into a crown. This "Wienjec" was decorated with nuts, flowers, and apples. A procession of harvesters was led by a girl wearing the Wienjec. When the procession reached the farmhouse, the farmer threw buckets of water at the girl until she was thoroughly drenched. Perhaps this was meant to ensure rain for the next growing season.

Central and South America. In ancient times, the **Mayas** held many religious festivals that demonstrated how important corn was to them. One festival honored the corn god, Yum Kax, who was believed to have created the Mayan people out of corn. The Mayas also held a rain festival and a celebration of harvest after gathering the crops. At the harvest feast, turkey and squash were served. If there was not enough turkey for everyone, dog meat was used to supplement the meal. When the newly harvested corn was popped into popcorn, young girls threw handfuls at the spectators.

Xilonen was the **Aztec** name for their harvest goddess. They gave her two nicknames. When the harvest was good, she was called Chalchiuhcihuatl, meaning "woman of precious stone." In lean years she was called Chicomecoatl, which means "serpent of seven heads" (Penner, 1986, p. 43). Her festival was celebrated on September 15 only in years when the harvest was good. A week before this festival, the Aztecs ate only scraps of old tortillas and drank only water. During this entire week, a slave girl danced. Representing the goddess Xilonen, she was dressed in a beautiful costume and precious stones, with her face painted yellow and red, and her head crowned with a hat decorated with green plumes. On the day of the feast, she was slain as a sacrifice. This was followed by an enormous feast.

The **Incas,** who lived in the Southern Hemisphere, held their harvest festival in May, when it is autumn there. During this time they made offerings of the first corn to their gods.

Modern Thanksgiving and Harvest Holidays Around the World

Africa. Tribal farmers observe harvest festivals in which they thank their ancestors for keeping the people well and sending rain. The African-American community in the United States has begun the annual celebration of Harambee. Harambee is the Swahili word for "let's pull together" or "unity." It is observed on the fourth Saturday of October as a time to celebrate African-American culture.

Canada. The Canadians celebrate Thanksgiving on the second Monday in October. Because of Canada's short growing season and early harvest, October was chosen for the thanksgiving celebration rather than November. The Canadian holiday is very similar to the one celebrated in the United States, with families gathering to enjoy traditional foods.

China. The "moon's birthday" set for the day of the full moon closest to the fifteenth day of the eighth month, is the start of the Chinese harvest festival called Chung Ch'ui, a time to give thanks and to remember a victory over an invading army. Chung Ch'ui is a family celebration that lasts for three days. An altar is built in each home and five plates are arranged on it. In the center of each plate is a round, yellow moon cake made of newly harvested grain with red or green decorations, surrounded by round fruits. Because the Chinese believe they see the outline of a rabbit on the moon's surface, each cake is stamped with the image of a rabbit. Chinese families celebrate with great feasts of roast pork, fruit, and moon cakes. During this time, they believe that flowers fall from the moon and that anyone who is able to see them will have good fortune throughout the year.

India. In September, Hindu women honor Gauri, the goddess of harvest and the protector of women. In the Indian household, an unmarried daughter carries a bundle of aromatic plants throughout the house for three days. As she walks from room to room, other female members of the family ask her what she has brought. The answer varies depending on the room — delicious food, prosperity, or beautiful children. The other women respond, "Come on golden feet and stay forever" (Penner, 1986, p. 110). Afterward, Gauri is offered milk and sweets. On the second day of the festival, the women feast. On the final day, a servant takes the bundle to a stream and throws it into the water, bringing back some earth from the bank of the stream.

This earth is considered sacred, representing the land where the first farmers planted crops.

Japan. Before World War II, the Japanese people had two harvest festivals, Kanname-sai and Niiname-sai. Kanname-sai was held on October 17, in honor of a legend in which Princess Yamatohime received rice from a crane. After preparing a meal from the rice, she made an offering to the sun goddess. Each year, gifts of rice and saki, a rice wine, were offered to the ancestors of the royal family.

The second festival, Niiname-sai, was celebrated on November 23 at the emperor's palace (Penner, 1986, pp. 105–106) This holiday honors the time when the imperial grandson, Prince Ninigi, came down to earth and was given new rice by the local gods. On this date, the emperor honored his ancestors by offering their spirits the first fruits of the harvest.

Since World War II, Thanksgiving is a national holiday celebrated on November 23. It no longer honors the imperial grandson or the emperor's ancestors, but instead is a time to give thanks for blessings.

Korea. On the fifth day of the fifth lunar month (approximately early June), Koreans observe a festival called Tano Day, whereby they offer prayers for good harvests.

Northern Europe. In many parts of northern Europe, November 11 is called Martinmas and is designated as a day of thanksgiving. During the Middle Ages, people gave harvest feasts for beggars on the anniversary of the day that St. Martin, the patron saint of beggars, was buried. Today, in **Holland,** children go begging for cake, fruit, and candy on St. Martin's Day, an interesting carryover of the traditions of earlier times associated with Martinmas.

In **Switzerland** and **Sweden**, on their holidays celebrating the harvest, children carry lanterns made from vegetables. These lanterns are made much the same way as jack-o'-lanterns are made from pumpkins. In Sweden the celebration is held on Martinmas, but in Switzerland the holiday is observed on the Monday before the last Thursday in November.

In America: A Time to Remember. In the United States, Thanksgiving is celebrated on the fourth Thursday in November. It is a time to remember the early European settlers who left their homes in search of freedom of worship and to make better lives for themselves. It is also a time to remember all people who have struggled for freedom. Finally, it is a time to give thanks for a bountiful harvest and to participate in the traditional Thanksgiving feast. Families and friends generally sit down for a meal of turkey, stuffing, cranberry sauce,

sweet potatoes or yams, and pumpkin pie. These items form the traditional meal because, according to popular belief, they represent some of the foods the Pilgrims may have eaten at their celebration.

Although the Thanksgiving meals served in the United States tend to be similar, there are regional variations. Stuffing for the turkey in the South is made from corn bread, while in other parts of the United States, the stuffing may contain oysters, chestnuts, rice, white breadcrumbs, or a variety of other ingredients.

The activities in the next section can be used to expand this unit by directly involving your students.

Instructional Activities

Activity 3.1: Thanksgiving Customs around the World

Have students collect information about various thanksgiving, harvest, and planting customs around the world. Ask them to discuss what they can infer about a country or culture based on this information. Compare the various customs to determine similarities. A good starting place for this project is the References and Bibliography list at the end of this section.

Activity 3.2: Researching Your Own Family Thanksgiving Celebrations

After a discussion of different thanksgiving customs and traditions around the world, students can be given a copy of the chart "How We Celebrate Thanksgiving" to complete by interviewing members of their family. In addition, students might collect recipes from parents, grandparents, relatives, or neighbors. The class could then develop a book of Thanksgiving Festival Recipes. Each student should include interesting

information related to the tradition of using that food for his or her family's celebration.

If your class is composed of children from many different cultures and backgrounds, the chart supplied here may be appropriate. However, if the class population is very similar in nature, you may want to adapt the form.

Activity 3.3: Understanding the Symbols of Thanksgiving

Each student should select a word from the boxed list to research its origins or symbolism for Thanksgiving. After completing the research, the student can expand the project by creating a small booklet including information, illustrations, and examples of usage of the word.

You may want to make a class book instead. Each student should be given a page that is shaped like a Thanksgiving symbol, such as a turkey or cornucopia. After students have completed their assignments, all the pages are assembled.

Thanksgiving Words

Thanksgiving	Thursday	Puritan
Pilgrim	corn	November
turkey	feast biscuit	cranberry
squash	pumpkin	ancestor
yam/sweet potato	succotash	others?

Suggested Reading

Barth, E. (1979). *Turkeys, Pilgrims and Indian corn: the story of the Thanksgiving symbols*. New York: Clarion Books.

Graham-Barber, L. (1991). *Gobble: the complete book of Thanksgiving words*. New York: Bradbury Press.

Penner, L. R. (1986). *The Thanksgiving book*. New York: Hastings House.

Funk, C., & Earle, C. (1958). *Horsefeathers and other curious words*. New York: Harper & Row.

The Oxford dictionary of English etymology. (1966). Oxford: Clarendon Press.

HOW MY FAMILY CELEBRATES THANKSGIVING

In our family, we call our thanksgiving celebration: _____

_____

We celebrate the holiday during (month): _____

Our special practices and customs are: _____

_____

_____

_____

_____

Our traditional meal for this occasion usually is: _____

_____

_____

_____

_____

We eat this type of food or practice this custom because: _____

_____

_____

Activity 3.4: Community Food Bank— A Social Action Project

The class can organize a schoolwide drive in cooperation with a local food bank or service organization. Students can publicize the project and collect or contribute canned and nonperishable foods for distribution to needy families. Some students may want to volunteer to help in the actual distribution of the items.

Activity 3.5: Why Did the Turkey Cross the Road? or Let's Have Fun

Establish a humor corner where students can collect or write original Thanksgiving jokes, riddles, puns, or stories. For example: What do you get when you breed a turkey with an octopus? Answer: A turkey with enough drumsticks for everyone! Often many students will have a large repertoire of sayings and jokes that they can share with the class. From this activity, students may see that many jokes belong to what folklorists call motifs. That is, they are repeated over and over in various cultures, using similar themes and characters, but are changed as needed to meet the intent of the joketeller.

References and Bibliography

Barkin, C., & James, E. (1987). *Happy Thanksgiving*. New York: Lothrop. Collection of creative ideas for celebrating Thanksgiving and developing new traditions for that holiday.

Barth, E. (1979). *Turkeys, Pilgrims, and Indian corn. The story of the Thanksgiving symbols*. New York: Clarion Books. Presents information about the Pilgrims, their lifestyle, a brief history of Thanksgiving, and a list of sources for stories, poems, pageants, and plays.

Bartlett, R. (1965). *Thanksgiving day*. New York: Thomas Crowell. Presents a well-developed history of Thanksgiving, beginning with an introduction of early Thanksgiving celebrations.

Graham-Barber, L. (1991). *Gobble! The complete book of Thanksgiving words*. New York: Bradbury Press. Provides etymology and anecdotes about the Thanksgiving vocabulary, as well as historical information about the holiday.

Hannum, D., et al. (1985). *Thanksgiving handbook*. Elgin, IL: Child's World. Collection of activities, decorations, suggestions for learning centers, songs, poems, and stories. Resource guide for teachers of grades K-3.

Luckhardt, M. C. (1966). *Thanksgiving: feast and festival*. Nashville: Abingdon Press. Collection of historical accounts, stories, and poems about Thanksgiving.

Penner, L. R. (1986). *The Thanksgiving book*. New York: Hastings House. History of Thanksgiving celebrations from different periods and countries. Includes recipes. Presents wealth of information about Native American practices.

November's Potpourri of Teaching Ideas

The purpose of each month's Potpourri of Teaching Ideas is to provide additional resources from which to build your curriculum. Most, but not all, of the activities listed each month relate directly to that month. It is not intended that you use them all, but rather that you choose those which are appropriate for your program. Although the topics are written for a particular month, many of them would be appropriate for use throughout the year. How you use these activities will depend on your curricular goals. You may wish to use some of the activities as they are presented, and you may need to modify some to meet your needs. Perhaps some of them will give you ideas for entirely different potpourris.

Day of the Dead

In Mexico, the first day of November is remembered as the Day of the Dead. This day is a time to honor the dead, not with mourning, but rather with a spirit of friendliness and good humor. Tradition holds that departed souls come back to earth on Halloween and then return to heaven on the Day of the Dead. This observance actually begins during late October, when "dead man's bread" is sold in bakeries and markets in villages and around the countryside. These round loaves are decorated with skulls made from sugar and are called *pan de muetros* in Spanish. The bread is specifically prepared and offered to the spirits, along with fruit, tamales, beverages, and other foods, for the journey the departed souls will make back to heaven.

This also is a time to visit cemeteries to decorate the graves with flowers. Altars and gravesites customarily are decorated with marigold flowers called *zempasuchitl*. The golden colors of these flowers, along with the deep maroon blossoms of cockscomb, symbolize death. Many candles are placed on altars to provide light for the spirits on their journey. Faithful followers often will remain all night at the cemetery, or before their home altars, praying for protection on behalf of the departed spirits.

People also honor the dead by displaying photographs of the deceased and by placing pictures or images of the Virgin of Guadalupe on the altars. In many parts of Mexico, it is believed that the trip made by the dead can be long and arduous. Sometimes new shoes are left on the altar to make the spirits' journey more comfortable.

Try These Activities

1. Death is a real, although fearful, part of the lives of many students. For older, more mature students, a

discussion of death and the mysticism and fears that surround it may be appropriate. A number of juvenile books that deal with this subject are available at most public and school libraries. One notable example is *Bridge to Terabithia* by Katherine Paterson (1977; New York: Harper & Row), which tells of the death of twelve-year-old Leslie and the reaction of her best friend, Jess.

2. If there are students in your class who have recently immigrated to the United States from Mexico, they may be willing to share with the class some of their experiences related to this custom.

3. After learning about the Day of the Dead, students can research customs and rituals related to death in different parts of the world, including ancient as well as modern civilizations. In Vietnam, for example, families visit the graves of ancestors on Thanh-Minh Day, a tradition similar to Mexico's Day of the Dead. Students can research the customs of the two countries and compare the rituals and practices of each.

Let's Bake Some Bread

Bread, the "staff of life," is thought to be the oldest food made by humans and is certainly the most widely eaten. The earliest bread was hard and flat and was probably baked by the sun or on hot stones. Unlike earlier times, most bread today is baked with a leavening agent such as yeast or baking powder to make it "rise."

Every culture makes some type of bread or bread substitute (grains and cereals). The most popular grain for breadmaking in the United States is wheat. However, both here and abroad, people make bread from oats, barley, corn, rye, rice, or a combination of these and other grains. For many families today, the principal source of bread is the local bakery or supermarket. A few generations ago, however, almost all bread eaten by a family was made at home.

To illustrate the importance of bread to various cultures, discuss with the class the breads eaten by different families. Suggest that the students make homemade bread for their families. They probably will receive positive responses for this project, especially if they promise to clean the kitchen afterward. Many types of bread are made by hundreds of world cultures, so you should have little difficulty locating a simple and acceptable recipe. However, as examples, three basic bread recipes are included here: French bread, corn pone from the South, and flour tortillas from Mexico.

Basic French Bread

This is an easy recipe for French bread or, as it is called in France, pain ordinaire. *Almost every French family is served bread very similar to this every day.*

INGREDIENTS:

1 cup milk	1 envelope dry yeast
1 Tbs. butter	½ cup warm water for yeast
1 Tbs. sugar	6 cups white flour
2 tsp. salt	egg whites
1 cup hot water	corn meal

DIRECTIONS:
Scald milk and stir in butter, sugar, salt, and 1 cup of hot water. Allow to cool. Dissolve package of yeast in ½ cup of warm water. Pour this into the milk mixture and stir. Add the flour (about 6 cups) to form a soft dough. Knead on a lightly floured board until the dough forms small air bubbles or blisters on top. Place the dough in a greased bowl and cover with a cloth. Let rise in a warm place until doubled in size (about 45 minutes to an hour). Punch the dough down and knead for 5 minutes. Let the dough rise again.

Punch the dough down a second time, and divide it in half. Knead each half and shape into a long loaf. Place the two loaves on a lightly oiled cookie sheet sprinkled with cornmeal. Brush the loaves with warm water and dust the top of each with cornmeal. Set the loaves in a warm place and allow them to rise until almost doubled. Bake at 375 degrees for 30 minutes. Remove loaves from oven and brush generously with stiffly beaten egg whites. Return loaves to oven and continue baking for another 10 minutes or until golden brown.

Hot Water Corn Pone

In the South, corn often was used for making bread. Corn-bread and corn pone are two types of quick breads. While the basic ingredients are nearly the same, corn bread and hot water corn pone differ in the way they are prepared.

INGREDIENTS:
½ cup flour
1 cup yellow corn meal
1 tsp. salt
2 Tbs. sugar
2 Tbs. shortening
1 cup boiling water
2 tsps. baking powder
Oil for frying

DIRECTIONS:

Mix together flour, corn meal, salt, sugar, and shortening. Add boiling water and stir well. Mix in baking powder. Shape into small balls (balls may be flattened or rolled into oblong "fingers" if preferred). Fry in hot oil in skillet. Serve hot.

Corn Tortillas

Tortillas are a staple food in many Mexican-American homes. They are easy to make and store. Besides being eaten as bread, they can be left flat and spread with ingredients to make chalupas, folded in half for tacos, or rolled to hold the filling of enchiladas.

INGREDIENTS:

2 cups masa harina
1/2 tsp. salt
1 1/2 cups water
Oil

DIRECTIONS:

Mix masa harina and salt with water and shape into 12 balls. Pat out flat with hands or tortilla press. Cook tortillas on hot griddle smeared with oil until brown. Turn and cook other side until brown. Note: Masa harina is available at many stores (particularly in regions where there is a large Hispanic-American population) in the baking section where flour and cornmeal are sold.

Kristallnacht: *Night of Broken Glass*

Kristallnacht, or "night of broken glass," is seen as the event that began the violence of the Holocaust prior to World War II. On November 9, 1938, Nazis dressed in civilian clothes and armed with hammers and axes took to the streets, shouting "Down with Jews." This activity attracted others, and soon angry mobs had formed. For the next twenty-four hours, throughout Germany and Austria, mobs roamed the streets, setting fires and destroying Jewish places of business and worship, and demolishing and looting Jewish homes. The Jewish people were made to pay for the damages. Thirty thousand Jews were then arrested and sent to concentration camps. It was a day of infamy.

In the weeks that followed, other persecution occurred. Some events were mob related, but some were brought about by law or decree, as was the case when, on November 15, 1943, the Gypsy Condemnation Order was issued. Approximately half a million Gypsies were put to death in the Holocaust as a result of this act.

Try These Activities

1. Call to Social Action. Ask students to imagine the following. You are a citizen living in Germany or Austria at the time of the Kristallnacht, and you are appalled at the government's response to the mob's actions. You decide to meet with other people who feel the same way you do.

Brainstorm three or four possible actions your group can take.

Identify those who would be against your position. Determine the type of argument you could make to present your opposition to the violence.

Develop a plan for putting one of your possible actions into practice.

Write a mock letter supporting your position to the Berlin *News* for inclusion in the Letters to the Editor section of the paper.

2. Researching Kristallnacht. Students can use library resources to research the topic for in-depth accounts of the infamous night. They can begin with the books listed under "Suggested Reading."

3. In Their Shoes: How Does It Feel? To help students imagine their feelings of frustration, fear, and anger if they had been a part of this horror, you can lead them through a visualization experience. The following paragraphs should be read orally and with proper emphasis and emotion to set the stage for empathy. Note: This activity may be considered too emotional or controversial by some parents. Before you attempt this, you should know your students, parents, and community quite well. Perhaps a letter to parents discussing your teaching objectives and requesting permission for their children's participation would be advisable.

> *Teacher:* Today we are going to participate in a visualization exercise. You must be very quiet. Close your eyes.—Picture yourself in your home at night. Look around.—What room are you in? What does it look like? The room is dark. You want to turn on the light. Walk over to the wall to switch it on. Look around again.—Who is with you? Look down at yourself.—What are you wearing? Look at your watch. What time is it? You stop and stand perfectly still.—There is not a sound in the house. You hear the drone of noises from outside. How does it sound? Are you hearing traffic? A parade? An airplane or train? *(Pause for several seconds to allow time for the imaginative experience to build.)*

Teacher continues: The noises become closer and louder. You now hear a babble of voices. These are not distinct, but they sound angry. The voices get louder; they must be moving closer and closer.—You want to run to the window to see what is happening, but somebody stops you. Who is it? The voices from the street are much closer now. Perhaps next door. You hear distinct words. What are they?—Somebody in the room runs to turn off the lights. Lights from outside are flashing through the windows. Someone quickly moves to close the curtains. The voices become loud, angry, shrill shouts, and they do not move on. They seem to be centered on the street in front of your home.—You are pushed to the floor and told to lie down under some furniture. You hear one or two voices moving toward your door.—A mob is screaming in the background: "Scum, Scum. We know you are there! Dirty. . . ."—Footsteps are moving closer to your house. *(Wait five seconds and then ask students to open their eyes and to write in their journals.)*

Reaction: The students should write about their feelings of frustration, fear, and anger in the "lived-through" experience. Some students may wish to express their response through pictures rather than words.

Suggested Reading

Chaikin, M. (1987). *A nightmare in history: the Holocaust 1933–1945.* New York: Clarion Books.

Finkelstein, N. H. (1985). *Remember not to forget: a memory of the Holocaust.* New York: Franklin Watts.

Lewis, B. A. (1991). *The kids guide to social action. How to solve the social problems you choose and turn creative thinking into positive action.* Minneapolis: Free Spirit Publishing.

Celebrating Children's Book Week

The class can celebrate this week set aside to honor children's books in two ways. The first is to read a children's or young adult book that has won an international award. The second is to read a book in which the main character is a child who immigrated to the United States.

International Award Winners

Most students have heard of the two American awards given each year for outstanding children's literature. The **Caldecott Medal** is awarded by the American Library Association to the illustrator of the most distinguished picture book for children published in the United States during the previous year. The **Newbery Medal,** also awarded each year by the American Library Association, is given to the author who has made the most distinguished contribution to children's literature published in the United States during the previous year. Although restricted to U.S. publications, these awards are also international in scope. Most of the award-winning books are reprinted in many languages and distributed worldwide.

The **Kate Greenaway Medal** is sponsored by the British Library Association for the most distinguished work in illustration of a children's book first published in the United Kingdom during the previous year.

The **Carnegie Medal,** also sponsored by the British Library Association, is awarded to recognize the author of the most distinguished children's book first published in English in the United Kingdom during the previous year.

The Canadian Library Association awards the **Almerlia Frances Howard-Gibbon Medal** to the illustrator of the most distinguished children's book published in Canada during the previous year. The **Canadian Children's Book of the Year Award** goes to the author of a children's book of outstanding literary merit. Two awards are presented: one for a book published in English, the other for a book published in French **(Le Venerable François de Montmorency-Laval).**

The **Australian Children's Book Council** presents three awards for outstanding children's books each year: Picture Book of the Year for Younger Readers, Picture Book of the Year Award, and Children's Book of the Year for Older Readers.

Major Awards for Children's and Young Adult Books

Caldecott Medal (U.S.)
Newbery Medal (U.S.)
Kate Greenaway Medal (Great Britain)
Carnegie Medal (Great Britain)
Almerlia Frances Howard-Gibbon Medal (Canada)
Canadian Children's Book of the Year Award (Canada)
Australian Children's Books of the Year Awards (Australia)
Esther Glen Award (New Zealand)
Russell Clark Award for Illustrations (New Zealand)
Mildred Batchelder Award (U.S.)
Laura Ingalls Wilder Award (U.S.)
Hans Christian Andersen Prize (International)
Coretta Scott King Award (U.S.)
Scott O'Dell Award for Historical Fiction (U.S.)

THE WAY IT WAS BACK HOME: INDIVIDUAL ACTIVITY

As you read your book, think about the practices or customs described. While reading, complete this chart.

Name of book:_____

Author: _____

Publisher: _____

Country of Origin: _____

Main Character(s): _____

_____

What I learned about the country: _____

_____

_____

_____

_____

List the customs or traditions in the United States that the characters in your book find unusual or strange.

_____

_____

_____

_____

New Zealand sponsors the **Russell Clark Award for Illustrations** and the **Esther Glen Award** for the author of the most distinguished contribution to New Zealand children's literature.

The International Board on Books for Young People presents awards every two years to outstanding authors and illustrators whose complete works have made international contributions to children's literature.

The **Mildred Batchelder Award** is presented by the American Library Association to the American publisher of children's books considered to be the most outstanding (1) published in a country other than the United States, (2) in a language other than English, (3) translated into English, and (4) published in the United States.

The **Laura Ingalls Wilder Award** is presented every five years by the Association for Library Services to an author or illustrator whose works, published in the United States, have made a major contribution to children's literature.

The **Hans Christian Andersen Prize** is presented every two years to a living author whose works have made a substantial and international contribution to children's literature.

The **Coretta Scott King Award** is presented by the American Library Association to the African-American author and illustrator whose children's books make distinguished inspirational and educational contributions to children's literature.

The **Scott O'Dell Award for Historical Fiction** is given by the Bulletin of the Center for Children's Books to the author of a distinguished work of historical fiction set in the New World and published in English.

The Way It Was Back Home

A second way to commemorate Children's Book Week is to read a story with a multicultural emphasis. For this activity, you or the librarian can recommend books in which the main character is an immigrant child to America (see the "Suggested Reading" list). When students finish reading, they can complete the chart "The Way It Was Back Home: Individual Activity."

Synthesis: When students finish reading their books and have completed their individual charts, you can group together those students whose books contained characters from the same country. Each group should develop a chart similar to "The Way It Was Back Home: Group Activity."

THE WAY IT WAS BACK HOME: GROUP ACTIVITY

Country: _____

Foods	Customs	Special Holidays	Vocabulary

Analysis. In some of the books, the main character may note American customs that seem strange. For example, in *Children of the River* (Crew, 1989), the main character talks about the way Americans touch babies or young children on the head and how that custom would be taboo in her homeland. Students should collect such information and then try to explain how or why common customs in one country or culture appear unusual or strange to outsiders.

Suggested Reading

Ashabranner, B. (1986). *Children of the Maya: a Guatemalan Indian odyssey*. New York: G. P. Putman's Sons.

Ashabranner, B., & Ashabranner, M. (1987). *Into a strange land: unaccompanied refugee youth in America*. New York: G. P. Putman's Sons.

Beatty, P. (1981). *Lupita manana*. New York: William Morrow.

Bernstein, J. (1981). *Dmitry: a young Soviet immigrant*. Boston: Houghton Mifflin.

Crew, L. (1989). *Children of the river*. New York: Delacorte.

Huynh, Q. N. (1982). *The land I lost*. New York: HarperCollins

Lord, B. B. (1984). *In the year of the boar and Jackie Robinson*. New York: Harper.

Thomas, J. C. (Ed.). (1990). *A gathering of flowers: stories about being young in America*. New York: Harper & Row.

Yep, L. (1977). *Child of the owl*. New York: Harper & Row.

Section Two: Winter

If Winter Comes . . .

In the Northern Hemisphere, the three-month period between December 21 and March 21 is called winter. In most regions located in the Temperate Zones, temperatures fall below freezing and the climate is often stormy. In the subtropical areas, however, changes caused by the coming of winter are often so minor that they escape notice. Because the earth's axis is tipped about 23 degrees from a line perpendicular to its orbital plane, the sun's rays fall directly over parts of the Southern Hemisphere during this time. As a result, when it is winter in the United States, it is summer in countries south of the equator.

Some people view winter as a time of cold and unpleasant weather that forces them to spend their leisure time indoors. Those who love the ice and snow look forward to outdoor sports such as skiing, ice skating, and ice hockey. In Canada and the northern United States, winter sports abound. Many cities hold annual ice or winter carnivals during the coldest part of winter.

Major holidays are associated with the winter solstice. Christmas, a significant religious holiday for Christians, occurs at the beginning of the winter season. In cultures that use the Gregorian calendar, such as the United States, Canada, and most European countries, celebrations marking the beginning of the new year are important. Holidays honoring significant figures in United States history, such as Martin Luther King, Jr., Abraham Lincoln, and George Washington, are observed. People who practice the Catholic religion mark several important religious occasions during winter. Some cities plan Mardi Gras celebrations on the Tuesday before the beginning of Lent.

Those who must endure the long cold days of winter can find hope in the words of poet Percy Bysshe Shelley, who wrote, "O Wind, if winter comes, can spring be far behind?"

Chapter 4

That Brief December Day

The Romans, who were responsible for naming most of the months of the calendar that we came to adopt, began using numbers for the names of the months beginning with the seventh. Thus, *December* is derived from the Latin word for ten, because it was the tenth month of the old Roman calendar.

December is a month of significance for many cultures and groups. For example, during this month Christians throughout the world celebrate the birthday of Christ, the religion's founder. In many other cultures, December celebrations occupy a special place in the year's events. This may stem in part from the fact that, at least in the Northern Hemisphere, the shortest day of the year falls in December. Many early groups saw the winter solstice as a time when the world had reached a point where darkness and cold were especially threatening to one's well-being. The words of the American Quaker poet, John Greenleaf Whittier, serve to express quite well this view:

> *The sun that brief December day*
> *Rose cheerless over hills of gray,*
> *And, darkly circled, gave at noon*
> *A sadder light than waning moon.*

A poet living in the Southern Hemisphere might write an ode to summer in December, lauding the sunny times and long days.

If one traveled the world during this month, one might happen upon Christian observances of not only the birth of Christ, celebrated on December 25, but also of Saint Nicholas Day (Netherlands) on December 6, Guadelupe Day (Mexico) on December 12, and Saint Lucia Day (Italy and Sweden) on December 13. In addition, Jewish people everywhere celebrate an eight-day festival of lights called Hanukkah (although, in some years, this period may fall in November). The African-American observance of Kwanzaa, a seven-day celebration of their culture, begins on December 26 and concludes on the first day of January.

December

	Sunday	Monday	Tuesday	Wednesday	Thursday	Friday	Saturday

DECEMBER

People, Places, and Events of December

What's Happening in December:
Universal Human Rights Month

Other December Events:

First Monday: Christmas Lights Across Canada. Simultaneous lighting of Canadian legislative sites across Canada.

Events Scheduled According to Non-Gregorian Calendar Usually Occurring in December:

Hanukkah

December's Daily Calendar

1

Becky Thatcher Day. Honoring women who inspired or wrote great literature. Observed on the birthday of Laura Hawkins, Mark Twain's model for Becky Thatcher in *Tom Sawyer*.

Iceland Independence Day. Gained independence from Denmark in 1918.

Rosa Parks Day. Commemorating anniversary of the arrest of Rosa Parks in 1955.

World AIDS Day. Designed to increase awareness in the fight against acquired immune deficiency syndrome.

Birth anniversary of:
Lee Trevino (1939–). Mexican-American golfer.

2

Anniversary of the first self-sustaining nuclear chain reaction. Led by Enrico Fermi, a team of scientists produced the first nuclear chain reaction in 1942.

Anniversary of the Monroe Doctrine (1823).

United Arab Emirates National Day. Merger created independent state and freedom from British control in 1971.

Birth anniversary of:
Georges Pierre Seurat (1859–1891). French painter.

3

Bhopal poison gas disaster (1984). World's worst industrial disaster occurred in India, killing two thousand and injuring two hundred thousand.

Illinois Admission Day. Became twenty-first state to join Union (1818).

Laos National Holiday. Commemorating the establishment of Lao People's Democratic Republic in 1975.
Birth anniversary of:
Joseph Conrad (1857–1924). British novelist (born in Poland).
Gilbert Charles Stuart (1755–1828). Painter; most famous for his portrait of George Washington.

4

Founding of Mission Santa Barbara (1786).
Birth anniversary of:
Thomas Carlyle (1795–1881). Scottish writer and historian.

5

Haiti Discovery Day. Commemorating Columbus's arrival in Haiti (1492).
Death of Wolfgang Amadeus Mozart (1756–1791).
Birth anniversary of:
Martin Van Buren (1782–1862). Eighth president of the United States; born in New York.

6

Central African Republic National Day. Commemorating military coup of 1965.
Day of Quito, Ecuador. Commemorating the founding of Quito in 1534 by the Spanish.
Finland Independence Day. Declared independence from Russia in 1917.
St. Nicholas Day. Noted for his charity, "Santa Claus" and the custom of gift giving is said to derive from this fourth-century saint.
Birth anniversary of:
Ira Gershwin (1896–1983). Songwriter.

7

Armenian earthquake (1988). More than sixty thousand killed.
Côte d'Ivoire National Day. Became independent of France in 1960; West African country officially changed its name from Ivory Coast to Côte d'Ivorie.
Delaware became first state to ratify Constitution (1787).
Pearl Harbor Day (1941). Japanese aircraft bombed Pearl Harbor, killing nearly three thousand.
Birth anniversary of:
Willa Cather (1873–1947). Midwestern author.

8

Soviet Union dissolved (1991)
Birth anniversary of:
Sammy Davis, Jr. (1925–1987). African-American singer, dancer, and actor.

Diego Rivera (1886–1957). Mexican artist famous for his mural paintings.
James Thurber (1894–1961). Author and illustrator.

9

Tanzania Independence and Republic Day. Located in southern Africa; gained independence from Britain in 1961.
Birth anniversary of:
Clarence Birdseye (1886–1956). Developed process of freezing foods.
Joel Chandler Harris (1848–1908). Creator of the Uncle Remus stories.
John Milton (1608–1674). English poet.

10

Mississippi Admission Day. Became twentieth state to join Union (1817).
Nobel Prize award ceremonies. Given in Norway and Sweden from bequest of Alfred Nobel.
Ralph Bunche awarded Nobel Peace Prize (1950). First African-American to be awarded Peace Prize.
Death of Red Cloud (1909). Sioux Indian chief; leader and defender of Native American rights.
United Nations Human Rights Day.
Birth anniversary of:
Melvil Dewey (1851–1931). Creator of the Dewey decimal library classification system.
Emily Dickinson (1830–1886). Poet.
Thomas Hopkins Gallaudet (1787–1851). Established first American school for the deaf in 1817.

11

Indiana Admission Day. Became nineteenth state to join Union (1816).
Birth anniversary of:
Annie Jump Cannon (1863–1941). Astronomer and discoverer of five stars.

12

Mexico: Day of Our Lady of Guadalupe. Commemorating the legend of saint's appearance near Mexico City in 1533 to Juan Diego.
Joseph Hayne Rainey became first African-American to serve in U.S. House of Representatives (1870).
Kenya National Republic Day. Gained independence from Britain in 1963.
Pennsylvania became second state to ratify Constitution (1787).
Birth anniversary of:
William Lloyd Garrison (1805–1879). Poet, journalist, and antislavery leader.

13

Malta Republic Day. Became republic in 1974; gained independence from Britain in 1964.

Santa Lucia Day. Observed with festival of lights, particularly in Sweden.

14

Alabama Admission Day. Became twenty-second state to join Union (1819).

Halcyon Days. Seven days before and seven days after winter solstice. Named for legendary bird that calmed the winds and seas.

Roald Amundsen party reached the South Pole (1911)

Birth anniversary of:
    Margaret Chase Smith (1897–). First woman to be elected to both houses of Congress.

15

Bill of Rights Day.

Death of Sitting Bull (1834–1890). Sioux leader, medicine man, and warrior.

Birth anniversary of:
    Alexandre-Gustave Eiffel (1832–1923). French engineer noted for designing the Eiffel Tower in Paris.

Lazarus Ludovic Zamenhof (1859–1917). Developer of international language known as Esperanto, meaning "he who hopes." International Language Week is observed in connection with his birth anniversary.

16

Mexico: Posadas. Begins nine-day celebration leading to Christmas.

Birth anniversary of:
    Jane Austen (1775–1817). English novelist.
    Ludwig van Beethoven (1770–1827). German composer.
    Margaret Mead (1901–1978). Anthropologist and author.
    George Santayana (1863–1952). Spanish-born philosopher and author. Credited with the statement, "Those who cannot remember the past are condemned to repeat it."

17

Wright Brothers' first powered flight (1903).

Birth anniversary of:
    John Greenleaf Whittier (1807–1892). Poet.

18

New Jersey became third state to ratify Constitution (1787).

Thirteenth Amendment to the U.S. Constitution ratified, abolishing slavery in the nation (1865).

Birth anniversary of:
    Tyrus Raymond ("Ty") Cobb (1886–1961). Baseball player.
    Joseph Grimaldi (1778–1837). English actor. Said to be "greatest clown in history."

19

Birth anniversary of:
    Mary Ashton Livermore (1821–1905). Reformer and women's suffrage leader.
    William Parry (1790–1855). Englishman who explored the Arctic and sought the Northwest Passage.

20

Louisiana Purchase Day (1803). More than a million square miles of land was purchased from France for approximately $20 per square mile.

Death of Sacagawea (ca. 1787–1812). Native-American interpreter and guide for Lewis and Clark expedition in 1803.

Birth anniversary of:
    Harvey S. Firestone (1868–1938). Industrialist and founder of the Firestone Tire and Rubber Company.

21

Pilgrims landed at Plymouth Rock (1620).

Yalda: Iranian observance related to longest night of the year.

Birth anniversary of:
    Benjamin Disraeli (1804–1881). British statesman and prime minister.
    Andor Foldes (1913–1992). Hungarian pianist.
    Joseph Stalin (1879–1953). Russian dictator.
    Henrietta Szold (1860–1945). Teacher, writer, social worker, and founder of the Zionist movement.

22

Birth anniversary of:

James Edward Oglethorpe (1696–1785). English leader and colonizer of Georgia; founded the city of Savannah.

Giacomo Puccini (1858–1924). Italian composer.

Edwin Arlington Robinson. (1869–1935). Poet (*Spoon River Anthology*).

23

Japan: National Day. Celebrating birthday of the emperor.

Birth anniversary of:
> Joseph Smith (1805–1844). Religious leader and founder of the Mormon Church.

24

Austria: Anniversary of the Christmas carol "Silent Night, Holy Night" (1818).

National Roof-Over-Your-Head Day. Designed to call attention to the plight of homeless people across America.

Birth anniversary of:
> Christopher "Kit" Carson (1809–1868). Frontiersman, soldier, and guide.

25

Christmas Day. Christian festival to commemorate the birth of Jesus.

Birth anniversary of:
> Clara Barton (1821–1912). Nurse and founder of the American Red Cross.
>
> Humphrey Bogart (1899–1957). Stage and movie actor.
>
> Evangeline Cory Booth (1865–1950). Leader and general in Salvation Army.
>
> Mohammed Ali Jinnah (1876–1948). Founder of the Islamic Republic of Pakistan.
>
> Isaac Newton (1642–1727). Mathematician and scientist who formulated the laws of motion.

26

Ireland: Day of the Wren. Merrymakers, wearing masks, go from house to house asking for money.

Beginning of Kwanzaa (December 26–January 1). Cultural celebration observed by many African-American families.

Birth anniversary of:
> Mao Tse-tung (1893–1976). Communist leader of the People's Republic of China.

27

Birth anniversary of:
> George Cayley (1773–1857). English scientist and inventor, called the "Father of Aerodynamics."
>
> Johannes Kepler (1571–1630). German astronomer, called the "Father of Modern Astronomy."
>
> Louis Pasteur (1822–1895). French chemist. Discovered inoculation against rabies; pasteurization process named in his honor.

28

Holy Innocents Day (Childermas). Commemorating massacre of children in Bethlehem following birth of Jesus.

Iowa Admission Day. Became twenty-ninth state to be admitted to the Union (1846).

Messina (Sicily) earthquake (1908). Nearly eighty-thousand died.

Nepal National Holiday. Public holiday honoring the birthday of the king.

Birth anniversary of:
> Woodrow Wilson (1856–1924). Twenty-eighth president of the United States; born in Virginia.

29

St. Thomas of Canterbury Feast Day. Commemorating the death of Thomas à Becket (1118–1170), archbishop of Canterbury.

Texas Admission Day. Became twenty-eighth state admitted to the Union (1845).

Wounded Knee massacre (1890). More than two hundred Native Americans were killed in South Dakota when U.S. Seventh Cavalry suppressed ceremonial religious practice.

Birth anniversary of:
> Pablo Casals (1876–1973). Spanish cellist.
>
> William Ewart Gladstone (1809–1898). British author and statesman; prime minister for four terms.
>
> Andrew Johnson (1808–1875). Seventeenth president of the United States; born in North Carolina.
>
> Grigori Efimovich Rasputin (1871–1916). Russian monk and mystic referred to as "mad advisor" to Czar Nicholas II.

30

Philippines: Rizal Day. Commemorating the martyrdom of Dr. José Rizal.

Birth anniversary of:
> Rudyard Kipling (1865–1936). English poet and author, born in India. Noted for *The Jungle Book.*
>
> Hideki Tojo (1884–1948). Japanese prime minister during World War II.

31

Japan: Namahage. Men dressed as devils go from house to house seeking sluggards and offering them the opportunity to become diligent.

New Year's Eve. Festive occasion the evening before the new year begins for those who follow the Gregorian calendar.

St. Sylvester's Day. Commemorating the death of Pope Sylvester I. Celebrated in Belgium, Germany, France, Portugal, and Switzerland.

Western Samoa Fire Dance. Celebrating achievement of full independence on January 1, 1962.

Winter Holidays around the World

Teaching Unit for December

A Word about This Unit: This unit provides students with the opportunity to study the variety of ways in which winter holidays are celebrated around the world. The two major topics of this unit are worldwide Christmas celebrations and New Year observances.

Celebrations of holidays are important aspects of cultures. Although the same holidays, such as Christmas or New Year's Day, may be observed by a variety of cultures, they are marked by differences in their observance. The Christmas section of this unit includes more than the traditional material found in most books on this holiday. New Year's observances are included in a second section because people throughout history have marked the beginning of a new year in some manner. Almost all groups of people have recognized how astronomical cycles affect the seasons and the climate in which they live. The way in which the beginning of a new year is celebrated in various countries and the dates chosen to mark the occurrence have been included. Presented here are examples of Christmas and New Year's celebrations from around the world.

Part I: Christmas in Many Lands

The birth of Jesus is celebrated by Christians around the world. However, not all groups who observe this religious holiday do so in the same manner. Environmental conditions and specific cultural traditions influence Christmas celebrations. Although this topic is narrow in focus, dealing with only one of the major religions of the world, it can serve as a stimulus to the investigation of other religions and their special holidays and observances.

It should be noted that this topic necessitates a marked sensitivity on the part of the teacher. As a result of court decisions, many public schools hesitate to include the study of religions in the curriculum. The courts have held to a distinction between the "study of" and the "practice of" religions. This unit has been prepared with the former goal in mind. The study of religious practices and traditions is an appropriate subtopic within the context of social studies. We live in a society marked by diversity, and if we are to grow in our understanding of one another, and are to tolerate differing sets of beliefs and to live civilly together, then this topic certainly is valid for inquiry.

Just as the unit on Thanksgiving led to a more thoughtful understanding of what the day "means," so this unit serves to promote your students' understanding of such matters as why gifts are given during the Christmas season. It may also provide an opportunity to note why it is particularly appropriate at this time of year to contemplate what might be done to provide for those less fortunate and to concentrate on the less material aspects of the occasion.

Motivation. For many students, no time of the year (with the possible exception of summer vacation) is looked forward to with more expectancy and excitement than the December holidays. Begin this unit by discussing how the students' families prepare for the holiday season. Then raise questions about how the holidays might be observed by other cultural groups in the United States and in other areas of the world.

Immersion. Once the students' curiosities have been aroused, encourage them to seek information about other customs using books, magazines, and newspaper articles. Older family members, relatives, neighbors, and others in the community may be sources of information.

Information. According to the beliefs of traditional Christianity, an infant named Jesus was born of a virgin nearly two millennia ago in a small village far from the center of the leading western empire of the times.

From the perspective of many Christians, this event, in conjunction with their belief in the resurrection of Jesus, remains one of the most significant events in human history. Christianity is one of the major religions of the world. Its adherents form the largest religious group on each continent, except Asia. Christians, however, are not the only group that sees the approach of the solstice (winter in the Northern Hemisphere, summer in the Southern Hemisphere) as signaling a time of celebration or festive occasions.

Pre-Christian Winter Solstice Festivals. This time of the year was considered to be special long before the birth of Christ. In northern climes, days had been growing shorter. People may have become concerned that the sun would fade away completely and fail to return to warm and light up the earth. The winter solstice may have been viewed as marking the gradual rebirth of the sun.

Groups that inhabited western Europe, what is now France and Germany, saw this as a festive time. Slaughtered livestock were roasted over fires in preparation for feasts. These feasts may have had their origins in a very practical concern, for the coming of winter meant that the grasses in the fields were drying up and that there would be little sustenance for the stock. Some pragmatic person may have suggested that the animals might as well be cooked and eaten, since most would fail to survive the long winter months.

A term often associated with this season is "yuletide." The old English origins of "yule" may be rooted in these feast times, designating the name of either the month during which the solstice falls or the festival that occurs during this period. Indeed, yule logs may have been large sections of special trees that would be cut with much ceremony to provide both warmth and light during this time of the year.

The yule log likely had both literal and symbolic meaning. As it burned, it provided warmth against the winter's chilly dampness. The log's significance for those huddled around it went far beyond this, however. This symbolic meaning is crucial as well, for the light given by the giant log offered a haven from the outer darkness and cold. The members of the group settled around the hearth, the symbolic center of the home, were also provided with a sense of community and family as the yule log burned. It was a natural time for stories to be shared and for traditions to be passed down from one generation to the next by elders of the group. As already noted, the selection, cutting, and cumbersome chore of dragging the log into the home required much effort and was likely a time of ceremony among the members of the family.

Various pagan customs have found their way into later practices closely associated with the Christian holidays. For example, the likely origin of the Christmas tree stems from the role of such evergreen (and by implication, "ever living") trees in the religious practices of certain Teutonic (Germanic) tribes. The tradition of the Christmas tree in American homes is fairly modern. Although the date of the first such event is debated, it did not occur until well into the nineteenth century. As one might expect, a family that had emigrated from Germany instituted this popular custom.

The winter solstice has long been a period of celebrations and rites for many groups. Today, however, as the month of December rolls around, thoughts of Christmas are evoked throughout the world. In the coldest and warmest climes of the earth, Christians look forward to this time.

Christian Observances of the Birth of Jesus of Nazareth. The variety of ways in which the birth and other events associated with this religious figure are celebrated represents a good example of how different cultures incorporate shared beliefs and customs in their own particular manner. Even the religious services devoted to the celebration of Jesus's birth occur on a variety of dates during the period. Typically, members of Protestant and Roman Catholic churches conduct their services of celebration on Christmas Eve, the twenty-fourth of December. Many other Christian groups hold their services at later times. The Greek Orthodox Church, as well as Ethiopian and Syrian Christians, celebrate on the sixth of January, and the Armenian Church as late as the eighteenth of January. Other festive occasions associated with the Christmas season frequently occur both before and after the solstice.

Christmas Celebrations around the World. Early in December, children in the Netherlands look forward to the visit of the good Saint Nicholas, who along with Black Peter (his faithful cohort, who helps determine whether a child has been "naughty or nice") traverses the Netherlands bringing good cheer and, more importantly, gifts to the good children. The Santa who visits homes all over the United States is likely a descendant of this figure. The American Santa has become efficient enough to employ a set of elves in the polar region to assist in the effort of producing a sufficient supply of gifts.

It is not always a saint or even a male who delivers the gifts. In Italy, a type of witch, albeit a friendly one, provides the gifts for the children. In Puerto Rico, children must wait until early in the new year before the Magi deliver their presents. In every case, however, good children are rewarded with gifts, while those who may have been bad receive something unwanted. This may be a lump of coal, a bundle of sticks, or other evidence of one's neglectful behavior during the year.

In many countries, children will leave cookies for Santa (or whoever is the gift bringer), hay or straw for his reindeer, and in Westphalia children will often leave notes for the *Christkind*.

The principal holiday symbol used in the home varies among cultures. In many American homes, a Christmas tree (of different types although almost always an evergreen one) is often the center of the celebration, if only because the presents are often placed beneath its branches. In French and Italian homes, a crèche or presepio (crib or manger) is likely to be the focal point.

Garlands of greens, candles, and sprigs of holly, ivy, and mistletoe are also used as decorations, each having its own significance (as romantically inclined individuals well know in the case of mistletoe). In India and Pakistan, the leaves of banana trees are used as decorations at this festive time.

Seasonal "Goodies" around the World. Almost every family has particular foods or special treats that are an expected part of Christmas or seasonal holiday meals. The foods eaten on such occasions have meaning and significance far beyond their nutritional value. A sample menu of the varied viands consumed throughout the world during this period of the year might include the following:

Rye bread dipped in the juices of a ham cooked for the
    Christmas meal (Sweden)
Goose, turkey, or ham (France, although oysters are a
    favorite in Paris)
Turkey and other meats, currant bread, and spaghetti
    (Italy)
Poppyseed rolls and dumplings (Hungary)
Kourabiedes, or honey-soaked cakes sprinkled with
    powdered sugar (Greece)
Plum pudding (England)
Gingerbread baked in the shapes of animals and other
    figures (Finland)
Cakes shaped and decorated to look like yule logs
    (France)
Mattak, or strips of blubber wrapped in whale skin
    (Inuit)

If you're still hungry, drop in on the feasts of the Navajo in New Mexico and Arizona, where a stew of meat, potatoes, beans, and onions can be enjoyed.

Secular Celebrations. Many Christmas customs owe their origins to pagan practices. Some traditions associated with Christmas today have little to do with the religious roots of this holiday. For example, it is difficult to link the modern image of St. Nicholas with a Christian bishop and saint of centuries long ago. (In this case, even historians might argue as to whether such an individual actually existed at the time and in the region in which he purportedly lived.) Even in the secular state of the former Soviet Union, Santa Claus was embodied in a figure called "Grandfather Frost" who gave gifts to children.

Instructional Activities

Christmas is celebrated in different ways by various cultural groups. Even within the same culture, there may be marked differences in customs because of varied geographical settings or particular family traditions.

A variety of activities can be utilized in the classroom to increase students' level of awareness of other cultures, as well as to develop research skills. Each of the activities presented here has been selected to provide students with the opportunity for increased awareness of the wide range of cultural traditions and the specific practices and customs associated with the celebration of Christmas. They may also serve to illustrate unique family seasonal traditions that have grown over time and been passed on as part of the family's heritage.

Activity 4.1: How Does Your Family Celebrate Winter Holidays?

Ask students to investigate how their own families celebrate the holidays during this season. They can research such questions as:

What special winter holiday does my family celebrate? When do we celebrate it?
What special symbols are associated with this holiday?
What special activities do we enjoy?
What special foods do we eat?

Once the information is collected and organized, the students can make a classroom collage.

Looking for Symbols. Many similar items are used as symbols during this holiday season by different groups. For example, candles are used during St. Lucia Day in Sweden, for the Jewish holiday of Hanukkah, and during the African-American celebration called Kwanzaa. The students can speculate as to the symbolic significance of candles or lights during this time of year.

These activities will provide students with the opportunity to share the results of their inquiry in a classroom setting. They can collect and report the data through the use of personal journals, posters, and stories describing past and present family activities.

Activity 4.2: My Grandfather's Holidays

This activity engages the students in researching generational differences regarding family holiday traditions. Having investigated the activities that their family engages in at this season, students should be urged to ask their parents or grandparents how holidays were celebrated within their immediate families when they were the student's age. Other older relatives or acquaintances can be interviewed to determine how they celebrated the holidays in their homes.

Activity 4.3: Holiday Decorations

In many homes in the United States, the Christmas tree has become an integral part of the celebration of the season. "O Tannenbaum" ("O Christmas Tree") is one of the songs sung by many families as they gaze upon the lighted tree. A number of questions can be asked of students regarding the Christmas tree tradition:

Does your family use a tree as a part of its Christmas decorations or do you use some other symbol? If so, what?

Does your family try to have the same type of tree each year? If so, why?

How does your family obtain its tree? Do you buy it, or do you usually cut your own tree? If so, who is responsible for selecting and cutting the tree?

When does your family put up the tree? Is there anything special about this occasion?

Are there any special decorations on the tree, such as, certain ornaments that have been in the family for generations? Are special meanings associated with them? For example, an ornament may have been made by a member of the family in the past, or an ornament may have been received as a gift, or purchased at a special place, or may even have been brought to this country from another when a family member emigrated.

Do you have lights on your tree? What kind of lights? Obviously, before the invention of electric lights, trees were illuminated with candles. Within certain traditions this is still done, and the lighting of the candles is a significant family event. As the students might suggest, this practice is rather unsafe, and many homes had a bucket or two of water to douse errant flames. Older members of families may have stories to share with the class about such events. For many, lighted candles shining in the darkness was a memorable experience.

For many children, a highlight of this time of year is when "the stockings are hung by the chimney with care," for each child hopes that "Saint Nicholas soon will be there." The origins of this custom are arguable, but the practice itself is firmly fixed in many American households. What sorts of items are placed in Christmas stockings? What sorts of items did the students' parents or grandparents receive in their stockings?

Activity 4.4: Celebrations throughout the World

After students have surveyed the customs within their own families, they should share their findings with other members of the class. Students' families may have brought with them many practices from their lands of birth. In this way, customs emigrate as well. As students discuss their own traditions regarding the celebration of winter holidays, jot them down. The origins of these different traditions can be illustrated on a large map of the world.

Students may discover that certain traditional practices had to be modified when they or their parents came to this country. These changes may be attributable to differences in climatic or geographic conditions. For example, a student's family that emigrated from Australia (or some other part of the Southern Hemisphere) might have become accustomed to having a Christmas picnic as they swam and cavorted on the beach. In most places in the United States (although there are exceptions), this might prove to be a "chilling" experience.

Activity 4.5: Researching the Symbols of the Season

Each student should select a term from a list compiled by the class that refers to some practice or activity associated with this time of the year. They can then search out its origin or significance within a particular culture or country. When their investigations are complete, they can report the results in a variety of ways. For example, they can construct small bulletin boards giving the origin of the term or symbol, a description

Winter Holiday Symbols

Yule log	Black Peter	Saturnalia
Kiviak	waits	Pepparkakor
tannenbaum	crèche	Kris Kringle
Bara Din	Befana	Saint Lucia Day
Three Kings Day	dreidel	menorah
Nguzo Saba	Umoja	mistletoe
latkes		

of its meaning or significance, and the location or group with which it is usually associated. The box includes examples of symbols associated with winter holidays. You and your students may add others.

Activity 4.6: Celebrating the Holidays in Our Community

Students can interview religious, government, and other community leaders to obtain answers to the following questions:

How does our community celebrate the winter holiday season?

Which of these events are purely secular in nature? Which are religious?

What traditions have arisen in our community with respect to the holidays?

What are some of the interesting and humorous stories told about past holiday seasons? For example, what was Christmas like during the depression, some wartime period, or some particularly happy or unhappy occasion in the community's past?

Which holiday season was most memorable for you? Why?

Students should be urged to obtain a wide sampling of community opinion. In addition to interviewing individuals, they should be encouraged to seek out other sources of information. They might first survey newspapers, beginning with present practices and working back to earlier times. They could then formulate and validate hypotheses that explain why various changes may have occurred.

Part II: Celebrating the New Year

Motivation. The streets ring out with cries of *Buon Capo d'Anno, Szczesliwego Nowego Roku, Gott Nytt Ar,* and *Feliz Año Nuevo.* All over the world, people wish each other a Happy New Year, but not all on the same day. Nor do they celebrate the occasion in the same way. Where do people throw water on each other? Where do people wish their animals a good year? How or why did some of these customs begin?

Immersion. In this part of the unit, students gather information about the topic. You can either read the short excerpts of information included in this text, read from

a variety of trade books, or direct students to seek information in appropriate books, encyclopedias, almanacs, and other sources.

Information. New Year celebrations are important holidays because they provide a time to look back at what happened during the past year and to look forward to a new beginning, a time to make a fresh start. Around the world, the new year is not always celebrated on December 31 or January 1, as in the United States. Many cultures use different calendars for marking the year. Several cultures base their celebrations on lunar calendars rather than on the Gregorian calendar used for business in the United States. When lunar calendars are used, the holiday will not always fall on the same date, because a year based on a lunar cycle does not correspond exactly to the 365 days that the earth travels around the sun (for information about calendars, see Chapter 1).

For some people in the world, the beginning of a new year is a religious celebration; for others it is a public holiday. Although many cultures and religions of the world observe a New Year holiday, this occasion is celebrated in diverse ways.

Religious Celebrations

Buddhists call their New Year's holiday Songkran. It takes place in the middle of April. At this time, the Buddhists of Thailand wash the pictures and statues of the Buddha. For fun, people throw water at each other, perhaps to wash away evil.

Hindus celebrate Baisakhi in April or May. Devout Hindus in India view this time as a holy consecration and bathe in sacred water to protect themselves from evil. People go to the temples to listen to the reading of the calendar and to offer prayers.

Jewish people around the world celebrate the religious holiday of Rosh Hashanah, which usually occurs in September (sometimes in October). It lasts for one or two days, depending on where a particular Jewish family lives and on the movement within Judaism to which they belong. This is a time of quiet reflection about one's behavior during the past year and a time to pray that the new year will be one of prosperity, peace, and good health for the individual and for all the world.

Muslims in India celebrate Morharram in January or February. During this holiday, boys and men perform special dances dressed as "dervishes," who are holy men who live in monasteries and take vows of poverty.

Native Americans. Religious celebrations welcoming the new year were also practiced by Native Americans. The ancient Cherokee nation took part in a friendship ceremony called Atohuna, a celebration to grant each person a fresh start. In this ceremony, they burned their old clothing and household items, aired out what they wanted to keep, and scrubbed their homes. They drank a dark-colored liquid to cleanse their bodies and took part in tribal dances. The people gathered embers from a special sacred fire lit in the council house and carried them to their homes to rekindle their own fires. Everyone looked forward to good fortune and honor for the coming year.

New Year Celebrations by Region

Celebrations and Customs in Asian Countries. The celebration of the **Chinese** New Year, called Yuan Tan, may continue for five days. It is a time for the family to come together, a time to honor ancestors, and a time to thank the gods for blessings. The Chinese add a year to their age on the day of the new year, regardless of their true date of birth. The Chinese New Year is based on the ancient Chinese lunar calendar. As a result, it may occur between mid-January and mid-February. Each Chinese year is given the name of one of the twelve animal symbols on the Chinese zodiac.

During the New Year celebration, homes are filled with flowers and fruit. Oranges and apples are used as decorations and gifts. The Chinese believe that red and orange are colors of joy. Orange is also a symbol for good luck. Children are given a gift of "good luck money" wrapped in red paper.

One part of the celebration of the new year is the Festival of Lanterns. During this festival, public offices are closed, children wear new clothes, and people eat special foods. Lanterns are placed everywhere to light the way for the new year. During the celebration, dancers carry papier-mâché heads of lions and perform "lion dances" in the streets in front of businesses and homes. The Golden Dragon Parade is held at night. This is a time when the full dragon appears to wish the people peace, prosperity, and good luck. Firecrackers traditionally are exploded to scare lazy and evil spirits.

In **Japan,** New Year's Day is celebrated on the first of January.

During the New Year holidays, Japanese homes are decorated with many symbols: branches or bamboo stand for health and long life, while ropes symbolize happiness and good luck. On New Year's Eve, a gong is struck 108 times to announce the arrival of the new year and as a reminder of the 108 commandments of Buddha. When people hear these sounds, they begin to laugh, continuing for as long as they can, for laughter is believed to bring good luck. People walk to shrines to pray for a happy and prosperous new year. Certain foods are prepared to symbolize good luck and blessings for a long life. A gruel of seven herbs is eaten on the seventh day to rid the mind and body of evil during the coming year.

In **Burma** and **Madagascar,** people want to start the new year with a "clean slate," so they pour water over their heads.

Tet Nguyen Dan, or Tet, falls between January 21 and February 19 and is the three-day New Year holiday for the **Vietnamese.** The exact dates vary from year to year because Vietnam operates on a lunar calendar. The Vietnamese people believe that protective "kitchen gods" live in their houses and that once a year these gods travel to heaven to report about the family. Before Tet begins, in order to ensure a good report, the family will present gifts to the gods. When Tet arrives, the gods depart for heaven amid an explosion of firecrackers. During Tet, candles are lit for dead relatives, presents are left for the gods, and everyone tries to be happy to bring good luck.

Celebrations and Customs in African Countries. Because the rains begin in March or April in **Sierra Leone,** some Mandingo people use the New Year holiday to celebrate the ending of the dry season. On New Year's Eve, people clean their houses and yards. The next day, while the women and children sing and dance in the village, the men walk to a stream to fill as many buckets as they own. They place the buckets on their heads and march back to the village.

Celebrations and Customs in European Countries. Many New Year customs in Europe are similar from country to country. European countries generally use the Gregorian calendar and thus, as in the United States, New Year's Day falls on January 1. However, because of the variety of cultural and ethnic backgrounds found in Europe, many New Year beliefs and celebrations differ from one country to another.

For example, in **Belgium,** farmers wish their animals "Happy New Year" on the first day of the year. An ancient custom in **England** allowed young boys to "wassail" the fruit trees. They did this by marching around the trees, singing songs, and beating the trees with branches. This was believed to make the trees bear more fruit during the coming year. The **Danes** have a custom whereby the new year is "smashed in." Young people go from house to house banging (smashing) on their friends' doors. The **French** eat pancakes to bring good luck for the rest of the year, and in **Spain,** many people eat twelve grapes or twelve raisins at the stroke of midnight to bring good luck. This custom is also practiced in many Latin American countries. A drop of cream falling to the floor is supposed to bring good luck in **Switzerland**. If you are the last out of bed on New Year's Day, you are called a "Sylvester," which implies that you are lazy.

In **Greece**, January first is a day to honor St. Basil, the bishop of Caesarea in the fourth century. Carolers carrying a miniature "St. Basil's ship" go through the streets singing. Basil cakes eaten on New Year's contain a small silver coin. Whoever gets the piece with the coin is believed to have good luck for the new year. An important part of the holiday preparation, women wear their best clothes and jewelry while baking these round, flat, savory cakes. It is said St. Basil fills children's shoes with presents on New Year's Eve.

Romania also combines New Year's and St. Basil celebrations. There, too, young people go from house to house singing New Year's greetings, but they ring bells and carry whips. On the following day, people throw corn at each other for good luck.

Celebrations and Customs in Latin American Countries. Año Viejo is the holiday that families in **Ecuador** celebrate at the end of the "Old Year." Family members make and dress a scarecrow, which they call the "old man." Someone then writes a "family will," listing each member's faults. At midnight this will is read to the scarecrow. A fire is lit, and the scarecrow and the family will are burned to ashes. The family watches as the faults and the scarecrow disappear, allowing everyone to start the new year fresh. Last year's faults have been forgotten.

In **Mexico,** a wooden frame shaped like a tower is built and strung with firecrackers. When the first firecracker is lit, it sets off the next one, and in domino fashion all the firecrackers on the tower are soon exploded.

Buckets of water are emptied from balconies or windows in **Puerto Rico**. This custom is believed to rid the house of evil spirits.

Celebrations and Customs in Middle Eastern Countries. No Ruz is the name **Iranians** give to their New Year celebration. No Ruz begins on March 20 and lasts for thirteen days. People eat a meal of eggs and pilaf, a rice dish, to bring good luck. After the meal, friends bring gifts of fruit, flowers, and colored eggs. Iranians believe that the earth shakes when the new year begins. At midnight, the family sits around a table and each member is given a mirror and a colored egg. When the new year begins, everyone puts their eggs on the mirrors. The eggs begin to shake when a cannon is heard in the distance. Then the family eats a festival meal of chicken, fruits, bread, and sweets. Afterward, someone reads from the Koran, the holy book of the Islamic faith. On the thirteenth day, Iranian tradition holds that it is unlucky to stay indoors, so people pack lunches and travel to the country. Children bring bowl gardens that they planted earlier at home and toss

NEW YEAR'S CUSTOMS

Country	Custom	Reason for Custom

them into country streams as a symbol of discarding or throwing away bad luck.

Instructional Activities

Activity 4.7: Happy New Year!

Many regions have local customs or traditions for celebrating the beginning of a new year in order to ensure good luck and prosperity. Students can interview family members, neighbors, and community leaders to learn about local or individual customs. The class can then make a book of New Year Celebrations.

Working in groups, students can conduct library research into how the new year is celebrated in a particular country. They can also question community members who are originally from that country. When the information is collected, students can make a collage or poster illustrating these customs.

Students can consult encyclopedias or dictionaries to learn to say "Happy New Year" in as many different languages as possible. Direct them to use encyclopedias or *Red Letter Days* by Elizabeth Sechrist (1940) to trace the history of customs used in the United States to celebrate the new year.

Activity 4.8: Customs and Symbolism

Using a variety of sources or information from their reports about New Year's customs around the world, students should look for uses of symbolism. For example, in many countries water is thrown on others or on oneself in a symbolic gesture of cleansing. Completing the chart "New Year's Customs" will help students organize the information. Then they should look for customs common to several countries and trace their background.

References and Bibliography

Behrens, J. (1982). *Gung hay fat choy: happy new year*. Chicago: Childrens Press. Easy-to-read book with color photographs which explains the significance of how the Chinese New Year is celebrated by Chinese-Americans.

Davidson, J. (1983). *Japan: where east meets west*. Minneapolis: Dillon Press. Short introduction to both the history and the customs of Japan. This book includes chapters about Japanese legends, festivals, sports, and schools. Appendices explain hiagana symbols, and how to make a kimono. A glossary of Japanese words is included.

Dobler, L. (1962). *Customs and holidays around the world*. New York: Fleet Press.

Dobler, L. (1968). *National holidays around the world*. New York: Fleet Press.

Greene, C. (1982). *A new true book: holidays around the world*. Chicago: Childrens Press. Briefly describes various holidays celebrated throughout the world. Very easy to read with many color photographs.

Kelley, E. (1984). *Happy new year*. Minneapolis: Carolrhoda Books. Short, easy-to-read summaries of how New Year's is celebrated in several different countries: Ecuador, Iran, Japan, Vietnam, Sierra Leone, and China.

Perl, L. (1983). *Piñatas and paper flowers: Holidays of the Americas in English and Spanish*. New York: Clarion Books. Information about various holidays. Facing pages are written in English and Spanish.

Sechrist, E. (Ed.). (1940). *Red letter days: a book of holiday customs*. Philadelphia: Macrae-Smith. Explains the historical origins of many of the holidays celebrated in the United States, a number of which are rooted in other countries.

December's Potpourri of Teaching Ideas

The purpose of each month's Potpourri of Teaching Ideas is to provide additional resources from which to build your curriculum. Most, but not all, of the activities listed each month relate directly to that month. It is not intended that you use them all, but rather that you choose those which are appropriate for your program. Although the topics are written for a particular month, many of them would be appropriate for use throughout the year. How you use these activities will depend on your curricular goals. You may wish to use some of the activities as they are presented, and you may need to modify some to meet your needs. Perhaps some of them will give you ideas for entirely different potpourris.

In Celebration of Kwanzaa

Kwanzaa is an African-American holiday that is celebrated from December 26 to January 1. This holiday was created in 1966 by by Dr. Maulana Karenga, an African-American scholar and social activist, to teach others about their heritage. The term *Kwanzaa* is derived from the Swahili word for *first* and, by extension, the first fruits of the harvest. The Swahili word ends with one *a*, but a second was added to correspond with the seven symbols associated with the holiday, each representing an important concept: (1) a placemat, which stands for history; (2) a large cup, which is a symbol for unity; (3) fruits and vegetables, which represent harvest and the work associated with it; (4) corn, or *muhindi*, which stands for children; (5) a candle-holder for seven candles, which represents the people who lived in Africa; (6) the seven candles which light the way; and (7) *zawadi*, or gifts for the children.

Candlelighting is a significant observance related to this holiday. On the first night of Kwanzaa, a child lights the center candle, which is black. Each night for the remainder of the festival, another candle is lit. These candles are lit in a specific order: black, red, then green, each time beginning with the one closest to the center. After the candle for the day is lit, the child talks about one of the reasons, or principles, for this holiday. There are seven principles, or Nguzo Saba: unity, self-determination, collective work and responsibility, co-operative economics, purpose, creativity, and faith.

Try This: Ask a group of students to prepare a poster or small display of the different symbols for Kwanzaa and to explain the significance of these objects. The students can also give the Swahili words for these symbols preferred by the founder, Dr. Karenga.

Suggested Reading

Chocolate, D. M. N. (1992). *My first Kwanzaa book.* New York: Scholastic.

Hoyt-Goldsmith, D. (1993). *Celebrating Kwanzaa.* New York: Holiday House.

Pinkney, A. D. (1993). *Seven candles for Kwanzaa.* New York: Penguin Books USA.

Porter, A. P. (1991). *Kwanzaa.* Minneapolis: Carolrhoda Books.

About Dewey's Decimals

As a young man, Melvil Dewey (1851–1931), revolutionized the method that librarians use to organize books. He was a founder of the American Library Association, but is best known as the creator of the system that bears his name: the Dewey Decimal System of Classification. Most students will be familiar with the Dewey decimal system, but they may be unaware of its origin. This activity is designed to extend students' knowledge and encourage them to spend time in the library.

Try These Activities

Who was Dewey and What Did He Know about Decimals? Direct students to use the resources of the library to find answers to the following:

Who was Melvil Dewey?
What did he do that was important for schools?
Why is his system of classification called the "decimal" system?

What might be the result if we did not have a system of book classification?
What methods other than the decimal system could Dewey have used to classify books?

From 000 to 999: Where Is the Book? Using the chart "Where Is the Book" should encourage students to explore the entire library rather than only those sections pertaining to their immediate interest.

And the Award Goes to John Newbery!

John Newbery was known as a friend of children, for he was the first publisher to concentrate on producing books for children. Before his time, most children's books were adult books that young people "adopted" as their own. These included works like John Bunyan's *Pilgrim's Progress* and Daniel Defoe's *The Life and Strange and Surprising Adventures of Robinson Crusoe.*

Although Newbery may have done some writing, he was first and foremost a publisher who realized a need for books written primarily for children. In 1765, he published *Mother Goose's Melodies,* which is believed to be the first English edition of a book of nursery rhymes. He published a wide assortment of materials, such as small volumes of didactic stories of interest to both boys and girls, including *The History of Little Goody Two Shoes.*

In 1921, Frederic J. Melcher was instrumental in establishing an annual award to be given by the American Library Association to the author of the "most distinguished contribution to American children's literature published during the preceding year." Because of work done by John Newbery nearly two centuries earlier, the award was named in his honor. Since 1922, when the first Newbery medal was awarded to Hendrik van Loon for *The Story of Mankind,* authors of more than seventy books have received the honor.

Try These Activities

In What Country? As stated in the rules, authors awarded the Newbery medal must be American citizens. However, the characters and settings of their books often are international, representing a world community. After discussion and research related to Newbery Award books, students can complete the "In What Country?" chart. You may also wish to use the "Where in the United States?" chart for regional studies.

When Did It Happen? Many of the Newbery Award books are historical fiction. Have students identify those books that are based on historical events or set during historic periods. They can then construct a chart similar to "People, Places, and Events."

WHERE IS THE BOOK?

Number	Category
000-099	General Works

Call number, author, and title of a book in this category that interests me:

_____

_____

100-199	Philosophy, Psychology, Ethics

Call number, author, and title of a book in this category that interests me:

_____

_____

200-299	Religion and Mythology

Call number, author, and title of a book in this category that interests me:

_____

_____

300-399	Social Sciences

Call number, author, and title of a book in this category that interests me:

_____

_____

400-499	Philology (language and dictionaries)

Call number, author, and title of a book in this category that interests me:

_____

_____

500-599	Science

Call number, author, and title of a book in this category that interests me:

_____

_____

600-699	Useful Arts

Call number, author, and title of a book in this category that interests me:

_____

_____

700-799	Fine Arts

Call number, author, and title of a book in this category that interests me:

_____

_____

800-899	Literature

Call number, author, and title of a book in this category that interests me:

_____

_____

900-999	History, Geography, Biography, Travel

Call number, author, and title of a book in this category that interests me:

_____

_____

IN WHAT COUNTRY?

Title of Book	Country
The Trumpeter of Krakow	_____
The Cat Who Went to Heaven	_____
Young Fu of the Upper Yangtze	_____
Dobry	_____
The White Stag	_____
Call It Courage	_____
Adam of the Road	_____
The Twenty-One Balloons	_____
King of the Wind	_____
The Door in the Wall	_____
Secret of the Andes	_____
The Wheel on the School	_____
The Bronze Bow	_____
Shadow of a Bull	_____
I, Juan de Pareja	_____
Number the Stars	_____

WHERE IN THE UNITED STATES?

Title of Book	Region or State
Waterless Mountain	_____
Caddie Woodlawn	_____
The Matchlock Gun	_____
Strawberry Girl	_____
The Witch of Blackbird Pond	_____
The Island of the Blue Dolphins	_____
It's Like This, Cat	_____
From the Mixed-up Files of Mrs. Basil E. Frankweiler	_____
Julie of the Wolves	_____
Roll of Thunder, Hear My Cry	_____
Bridge to Terabithia	_____
Jacob Have I Loved	_____
Dear Mr. Henshaw	_____
Sarah, Plain and Tall	_____

PEOPLE, PLACES, AND EVENTS

Title	Time Period	Location	Historic Event
Number the Stars	Early 1940s	Denmark	Wolrd War II
Rifles for Watie	_____	_____	Civil War
Johnny Tremain Etc.	_____	_____	_____

Gift Bearers around the World

Gift giving is an integral part of the holiday season. Students may find it interesting to investigate the names of mythical individuals who bring gifts to children. Children in many countries anticipate the arrival of essentially the same "folk" character. For example, Father Christmas (England), Père Noel (France), Papa Noel (Brazil), and Dun Che Lao Ren (Hong Kong and Chinese Taiwan) represent the same figure in several different languages. Similarly, Christkind and El Nino Jesus are German and Spanish words that indicate that children in these countries receive their gifts from the Christ child. In many cases, various helpers assist the gift giver.

Children can share their own experiences in this regard and then seek further information from books and other sources. The students can prepare a chart, working as a class or in groups, listing particular types of gift givers. Representative illustrations or collages can be used to represent the gift bearer, the country or culture in which this custom is practiced, and the time of year or occasion when gifts are given.

Santa Claus is a familiar figure to most American youth, but few would recognize other characters. The English "Father Christmas" is traditionally pictured quite differently from our Santa Claus, as is the case with the other gift givers. After collecting illustrations or drawing pictures, students can put together a bulletin board display.

" 'Santas' of the World" is an example of a chart that can be constructed. A similar chart could list the names of those involved in "assisting" or helping the gift givers in their tasks.

Human Benefactors: Those Who Have Given Gifts of Technology

The month of December is the time of the year when gifts are exchanged among individuals in many cultures and countries. It seems appropriate to highlight a sampling of individuals who have given gifts of another sort to humanity. The gifts of the inventor and the creative scientist are the most enduring of all. They provide us with the technology and the knowledge to make our lives longer, healthier, easier, and more pleasurable.

Obviously, the birth dates of inventors and scientists and the anniversaries of scientific discoveries and technological advancements are distributed throughout the year. However, a number of notable individuals were born in December, so it is an appropriate time to remember their "gifts" to the human race: Alexandre-Gustav Eiffel, the French engineer who designed the Eiffel Tower in Paris; Johannes Kepler, the German astronomer who evolved the laws of planetary motion; Louis Pasteur, the French bacteriologist; and Englishman Sir Isaac Newton, the physicist and mathematician who laid the groundwork for the science of spectroscopy, derived the law of gravitation,

"SANTAS" OF THE WORLD

Location	Gift Giver	Date
Netherlands	Sinter Klass	December 5
U.S./Canada	Santa Claus	December 25
Italy	Befana	January 5
Puerto Rico	Magi (Three Kings)	_____
Russia	Grandfather Frost	_____
Hong Kong Etc.	Dun Che Lao Ren	_____

and developed the laws of motion. The month of December also marks the anniversaries of the first powered flight by the Wright Brothers at Kitty Hawk and the first sustained nuclear reaction, primarily the work of Italian-born physicist Enrico Fermi.

Students should be encouraged to learn more about these and other noted scientists and inventors, from countries around the world. Be sure to point out the contributions of minority populations, including women. A timeline is an effective way to present this information, showing not only the specific "gifts" of individuals but also when and where the work was done.

Chapter 5

The Cold Blasts of January

"BLASTS OF JANUARY would blow you through and through," wrote Shakespeare four centuries ago. This is still true today in cities and villages in the Temperate Zone of the Northern Hemisphere. January, the coldest month of the year for those who live north of the equator, is the hottest month for those in the Southern Hemisphere.

The Gregorian calendar places January as the first month of the new year. This was not always so. In many early cultures, the month we call March was the beginning of the new year, and January was one of the last months. Numa Pompilius added January and February to the end of the ten-month Roman calendar. In 46 B.C., Julius Caesar changed the calendar to place January as the first month. January is named for the Roman god Janus. Other cultures called the month by different names. The Norsemen called it Thor after their god of thunder and storms, and the early Anglo-Saxons named it Wolfmouth because during this time wolves came into their villages in search of food.

Several special events occur in January, including New Year's celebrations in many countries of the world. Many Christian religions celebrate Epiphany on January 6. This is believed by some groups to be the traditional date of the coming of the wise men to visit the Christ child. In the United States, Martin Luther King, Jr., is honored by a special day to celebrate his birth and to commemorate his achievements. Martin Luther King, Jr., Day is observed on the first Monday following his birthday of January 15.

January

Sunday	Monday	Tuesday	Wednesday	Thursday	Friday	Saturday

JANUARY

SELECTED EVENTS

1 New Year's Day
   Emancipation Proclamation signed (1863)
2
3 Lucretia Mott (1793–1880)
   Anna Pavlova (1885–1931)
4 Louis Braille (1809–1852)
   Jacob Grimm (1785–1863)
5 First woman governor (1925)
   Jeannette Ridlon Piccard (1895–1981)
6 Epiphany
   Joan of Arc (1412–1431)
7 Japan: Nanakusa Festival
8 Greece: Women's Day
   Elvis Presley (1935–1977)
9 Carrie Lane Catt (1859–1947)
10 Ethan Allen (1738–1789)
   League of Nations formed (1920)
11 Eugenio Maria de Hostos (1839–1903)
   Alice Paul (1885–1977)
12 Charles Perrault (1628–1703)
   Jack London (1876–1916)
13 India: Makara Sankranti/Pongal
14 Albert Schweitzer (1875–1965)
15 Martin Luther King, Jr. (1929–1968)
16 Robert William Service (1874–1958)
17 Benjamin Franklin (1706–1790)
18 Tunisia Revolution Day
   A. A. Milne (1882–1956)
19 Robert E. Lee (1807–1870)
   Edgar Allan Poe (1809–1849)
20 Inauguration Day
21 Roger Nash Baldwin (1884–1981)
22 André Ampère (1775–1836)
23 Bulgaria: Babin Den
   John Hancock (1737–1793)
24 Gold discovered in California (1848)
   Maria Tallchief (1925–)
25 Robert Burns (1759–1796)
26 Australian Day
27 Wolfgang Amadeus Mozart (1756–1791)
28 *Challenger* space shuttle explosion (1986)
29 Anton Pavlovich Chekhov (1860–1904)
   Thomas Paine (1737–1809)
30 Death of Mohandas Gandhi (1948)
31 Jackie Robinson (1919–1972)
   Franz Schubert (1797–1828)

People, Places, and Events of January

What's Happening in January:

First week: Universal Letter Writing Week
January 1–9: Philippines Black Nazarene Fiesta

Events Scheduled According to Non-Gregorian Calendar Usually Occurring in January:

Christmas (Eastern Orthodox)

January's Daily Calendar

1

New Year's Day. First day of the year according to the Gregorian calendar. Some countries, such as China and several other Asian nations, add a year to everyone's age on this date. In those countries, New Year's Day is "everybody's birthday."

Cameroon Independence Day. Gained independence in 1960. French Cameroon and British Cameroon, located in central Africa, merged and restructured to become Cameroon.

Cuba Liberation Day. National holiday celebrating end of Spanish rule in 1899.

Ellis Island opened (1892). A symbol of freedom for immigrants. More than twenty million people entered the United States through this entry station.

Emancipation Proclamation signed by President Abraham Lincoln (1863).

St. Basil's Day. Observed in Eastern Orthodox churches. A St. Basil cake with a coin baked inside is traditionally served.

Sudan Independence Day. Gained complete independence from Britain in 1956.

Birth anniversary of:

Paul Revere (1735–1818). Silversmith and patriot, remembered for his "midnight ride" warning of the advance of British soldiers.

Betsy Ross (1752–1836). Reputed by her grandson, nearly a century later, to be the creator of the first stars and stripes flag in 1775. No evidence proves that she actually was the seamstress who made this famous banner.

2

Georgia became the fourth state to ratify the Constitution (1788).

3

Alaska Admission Day. Became the forty-ninth state admitted to the Union (1959).

Birth anniversary of:

Lucretia Mott (1793–1880). Teacher, antislavery leader, and early founder of women's rights movement.

Anna Pavlova (1885–1931). Russian ballerina believed by many to be the world's greatest dancer.

4

Myanmar Independence Day. Formerly known as Burma. Gained independence from Britain in 1948.

Utah Admission Day. Became the forty-fifth state to join the Union (1896).

Birth anniversary of:

Louis Braille (1809–1852). French inventor of a reading and writing system for blind persons.

Jacob Grimm (1785–1863). With his brother Willhelm, collected and published *Grimm's Fairy Tales*.

5

First woman governor. Nellie Taylor Ross became governor of Wyoming in 1925.

Birth anniversary of:

Jeannette Ridlon Piccard (1895–1981). In 1934, became the first American woman to qualify as a free balloon pilot.

6

Epiphany or Twelfth Day. Observed twelve days after December 25. Celebrated by many Christians to commemorate the visit of the Magi, or wise men, to the Christ child. Also celebrated as Three Kings Day in many parts of the world.

Italy: La Befana. Festival with gifts and toys for children.

Jamaican Maroon Festival. Commemorating freedom for fugitive slaves when the Spanish were driven from Jamaica in 1655.

New Mexico Admission Day. Became the forty-seventh state admitted to the Union (1912).

Birth anniversary of:

Carl Sandburg (1878–1967). Poet and folklorist.

Joan of Arc (1412–1431). French heroine of the siege of Orléans.

7

Japan: Nanakusa Festival. Relates to seven plants that are believed to have medicinal powers.

Birth anniversary of:

Millard Fillmore (1800–1874). Thirteenth president of the United States; born in New York.

8

Battle of New Orleans Day. Observed in Louisiana and Massachusetts to commemorate U.S. victory over the British in 1815.

Greece: Women's Day. Honoring Greek women. Women spend time in cafés; men stay home to tend the children and do household chores.

Birth anniversary of:

Elvis Presley (1935–1977). Remembered by many as the "King of Rock and Roll."

9

Connecticut became the fifth state to ratify the Constitution (1788).

Birth anniversary of:

Carrie Lane Catt (1859–1947). Leader for women's rights and founder of the National League of Women Voters.

Richard Milhous Nixon (1913–1994). Thirty-seventh president of the United States; born in California. The only U.S. president to resign from office.

10

League of Nations established (1920).

Birth anniversary of:

Ethan Allen (1738–1789). Revolutionary war leader of the Green Mountain Boys of Vermont.

Robinson Jeffers (1887–1962). Poet and playwright.

11

Birth anniversary of:

Eugenio Maria de Hostos (1839–1903). Puerto Rican patriot and author.

Alice Paul (1885–1977). Founded the National Woman's Party (1913).

12

Birth anniversary of:

Jack London (1876–1916). Author.

Charles Perrault (1628–1703). French author and collector of fairy tales.

13

India: Makara Sankranti/Pongal. Five-day festival celebrating harvest and thanksgiving. Followed in the evening by a "Battle of the Kites."

First radio broadcast (1910). Lee De Forest broadcast voices of opera stars to listeners in New York City.

14

Singapore: Pongal Harvest Festival. Beginning of four-day festival of thanksgiving for southern Indians.

Bulgaria: Vinegrower's Day. Ancient festival believed to produce a bountiful harvest of grapes. The ritual is followed by feasting and festivities.
Birth anniversary of:
Benedict Arnold (1741–1801). Deserted to the British during the American Revolution; name became synonymous with treason.
Albert Schweitzer (1875–1965). Philosopher and physician; awarded Nobel Peace Prize in 1952 for work in Africa.

15

Japan: Adult's Day. National holiday honoring youth who have reached adulthood during preceding year.
Birth anniversary of:
Martin Luther King, Jr. (1929–1968). African-American minister and civil rights leader. National holiday celebrating his life is observed on the third Monday in January.

16

Birth anniversary of:
Robert William Service (1874–1958). Canadian poet best remembered for "The Cremation of Sam McGee" and "The Shooting of Dan McGrew."

17

Birth anniversary of:
Benjamin Franklin (1706–1790). Scientist, author, publisher, and the oldest signer of the Declaration of Independence and the Constitution.

18

First African-American cabinet member. In 1966, Robert Clifton Weaver became secretary of housing and urban development.
Birth anniversary of:
A. A. Milne (1882–1956). English author (*Winnie the Pooh).*
Peter Mark Roget (1779–1869). English scholar best remembered for *Thesaurus of English Words and Phrases* (1852).

19

Birth anniversary of:
Robert E. Lee (1807–1870). Military commander and leader of the Confederate army.
Edgar Allan Poe (1809–1849). Author best remembered for poems and tales of suspense.
James Watt (1736–1819). Scottish inventor, noted for developments improving the steam engine.

20

Brazil: Nosso Senhor do Bonfim Festival. Observed especially in the town of Salvador. Festival culminates in a ritual designed to cleanse citizens of their impurities.
Inauguration Day. Every four years, a newly elected U.S. president is inaugurated to begin a new term of office.
Lesotho Army Day. Commemorating the beginning of a military coup in 1986 in this southern African country.

21

Roger Nash Baldwin (1884–1981). Founder of the American Civil Liberties Union.

22

Birth anniversary of:
André Ampère (1775–1836). French physicist and founder of the science of electrodynamics. The ampere, a unit of electrical current, is named for him.

23

Bulgaria: Babin Den. Traditional celebration honoring grandmothers.
National Handwriting Day. Observed on the birth anniversary of John Hancock (1737–1793) to encourage more legible handwriting.

24

Gold discovered in Coloma, California (1848), precipitating the great gold rush of 1849.
Birth anniversary of:
Maria Tallchief (1925–). Osage Indian and one of America's greatest ballerinas.

25

Birth anniversary of:
Robert Burns (1759–1796). Scottish poet, famous for the lines, "Oh wad some power the giftie gie us/to see oursels as ithers see us!"

26

Australian Day. Commemorating the first British settlement in Australia (1788).
Dominican Republic National Holiday. Honoring founding father Juan Pablo Duarte.
India Republic Day. Became democratic republic in 1950.
Michigan Admission Day. Became the twenty-sixth state admitted to the Union (1837).
Birth anniversary of:
Douglas MacArthur (1880–1964). U.S. soldier and commander during World War II.

27

Birth anniversary of:

Charles Lutwidge Dodgson (1832–1898). English mathematician, best known as the author of *Alice's Adventures in Wonderland* (using the pseudonym of Lewis Carroll).

Wolfgang Amadeus Mozart (1756–1791). Austrian composer and musician.

28

Challenger space shuttle explosion. In 1986, seven people, including schoolteacher Christa McAuliffe, died in an explosion seventy-four seconds into the flight.

Birth anniversary of:

Henry Morton Stanley (1841–1904). English explorer and leader of the African expedition to find missing missionary David Livingston.

29

Kansas Admission Day. Became the thirty-fourth state admitted to the Union (1861).

Birth anniversary of:

Anton Pavlovich Chekhov (1860–1904). Russian playwright and author of short stories.

William McKinley (1843–1901). Twenty-fifth president of the United States; born in Ohio. Died from an assassin's bullet.

Thomas Paine (1737–1809). Supporter and leader of the American Revolution.

30

Assassination of Mohandas Gandhi. Indian religious and political leader assassinated by a Hindu extremist in 1948.

Birth anniversary of:

Franklin Delano Roosevelt (1882–1945). Thirty-second president of the United States; born in New York. Only president to serve more than two terms.

31

Republic of Nauru National Holiday. Located in the western Pacific Ocean; became independent of Britain in 1968.

Birth anniversary of:

Zane Grey (1875–1939). Author of western frontier stories; best remembered for *Riders of the Purple Sage*.

Jackie Robinson (1919–1972). First African-American to play major league baseball.

Franz Schubert (1797–1828). Austrian composer and musician.

A Simulation Trip to Africa— Capturing Endangered Animals

Teaching Unit for January

A Word about This Unit. Students become more active learners when teachers plan and structure class activities that engage them both cognitively and emotionally. One way to achieve this is to develop lesson plans that incorporate opportunities for role playing. Role playing as an instructional motivation allows integration of social studies content with reading and writing strategies nested within the dramatic experience, making it possible not only to teach relevant social studies concepts, but also to improve students' writing and reasoning skills. In addition, the use of drama draws students into an awareness of social problems. Role playing becomes a vehicle for helping students view problems from different perspectives.

Research in language-arts education supports instruction that integrates different areas of subject matter and that includes various types of purposeful and meaningful reading and writing activities. Whole language theory advocates planning meaningful writing experiences in a variety of subject areas (Pappas et al., 1990). The purpose of this unit is to provide a way to integrate whole language strategies within the area of social studies.

Drama, as used in this lesson plan, refers to "role drama" as discussed by Tarlingon and Verriour (1991). The purpose of role drama is to promote a change in understanding or to provide insight on the part of participants. It allows students an opportunity to explore thoughts and feelings by responding and behaving as if they were actually involved in a given situation. As Tarlingon and Verriour (1991, p. 9) explain: "In role drama, teachers set up imagined situations which students and teachers enter together, *in role*, to explore events, issues, and relationships. What distinguishes role drama from other kinds of drama is that the teacher takes a role within the drama."

The unit described in this chapter is the study of Africa. However, the vortex around which instruction revolves is a role-playing situation. In the example used here, students will become part of a team that is being employed to plan, capture, and bring back unharmed to the United States an endangered animal that lives in Africa. Because the continent is so large and the countries so varied, you may want to plan other types of quests for the study of North Africa or countries within the great horn of Africa. For example, if the class is studying northern Africa rather than Central or East Africa, the group could be planning an expedition seeking important manuscripts written at the time of Muhammad. The reason for the quest or the trip is merely the core around which activities are planned. Although activities such as these may appear to be contrived, students enjoy them as a way to integrate various aspects of learning activities or projects.

Themes to Be Explored

The conceptual outcomes developed in this unit include learning about the geography and history of a country, and about the use and misuse of political power in terms of European colonization and the search for independence by colonized African nations. In addition, students will develop an understanding of the cost of maintaining habitats for endangered species.

Motivation. To attract the students' attention and to involve them in the lesson immediately, the teacher assumes the role of a zoo director in order to invite the class to take part in a safari to capture, unharmed, a rare animal native to Africa. To draw the students into the drama, the teacher and the students brainstorm about the type of person who would be needed to attempt this project. Afterward, each student chooses a role of a likely person who would participate in such an expedition. Several students may choose the same role—for example, veterinarian, guide, caretaker, or cook.

Immersion. In this part of the unit, students gather information about the topic. You can either read the short excerpts of information included in this text, read from a variety of trade books, or encourage students to seek additional information in appropriate reference sources.

Required:

1. Travel brochure describing the outstanding sights (natural and manmade), climate, and location of the target country
2. Topographical map: a two- or three-dimensional product
3. Fine arts performance: storytelling, music, dance, crafts, or art
4. Development and participation in a simulated "World Court"

Optional:

1. Map of the natural resources of the target country
2. Chart of the governmental bodies of the target country and their relationships
3. Map showing the locations of ethnic groups in the target country

Individual Student Activities:

1. Passport
2. Short biography of a famous person from the target country
3. Writings: diaries, reflections, etc.
4. Performance or reading of a folktale
5. Preparation for a debate in a mock "World Court"

Information and Background

A Note to the Teacher. This short summary of African history is intended to show some of the important aspects of the continent prior to European colonization. Many of the regions of Africa had developed rich cultures. This segment of the unit serves to counter the stereotypical image of Africa as the "dark and mysterious continent." African history can be viewed as comprised of three eras: precolonial, colonial, and postcolonial. When presenting this unit, the teacher will need to guard against oversimplification and the creation of new stereotypes while attempting to assist students to recognize the inaccuracy of established ones.

Information. The early stereotypical view of Africa as the dark and mysterious continent likely arose in the minds of Europeans because they knew so little about it. Historical study reveals that Africa was the seat of great civilizations and cultures that grew, flourished, and declined long before the age of European exploration. This continent, almost completely surrounded by oceans, is approximately eleven and one-half million square miles in size, the second largest land mass in the world. It contains many different geographical regions, a rich diversity of peoples and cultures, and an abundance of natural resources. In it are countries with beautiful beaches, tropical rain forests, savannas, deserts, and mountains. Some of the countries in Africa are located on the equator.

Africa is sometimes called the "cradle of civilization" because many early societies and cultures began there. The bones of one of the earliest direct ancestors of humans, named Lucy, who lived approximately five million years ago, was discovered in Ethiopia in 1974. Bone fragments and tools which suggest that ancestors of humans also lived in Tanzania over two and one-third million years ago were found by two scientists, Mary and Louis Leakey. Two million years ago, several varieties of australopithecine man lived throughout much of central, eastern, and southern Africa (Maquet & Rayfield, 1972).

Throughout Africa's history, people have become efficient masters of their environments (Fritz et al., 1992). In the earliest years, people living in the rain forests took metals from the earth and made tools and weapons. In the savanna land and plains, people planted and harvested crops and tended herds. Along the bands of the great rivers, people established trade and cultural exchanges, developed commercial centers where cities grew, and practiced the fine arts. There is evidence that ancient kingdoms in Africa, including Egypt, Kush, and Ethiopia (Sheba), had developed great cultures before the birth of Christ. Egyptians created one of the earliest and greatest cultures in the ancient world, dating back to 8000 B.C. These civilizations grew and flourished until invasions by Arab armies, other African kingdoms, the Crusades, and Europeans and the beginning of the slave trade led to their decline.

From the fourth to the tenth centuries, the ancient kingdom of **Ghana** was the first West African empire below the Sahara to flourish as an important trade and cultural center. Ancient Ghana was about five hundred miles northwest of present Ghana. In 1076, invaders from the north began attacking Ghana's smaller city-states and forcing many of the people to become Muslims. This military action disrupted Ghana's government and, after a series of defeats, Ghana began to decline. Many refugees fleeing from the new invaders migrated south to what is present-day Ghana.

Mali grew out of the ruins of old Ghana. Mali and **Songhai** were powerful kingdoms from A.D. 500 to 1500. These kingdoms had become famous for their gold and salt trade. After leading a rebellion against the Sosso in 1235, the Malis became the leaders of military trade and political power in the region for the next two hundred years. Eventually, Mali became the size of western Europe. During that time, one of the largest libraries in the world was located in the city of Timbuktu. There is a story that Mali's ruler, Mansa Musa, needed one hundred camels to carry the gold and gifts he took with him when, in 1324, he made a trip to Mecca, the holy city of the Muslims.

In 1364, Sunni Ali the Great became the leader of Songhai. He captured Timbuktu and Jenne. By 1473, the government of Songhai had established one of the largest universities for the training of doctors in Jenne. Here, doctors isolated the mosquito as the cause of malaria and performed cataract operations on humans. Universities also were founded in Gao and Timbuktu. Gao, on the Niger River, had a reputation as a craftsman's paradise. Its goldsmiths, leather workers, blacksmiths, weavers, and potters were famous. By 1600, Moroccan soldiers had defeated the Songhai and the empire disintegrated to become parts of Hausa, Bornu, and Kanem.

East Africa has been explored constantly for more than two thousand years (Crofts, 1988, p. 19). The **Swahili** were the powerful rulers of the east African sea trade. From the twelfth through the fifteenth centuries, they traded gold, ivory, spices, iron, cloth, and pottery to Kilwas, Mombas, Sofala, Malindi, and Zanzibar. Swahili sailors used compasses and charts, making it possible to trade with India, Indonesia, Ceylon, and China for centuries. Later, the Portuguese disrupted the Indian Ocean trade and burned and sacked Kilwa, ending Swahili rule.

From A.D. 800 to 1600, other city-states became important trading centers as well. **Kilwa,** on the East African coast, became a trading center for African gold, iron, and ivory, which was traded for goods from Arabia, India, and China. **Benin,** located in today's Nigeria, became a great civilization. **Monomotapa,** with Gradt Zimbabwe as its capital, had great temples.

Between the eighth and eleventh centuries, Islam spread from Mecca throughout the Arab world and traveled across North Africa. Traders carrying goods and the message of Islam helped make North Africa part of the Muslim empire.

In 1434, a Portuguese captain was able to sail beyond the coast of Rio de Oro and return home. This opened the way for the European exploration and colonization of Africa. Before this time, Europeans knew of the riches of Africa but were unable to travel there because the Muslims would not allow them to trade and travel in northern Africa. The headwinds along the Moroccan coast prevented the ships from returning home, as they were unable to sail beyond the sight of land because they had no navigational instruments. When better ships, instruments, and sailing techniques were invented, the Europeans equipped their sailing vessels with compasses and astrolabes—instruments brought to Europe by Arab traders who had learned about them from the Chinese. With these improvements, exploration of Africa was begun by the Europeans.

The kingdom of the **Congo** was explored by the Portuguese in 1490. The king, Nizinga Mbemba, welcomed them because they had a common interest in trading. Weapons were added to the trading list in exchange for prisoners of war.

These prisoners of war probably became the early slaves brought to the Americas. When the demand for slaves exceeded the supply by the Congo, the Portuguese began taking the Congolese people. When Affonso, the king of the Congo, sent young men to become educated in Portugal, they, too, became slaves. Affonso asked the king of Portugal to stop taking his people as slaves and instead allow them to become priests, teachers, physicians, apothecaries, and surgeons. He was ignored and the slave ships kept returning. After the death of Affonso, the Congolese people divided into warring factions, with the Portuguese taking captives on all sides. By 1667, the Portuguese had sacked the Congo.

The **Ivory Coast** (Côte d'Ivoire) was first inhabited by humans approximately thirty-five thousand years ago. These early people lived along the edges of coastal lagoons and the estuaries of the major rivers. Beginning in the 1100s, other African groups left the northern countries and moved to the south to begin new independent communities in what is now Côte d'Ivoire. These people were hunters and gatherers, living in small groups. Beginning in the sixteenth century, Malinke people from northwestern Africa moved to the territory of the Senufo, forcing them to move south and east and into the Côte d'Ivoire. The Malinke people were Muslim traders who, looking for cola nuts and other forest products, established major trading routes on the Niger River.

Portuguese and other Europeans may have reached Côte d'Ivoire as early as the 1300s. However, it was not until 1637 that the first French landed at **Assine.** These were missionaries who founded settlements that lasted only a few years. In 1842, the French government undertook massive exploration of the West African coast in order to acquire colonies.

In 1652, the Dutch East India Company set up a supply station at Table Mountain at the tip of **South Africa.** The indigenous people who lived there, the Khoi-khoi, were hunter-gatherers who kept cattle. Although the Dutch settlers began by bartering with the Khoi for meat and for land, differing attitudes soon led to conflicts. Jan Van Riebeeck, the Dutch leader, noted that the Khoi complained that the Dutch were taking more and more of their land. The Khoi asked ". . . if they [the Khoi] would be allowed to do such a thing supposing they went to Holland [sic]" (Hayward, 1989, p. 7).

Other Europeans entered southeast Africa—the British into **Zimbabwe, Zambia,** and **Malawi,** the French into **Mauritius** and **Reunion.** These Europeans, with their powerful weapons, quickly put an end to uprisings and took over the land, even though they constituted a small percentage of the total population. By 1893, most of Africa was under European rule and by 1900 had been divided into formal colonial empires. Seven countries—Britain, France, Belgium, Portugal, Germany, Italy, and Spain—had occupied the entire continent. The French also controlled **Algeria, Morocco,** and **Tunisia** in North Africa. The countries of West Africa were colonized by the British, the French, and the Germans. The Portuguese laid claim to **Angola.** In South Africa, the Boers (descendants of Dutch settlers), the British, and the Germans established empires. East Africa was claimed by the Onani Arabs, the British, the Germans, the Portuguese, and the Italians. King Leopold II of Belgium claimed the inland country of the Congo basin.

Although there was some peaceful occupation by agreement, more often it came through armed conflict and small wars. Sizable forces were used to impose rule, and spears, arrows, and clubs were no match for rifles and machine guns. Moreover, there were armed uprisings and revolts during World War I. After the war, Germany lost its African colonies to other European countries. Vast numbers of Africans who were involved in the war effort either economically or militarily received none of the compensation that usually comes with victory.

World War II marked the turning point in the colonial history of Africa (Baynham, 1987). At the sixth Pan-African Conference (PAC) held in Manchester, England, in 1945, the delegates from Black Africa demanded autonomy and independence, stating, "We will fight in every way we can for freedom, democracy, and social betterment" (Davidson, 1971, p. 100). In 1946, at a meeting in Bamako, the African Democratic Alliance was born. This was an all-territory freedom movement for the French-African colonies. The Black African soldiers, returning home after having fought against fascism and racism, wanted equal rights with other citizens in their countries.

Educational and economic developments after World War II, India's independence from England, and the emergence of the United States and the Soviet Union as world powers were factors leading to moves for independence by the colonial countries in Africa. Almost fifty African countries have gained independence since the end of World War II (Baynham, 1987, p. 13). **Libya,** in northern Africa, was one of the first, gaining independence in 1956.

In Zimbabwe (then called Rhodesia) during 1965, the white minority rebelled against British colonial rule. However, they did this to form their own set of rules, which denied political and civil rights to Black Africans within this country.

In the 1960s, the inhabitants of Malawi, Madagascar, and Mauritius regained their independence. However, Zimbabwe and Zambia were in conflict into the early 1980s.

Although many of the countries became independent of European rule, this did not bring an end to conflict. The borders that were drawn up by the Europeans as they formed colonies were artificial and did not always consider the major groupings within Africa. Ethnic groups were forced to live together because their separate territories had become one country. No attention was paid to whether these groups had been traditionally friendly or hostile. Most Africans are more loyal to ethnic groupings than to national boundaries. For this reason, the time after independence was often one of civil and military conflicts and sometimes resulted in the abolition of the legal system. Thus, in some countries the only way to change presidents and prime ministers was through violence and military coups. At least thirty-one of the African state have staged successful coups, with sixteen of them having more than one. Sometimes the violence has forced governments to request the United Nations to intercede and send in troops to restore order.

The **Masai** represent the plight of threatened African groups. The Masai are a nomadic people whose territory once crossed the present-day borders of Kenya and Tanzania. When the Europeans carved up Africa in the 1800s, Masailand was splintered into parts of Tanganyika, Kenya, and Uganda. Even when the new African leaders came to power, they did not honor these ancestral claims and instead restored the old colonial boundaries. This led to boundary disputes, wars and competition for diminishing resources. Today, Masai compete with other ethnic groups and national game parks for the savannas where they had lived for centuries. Most Masai have less than half the land they need to sustain their herds. A drought in the 1960s killed approximately one-third of their cattle (Davidson, 1993).

In addition to civil unrest, today many African countries are suffering from poverty, overpopulation, and disease. Each month, the population of Africa grows by a million people. Diseases such as cholera, diphtheria, yellow fever, malaria, and AIDS have spread across Africa. There is low output within the agricultural sectors.

However, there are countries that are successful. The Ivory Coast and Malawi have established stable, orderly, and prosperous regimes. Stable governments have formed in Senegal, Cameroon, and Tanzania.

Apartheid. No discussion of the African continent is complete without mentioning the former practice of apartheid in South Africa. Apartheid means "apartness" of people based on the color of their skins. This system of racial laws ensured white rule over the African ethnic groups and led to inferior education, unequal land distribution, low monthly earnings, and poor working conditions for Africans and for people of mixed race (Hayward, 1989). This philosophy of government based on racial differences and inequality (Hayward, 1989, p. 5) was put into place in 1948 by the National Party, although it had been in existence before that.

The first European settlers were the Dutch, who eventually wiped out the San and the Khoi, who were the aboriginal ethnic groups in the area. The few remaining Khoi were either enslaved by the Dutch colonists or sent to the Dutch East Indies as slaves. After the Dutch were defeated in 1815 in the Napoleonic wars in Europe, the settlements in the Cape Colony passed to the British, who abolished slave labor in 1834. From 1836 to 1840, the Dutch farmers (called the Boers) moved to the interior looking for farmland on which they could keep slave labor. Because there was a large-scale war among the African chiefs in the interior, the Boers and the British conquered the African kingdoms. The Boers formed two independent republics, the Orange Free State and the Transvaal. The British expanded the Cape and took over Natal. The African farmers found themselves forced to work on white farms to pay the taxes introduced by the British and Boer governments. The discovery of diamonds and gold in South Africa eventually led to war between the Boers and the British. The Parliament Act of Union in 1910 united the former British colonies and the independent Boer republics. This new country of South Africa was to be governed by a parliament that met in Cape Town but whose seat was in Pretoria. The vote was still denied to Africans who lived in the Transvaal and in the Orange Free State.

In 1912, a group of African chiefs, Christian ministers, and intellectuals formed the South African Native National Congress as a reaction to the injustices of the Act of Union. This group had little success in convincing the British or other Africans that the Africans should be a united people rather than separate ethnic groups.

In 1914, the Natives' Land Act divided South Africa into black and white areas. This forced hundreds of thousands of Africans to be relocated from their farms to black areas. In 1922, the Afrikaner National Party came to power and passed a series of acts that made racial discrimination the law. From 1934 onward, the National Party made an effort to unite Afrikaners behind them.

During World War II, many Africans were allowed to work in semiskilled factory positions. Many whites felt that too many Africans were living or working in white areas, paving the way for a party that would develop laws to truly separate Africans from whites.

During the 1948 election, Dr. Magnus Malan used the word "apartheid" in his election slogan, formally declaring it as the party manifesto. This led to the Population Registration Act of 1950, which classified persons by race, the Prohibition of Mixed Marriages Act, and the Immorality Act. These acts made it possible for the white minority to have absolute control over the African majority.

The African National Congress (ANC), which had begun as a moderate black organization, formed a Youth League. During the 1949 ANC conference, Nelson Mandela, among others, pushed for a program of action to abolish discrimination through boycotts, strikes, and civil disobedience. After the joining together of the ANC and the Indian Congress, volunteers began openly to break segregation laws. These protesters were sent to jail by the hundreds. In retaliation, the government laid down heavy penalties for those accused of influencing Africans to break laws. In 1953, Albert Luthuli became president of the ANC. He led the fight for the Freedom Charter, which declared that South Africa belonged to all inhabitants and which called for a nonracial democracy with equal opportunities for all citizens (Hayward, 1989). The government responded by arresting 156 of the leading delegates and charging them with treason. Because "violent means" had not been used, all were acquitted four and a half years later.

In 1961, the people of South Africa voted to leave the British commonwealth. Because ANC and PAC members felt that peaceful resistance was not working and that violent measures were necessary to achieve their goals for change, the government, led by Hendrik Verwoerd and later by Vorster, passed laws of repression. The police were empowered to arrest without a warrant and hold for ninety days anyone whom they suspected of being involved with antigovernment activities. They also were allowed to detain suspects immediately after release. By 1966, this law had been changed so that a suspect could be held for an unlimited time. One hero of black resistance was Nelson Mandela, who was imprisoned in 1962 on minor charges. He was not released from jail until 1990.

In 1976, nearly a thousand students in Soweto, a black township, revolted against the poor schooling conditions for Africans. White police moved in and killed young black people, including children. Those taken into detention were assaulted, beaten, and tortured to force them to sign statements admitting guilt (Hayward, 1989). One hundred and seventy-six people were killed by the police and more than one thousand were wounded. In 1986, a state of emergency declared by the South African government gave the police greater powers to arrest, ban public gatherings, and enforce press censorship.

The problem continues, but changes have occurred to break down the barriers. Many whites have left South Africa because they feel that the government's policies have been morally wrong. Others struggle to change the system. Political parties have developed that work toward moderation and full democracy for all citizens of South Africa.

After a brief overview of the early history of the continent, the first part of the unit will concentrate on the countries of Botswana, Burundi, Kenya, Lesotho, Mauritius, Namibia, Rwanda, South Africa, Swaziland, Tanzania, Uganda, Aaire, Zambia, and Zimbabwe. These countries encompass a wide range of habitats—savannas, forests, wetlands, deserts—and thus support a variety of wildlife. Because the premise of this unit is the search for and capture of endangered species, these countries were chosen for study.

Instructional Activities

This unit opens immediately with the teacher taking on the role of a director of a zoo or a leader of an expedition. Some of you will want to dress for the part, others will prefer to introduce their students to the activities that follow by discussing them first or by discussing the use of drama for "let's pretend" or "what if."

What follows is a suggested "script." Activities are embedded throughout the script, so you read this section in its entirety before trying it in class.

Teacher (in role): "Good morning and thank you for answering my advertisement and coming to our meeting today to discuss the capture and preservation of rare or endangered African wildlife species. I know that each of you has particular skills, knowledge, and practices that we will need if we are to make our trip a success.

"Capturing and transporting these animals will take many people who are seriously committed to the project. What types of people will be needed to capture and transport these animals?"

Teacher writes the students' suggestions on the chalkboard and then helps students visualize themselves in a role with the following.

Teacher continues: "Close your eyes. It is ten years from now and you are going on an expedition to capture rhinos. Visualize yourself as an adult. How old would you like to be? How do you look? How tall are you? What are you wearing? Now look closer. What is your hair like? How long is it, and what style is it? What about your face? Have you aged well? Do you have any wrinkles on your face? What kind of expres-

sion do you have? Are you happy with the work you do? How did you decide on the occupation you have chosen? What happened to you that made you decide that being a _____ would be interesting?"

The teacher helps students to formalize their roles by having them write a biographical sketch.

Teacher continues: "Write about how you decided to become a _____. This type of writing is called autobiography. What would you include to make your writing interesting to the reader? Your reader will not know you, so you must explain at what age you decided to become a _____. What do writers do to make these kinds of books interesting? You could tell something that happened to you or to someone you know. You might have had a conversation with someone or you might have known someone who was a _____ and, because you admired them, you wanted to be like them. Open your eyes. Now, write about the person you are who is going on this expedition."

At this point during the visualization stage, the essential elements of biography can be introduced. The students should write a short "autobiography" that tells how they became interested in their "occupation," the schooling and job experiences they have had, and why they are interested in going on this hunt. If students have not had the opportunity to write in this format, read some excerpts from appropriate biographies or autobiographies.

Allow some of the students to tell which of the people they have chosen to be. Although this writing has elements of biography, its goal is to be persuasive. It is a way of highlighting the activities that make one a suitable candidate for this trip.

Have students *share their first drafts in groups.* Because the director of the zoo must submit a portfolio to the people funding the trip, students must rewrite their rough drafts into a suitable format for inclusion in the report. They can also share these biographies by publishing them in a "Who's Who" or by interviewing for the job with the leader of the expedition who can be represented by either the teacher or another student in the role.

Students will use these biographies to fill out applications for positions on this imaginary quest.

Teacher: "You know we can't take everyone on this trip; therefore, we need to create an application form."

The class designs an application form, which everyone completes. Afterward, the students form groups, with members taking on various roles of required personnel; if several choose to be veterinarians, one veterinarian should be on each team. Students make name tags showing the occupation of the person they will role play.

Teacher: "It is necessary for you to sign some papers that state that you will not hold the zoo responsible for your safety and that if something does happen to you, the zoo will not have to pay any damages. After all, what could happen on an expedition to an unknown country to trap wild animals?

"What is this type of paper called? What type of information is on it? What type of language is used? Please work with a partner to draw up this paper. Draft a letter to the government of _____ for permission to capture and transport endangered animals."

Teacher in role as director of zoo: "Well, staff, I'm glad that you were able to finish feeding the animals early so that we could have our staff meeting. I know that working in the zoo is tiring and you want to go home, but I have just received a reply to our letter to the government of _____ requesting permission to capture and transport the rhinos. Let me read it to you:

Dear _____:

The government of _____ is very concerned about the black rhinos and wants to protect this endangered species from extinction. However, our very limited resources make it necessary for us to concentrate on human needs first. Therefore, we agree to allow you to collect two black rhinos under the following conditions:

1. You ensure the safety of the rhinos by bringing a qualified staff to capture and transport the animals.
2. You provide the animals with cages large enough to make their transport comfortable.
3. You capture the rhinos without endangering the herd or any other animals that live in the same habitat.
4. You provide an environment in your homeland that is similar to the environment in which the animals lived.

Sincerely,

_____

"You see that we have our work cut out for us."

At this time, students need to design some type of identification badge to be worn whenever they are in role on the journey or as experts on a particular country or personality.

Teacher: "Before we leave, I think you should know something about the country in which we will be traveling. With the help of reference books and the information I will give you, I think we will become reasonably acquainted with the country we are visiting."

Activity 5.1: Developing a Travel Brochure

Teacher: "The next activity is to write a travel brochure about the country your team will visit to capture the animal. A travel brochure must inform the reader about the country in general and about the specific sights a visitor might see. It should include information about both rural and urban areas."

Each team is responsible for developing a travel brochure about the country of the endangered animal it is capturing. Either *in role* as a travel agent or the zoo director, you should model the elements of this type of writing. Constructing such brochures provides an opportunity for students to learn about the geography and political system of the country they plan to "visit." Travel folders should include geographic facts, information about the country's people, and details about specific sites.

Place sample travel folders around the room as models for the students to use. However, none of the brochures should be about countries in Africa.

Constructing a Travel Brochure

A travel brochure should be produced by each group. Pictures from magazines, textbooks, and trade books can be used as illustrations. Information within the brochure should include terrain, major cities, important sites, and maps.

Students should be given class time to work on the brochures. In some schools, computers may be used as a means for formatting, or students can make a large outline map of each country and draw or paste illustrations of important cities, minerals, geographic features, and resources. These could be hung from the ceiling over different areas within the classroom after each group makes its presentation to the class. The next activity is optional, depending on the class.

Teacher: "Finally, the day of departure is here, and we've arrived at the airport. They are calling our flight, so let's get in line to board the plane. (*If possible, the students should arrange their chairs in rows similar to airplane seats.*) Don't forget to take your bags. OK, let's get seated and ready for takeoff. Buckle your seat belts. (*Ask for a volunteer to play the role of the flight attendant to tell the safety rules.*)

"Introduce yourself to the person seated next to you. Before we land, I would like to remind you that we will be guests of this country and so we will do our best to honor the customs, traditions, and sensibilities of the people who live there. Therefore, refer to the inhabitants of this continent either as Africans or, better, as members of a particular nationality or ethnic group—for example, the Togolese. The interior regions are described as 'bush,' 'country,' or 'rain forest,' rather than 'jungle.' Some of the people we will see will wear 'traditional clothes,' not 'native costumes' (Suttles & Suttles-Graham, 1986, p. 6).

"Each of us will keep a diary of this trip. Your first entry will be made while in the airplane. Think about all of the things you did to get ready for this trip. Think about how you said goodbye to your family. You are going to a place you have never been before; you are going to help capture a large and rather dangerous wild animal. This is a big adventure. What if you become frightened or badly injured? How do you feel? What are you thinking about? Write these thoughts in your diary."

Allow students to write.

Teacher: "We've been flying now for fifteen hours. It is time to land and deplane. Stand up and stretch. It was a long flight. I'm glad we're here. Let's gather our bags and meet in the airport terminal.

"You are in the airport. Look around you. The people are wearing various types of dress and carrying interesting objects. However, we can't spend too much time here. Pick up your belongings and go through customs."

Students then break into groups and, using the book *Ashanti to Zulu* (Musgrove, 1976), describe or explain some of the specific dress and artifacts of ethnic groups from their country of study.

Teacher (before students give their reports): "This is so interesting that you make brief notes in your diary about what you see. You plan to write to your family later on. What form will these notes take? What do writers keep in their notebooks that will help them to remember something later on?

"We need to move to our camp headquarters and prepare for the night. What do we need to do to set up camp?"

Groups should get together to plan their working space for the rest of the enactment of the expedition. Each group will find a work space and collect materials. This workplace should be called by the name of a major city of the country in which the group will search for its animal.

Activity 5.2: Mapmaking

Teacher: "It is time for us to get down to business. We will break into groups and draw maps."

Hand out pieces of board and crayons, allowing each group to map a quarter section of the territory. When all groups are finished, one person from each group will explain what they saw as they scouted the terrain. Place the maps in a prominent place so they can be referred to later. An alternative activity to making geographic or political maps would be to make elevated models from papier mâché.

Teacher: "We have not been able to make plans for the capture because we were unsure of the terrain that the animals would be in during this time of the year and whether there would be sufficient water available for them to stay in this terrain. I think it is time for us to make plans. Break into groups of three or four and come up with a way to capture this big animal. Remember, we cannot hurt it. When you have devised a plan, practice acting it out to show the others. Act it out in slow motion so that we can see how it will happen. Use the map to show us what part of the terrain you are occupying."

Students then present their plans for capturing the animal.

Activity 5.3: Storytelling, Dance, or Song

Sharing the folk literature of a country helps students to understand the values and lessons important to the people who tell them. Students from each group will prepare to tell or to read a folktale from the country they are "visiting." If you are working on a team or with another teacher, students can be helped to read aloud in a dramatic way or to learn about elements of storytelling. Allow students the time and opportunity to visit either the school or public library to obtain books on African folk literature (see the Suggested Reading list).

Teacher: "It is the night before we move to capture the animals. We have just finished dinner; everyone has checked all the equipment and knows what his part will be. It is time to go to bed. Go into your tent and climb into your sleeping bag. Listen, there is soft singing in the night, and perhaps the noise of drums. It is the chanting of the trackers."

Students read a folktale from their country, perform music, or dance.

The next activity is optional, but it allows students the opportunity to problem solve as they prepare a pantomime showing how the group captured its animal.

Teacher: "Close your eyes and think about the capture tomorrow. Think about the plan and what could go wrong. You fall asleep and have nightmares. You awake with a start and to assure yourself that you are safe, you write your nightmare in your diary.

"Good morning, everyone! I hope you had a good night's sleep. Today is the day. Did you have sweet dreams? No? Tell us."

Groups perform or act out their plan for capturing the animal as if it were in a nightmare. Slow motion is one way to make the performance appear as a nightmare. After the performance, or in place of it, ask students to write about the capture from their own perspectives.

Teacher: "Now we have captured the animals. We're back in camp and it's time to rehash the excitement. Think about who you are. What did you do in the capture? Write yourself a note in your diary."

Students, in their roles as professionals, should tell what they did during the capture.

Suggested Readings

Aardema, V. (1973). *Behind the back of the mountain: black folktales from southern Africa.* New York: Dial.

Aardema, V. (1975). *Why mosquitoes buzz in people's ears.* New York: Dial.

Aardema, V. (1977). *Who's in rabbit's house? A Masai tale.* New York: Dial. Includes illustrations of costumes and masks that could be used as this tale is told.

Aardema, V. (1979). *Half-a-ball of kenki.* New York: Warne, Frederick.

Aardema, V. (1981). *Bringing the rain to Kapiti Plain: A Nandi tale.* New York: Dial.

Bryan, A. (1971). *The ox of wonderful horns and other African folk tales.* New York: Atheneum.

Cowlander, H. (1982). *The crest and the hide and other African stories of heroes, chiefs, bards, hunters, sorcerers and common people.* New York: Coward.

Dayrell, E. (1968). *Why the sun and moon live in the sky: An African folktale.* Boston: Houghton Mifflin.

Domanska, J. (1978). *The tortoise and the tree.* New York: Greenwillow Books.

McDermott, G. (1972). *Anansi the spider.* New York: Holt, Rinehart & Winston.

Mollel, T. (1992). *A promise to the sun.* Boston: Little, Brown.

Prather, R. (1978). *The ostrich girl.* New York: Charles Scribner's Sons.

Serwadda, W. (1974). *Songs and stories from Uganda.* (H. Pantaleoni, Trans. & Ed.) New York: Thomas Y. Crowell.

Recordings

Africa: ceremonial and folk music. Nonesuch (H-72063).
Dance music of Zimbabwe. Carthage Records (CGLP 4411).
Shona Mbira music. Nonesuch (H 72077).

Films

African wildlife; Lions of the African night; and *The rhino war.* Washington, DC: National Geographic Society.

Activity 5.4: Biography

This is the time in the study of Africa when students focus on the important people who have helped shaped the countries within that continent. Students can suggest or research names from their countries of study or use the names included in this activity.

Teacher: "Before we go home, we will have the opportunity to participate in one of two activities: We can either plan a dinner party with a famous person of the past or present, or we can visit a wax museum where the models talk and tell us about their lives."

Each group will decide how it wants to present the information about important people in the history of the country it has studied. If the group plans a dinner party, then each member of the group will research an important person in the country and assume the role of that person at the dinner party. The presentation to the entire class will be the dinner party, where the audience learns about the important people either through what they say about each other or what the character says about himself or herself. The group will need to plan this carefully so that each person is introduced and the audience learns something.

A second option is the establishment of a "wax museum." For this activity, each member of the group will research an important person from the country of study and will write a short biography about that person. To make the museum, the group will sit together in an interesting pose, "frozen" in place. The lights will be turned off; then, using a flashlight to illuminate one of the "characters," the tour guide will introduce that character. The person will then stand and tell something about his/her life, accomplishments, and beliefs.

Biography. The students will prepare short biographical summaries of famous Africans, either current or historical. Biography is included in the unit to help students learn about a historical period or social/political movement or current events, as well as information about a specific individual. A good biography helps characterize the subject as an individual and relates that individual to humanity. It gives the basic facts of where and when that person lived and why he or she is remembered today. In addition, it provides background information, including the social, cultural, and economic forces in the environment in which the person lived. Biographies use original materials such as birth certificates, school records, diaries, and letters as evidence. Therefore, students can study the original writings of the individual or learn about the person through secondary or other sources of information.

One strand that these biographies can take is for the students to structure their reports in order to highlight how the subject of the biography helped his or her country move to the aim of article 3 of the Atlantic Charter: "Respect for the right of all peoples to choose the form of government under which they live."

Côte d'Ivoire: Felix Houphouet-Boigny; François-Joseph Amon d'Aby (playwright)

Ghana: General A. A. Africa; General Frederick Akufo; Anne Ruth Jiagge (first woman lawyer in Ghana; supreme court justice, chairperson of the United Nations commission on the status of women); Dr. Kwame Nkrumah; Jerry John Rawlings

Guinea Bissau (Portuguese Guinea): Amilcar Cabral

Kenya: Jomo Kenyatta

Malawi (Nyasaland): John Chilembwe

Mozambique: Samora Macel (president)

Nigeria: Nnamdi Azikiwe; Wole Soyinka (first African to win the Nobel prize for literature)

Senegal: Leopold Sedar Senghor

South Africa: Steve Biko; Allen Boesack; Pieter Willem Botha; Mangosuthu Gatsha Buthelezi; Magnus Malan; Nelson Mandela; Winnie Mandela; Es'kia Mphahlele (musician); Beyers Naude; Alan Paton; Shaka (Zulu king); Walter Sisulu; Robert Sobukwe; Helen Suzman; Oliver Tambo; Archbishop Desmond Tutu; Hendrik Verwoerd

Tanzania: Julius Nyerere

Uganda: Dr. Milton Obote; King Mutes II; Idi Amin Dada; David Livingstone

Zaire: Mobutu Sese Seko

Zambia: Kenneth Kaunda

Zimbabwe (Rhodesia): Abel Muzorewa (African National Council of Rhodesia–Zimbabwe); Cecil Rhodes (Rhodesia); Ian Smith (Rhodesia); Joshua Nkomo (Zimbabwe); Robert Mugabe (Zimbabwe); Sir Garfield Todd (former prime minister of Southern Rhodesia)

Activity 5.5: Debate

Teacher: "After the tour of the wax museum we will visit the World Court, which has been set up to listen to and rule on grievances that have been brought in front of it by international organizations or because of violation of a group's civil rights. The two cases we will hear are a complaint by a wildlife interest group about the destruction of habitat and illegal poaching of animals, and one from the International Committee on Human Rights, which is urging South Africa to move faster to complete integration of its population."

Students are divided into two groups, one to simulate a court case against destruction of animal habitat and the other to debate the former apartheid policy of South Africa. In each group, three students serve on the court as justices, three present the defense, and three act as the prosecution. Students acting as the lawyers call forward their witnesses to present testimony to the court. The justices of the court set the rules and time limits and, having spent some time developing their own background of information about the cases, make a ruling based on the presentation of the witnesses.

Students are given three days to research their position and to prepare their presentation for the court. On the fifth day, the court convenes to hear the cases before it. The justices then deliberate and present their ruling.

To aid the students in selecting relevant facts to present their positions, the following guidelines are suggested.

Case 1: Preserving Endangered Species

Witnesses for:

Representative of a wildlife federation: Joan, is a member of a team who has studied animals all over the world, and she is convinced that all animals serve vital links in ecosystems. The destruction of a species leaves all of us poorer in our understanding of the natural order.

Representative of the government of the local country: Peter is convinced that the country can make money by bringing in tourists to see the many areas that have unusual native plant and animal wildlife.

Expert on soils and forestry: Wendy is sure that destruction of animal habitats will lead to soil erosion, which in turn will lead to desertlike conditions.

Witnesses against:

John is a poor farmer whose lands border the wildlife area under discussion. If he is unable to expand the area for planting crops, his family will slowly starve.

Rami is a father of ten children who has been unable to find work after having lost his farm to the drought. He makes money to feed his family by selling rhino horns to foreign countries. He often kills animals in the reserve to feed his family.

Henry is a professional guide. He makes his money by leading groups of big-game hunters. If he cannot lead hunting groups, he will be unable to take care of his family.

Decision-making strategies to be brought out by the lawyers (based on Parisi, undated):

Defining the issue: What is the value of an animal species?
Recognizing interests and values
Locating and using information
Identifying alternatives
Identifying probable consequences
Selecting a course of action

Case 2: Apartheid

One advantage of a dramatic activity involving role playing is that students are forced to take different perspectives on an issue as they develop a character and his or her justification for holding a particular point of view. Although conditions recently have changed within South Africa, this World Court simulation can be introduced as an opportunity to understand the different positions and rationale for separation and for inclusion of the various groups within South Africa. You need to state to your students, "Let's pretend as if South Africa were the same as it was before 1994."

Witnesses for:

Jacques' family have been citizens of South Africa for five generations. They carved their farm out of the wilderness and have made it a profitable business.

Alice is a career government employee. She fears that if blacks are given power, they will not know how to use it in a constructive manner. She cites, as examples, the history of many of the other countries in Africa, points out that blacks do have their own *banstustans*, or "homelands."

George owns a large manufacturing plant in South Africa. He is afraid that if blacks are given power, they will want to take control of industries. He is also afraid that the white minority will not retain any status in the country.

Witnesses Against:

Randolph's family have been victims of the many riots in order to have equal rights. He also cites the underemployment and other restrictions on the black residents. Although the government is making some progress, it is not fast enough to ensure that his children will have access to education and jobs.

Margo is a representative of the Human Rights Commission and has been investigating allegations of violations of human rights and discrimination against black citizens.

Mnugam represents his ethnic group. His people have been owners of land in South Africa from the time before it was colonized. Some of his tribal lands have been taken away and given to white citizens without adequate compensation. He wants the court to return what historically has belonged to his people.

Decision-making strategies to be brought out by the lawyers (based on Parisi, undated):

Defining the issue: What is the value of a human?
Recognizing interests and values

GROUP'S WEEKLY PLANS

Summary Sheet

Country_____ Week of _____

Day	Goal(s)	Sources	Outcomes
Monday			
Tuesday			
Wednesday			
Thursday			
Friday			

A COUNTRY IN BRIEF

Name of Country: _____

Location:

    Relative (Neighbors and Boundaries): _____

    _____

    Absolute: _____

Capital: _____

Official Language(s): _____

_____

Religion(s): _____

Currency (Units and U.S. Equivalents: _____

_____

Population: Number and Major Groups: _____

_____

Special Geographic Features:

_____

_____

Important Holidays: _____

Other Interesting Facts: _____

Illustration of Flag: _____

Locating and using information
Identifying alternatives
Identifying probable consequences
Selecting a course of action

Activity 5.6: Home Again

Teacher: "Finally, we are back home. You are going to be interviewed on a morning or late-night television talk show or by a reporter from the local newspaper."

An alternative activity would be to have each team write a book about its adventures using the diary notes of the members. These books could be picture books to be shared with younger students.

References and Bibliography

Barker, C. (1995). *A family in Nigeria*. Minneapolis: Lerner Publications.

Baynham, S. (1987). *Conflict in the 20th century: Africa from 1945*. New York: Franklin Watts.

Bernheim, M. & Bernheim, E. (1969). *A week in Aya's world: the Ivory Coast*. London: Crowell-Collier Press.

Canesso, C. (1989). *Places and peoples of the world: South Africa*. New York: Chelsea House.

Carr, A. (1980). *The land and wildlife of Africa*. Alexandria, VA: Time-Life Books.

Cheney, P. (1990). *The land and people of Zimbabwe*. Philadelphia: J. B. Lippincott.

Chiasson, J. (1987). *African journey*. Scarsdale, NY: Bradbury Press.

Cohen, D. (1973). *Shaka, king of the Zulus: a biography*. New York: Doubleday.

Crofts, M. (1988). *Visual geography series: Tanzania in pictures*. Minneapolis: Lerner Publications.

Davidson, A. (1993). *Endangered peoples*. San Francisco: Sierra Club Books.

Davidson, B. (1969). *The African genius. An introduction to African cultural and social history*. Boston: Little, Brown.

Davidson, B. (1971). *A guide to African history*. Garden City: Doubleday.

GROUP WORKSHEET FOR ROLE PLAYING

1. Participants

    Name of lawyer(s) representing this side: _____

    Participants/witnesses:

    Name _____ Name _____

    Name _____ Name _____

2. Values and positions to be clarified

    (a) _____

    (b) _____

    (c) _____

    (d) _____

3. Collecting information

    What we know:

    _____

    _____

    _____

    Issues we need to learn more about:

    _____

    _____

    _____

    Other questions we have:

    _____

    _____

    _____

    Possible sources of information:

    _____

    _____

    _____

    What we learned and sources used:

    _____

    _____

    _____

4. Arguments to be made by the lawyer to support our side
    Course of action your group proposes (i.e., your position in this case):

    _____

    _____

    _____

    Reasons that support your position (based on role cards and research):

Reason	Support
_____	_____
_____	_____
_____	_____
_____	_____

5. Benefits to the community if your position is followed

    _____

    _____

    _____

    or Your Position for Alternative Course of Action

    _____

    _____

    _____

6. Summary
    Reiterate your position:

    _____

    _____

    _____

    Briefly explain your reasons and evidence for supporting your position:

    _____

    _____

    _____

    If your exact position is not accepted, what is an alternative?

    _____

    _____

    _____

WORKSHEET FOR JUDGES

You are charged with making a decision as to which side you would support based on the evidence presented. You are not to let your own emotions make that decision.

1. What is the issue?_____ _____

    _____

    _____

    _____

2. Before the hearing, what questions do you have?

    _____

    _____

    _____

3. What type of research will you need to complete to build your background on the issues?

    _____

    _____

    _____

4. Which member of court will research which issue/question?

    Name   Issue

    _____   _____

    _____   _____

    _____   _____

    _____   _____

5. Possible questions to ask each group

    Questions for those for the issue:

    _____

    _____

    _____

    Questions for those against the issue:

    _____

    _____

    _____

6. What would you consider a reasonable compromise or alternative?

    _____

    _____

    _____

JUDGES: HOW TO RUN THE TRIAL

1. Announce the purpose of the hearing.

2. Set the rules:

    Lawyers must state their position.

    Set the number of witnesses that may be called.

    Each witness should state his or her name.

    Set time limits for each witness to make presentation.

    Establish rules for cross-examination by the other lawyer.

3. Maintaining control:

    Be sure that the lawyers and witnesses state their names, and, if possible, their professions.

    Enforce the set time limits, with the same limits for each side

    Those who wish to speak who are not on the docket must raise their hands and seek your permission to do so.

    Question lawyers, but do not fight with them or let them know your bias.

    Be sure that the tone and level of the presentations are appropriate to a court.

    Be sure each side is given the opportunity to present closing arguments.

4. Your role:

    Keep and maintain order.

    Keep notes on the presentation of both sides.

    Ask for clarification or evidence to support positions taken.

    Ask for alternatives.

    Based on the evidence, render a decision.

Diakiw, J. (1990). Children's literature and global education: understanding the developing world. *Reading Teacher, 43*(4), pp. 296–300.

Elliott, K. (1979). *Benin: An African kingdom and culture.* Minneapolis: Lerner Publications. Describes this western African kingdom as it existed in 1472.

Ellis, V. (1989). *Afro-bets: First book about Africa.* Orange, NJ: Just Us Books.

Faul, M. (1991). *The story of Africa & her flags to color.* Santa Barbara, CA: Bellerophon Books.

Feelings, M. (1971). *Moja means one: Swahili counting book.* New York: Dial.

Feelings, M. (1975). *Jambo means hello: Swahili alphabet book.* New York: Dial.

Fodor's North Africa: Algeria, Morocco and Tunisia. (1988). New York: Fodor's Travel Publications.

Foster, F. B. (1981). *East central Africa: Kenya, Uganda, Tanzania, Rwanda, and Burundi.* New York: Franklin Watts.

Fritz, J., Paterson, K., McKissack, P., McKissack, F., Mahy, M., & Highwater, J. (1992). *The world in 1492.* New York: Henry Holt. Africa in 1492, pp. 67–96.

Hayward, J. (1989). *Witness history series: South Africa since 1948.* New York: Bookwright Press.

Hintz, M. (1987). *Enchantment of the world: Ghana.* Chicago: Childrens Press.

Hopf, A. (1978). *Biography of a giraffe.* New York: G. P. Putnam's Sons.

Jacobson, K. (1992). *A new true book: Ghana.* Chicago: Childrens Press.

Khalfan, Z. & Amin, M. (1984). *We live in Kenya.* New York: Bookwright Press.

Laure, J. (1988). *Enchantment of the world: Zimbabwe.* Chicago: Childrens Press.

Mack, J. (1981). *Zulus.* Morristown, NJ: Silver Burdett & Ginn.

Maquet, J., & Rayfield, J. (1972). *Civilizations of black Africa.* New York: Oxford University Press.

Maren, M. (1989). *The land and people of Kenya.* Philadelphia: J. B. Lippincott.

Moss, B. (1991). Children's nonfiction tradebooks: a complement to content area texts. *Reading Teacher, 45*(1), pp. 26–31.

Murphy, E. J. (1978). *Understanding Africa.* New York: Thomas Y. Crowell.

Musgrove, M. (1976). *Ashanti to Zulu: African traditions.* New York: Dial.

Nelson, H. D. (1983). *Zimbabwe, a country study.* Washington, DC: U.S. Government Printing Office.

Nicholson, M. (1985). *Across the Limpopo. A family's hazardous journey through Africa.* London: Robson Books. This book is excellent for reading aloud, as the author recounts a trip through South Africa, Zimbabwe, Zambia, Malawi, Tanzani, Kenya, Sudan, and Egypt. The teacher should read it through before reading aloud, as parts of it may be inappropriate for a classroom setting.

Nolting, M. (1990). *Africa's top wildlife countries*. Pompano Beach, FL: Global Travel Publishers.

Norton D. (1990). Teaching multicultural literature in the reading curriculum. *Reading Teacher, 44*(1), pp. 28–40.

O'Neill, C. (1985). Imagined worlds in theatre and drama. *Theory into Practice, 24*(3), pp. 158–165.

Parisi, L. (undated). *Creative role playing exercises in science and technology*. Boulder, CO: Social Science Education Consortium.

Pappas, C. C., Kiefer, B. Z., & Levstick, L. (1990). *An integrated language perspective in the elementary school*. White Plains, NY: Longman.

Paton, J. (1990). *The land and people of South Africa*. Philadelphia: J. B. Lippincott.

Percefull, A. (1984). *The Nile*. New York: Franklin Watts.

Price, C. (1978). *The mystery of masks*. New York: Charles Scribner's Sons.

Reutzel, D., & Cooter, R., Jr. (1991). Organizing for effective instruction: the reading workshop. *Reading Teacher, 44*(8), pp. 548–554.

Rossellini, A. (1988). *Visual geography series: Côte D'Ivoire, Ivory Coast in pictures*. Minneapolis: Lerner Publications.

Shachtman, T. (1981). *Growing up Masai*. New York: Macmillan.

Suttles, S., & Suttles-Graham, B. (1986). *Fielding's Africa south of the Sahara*. New York: William Morrow.

Stanley, D., & Vennema, P. (1988). *Shaka: King of the Zulus*. New York: Morrow Junior Books.

Sterling, T. (1963). *Exploration of Africa*. New York: American Heritage.

Tarlington, C., & Verriour, P. (1991). *Role drama*. Portsmouth, NH: Heinemann.

Taylor, L.B., Jr. (1981). *South East Africa: Zimbabwe, Zambia, Malawi, Madagascar, Mauritius, and Reunion*. New York: Franklin Watts.

Weiss, R. (1986). *The women of Zimbabwe*. London: Kesho Publications.

Welch, G. (1965). *Africa before they came*. New York: William Morrow.

Wisniewski, D. (1992). *Sundiata: Lion king of Mali*. New York: Clarion Books.

Woods, H. & Woods, G. (1981). *The horn of Africa: Ethiopia, Sudan, Somalia, and Djibouti*. New York: Franklin Watts.

Africa threatened. (1990, December). *National Geographic*.

Namibia's LIFE project brings people and wildlife together. (1993, November/December). *Focus, 15*(6).

Protecting central Africa's forests from the ground up. (1993, November/December). *Focus, 15*(6).

January's Potpourri of Teaching Ideas

The purpose of each month's Potpourri of Teaching Ideas is to provide additional resources from which to build your curriculum. Most, but not all, of the activities listed each month relate directly to that month. It is not intended that you use them all, but rather that you choose those which are appropriate for your program. Although the topics are written for a particular month, many of them would be appropriate for use throughout the year. How you use these activities will depend on your curricular goals. You may wish to use some of the activities as they are presented, and you may need to modify some to meet your needs. Perhaps some of them will give you ideas for entirely different potpourris.

Independence Days

In several countries around the world, the month of January marks the anniversary of their independence. The "Independence Day" chart lists the names of several countries that declared independence during Jan-

INDEPENDENCE DAY

Country	Date	Gained Independence From	Colors of National Flag
Cameroon	1961	Britain/France/U.N.	Green, red, yellow
Haiti	1804	France	Red, black, white
Western Samoa	_____	_____	_____
Sudan	_____	_____	_____
Myanmar	_____	_____	_____
Chad	_____	_____	_____
Nauru	_____	_____	_____

uary. Find the country from whom they became independent and complete the chart.

"I Lift My Lamp Beside the Golden Door."

"I lift my lamp beside the golden door," is the last line of the poem inscribed on the base of the Statue of Liberty. The words were written in 1883 by Emma Lazarus, an American poet. To many people who immigrated across the Atlantic Ocean to the United States, the "New Colossus" was the sign that soon they would be entering a country in which the streets supposedly were paved with gold. After viewing this famous landmark at the port of New York City, many saw another landmark, Ellis Island. This was the portal through which thousands of poor immigrants passed before beginning their new lives. The term "poor" is used here because first- and second-class passengers on the ships that brought the immigrants were examined on board before being allowed into the United States. Only those passengers who traveled steerage, the cheapest way, had to pass through Ellis Island.

Ellis Island was the main port of entry to the United States from 1892 until World War I. Since then, this island has been used as a hospital, a holding center for prisoners of war, and a Coast Guard station. In 1990, Ellis Island opened as an immigration museum.

Although many people entered the United States through Ellis Island, others came legally or illegally through other ports or across our borders to the north and south. Some came because they sought a better life; others because they wanted political or religious freedom; still others because they were kidnapped or were in some way forced to come. No matter how people arrived, everyone who lives in the United States has ancestors who at one time or another came from other parts of the world. Family ancestors of some Native Americans crossed the land bridge between Asia and Alaska before recorded history; some families are recent immigrants.

Try These Activities

Studying the role of Ellis Island as part of understanding immigration allows you to begin discussion of related issues and to read books about the immigrant experience.

1. A group of mature students may want to explore America's immigration policies. Students should be given the opportunity to research positions and prepare a debate.

   Should there be a "favored nation" immigration policy? Should immigrants from particular nations be allowed to immigrate in larger numbers than those from other countries? For example, in 1870 the U.S. Congress enacted a law that allowed only Caucasians and those of African descent to become citizens. In 1882, Congress passed the Chinese Exclusion Act, limiting or suppressing the number of Chinese who could enter this country. In 1952, President Truman vetoed a law that would allow immigrants from northern Europe to enter this country more easily than other immigrants.

2. Students who are interested in learning about immigration may want to read books by and about immigrants as they left their homelands and entered this country. They can share with the class some of the trials and tribulations these new immigrants faced, as well as the strange customs they encountered in the new country.

Suggested Readings

Anderson, M. (1980). *The journey of the shadow bairns*. New York: Random House.

Ashabranner, B. (1983). *The new Americans: Changing patterns in U.S. immigration*. New York: Dodd Mead.

Beatty, P. (1981). *Lupita mañana*. New York: William Morrow.

Blaine, M. (1979). *Dvora's journey*. New York: Henry Holt.

Bosse, M. (1981). *Ganesh*. New York: Thomas Y. Crowell.

Bunting, E. (1988). *How many days to America? A Thanksgiving story*. New York: Clarion Books.

Colman, H. (1978). *Rachel's legacy*. New York: William Morrow.

Coutant, H. (1974). *First snow*. New York: Alfred A. Knopf.

Cummings, B. (1979). *And now, Ameriky*. New York: Atheneum.

Fisher, L. E. (1980). *A Russian farewell*. New York: Four Winds Press.

Freedman, R. (1980). *Immigrant kids*. New York: E. P. Dutton.

Levine, E. (1993). *If your name was changed at Ellis Island*. New York: Scholastic.

Whelan, G. (1992). *Goodbye, Vietnam*. New York: Alfred A. Knopf.

All for One and One for All: The League of Nations

The League of Nations was established in January 1920 to maintain peace among the nations of the world. Headquartered in Geneva, Switzerland, its purpose was to defend the territory and independence of its member nations. It was dissolved in April 1946.

The United Nations was founded on October 24, 1945, to help people in many parts of the world to gain freedom and a better way of life. Like the League of Nations, its main goal was to help keep peace in the world. In June 1945, fifty nations signed the charter of

TWO ORGANIZATIONS FOR PEACE

	League of Nations	United Nations
Year Organized		
Headquarters		
Purpose	Protect member nations from aggression	World peace and betterment of humanity
Name of Organizing Charter	League Covenant	
Name of Governing Body		
Title of Head		
How is the Head Chosen?		
Major Successes		

the United Nations. The headquarters of the United Nations is in New York City. Using encyclopedias or other books, direct students to complete the chart "Two Organizations for Peace" and to be prepared to discuss these questions:

What are the major agencies of the UN?
Why has the UN been successful when the League of Nations was not?
Should the United States continue to belong to the UN? Why?

Joan of Arc, Maid of Orléans

A simple country girl, born in 1412, is remembered for saving her country from an invading enemy and leading the move to crown the rightful king of France. Joan of Arc, "knowing neither A nor B," told Charles, the uncrowned king, that she had had visions and heard voices which convinced her she was to deliver France from the armies of King Henry V of England. She persuaded Charles to place her in charge of an army of soldiers.

Joan, wearing shining armor and riding a white horse, appeared as a heaven-sent leader to her warriors and inspired them to attack the English like a thunderbolt. The Battle of Orléans was a major defeat for the English. Joan continued to lead her army to victory after victory. Her love of her country and her courage gave the French people new hope and a sense of patriotism. She seemed invincible to the English, who retreated in defeat.

In 1429, Joan paused in her conquest long enough to go to Reims, the traditional site for the coronation of French royalty. This young peasant girl felt it her duty to see that Charles, her leader and king, was properly crowned king of France. In a traditional ceremony held in the Cathedral of Reims (for in Joan's mind this was the only acceptable site for a "real" king's coronation), Joan stood beside Charles as he became the people's ruler, the true king of France.

Soon afterward, Joan was captured, not by the English, but by Burgundians, allies of the English, who sold her to her enemies. She was tried by her English foes, convicted of heresy, and in 1431 was burned to death at the stake. Joan of Arc, the simple country girl, the Maid of Orléans, the seventeen-year-old aide to the king, was dead. But her memory lived on to inspire the French to eventually remove the English from French soil. Many believe she saved her country from almost certain destruction.

Try These Activities

They Made a Difference. Students can research the lives of ordinary people who have accomplished important deeds. There are many example—some well known, others not so familiar. Use the chart "They Made a Difference" as a guide for this activity.

In Joan's Footsteps. Joan's travels took her from her home in east central France to Orléans and surrounding areas, to Reims, and finally to her death at Rouen. Using a map of France, trace Joan's movements from the time she first heard the "voices" until her death.

Suggested Reading

Brooks, P. S. (1990). *Beyond the myth: The story of Joan of Arc.* Philadelphia: J. B. Lippincott.

Is There a Higher Law That Should Be Obeyed?

As young children, we became aware that we are to obey certain rules, whether within the home, the school, or the outside community. Laws had been passed and established to govern and regulate the behavior of those in our cities and nation. If we failed to obey these laws, we would be punished. Depending on the severity of our crime, the failure to obey a law would result in the imposition of sanctions that might take away our property (a fine), our liberty (imprisonment), or, in the most severe cases, even our lives. Obeying the law became a habit that our parents, our teachers, and others in society tried to ingrain in each of us.

Throughout human history, various individuals have raised questions as to whether some laws should not be obeyed because they were believed to be unethical or immoral when judged according to something more fundamental than the law. This standard might be some religious belief, such as the Ten Commandments, or some other religious or ethical principle. Even the dictates of an individual's conscience might serve as such a standard. What distinguishes these individuals is that they acted on their beliefs and suffered the consequences of their actions. Men, such as Henry David Thoreau in the nineteenth century and

THEY MADE A DIFFERENCE

Person	Time Period	Accomplishment
Joan of Arc	1429–1431	Led French army to defeat English
Leonard Grimes	Mid-1800s	Assisted fugitive slaves
Rosa Parks	1955	_____
Martin Luther	_____	Founder of Reformation movement
Alice Paul	_____	_____
Robert Weaver	_____	_____

Mahatma Gandhi and Martin Luther King, Jr., in the twentieth century, willingly suffered the consequences of disobeying the law, standing for what they believed to be higher principles. In some cases, their actions were effective, as well as ethical, for they led to changes in the law. By nonviolent means, or civil disobedience, they persuaded elected officials to alter laws that were originally in conflict with their higher moral principles.

Many women have engaged in similar activities in an attempt to change the laws in order to participate equally with men in the governance of the country or to redress other injustices. Notable examples include Susan B. Anthony and Rosa Parks. Many other individuals have committed acts of civil disobedience but are lesser known. They, too, have made contributions to the moral development of our society.

Try This: After students collect data about individuals who engaged in acts of civil disobedience, they might participate in a role-playing activity. In the role of the individual whom they researched, they could be interviewed by another student acting as a newspaper or television reporter. These interviews could be videotaped and shown to other classes.

African Cuisine

South African Geellrys (Yellow Rice with Raisins)

INGREDIENTS:
2 Tbs. butter
1 cup long-grain white rice
2 cups boiling water
1 cinnamon stick (2 inches long)
½ tsp. turmeric
pinch of saffron
1 tsp. salt
½ cup seedless raisins
pinch of sugar (optional)

DIRECTIONS:
Melt butter in a 2 or 3 quart saucepan. Add rice and stir until the grains are coated with butter; *do not brown.* Add boiling water and spices, stirring constantly over high heat until the mixture begins to boil. Reduce heat, cover pan tightly, and simmer until the rice has absorbed all the water and is tender (approximately 20 minutes). Remove from heat and discard cinnamon stick. Fluff rice with a fork and stir in raisins and sugar. Place a piece of waxed paper or aluminum foil directly on top of the rice and cover the pan with lid. Let stand for 20 minutes at room temperature. Fluff rice again and serve.

Suggested Readings

Berry, E. (1963). *Eating and cooking around the world. Fingers before forks.* New York: John Day. This is not a true cookbook with recipes, but rather the chapters present information about a country's typical food. The chapters explain the relationships among culture, climate, and foods.

Gulden, D. (Ed.).1989). *Betty Crocker's new international cookbook.* New York: Prentice Hall. Recipes from Algeria, Ethiopia, Ghana, Kenya, and Morocco.

Shapiro, R. (1962). *Wide world cookbook.* Boston: Little, Brown. Recipes from Ghana, Nigeria, Northern Rhodesia, and Uganda.

Van der Post, L. (1970). *African cooking.* New York: Time-Life Books. Books in this series contain both information and recipes. This book contains recipes from many different African countries.

Chapter 6

Excepting February Alone

AN EARLY CHILDREN'S RHYME has been quoted for generations to help us remember how many days are in each month. Although most people can recite the beginning lines, the entire poem is less familiar:

Thirty days hath September,
April, June, and November,
All the rest have thirty-one,
Excepting February alone,
Which hath but twenty-eight, in fine,
Till leap year gives it twenty-nine.

True to the old saying, February is the shortest month of the year. Today it is the second month in our calendar, but the early Roman calendar was composed of only ten months until Numa Pompilius added January and February to the end of the year, making February the last month. Originally it was called *Februarius*, a Latin word meaning to purify. In Roman times, this month, occurring just before the beginning of the new year in March, was a time for purification and readiness.

February has its share of important events. In the Christian world, Valentine's Day symbolizes love and the exchanging of greeting cards called valentines. This custom began centuries ago, for historians have found evidence of such as far back as the Middle Ages. February also marks the observance of Presidents' Day in the United States. Two of our most influential leaders, George Washington and Abraham Lincoln, were born during this month.

Although not an official holiday, Groundhog Day is celebrated by some. Popular belief holds that on the second day of February, the groundhog or woodchuck emerges from his winter burrow to survey weather conditions. If the sun is shining, the groundhog sees his shadow and knows winter is not over. He returns to his burrow for six more weeks of sleep. If, on the other hand, he does not see his shadow, he knows that spring is imminent and remains above ground to prepare for the days ahead.

Every four years during those years that are divisible by four, an extra day is added to February. This addition is necessary to keep our calendar in line with the solar year. The earth's orbit around the sun takes about 365 and a quarter days. Because our calendar is based on 365 days, eventually a discrepancy would occur between solar time and calendar time if no action was taken to rectify the situation. Therefore, nearly every four years, a twenty-ninth day is added to February.

February

Sunday	Monday	Tuesday	Wednesday	Thursday	Friday	Saturday

FEBRUARY

SELECTED EVENTS

1	Freedom Day
2	Groundhog Day
	Mexico: Dia de la Candelaria
3	Elizabeth Blackwell (1821–1910)
	Norman Rockwell (1894–1978)
4	Charles Lindbergh (1902–1974)
	Rosa Lee Parks (1913–)
5	Mexico Constitution Day
6	New Zealand: Waitangi Day
	"Babe" Ruth (1895–1948)
7	Charles Dickens (1812–1870)
8	Boy Scouts of America founded (1910)
	Jules Verne (1828–1905)
9	Amy Lowell (1874–1925)
10	Boris Pasternak (1890–1960)
11	Thomas Alva Edison (1847–1931)
12	Abraham Lincoln (1809–1865)
13	First public school opened in America (1635)
	Grant Wood (1892–1942)
14	Valentine's Day
15	Susan B. Anthony (1820–1906)
	Pedro Menendez de Aviles (1519–1574)
16	
17	National PTA Founders Day
18	George Peabody (1795–1869)
19	India: Shivaratri
	Nicolaus Copernicus (1473–1543)
20	Death of Frederick Douglass (1895)
21	First female dental school graduate (1866)
22	George Washington (1732–1799)
23	George Frideric Handel (1685–1759)
	Emma Hart Willard (1787–1870)
24	Wilhelm Carl Grimm (1786–1859)
25	Pierre Auguste Renoir (1841–1919)
26	Victor Hugo (1802–1885)
	Levi Strauss (1829–1902)
27	Henry Wadsworth Longfellow (1807–1882)
28	John Tenniel (1820–1914)
29	Extra day in leap year

People, Places, and Events of February

What's Happening in February:

Black History Month
National School Counseling Month
National Children's Dental Health Month
Human Relations Month

Other February Events:

First week: National Crime Prevention Week
Second week: Brotherhood/Sisterhood Week
Third Monday: Presidents' Day

Events Scheduled According to Non-Gregorian Calendar Usually Occurring in February:

Mardi Gras
Chinese New Year (sometimes in January)

February's Daily Calendar

1

Freedom Day. Commemorating Lincoln's signing of the thirteenth amendment, abolishing slavery.

2

Groundhog Day. Relates to the belief that if the sun shines on this day and the groundhog sees its shadow, six weeks of winter will follow.

Mexico: Dia de la Candelaria. Celebrated with dances, processions, and bullfights.

Treaty of Guadalupe Hidalgo. War between Mexico and United States officially ended in 1848. U.S. gained territory that became California, Nevada, Utah, and most of Arizona, New Mexico, Colorado, and Wyoming. Mexico also relinquished claim to Texas.

3

Birth anniversary of:
Elizabeth Blackwell (1821–1910). First woman physician; pioneer in women's medicine; established hospital in New York City with an all-women staff.

Norman Rockwell (1894–1978). Illustrator, noted for realistic depictions of family life for the *Saturday Evening Post*.

4

Birth anniversary of:

Charles Lindbergh (1902–1974). Aviator who flew alone nonstop from New York to Paris in 1927.

Rosa Lee Parks (1913–). Civil rights figure, noted for her now-famous bus ride in Montgomery, Alabama, in 1955.

5

Mexico Constitution Day. Commemorating the adoption of present constitution in 1917.

6

Massachusetts became sixth state to ratify the Constitution (1788).

New Zealand: Waitangi Day. Commemorating the signing of treaty between Maori and European peoples in 1840.

Birth anniversary of:

Ronald Reagan (1911–). Fortieth president of the United States; born in Illinois. Oldest president and first divorced person to become president.

George Herman "Babe" Ruth (1895–1948). One of the greatest heroes of baseball.

7

Grenada Independence Day. Gained independence from Britain in 1974.

Birth anniversary of:

Charles Dickens (1812–1870). English author noted for his many novels, including *A Christmas Carol*.

8

Boy Scouts of America founded in 1910 by William Boyce.

Martha Griffiths' speech. Her 1964 speech resulted in the addition of civil rights protection for women in the 1964 Civil Rights Act. Her work was largely responsible for the Equal Rights Amendment (not yet ratified).

Birth anniversary of:

Jules Verne (1828–1905). French writer of science fiction, including *Twenty Thousand Leagues Under the Sea*.

9

Birth anniversary of:

William Henry Harrison (1773–1841). Ninth president of the United States; born in Virginia. His was the shortest term in U.S. history (thirty-two days).

Amy Lowell (1884–1925). Poet.

10

Birth anniversary of:

Boris Leonidovich Pasternak (1890–1960). Russian novelist best known for *Doctor Zhivago*.

11

Iran National Day. Commemorating the fall of the shah and the takeover of Ayatollah Khomeini in 1979.

Nelson Mandela released from prison. In 1990, after more than twenty-seven years, Mandela was released from prison. He helped abolish the system of apartheid, which had been in effect for many years in South Africa, and in 1994 was elected president of the country.

Vatican City Independence Day. Independent state of Vatican City established in 1929.

Birth anniversary of:

Lydia Maria Child (1802–1880). Writer and feminist.

Thomas Alva Edison (1847–1931). Inventor.

12

Luxembourg: Burgsonndeg. Celebrating the end of winter.

Birth anniversary of:

Abraham Lincoln (1809–1865). Sixteenth president of the United States; born in Kentucky. First president to be assassinated. Noted for many accomplishments, but especially the Emancipation Proclamation.

13

First public school in America, the Boston Latin School, opened in 1635.

Birth anniversary of:

Grant Wood (1892–1942). Painter and sculptor.

14

Arizona Admission Day. Became forty-eighth state admitted to the Union (1912).

Oregon Admission Day. Became thirty-third state admitted to the Union (1859).

Valentine's Day. One of the most widely observed unofficial holidays.

15

Birth anniversary of:

Susan B. Anthony (1820–1906). Reformer and women's suffrage advocate.

Cyrus H. McCormick (1809–1884). Inventor of the reaper, which contributed greatly to the development of American industry.

Pedro Menendez de Aviles (1519–1574). Spanish explorer; established fort at St. Augustine, Florida, in 1565.

16

17

National PTA Founders Day
Birth anniversary of:
René Laennec (1781–1826). French physician and inventor of the stethoscope.

18

Gambia Independence Day. Located in west Africa; gained independence from Britain in 1965.
Birth anniversary of:
George Peabody (1795–1869). Philanthropist.

19

India: Shivaratri. Legend states that Lord Shiva, the Hindu god of destruction, danced his celestial dance on this date. Pilgrims travel to Shiva shrines for special prayers and celebrations.
Anniversary of Japanese internment. In 1942, more than one hundred thousand Japanese people living in the United States were placed in internment camps across western states.
Birth anniversary of:
Nicolaus Copernicus (1473–1543). Polish astronomer whose theory placed the sun at the center of our solar system.

20

Death of Frederick Douglass. African-American journalist and antislavery leader (1817–1895).

21

Lucy Hobbs became the first female dental school graduate in 1866.

22

St. Lucia Independence Day. Independence attained from Britain in 1979.
Birth anniversary of:
Robert Baden-Powell (1857–1941). English army officer and founder of the Boy Scouts and Girl Guides.
George Washington (1732–1799). First president of the United States; born in Virginia.

23

Birth anniversary of:
George Frideric Handel (1685–1759). British (German-born) composer of the oratorio *Messiah.*
Emma Hart Willard (1787–1870). Educator and pioneer in higher education for women.

24

Estonia Independence Day. Proclaimed independence from the Soviet Union in 1990.
Hadassah. founded (1912). Largest and oldest Zionist women's organization in the world.
Birth anniversary of:
Wilhelm Carl Grimm (1786–1859). German folklorist who, with his brother Jacob, collected and published *Grimm's Fairy Tales.*
Winslow Homer (1836–1910). American painter.

25

Suriname Revolution Day. National Military Council gained control of government in 1982.
Birth anniversary of:
Pierre Auguste Renoir (1841–1919). French Impressionist painter.

26

Birth anniversary of:
William Frederic "Buffalo Bill" Cody (1846–1917). Frontiersman and showman.
Victor Hugo (1802–1885). French author of *Les Misérables.*
Levi Strauss (1829–1902). German immigrant and creator of first pair of denim jeans.

27

Birth anniversary of:
Henry Wadsworth Longfellow (1807–1882). Poet, remembered for *The Song of Hiawatha, Paul Revere's Ride,* and *Evangeline.*

28

Birth anniversary of:
John Tenniel (1820–1914). English illustrator, noted for illustrations in *Alice's Adventures in Wonderland.*

29

Occurs once in four years during leap year, a year divisible by four (or by 400, if the year ends in hundreds) using the Gregorian calendar.

Celebrating African-American History

Teaching Unit for February

A Word about This Unit. Whether your school population is diverse, representing students from many cultural backgrounds, or a homogeneous student body, the study of peoples from minority or nondominant cultures has important educational value. February is an ideal month to introduce a unit related to the study of African-American history. Martin Luther King, Jr. Day has recently past, Rosa Parks's birthday is nearing, and February is designated as "Black History Month."

Motivation. Begin the unit with a discussion of the contributions that African-Americans have made to our society. Students may offer examples of individuals that they have studied or know about. People who are famous as leaders, athletes, or performers probably will be named. Allow and encourage discussion about Martin Luther King, Jr., Arthur Ashe, Michael Jordan, Oprah Winfrey, and other celebrities. Continue the discussion with questions such as:

Who are African-Americans who have done good and important things for our society who may not be well known?

Who is Carl Burton Stokes? What did he do?

Who was Medgar Evers? What was his contribution?

What is Marian Anderson noted for?

Can an ordinary citizen, regardless of race, make a difference?

Who are some individuals who have been instrumental in changing the way society behaves?

Immersion. In this part of the unit, students gather information about a topic. You can provide opportunities for students to conduct research about African-Americans who have made valuable contributions to our society. Students should be encouraged to research individuals who have done important work or service but may not be well known.

Information. This unit, rather than providing information for you to share with students, presents a play written by a middle school English class. This class was composed of an ethnic mix of students, mostly African-Americans, Hispanic-Americans, and Anglo-Americans, with varying degrees of scholastic abilities.

After reading a story about Rosa Parks and the Montgomery bus boycott, the students asked the teacher if they could write a play presenting their version of what it might have been like on that December day in 1955. The only restriction imposed by the teacher was that the major events of the story be true. The students were given freedom to construct actions and conversations as they chose within the framework of the actual event. This is similar to what writers of historical fiction do when they take real people and construct a story around their lives and the historical events and setting of the period. The following is the students' script of *The Saga of Rosa Parks*.

Sometimes You Have to Say No!

The Saga of Rosa Parks

A skit written by middle school students in Fort Worth, Texas, in celebration of African-American History Week

Characters:

Narrator	Rosa Parks
Mr. Murphy (bus driver)	Mother and Lamont (small boy)
Miss Maudie and	
Mrs. Wainwright	Pearl
Old Man (African-American)	Young Woman (white)
Man (white)	
Second Policeman	First Policeman
	16 Passengers

Time: December 1, 1955

Setting: *Inside a bus on the streets of Montgomery, Alabama. The stage is set with 24 chairs to resemble the inside of a city bus, four seats to a row with an aisle down the middle. There is a slight division between the front twelve seats and the back twelve seats to separate the White Section of the bus from the Black Section. The bus driver sits in a chair (driver's seat) at the front of the bus (front left) and beside him is a box with a tin cup where bus fare is deposited. Two wooden blocks serve as the steps for the front and rear* entrances of the bus and are placed downstage in order that the audience may see and hear each passenger as he or she boards. Already seated on the bus are nine white passengers in the front part of the bus and eight African-American passengers seated in the rear of the bus.

Narrator (*Before curtain rises*): Today our class presents a celebration of African-American history entitled "Sometimes You Have to Say No!" In this program, we pay tribute to the African-American. We celebrate the contributions of some people who have inspired us by their selfless courage. Their names are indelibly written upon the pages of history dealing with the African race in America. It is our hope that in turning our attention to these men and women who have affected the lives of many, we will, in some way, be inspired to live more nobly ourselves.

In the saga of the African-American in the United States, there are many names that illumine the pages of history—names that symbolize courage, daring, compassion, and unselfish devotion. Who has not heard of Harriet Tubman or Martin Luther King, Jr.? However, in our skit today we are going to present a different heroine— an ordinary citizen of Montgomery, Alabama— one without special skills, special training, or high position—but one who saw injustice and abuse and tried to do something about them. Let us introduce you to Rosa Parks, a woman whose single act of courage changed the lives of us all!

It is the first day of December, 1955, a period of time when many rules and regulations in the South promoted segregation. Some of the worst abuse dealt with the transit system. In Montgomery, black passengers riding the bus were forbidden to board through the front door except to pay their fare. They got on the bus at the front door, paid their money, then got off, and boarded the bus again through the back door. They were allowed to take seats only in the rear section of the bus. Whenever a white person got on a bus with no empty seats, the black person sitting nearest the front had to give his seat to the white person. This was the situation when Rosa Parks started home from work on this Thursday afternoon.

AT RISE: Sixteen passengers are seated throughout the bus. Pearl is seated in the front of the Black Section. The seat beside her is vacant. There are three empty seats in the White Section and four empty seats in the Black Section. Bus Driver pretends to drive the bus. Passengers simulate movement of bus by bouncing slightly up and down when bus is moving. Mother and Lamont are waiting at bus stop. Driver brings bus to a halt. Passengers lean forward in seats to simulate stopping motion. Mother and Lamont get aboard. While Mother is fumbling in her purse for fare, the child runs to an empty seat in White Section.

Mother (*grabbing child by the arm to pull him back*): No, no, Lamont! Come back here! Don't do that! You can't sit there!

Lamont (*attempting to sit in an empty chair in front of bus*): Why, Mama? Why can't we sit here? These seats don't have nobody in them.

Mother Hush, Lamont! We have to go around to the back of the bus. (*With some effort she gets Lamont in hand. They get off the bus and go to the back door. As they go, the child continues to question his mother.*)

Lamont: Why, Mama? Why we doing this? I want to sit up front by the bus driver. Why can't I? Huh, Mama? Huh? (*They board at back and find seats in the Black Section. Lamont is still grumbling, and Mother is trying to quiet him.*)

(*The bus starts up again. Two white women wait at next stop. Driver stops and women come aboard.*)

Miss Maudie (*pleasantly, as she pays her fare*): Good afternoon, Mr. Murphy. Sure is a nice day, isn't it?

Driver: Yes Ma'am, Miss Maudie. It sure is, especially for December.

Mrs. Wainwright (*paying her fare*): Mr. Murphy, I'm going to need me a transfer. Will you be able to give me one?

Driver (*very nicely*): You bet, Mrs. Wainwright. Got one right here.

Mrs. Wainwright Thank you, Mr. Murphy. You're so nice. (*The two women take seats in the White Section.*)

(**Bus proceeds.** *Rosa is waiting at a bus stop. Bus comes to a halt.*)

Rosa (*stepping inside bus as she speaks to the driver*): Does this bus go as far out as Edmond Street?

Driver: (*brusquely*): That's right, Lady! That'll be fifteen cents.

(*Rosa pays fare and starts to back of bus.*)

Driver (*loudly*): Hey, Lady! Stop right there! You know you can't do that. Now get off and get on through the back door like you're suppose to!

(*Rosa slowly gets off at front of bus and goes to back door.*)

Driver (*yelling at Rosa*): You know, Lady, we don't have all day. Get your picking and choosing done! I've got a schedule to keep!

(*Rosa takes a seat beside her friend Pearl, the first seat in the Black Section next to the aisle upstage. Driver starts bus again.*)

Pearl (*to Rosa*): My, they're so mean, aren't they? Once I forgot to get off and go round to the back door. I started down the aisle, and the driver ran after me, grabbed hold of me, and pulled me to the door. Then he pushed me out and drove away. Just to be spiteful!

Rosa: You're right, Pearl. They can be very unkind. It's like they don't think we have any feelings!

(*Driver stops again as Old Man boards the bus to pay his fare.*)

Old Man (*taking out pennies from his pocket and beginning to count*): One, two, three. Oh, good day, Sir! Four, five, six . . .

Driver (*puzzled and annoyed*): Say, what are you doing?

Old Man (*respectfully*): Giving you the money, Sir.

Driver (*impatiently*): Just pay your money and sit down!

Old Man: Oh, yes Sir, yes Sir!! That's what I'm gonna do, right now!

(*Old man finishes paying fare and gets off at front and reboards at back of bus. Man is very old and it takes him a while to find a seat.*)

Driver (*annoyed*): Move along! Move along, Uncle! This bus has a schedule to keep, you know! We don't have all day to wait for you to find a seat!

Old Man: Yes, Sir! Yes, Sir! It's my back, Sir. I went to the doctor, Sir, and he said I needed this medicine.

Driver: Come on! Come on! Just sit down!

Old Man: It's real expensive, and if I buy that medicine, I won't be able to buy the car I've been looking at. It's a beauty, Sir, jet black with yellow . . .

Driver: I don't care what's wrong with you, and I don't want to hear about your car. Just sit down!

(*Old Man mumbles and talks, and Driver continues to drive bus on to next stop where a woman is waiting to get aboard.*)

Driver (*very friendly*): Hello there! Nice day, isn't it?

Woman: Oh, yes! It's a lovely day! And the sun is shining so nicely. I just love days when the sun shines.

Driver: You're pretty sunny yourself, you know. Nice to have you aboard.

(*The lady spends a long time choosing a seat, but Driver is patient.*)

Lamont: Why is she taking so long to find a seat, Mama? Huh? Why don't the driver make her sit down? Huh?

Mother: Hush, Lamont! You'll get us in trouble. Hush up!

(*Bus continues down the street.*)

Passenger (*yelling at the Driver*): Look out for that bump!

(*Bus hits an imaginary bump and all passengers bounce up.*)

Old Man: Oh, land's sake! It's my back again! My back's been paining me something awful, lately!

(*Bus stops at next bus stop. By this time all seats are taken. White Man gets aboard. He looks for a seat but can't find one and turns to the Driver.*)

White Man (*to Driver*): Could you get me a seat? These are all full.

(*Driver gets up and comes to Rosa.*)

Driver: You have to get up, Lady! This man needs a seat!

Rosa (*firmly but politely*): No! I've paid my fare just like he has!

Driver: Look here, Lady! This bus has rules. When there are no white seats left, then coloreds stand! And in case you haven't noticed, Lady, you're colored! So get up and let this man sit down!

(*Rosa ignores him and begins to talk to the lady beside her.*)

Rosa: Pearl, have you noticed how much groceries cost these days? They're just completely out of sight.

Driver: Are you going to get up or not?

Rosa (*with determination*): I said, "NO!"

Driver: Do you mean to tell me you expect this white gentleman to stand while you sit?

Rosa (*to Pearl as she continues to ignore Driver*): Did you hear Brother Johnson's sermon last Sunday? It was mighty good, didn't you think? It was all about right and wrong, and this time I know I'm right!

Driver: All right! This is your last chance. Either you get up and give this man your seat—or you'll never ride this bus again! You can walk until you've got no feet left—you can walk until your feet are just bloody stumps—and nobody's going to care!

(*Rosa sits in silence and turns her back to him.*)

Driver: Okay! You brought this on yourself, Lady! You're never going to see the inside of this bus again!

Driver (*going to front of bus, picking up the radio transmitter and speaking into it*): Hey, Chester Roy! This is Bobby Joe Murphy, here. Send me a squad car up here to Fourth and Magnolia. I've got one of them colored folks aboard that thinks she's white. She's sitting down all la-ti-da—right in front of a white gentleman who doesn't have a seat. Won't get up, she won't! Like she expects him to stand while she sits! (*Pause.*) Yeah!—Uh-huh!—That's right! Some of them sure don't know their place.—You'll be right over?—Okay! I'll be here! I'm not going anywheres!

(*Sets down the radio transmitter.*)

Driver (*turns to passengers and speaks*): Okay, folks. We're gonna sit right here until the police come because Miss Uppidy, there, won't get up and give this white gentleman her seat.

(*Driver sits back down. There is nervous, but subdued chatter among the passengers on the bus. They all look at Rosa, who remains quiet and calm. She does not speak, but stares straight ahead.*)

(*Police arrive and board bus.*)

First Policeman: All right! What's the trouble here?

Driver (*pointing to Rosa*): It's that woman there. She refuses to get up. This gentleman here doesn't have a seat. But she thinks coloreds should sit—while decent white folks stand!

Rosa: Sir, I paid my fare—just like he did. I was here first. It's not fair to make me pay the same price he does and then have to give him my seat.

Second Policeman: You know the rules, Lady. Colored folks sit down only if there's empty seats. You don't expect a white man to stand while you sit, do you?

Rosa: But I have as much right to a seat as he does. Why do I have to give him my seat?

Second Policeman: Why, Girl, you talk like you think you're white!

First Policeman: Can't you see he has a right to that seat! He's white and you're colored! And that's the law!

Rosa: It shouldn't matter what color we are. We both paid the same fare.

Second Policeman: That's crazy talk! Of course it matters! There's not one place in the whole southern United States of America where colored folks sit and make white folks stand! Whoever heard of such a thing?

Rosa: Maybe we need to change some things in the South!

First Policeman: Okay, that's enough! You're under arrest!

Rosa: What am I under arrest for?

First Policeman: Well now—it looks to me like you're disturbing the peace, that you've been unruly and insubordinate, that you've caused a great deal of commotion, and you've impeded an entire bus-load of people who were minding their own business.

Second Policeman: (*pointing to the white man*): And you're sure as fire guilty of causing embarrassment and harassment to this innocent man here!

Rosa: I've not done any of those things. I don't deserve to be arrested!

Second Policeman: You can tell it in court, Girl. Hold out them hands!

> (*Rosa is handcuffed and led from the bus. At the door she stops and lifts her head proudly, turns to the audience and speaks.*)

Rosa (*dramatically*): I don't know what's going to happen to me—but sometimes—sometimes—you just have to say NO!

> (*Policemen lead Rosa off stage. She continues to hold her head high.*)

Narrator: On that December day, with this simple act of courage, Rosa Parks struck what was to become a fatal blow to the abuse and injustice of the Montgomery Bus Company's segregation policies! She is given credit for what led to 381 days of the Montgomery bus boycott and the eventual ruling by the U.S. Supreme Court that segregation on Montgomery buses was illegal. Rosa Parks answered for all time the question, "What can one person do?" From her, we draw courage to live better, to live wiser, to live kinder!

Instructional Activities

Activity 6.1: Verification of Data

In the introduction to this unit, it was stated that the teacher of the students who wrote the play insisted that they base the major events on facts. Before performing this play, have your students research this account to verify the facts. Discuss with the class how historians verify information. For example, how do we know whether George Washington did or did not cut down a cherry tree?

Activity 6.2: Interviewing Local Citizens Who Made a Difference

Oral history is a technique used by historians to record events witnessed and remembered by people who experienced them. There are people living in almost every community who have seen or participated in historical and social action events. After a discussion of who these people are and how they might be located, the students will decide whom they wish to interview. The procedure for conducting oral history interviews is described in Chapter 10 of this book.

Activity 6.3: Creating an African-American Hall of Fame

This activity is a way to motivate students to conduct research about noteworthy African-Americans and to present that information in a dramatic way. After the students collect facts about individuals, direct them to write "I Am . . ." speeches. Later, schedule a performance to be staged similarly to the Hall of Presidents at Disney World. A group of three or four students form a "still-life." Slowly a person in the still-life becomes "alive" and performs his or her "I Am . . ." speech. As each member completes his or her speech, they return to their original still-life position. When the group is finished, another group of performers takes the stage.

You must decide the focus of this activity. For example, will each still-life be organized around a theme or is some other format more appropriate? The following are some thematic possibilities:

Historical theme: People famous for historical achievements.

Chronological theme: People who accomplished deeds within a particular time period. Each still-life would represent a different era, i.e., 1900–1920, 1920–1940, etc. In this mode, literary figures, artists, entertainers, and political figures could be included.

Civil rights theme: People who fought for civil rights.

"Famous firsts" theme: People who were the first person or first African-American to accomplish a particular task.

To begin this activity, you may wish to show the students how to conduct research and present a format for the "I Am . . ." speech. The speech should detail the contributions and feelings of the important personage. Three examples are given here.

Harriet Tubman

I am Harriet Tubman. They call me the Black Moses of my people. Why? Because I want people to be free! I remember when I first ran away—I was scared. I knew if I was caught, terrible things would happen to me, but I knew freedom was worth it. There was no road, no path, no trail. I followed the North Star, the Drinking Gourd, they called it. When daylight came, I had to hide—in bushes, behind rocks, in haystacks, in people's barns. I was cold and hungry and wet and tired, but I knew I *had to go on*—I knew that freedom doesn't come easy! At last, I was out of the South—I was free! I couldn't believe it. It was like glory! I had reached the Promised Land! But I knew I had to go back. Now that I knew the way, I had to show others. I've made nineteen trips—through the dark, following the star. I won't stop. They can't make me stop. Sure, I know it's terrible danger—but freedom's bought with a price. Someday we'll all sing: Free at last! Free at last! Thank God A-Mighty, I'm free at last! And when we can sing that—*all* of us sing that—then I'll rest!

Sojourner Truth

My name is Sojourner Truth. It is a name the Lord gave me because He gave me a job to do—a job that matches my name. He told me to go everywhere across this land and proclaim the truth! To speak out! He told me, "Sojourner, you're gonna be my conscience to people." He wants people to be free—free of slave owners and beatings, of hard work and barely getting by. Free of men who sell our babies and take away our husbands—who break our spirits with their mean and hard ways and expect us to say, "Thank you kindly, Sir—for this little bit of corn—thank you for this little piece of hog jowl!" I want everyone to hear the truth! They try to stop me—they beat me and stone me and threaten me with jail. But I won't be stopped! A man said to me, "Old Woman, do you think your talk about slavery does any good? Why, I don't care any more for your talk than I do for the bite of a flea." But I says to

him, "Perhaps not, but the Lord willing, I'll keep you scratching!" And I will!

Nat Turner

My name is Nat Turner. It's not such an unusual name, is it? Yet that name has the power to strike terror into the hearts of whites throughout the South, because it stands for what slave owners fear the most—violent resistance. I was born on a plantation in Virginia, the property of Benjamin Turner. I was made a "house boy" and learned to read, so I could read the Bible. One of my earliest memories is of the "Voices." I have always heard them. Voices telling me all manner of things. I remember especially hearing the Voices telling me I was destined for great things—that God had chosen me to lead my people out of bondage. I have prayed and fasted constantly since that time, whenever my duties would permit. I heard the Voices telling me to "slay thy enemies with their own swords." The Spirit gave me a sign and I knew I must obey. I had only a few men at first—but others came. Soon we had about seventy men. If only others had joined us—we could have set the Black Man free! My revolt lasted forty-eight hours, and we killed about sixty people. Now, I am in prison. I will be tried and hanged. The Voices have told me that I must suffer and be killed. Soon my skin will be made into a belt as a warning to Black People not to try for freedom! But they cannot stop us! We will be free!

Activity 6.1: Dramatic Presentations

Often teachers are asked to be responsible for assemblies, PTA programs, or other presentations. This unit lends itself well to dramatic and oral interpretations. Besides the plays and the "I Am . . ." speeches the students compose, you could expand this activity to include:

Readings from African-American folk literature
Choral readings of poetry by famous African-American writers
Songs reflecting the African-American experience

References and Bibliography

Gause-Jackson, A., & Banks-Hayes, B. (1989). *Champions of change: Biographies of famous black Americans.* Austin: Steck-Vaughn.

Griffin, J. B. (1970). *Nat Turner.* New York: Coward-McCann.

Lawrence, J. (1968). *Harriet and the promised land.* New York: Windmill:Dutton.

Ortiz, V. (1974). *Sojourner Truth.* New York: J. B. Lippincott.

Peterson, H. S. (1972). *Sojourner Truth: Fearless crusader.* New Canaan, CT: Garrard.

Rollins, C. H. (1964). *They showed the way: American Negro leaders*. New York: Thomas Y. Crowell.

Young, M. B. (1969). *Black American leaders*. New York: Franklin Watts.

February's Potpourri of Teaching Ideas

The purpose of each month's Potpourri of Teaching Ideas is to provide additional resources from which to build your curriculum. Most, but not all, of the activities listed each month relate directly to that month. It is not intended that you use them all, but rather that you choose those which are appropriate for your program. Although the topics are written for a particular month, many of them would be appropriate for use throughout the year. How you use these activities will depend on your curricular goals. You may wish to use some of the activities as they are presented, and you may need to modify some to meet your needs. Perhaps some of them will give you ideas for entirely different potpourris.

Grimm and Perrault: Collectors of Tales

Charles Perrault and Jacob and Wilhelm Grimm were born in the early months of the year. They were collectors and recorders of folk and fairy tales. Perrault, a Frenchman, published *Contes de ma Mere l'Oye* in 1729. Jacob and Wilhelm collected and transcribed old German folktales. For this activity the students should visit the library to find a folktale by either Perrault or the Grimm brothers. After reading the tale, they should prepare some way to present it to the class. They might read it aloud, prepare a puppet presentation, or construct a collage or poster. As an extension, they could compare and contrast these German and French folktales.

Thurgood Marshall: Mr. Justice

Thurgood Marshall was born in Baltimore, Maryland, on July 2, 1908. He became the first African-American associate justice of the U.S. Supreme Court. Marshall was a graduate of Howard University Law School when he began practicing law in 1933. Later, as chief counsel for the National Association for the Advancement of Colored People (NAACP) from 1938 to 1961, he earned the name "Mr. Civil Rights." He presented arguments before the Supreme Court in the case that ended racial segregation in public schools. He was appointed to the U.S. Court of Appeals in 1961 and became solicitor general of the United States in 1965. He was nominated for a place on the Supreme Court of the United States, the highest court in the land, by President Lyndon Johnson in 1967 and was seated on October 2, 1967.

THURGOOD MARSHALL: LEGAL COUNSEL FOR THE NAACP

Issues/Cases	Date	Level of Court	Results/Outcomes
_____	_____	_____	_____
_____	_____	_____	_____
_____	_____	_____	_____
_____	_____	_____	_____

Try This: Understanding the Supreme Court

1. Using an encyclopedia or an almanac, research the following:

What types of cases does the Supreme Court adjudicate?

How does a case get presented to the Supreme Court?

Who are the current members of the Supreme Court?

When was each of these members appointed?

How is each viewed? Is the member considered to be liberal or conservative in interpreting cases related to the Constitution?

2. Study the court cases in which Marshall was involved. Complete the chart "Thurgood Marshall: Legal Counsel for the NAACP."

Heads of State

February is often associated with presidents; two of our more noted leaders, George Washington and Abraham Lincoln, were born during this month. Under our democratic form of government, the president is the chief or head of our nation. The United States has been headed by a president for a little more than two centuries. In colonial times, we were ruled by a nation whose head of state was a king.

As students discuss world issues and events, it may be a suitable time to raise questions about the forms of government in the countries being discussed, as well as the names and titles of the heads of state. Students can consult a variety of reference resources, such as the Statesman's Yearbook and various materials distributed by embassies, to discover the titles of the heads of states of nations around the world.

Mapping the World. After collecting the information, students can color the countries on a map according to the titles of the heads of state. For example, the color red might be used to represent those countries headed by a monarch (king or queen), blue for those headed by a president, green for a prime minister, yellow for a dictator, and perhaps brown for those cases in which

there is some dispute among the researchers or cases where they were not able to conclude the appropriate title.

Raise questions to lead the students to consider other factors besides the title of the head of state. Upon further scrutiny and study, they may discover that there are some heads of state called "president" who are in fact quite indistinguishable from dictators of the worst sort. Students should be encouraged to investigate not only the title of a leader's office as head of state, but also (1) how such leaders selected, (2) the powers they have while serving in office, and (3) the duration of their term. After conducting these additional studies, they can record their new results on another copy of a world map, and make note of any differences in color that result from their more critical inquiries.

As a follow-up to this activity, students can conduct a similar study of the governmental structure of other political units, such as their state or the community in which they live. A table of offices and duties, terms of office, and titles might be constructed. An additional way of reporting the results would be to construct a chart similar to the one sketched out in "What Type of Government?" Students could also be asked to discover the derivation or origin of each term denoting a head of state.

As students are charting the results of their studies, they will discover that Great Britain has both a monarch and a prime minister. This may serve to stimulate further analysis of the meaning of the term "head of state."

New Zealand's Waitangi Day

We tend to think of our country as a nation of immigrants, shaped over time by the waves of settlers who came upon its shores and made it their home. This was not accomplished without conflict and turmoil. As a nation, we are still wrestling with the problems stemming from this phenomenon.

WHAT TYPE OF GOVERNMENT?

Monarchy	President	Prime Minister	Dictator	Other
Spain	United States	Great Britain	North Korea	_____
The Netherlands	_____	Canada	_____	_____
_____	_____	_____	_____	_____
_____	_____	_____	_____	_____

Other nations can recount similar experiences. One such area is New Zealand, a nation consisting of two islands stretching over about a thousand miles in the southern Pacific Ocean. Hundreds of years ago, the Maoris arrived from regions to the north and west and settled the islands. A skillful and artistically gifted people, they decorated their houses and large war canoes with elaborate designs. Many different chiefs vied for power, and there was almost constant warfare among the different tribal groups.

The situation was exacerbated when the first European settlers not only traded guns to the indigenous peoples, but also exposed them to diseases to which they were not immune. As a result, within the course of fifty years, almost half the Maoris perished. Both the recent British immigrants and the Maoris wished for a more peaceful and stable situation. On the sixth of February in 1840, a group of Maori chiefs and Captain William Hobson, representing the British government, signed a treaty at Waitangi, which means "weeping waters." This agreement stipulated that in return for the protection of their land and their political rights by the British, the Maoris would accept the British monarch as their ruler. Waitangi Day celebrates the birth of New Zealand as a nation.

Try This: After further research into the history of New Zealand and the Maori people, students could first dramatize the events leading up to the treaty. For example, they could describe the conflicts that the Maori engaged in with other tribes, the sufferings from disease that they had endured, and the hopes that they had for their meeting with the British naval representative. They could play out the roles of the individuals involved in the treaty, the discussions that would likely have occurred, the issues and concerns raised by both the British and Maori representatives, and finally the speeches that might have been delivered by the representatives after the treaty had been signed. They could also write a draft copy of a treaty similar to that which the parties might have drawn up to address the points of concern.

Stick Game from New Zealand

The Maori people of New Zealand play a game of throwing and catching sticks. The sticks look like thick dowel rods and are often about two feet long but may be made shorter. They usually are about one inch in diameter but may vary according to what is comfortable for the participants.

There should be an even number of players, with each player having at least one stick. As the participants become more proficient at this game, they may each try using two sticks. To play, two players face each other, approximately a foot apart. Players may stand, sit, or kneel while playing. When the leader says "begin," the sticks are tossed simultaneously by the two players. The goal is to catch the opponent's stick and to be ready to return it at the next beat. Although the first person to drop a stick loses, the fun is to continue the tosses as long as possible. Therefore, the tosses follow a rhythm and are aimed so that the opponent is able to catch the stick. If there are several pairs playing, when one of the partners drops out, the winners toss to each other until there is only one player remaining.

At the beginning of the game, the sticks are thrown back and forth slowly, but as the game progresses, the sticks are tossed faster. Sometimes this game is played while the players chant or while someone beats a drum to keep the rhythm. As players become proficient, they may add beats by hitting the floor with the sticks or by striking the sticks together before tossing them.

Section Three: Spring

... Can Spring Be Far Behind?

FOR THOSE WHO LOVE warm weather, there is comfort in the poet Shelley's words, "If winter comes, can spring be far behind?" In the Northern Hemisphere, spring begins on the day that the sun shines directly over the equator on its "march" north. The earth's tilt causes the perpendicular rays of the sun to move toward the north with each day of spring. In the Southern Hemisphere, this is the beginning of fall, which will eventually give way to winter. This occurs on about March 21 and continues until June 21, when the sun's rays have reached their most northern point, the Tropic of Cancer, located on a line around the earth's surface at about 23 ½ degrees north latitude.

Spring, whether north or south of the equator, has always been an occasion for celebration. The ending of the long, cold winter months, with hardships and limited food supply, was reason enough to rejoice. However, spring also meant not just an ending to winter, but a beginning—a new birth, a renewing, the budding of life. Historically, throughout the world, spring celebrations and festivals have been held by almost all cultures.

For farmers in the Northern Hemisphere, spring is a time for tilling soil and planting crops; for urban dwellers, it calls for preparation of small gardens and flower beds, making ready for spring blossoms; and for schoolchildren, it is a time of spring break and dreamy anticipation of the long, lazy days of summer that are not far away.

Many countries hold special spring celebrations. In America and many parts of the world, this is a time of Lent and Easter. For Jewish people, the important holiday of Passover occurs in spring. Countries that do not follow the Gregorian calendar often mark the beginning of their new year during this period.

For many people, spring is their favorite time of the year. Cold weather is over, the hot days of summer are still weeks away, and the earth is a panorama of color, with fragrant breezes rustling in the trees. Is it any wonder that Tennyson wrote, "In the spring a young man's fancy lightly turns to thoughts of love."

Chapter 7

Take the Winds of March with Beauty

BEFORE JULIUS CAESAR moved the beginning of the year to January, March was the first month of the new year. It was originally called *Martius,* in honor of Mars, the Roman god of war. In the Northern Hemisphere, March marks the beginning of spring with the vernal equinox. However, March also marks the beginning of autumn for people living south of the equator. Children in the United States, Canada, and many European countries begin anticipating the long, hot days of summer; at the same time, Australian and New Zealand children have been in school only two months.

For much of the world, March is an unpredictable month. The weather is neither cold nor hot, but often can be some of both. Snowstorms still occur in March in many states. However, hot windy days may come to some regions, particularly in the southern parts of the country. Sandstorms often plague regions of the Southwest, with strong blowing winds laden with blinding dust. Perhaps these events led to the saying, "March comes in like a lion but goes out like a lamb."

There are no national holidays in March in the United States. However, Irish people everywhere celebrate St. Patrick's Day on March 17. Depending on the year, March may also be the month for Easter in the Christian world and Passover for Jews. Jews also hold the festival of Purim during this month. Some countries observe the first day of spring as the beginning of their new year. In Iran this day is called Noruz. The Baha'is new year on this day is called Naw-Ruz.

March holidays are observed in several states. Texas celebrates the anniversary of its independence from Mexico on March 2. The anniversary of Penn's Charter on March 4 is remembered by Pennsylvanians, and the people of Maryland celebrate the arrival of their first colonists on March 25.

	Sunday	Monday	Tuesday	Wednesday	Thursday	Friday	Saturday
March							

MARCH

SELECTED EVENTS

1   Peace Corps founded (1961)
     Glenn Miller (1904–1944)
2   Texas Independence Day
     Sam Houston (1793–1863)
3   Alexander Graham Bell (1847–1922)
4   Casimir Pulaski (1747–1779)
5   Australian Labor Day
6   Elizabeth Barrett Browning (1806–1861)
     Michelangelo (1475–1564)
7   Luther Burbank (1849–1926)
8   International Working Women's Day
9   Amerigo Vespucci (1451–1512)
10   Marcello Malpighi (1628–1694)
     Lillian D. Wald (1867–1940)
11   Johnny Appleseed Day
12   Girl Scouts founded (1912)
     Charles Cunningham Boycott (1832–1897)
13   Percival Lowell (1855–1916)
     Joseph Priestly (1733–1804)
14   Albert Einstein (1879–1955)
     Lucy Hobbs Taylor (1833–1910)
15   Ides of March
     Andrew Jackson (1767–1845)
16   First African-American newspaper in the U.S.
     James Madison (1751–1836)
17   St. Patrick's Day
     Nat "King" Cole (1919–1965)
18   Grover Cleveland (1837–1908)
     Rudolph Diesel (1858–1913)
19   Australian Canberra Day
     David Livingstone (1813–1873)
20   Henrik Ibsen (1828–1906)
21   Vernal equinox
     Johann Sebastian Bach (1685–1750)
22   India's New Year Day
23   Pakistan Republic Day
24   Harry Houdini (1874–1926)
     John Wesley Powell (1834–1902)
25   Gutzon Borglum (1867–1941)
26   Robert Frost (1874–1963)
     Sandra Day O'Connor (1930–)
27   Wilhelm Konrad Roentgen (1845–1923)
     Sarah Vaughan (1924–1990)
28   Three Mile Island accident
29   John Tyler (1790–1862)
30   Francisco José de Goya (1746–1828)
     Vincent van Gogh (1853–1890)
31   René Descartes (1596–1650)
     Franz Joseph Haydn (1732–1809)

People, Places, and Events of March

What's Happening in March:

American Red Cross Month
National Women's History Month
Poetry Month
Youth Art Month

Other March Events:

First week: Newspaper in Education Week
Second week: Girl Scout Week
Second Monday: Canadian Commonwealth Day
Week that includes first day of spring: National Agricultural Week

Events Scheduled According to Non-Gregorian Calendar Usually Occurring in March:

Purim. Jewish holiday commemorating Queen Esther's role in saving the Hebrews from a plot by Haman to exterminate them.
Taiwan: birthday of Kuan Yin, goddess of mercy.
Lailat Al-Qadr. "The Night of Power," a Muslim festival.
Id Al-Fitr. Muslim feast marking the end of the month-long fast of Ramadhan.
India: Idu'l Fitar. Celebrates ending of Ramzan, a month of fasting for Muslims.

March's Daily Calendar

1

Nebraska Admission Day. Became thirty-seventh state admitted to the Union (1867).
Ohio Admission Day. Became seventeenth state admitted to the Union (1803).
Peace Corps founded in 1961.
Switzerland: Chalandra Marz. Traditional springtime event to celebrate ending of winter.
Wales: St. David's Day. Participants wear a leek on this day to celebrate the patron saint of Wales.
Birth anniversary of:
     Oskar Kokoschka (1886–1980). Controversial Austrian artist, playwright, and teacher.
     Glenn Miller (1904–1944). Bandleader and composer.

Morocco Independence Day. Became independent of Spain and France in 1956.

2

Texas Independence Day. Gained independence from Mexico in 1836.
Birth anniversary of:
 Sam Houston (1793–1863). Governor of Tennessee who became known as the "Father of Texas."

3

Florida Admission Day. Became twenty-seventh state admitted to the Union (1845).
Japan: Hinamatsuri. Doll festival; special day for Japanese girls.
Birth anniversary of:
 Alexander Graham Bell (1847–1922). Inventor of the telephone.
 Norman Bethune (1890–1939). Canadian physician who treated the wounded in World War I, the Spanish Civil War, and the Chinese Revolution.
 George Mortimer Pullman (1831–1897). Inventor and manufacturer of the railway sleeping car.

4

Vermont Admission Day. Became fourteenth state admitted to the Union (1791).
Birth anniversary of:
 Casimir Pulaski (1747–1779). Revolutionary war hero of Polish descent.

5

Australia: Labor Day. Commemorating the efforts to limit workday to eight hours during the nineteenth century.

6

Ghana Independence Day. Gained independence from Britain in 1957.
Guam: Magellan Day. Commemorating Magellan's arrival on Guam in 1521.
Birth anniversary of:
 Elizabeth Barrett Browning (1806–1861). English poet, known for *Sonnets from the Portuguese*.
 Michelangelo (1475–1564). Italian Renaissance painter and sculptor.
 Anna Claypoole Peale (1791–1878). Painter of miniatures.

7

Birth anniversary of:
 Luther Burbank (1849–1926). Naturalist.

8

International Working Women's Day.

9

Belize: Baron Bliss Day. Honoring Sir Henry Bliss, benefactor of Belize.
Birth anniversary of:
 Amerigo Vespucci (1451–1512). Italian navigator and explorer for whom the Americas were named.

10

Birth anniversary of:
 Marcello Malpighi (1628–1694). Italian physician, called the "Father of Microscopic Anatomy."
 Lillian D. Wald (1867–1940). Sociologist and founder of the first nonsectarian public health nursing service.

11

Johnny Appleseed Day. Commemorating death (1847) of John Chapman, planter of apple trees and friend to wild animals.
Lithuanian Independence Day. Declared independence from the Soviet Union in 1990.
Anniversary of outbreak of "Spanish" influenza (1918). More than five hundred thousand people died in the United States. Worldwide, more than twenty-two million lost their lives to the virus.

12

Girl Scouts founded in 1912.
Mauritius Independence Day. Located in the Indian Ocean east of Africa; gained independence from Britain in 1968.
Birth anniversary of:
 Charles Cunningham Boycott (1832–1897). The English word "boycott" comes from action precipitated by this man. In 1880, tenants in Ireland pleaded for reduced rents because of poor harvests. Boycott responded by serving eviction notices. The tenants, in turn, staged a "boycott." They refused further dealings with him.

13

Birth anniversary of:
 Percival Lowell (1855–1916). Astronomer and founder of the Lowell Observatory at Flagstaff, Arizona.
 Joseph Priestly (1733–1804). English clergyman and scientist; discoverer of oxygen.

14

Birth anniversary of:
Albert Einstein (1879–1955). German-born physicist known for his theory of relativity.

Casey Jones (1864–1900). Railroad engineer and folk hero.

Lucy Hobbs Taylor (1833–1910). First American woman to receive a degree in dentistry.

15

Hungarian National Day. Anniversary of 1848 revolution.

Ides of March. Julius Caesar assassinated on this day in 44 B.C.

Maine Admission Day. Became twenty-third state admitted to the Union (1820).

Birth anniversary of:

Andrew Jackson (1767–1845). Seventh president of the United States; born in South Carolina.

16

First African-American newspaper published in the United States; (1827).

Birth anniversary of:

James Madison (1751–1836). Fourth president of the United States; born in Virginia.

17

Camp Fire Boys and Girls Founders Day.

Ireland National Day. Honoring St. Patrick.

St. Patrick's Day. Commemorating the patron saint of Ireland, who brought Christianity to Ireland in about 432. The holiday is celebrated in many U.S. cities, as well as in Ireland and Northern Ireland.

Birth anniversary of:

Nat "King" Cole (1919–1965). African-American singer and entertainer. First black person to host a national television show.

Bayard Rustin (1910–1987). African-American pacifist and civil rights leader.

18

Birth anniversary of:

Grover Cleveland (1837–1908) Elected twice to the U.S. presidency as twenty-second and twenty-fourth president; born in New Jersey.

Rudolph Diesel (1858–1913). German engineer and inventor of the oil-burning engine that bears his name.

19

Traditional day when swallows return to San Juan Capistrano.

Birth anniversary of:

David Livingstone (1813–1873). Scottish physician, missionary, and explorer of Africa.

20

Tunisia Independence Day. Gained independence from France in 1956.

Birth anniversary of:

Henrik Ibsen (1828–1906). Norwegian playwright (*An Enemy of the People*).

21

International Day for the Elimination of Racial Discrimination. Begun by the United Nations in 1966 to remember sixty-nine African demonstrators killed in South Africa in 1960.

Noruz. Iranian New Year begins on first day of spring.

Naw-Ruz. Baha'i New Year's Day.

Birth anniversary of:

Johann Sebastian Bach (1685–1750). German composer and organist.

22

India's New Year Day.

23

Pakistan: Republic Day. All-Indian-Muslim League adopted a resolution calling for a homeland for the Muslim people in India in 1940.

24

Birth anniversary of:

Harry Houdini (1874–1926). Magician and escape artist.

John Wesley Powell (1834–1902). Explorer and geologist, best remembered for explorations of Grand Canyon.

25

Birth anniversary of:

Béla Bartók (1881–1945). Hungarian composer.

Gutzon Borglum (1867–1941). Sculptor remembered for creating sculpture of four presidents at Mount Rushmore.

26

Bangladesh Independence Day. Proclaimed independence in 1971; civil war followed.

India: Gangaur or Gauri Tritiya. A festival for women to honor the goddess Gauri and her consort, Lord Shiva.

Birth anniversary of:

Jane Delano (1858–1919). Nurse, teacher, and leader of the American Red Cross.

Robert Lee Frost (1874–1963). New England poet; remembered for such poems as "Stopping by Woods on a Snowy Evening." One of his last public acts, a week before his death, was to read a poem at John Kennedy's inauguration ceremony.

Sandra Day O'Connor (1930–). First woman appointed to the U.S. Supreme Court.

Tennessee Williams (1911–1983). Playwright *(A Streetcar Named Desire)* and *(Cat on a Hot Tin Roof)*.

27

Birth anniversary of:

Wilhelm Konrad Roentgen (1845–1923). German scientist and discoverer of X-rays.

Gloria Swanson (1899–1980). Actress and film star.

Sarah Vaughan (1924–1990). African-American jazz singer.

28

Three Mile Island nuclear power plant accident (1979).

29

Birth anniversary of:

John Tyler (1790–1862). Tenth president of the United States; born in Virginia.

30

Seward's Day. Commemorating the anniversary of the purchase of Alaska from Russia in 1867.

Birth anniversary of:

Francisco José de Goya (1746–1828). Spanish painter.

Vincent van Gogh (1853–1890). Dutch painter.

31

Eiffel Tower opened (1889).

Virgin Islands Transfer Day. Commemorating the purchase of the Virgin Islands from Denmark in 1917.

Birth anniversary of:

René Descartes (1596–1650). French mathematician and philosopher, known as the "Father of Modern Philosophy."

Franz Joseph Haydn (1732–1809). Austrian composer, called the "Father of the Symphony."

American Women of Achievement

Teaching Unit for March

A Word about This Unit. "American Women of Achievement" is the focus unit for this month because March is set as National Women's History Month. However, it would be better to integrate the achievement of women within all topics and subjects rather than to set aside one time during the school year to study the achievement of women. This unit relates to two important issues: (1) the limits set by role or gender stereotypes and (2) characteristics that make a hero. Both of these issues are valuable topics for study and discussion by children and adolescents.

The names of the women found in this unit came from many sources and were included for many reasons. All of these women have changed the world or our society in some way. Many were included because, in addition to being discriminated against because of gender, they have overcome other factors imposed by society.

As you work through this unit, you may want your students to research further one or more of the individuals listed here or use these short segments as models for research on other women. Suggestions for continued study and ideas for classroom activities follow the brief biographies. The women's names have been arranged in chronological order by birth date rather than by field of endeavor.

Motivation. Begin the unit by reading Anthony Browne's *Piggybook* (1986) and lead a discussion about roles and role stereotyping. *Piggy Book* is a story about a family in which Mother does all of the housework until she leaves the family. While she is gone, the family lives "like pigs." When Mother returns, we find that all members of the family help maintain the household. Following the discussion, ask students to write in their journals about their ideas of role stereotyping or stereotyping of any kind. Class discussion should follow the journal entries.

Immersion. People often talk about the pilgrim fathers, forgetting that there were women among those who founded that early settlement in Plymouth in 1620. Eighteen women were aboard the *Mayflower,* but by the spring only six were still alive. While the men were carving out the settlement, the women cooked, kept the house and children, sewed, nursed the sick, and shared the work. The student who is interested in more information about women who lived in the Plymouth colony should begin by reading the appropriate chapters in Penner (1986).

Information. Keep students interested and motivated by reading aloud each day from a biography or autobiography of a woman of achievement. Continue the oral readings throughout the unit. If you do not want to read aloud an entire book, read to the students one of the short vignettes that follows. After each of the readings, the class discussion or writing should focus on the individual's achievement as well as why this woman is included in a unit on women of achievement and how she helped us to understand our world.

Biographical Sketches

Anne Dudley Bradstreet (1612–1672). America's first European woman poet was born in England and immigrated to the Massachusetts Bay Colony in 1630. Her book of collected poems, *The Tenth Muse Lately Sprung Up in America,* includes a variety of poetic themes: religion, nature, and home life.

Sacagawea (1787?–1812). This guide for the Lewis and Clark expedition was a member of the Lemhi Shoshone tribe. As a youngster she was captured by the Hidatsas Indian tribe and became a slave. At sixteen she was allowed to marry a French Canadian, Charbonneau, who lived with the Hidatsas. Charbonneau and Sacagawea became guides for Lewis and Clark as they explored the great Northwest from St. Louis to Oregon. Relying on her childhood memories of the area, she led the group of male explorers through the wilderness to the Pacific Ocean.

Susan B. Anthony (1820–1906). One of the first leaders in the fight for women's rights, Susan B. Anthony founded the National Woman Suffrage Organization to work for an amendment to the U.S. Constitution to give women equal rights, including the right to vote. In 1872, when she led a group of women attempting to vote, she was arrested and tried in court. She lost the case and was fined $100. Women did not attain the right to vote until 1920, fourteen years after Anthony's death. When her image appeared on the silver dollar minted in 1978, Susan B. Anthony became the first woman in history to be so honored by the U.S. Treasury Department.

Emily Dickinson (1830–1886) is considered to be one of the finest poets of the nineteenth century. Born in Amherst, Massachusetts, she was well educated, attending the Amherst Academy and then graduating from Mount Holyoke Female Seminary. She lived with her parents after finishing her education, a common practice for unmarried women of this era. During this period, she wrote poetry and helped with the housework. Although only seven of her poems were published while she was alive, her sister was able to have 115 published after Emily's death. These led to so much interest by the public that hundreds more of Emily's poems were published over the next fifty-five years. During her lifetime, Dickinson wrote more than seventeen hundred poems. Although she lived almost in seclusion, never traveling far from her home, her poetry demonstrated the universal quality of intimate experiences and feelings. The poems depicted the relationship between the inner self and the external world, often reflecting feelings of loneliness and anxiety.

Mary McLeod Bethune (1875–1955). A daughter of former slaves and sharecroppers who lived near Mayesville, South Carolina, Mary McLeod Bethune grew up to become a builder of schools. The first school she attended, a five-mile walk from her home, was in session only three months during the year because the students had to help their parents plant and harvest crops. After this first schooling experience, Bethune received a scholarship to attend the Scotial Seminary in North Carolina. She then attended the Moody Bible Institute in Chicago in preparation to become a missionary. When she was unable to be placed as a missionary, she began teaching school in South Carolina and in Georgia. After her marriage, Bethune was sent to start a mission school in Florida. However, it was soon apparent that the need to teach young African-American children of the railroad workers who were moving to Florida was a more pressing issue than missionary work. In addition to building a school for these students, she began other community facilities. During her lifetime, Bethune was appointed to various government posts by Presidents Coolidge,

Hoover, Roosevelt, and Truman. She was President Roosevelt's special advisor on minority affairs from 1935 to 1944. As director of the division of Negro affairs of the National Youth Administration from 1936 to 1944, Bethune became the first African-American woman to head a federal agency. She also served as vice president of the Urban League and president of the Association of Colored Women, and founded the National Council of Negro Women. After her death, Bethune was buried on the campus of Bethune-Cookman College, one of the schools she built.

Jane Addams (1860–1935). This American social worker was born in a small town in Illinois to prosperous Quaker parents. She was one of the few women at that time to attend college. She always wanted to help others, but sometimes found that her options were limited because she was a woman. In 1889, she moved to Chicago and, with others, built a neighborhood settlement house known as Hull House and began a variety of other projects as a way to better the living conditions of recent immigrants. In addition, she organized groups to pressure the legislature to bring about social reform. In 1931, she became the first woman to be awarded the Nobel Peace Prize. She revolutionized the American attitude toward the poor.

Susan LeFlesch (1865–1915). The daughter of a Native American chief, LeFlesch was born on the Omaha Indian Reservation. In 1889, she became the first Native American woman to graduate from medical school. She returned to the reservation to practice medicine, beginning as a school doctor but soon becoming the government doctor for the entire reservation of 1,244 patients. She was dedicated to her people's welfare and tried to help them move from traditional ways that no longer worked to a new order so that they could gain control of their own destiny.

Alice Hamilton (1869–1970) was born in New York City but grew up in Fort Wayne, Indiana. She became a physician and a pioneer of industrial medicine. Working with Jane Addams in Hull House, Dr. Hamilton set up a well-baby clinic and emphasized preventive health care. Her work with the people of Hull House convinced her of the dangers present in many workplaces, factories, and steel mills. Her career in industrial medicine began in earnest in 1910 when she became director of a commission formed by the State of Illinois to identify and study dangerous trades. From 1911 to 1921, she worked as a consultant to the U.S. Department of Labor.

In 1919, Dr. Hamilton was invited to join the faculty of Harvard Medical School to teach industrial medicine. Because she was the first woman faculty member, she did not receive the privileges afforded other members. She could not use the Harvard Club, did not receive her quota of football tickets, and was not allowed to march in the commencement processions.

Willa Cather (1873–1947) was born in the East in Back Creek Valley, Virginia, but grew up to become a writer whose novels describe the lives of America's western settlers. While still a child, she moved from Virginia to Nebraska with her family and in 1891 entered the University of Nebraska. She wanted to study science, but had trouble with mathematics. When an English professor identified her talent for writing, she changed her major and began to study languages and literature. In 1893, while still in college, Cather became a drama critic for the *Nebraska State Journal*. After graduation, she worked as an editor of the *Home Monthly*, serving at one time or another as a telegraph editor, drama critic, book reviewer, and freelance newspaper writer. In 1901 she moved to Pittsburgh and began teaching. Her first book was published seven years later. By April 1906, she had returned to magazine work, this time *McClure's* in New York.

Cather frequently traveled throughout the West and Southwest—the settings for many of her novels. At the end of her life she settled in New York, traveling less frequently, and her novels became reflective. Her writings reveal the prairie and western settlements to those who live in a different place and at a different time. She helps us to understand the settlers' love of their land and the beauty of the prairie. Her books reflect her admiration of the hardy, sensitive immigrant women whose strength and determination made life bearable in the harsh and lonely prairies during the pioneer days.

Pearl S. Buck (1892–1973), an American author and a Nobel Prize winner, showed us about a country different from the United States and urged us to form a better understanding with the people of Asia. Born in Virginia, she was taken to China by her missionary parents when she was only a few months old. Because Chinese servants helped in the house and she played with the children near her, she became fluent in Chinese and English.

Buck's first published work, a letter about the deaths of her brothers and sisters, appeared in the *Christian Observer* in Louisville, Kentucky, when she was seven years old. She was awarded several prizes for her writing by the *Shanghai Mercury* shortly thereafter. She continued to write and to submit short stories and articles to magazines throughout her college

years in Virginia. After college, she returned to China to be with her parents and to teach in a missionary school. There she met and married John Buck, an agricultural teacher. She continued to live and travel throughout China.

Pearl Buck was awarded a Pulitzer Prize for her novel *The Good Earth* in 1932 (six years later she would win the Nobel Prize in literature). This book was about the life of a Chinese farmer named Wang Lung. The descriptive passages were so vivid that readers felt they knew what China was like and that they actually had been through some of the rituals. *The Good Earth* has been translated into thirty languages.

Later, Buck divorced her husband, married publisher Richard Walch, and moved to the United States. They formed a large family with four adopted children and two children from their previous marriages. In addition to her writing, Buck is known for the three foundations she started: the East and West Association to foster better relations between Asia and America; the Welcome Home Adoption Agency, which finds homes for children of mixed parentage; and the Pearl S. Buck Foundation, established to provide care and training for Asian children fathered by American servicemen.

Golda Meir (1898–1978) was a Russian-Jewish immigrant who came to the United States at the age of eight. Born Golda Mavovitz, she and her family emigrated from Kiev to Milwaukee, Wisconsin, in 1906. She was educated as a teacher and taught for a short period of time before immigrating, in 1921, to what was then Palestine to join a collective farm. In Israel she held several government posts (minister of labor, minister of foreign affairs, and secretary general of the Labor Party) before being elected prime minister, serving in that position from 1969 until 1974. As prime minister, she was concerned with the territorial conflict between Israel and its Arab neighbors.

Marian Anderson (1902–1993) was born in Philadelphia and became a world-famous contralto. However, for many years she was not permitted to sing at some of the major concert halls in America because of the color of her skin. Her career first began in Europe, where her audiences included royalty. In 1935, she returned to the United States to perform. In 1939, she was banned from giving a concert in Constitution Hall in Washington, DC. Instead, she performed at the Lincoln Memorial, where more than seventy-five thousand people came to listen. In 1955, at the age of fifty-three, Anderson was the first African-American to sing with the Metropolitan Opera Company. She was appointed the U.S. delegate to the United Nations in 1958 and was awarded the UN Peace Prize in 1977.

Rachel Carson (1907–1964) was born in Springdale, Pennsylvania, and grew up to become a marine biologist and author of popular books about science. At first she was discouraged from becoming a scientist, being told that a "lady biologist" could teach only in a high school or college. Despite this lack of encouragement, she went on to teach all of us about the interrelationships among all life-forms.

Carson was the first woman to take the Civil Service exam and become a full-time aquatic biologist with the U.S. Bureau of Fisheries. In 1950, she published her second book, *The Sea around Us*, which describes the biology, chemistry, and geology of the oceans. Her next book, *The Edge of the Sea*, about the seashore and the land surrounding it, was published in 1955. *Silent Spring*, her book warning about the wasteful and dangerous use of DDT and other pesticides, was published in 1962 amid controversy. On one side, she was accused of being a sentimentalist; on the other, she received awards from the Animal Welfare Institute, the National Wildlife Federation, and the American Geographical Society. She was the first woman to be awarded the Audubon Society's Medal for Achievement in Conservation.

Mother [Mary Harris] Jones (1830–1930) was once called the "most dangerous woman in America" (Peavy & Smith, 1985, p. 81) because of her work organizing local labor unions. She was born Mary Harris in Ireland in 1830 but immigrated to America at the age of eleven. In 1860, she married George Jones, a Memphis ironworker. Later, as "Mother Jones," she worked with fledgling labor unions to improve working conditions, especially in coal mines. Once she led two hundred children who worked in the mills a 125-mile march for twenty-two days to confront the president of the United States, Teddy Roosevelt. Unfortunately, this confrontation had little or no immediate impact. The first federal child labor law was not passed until forty years later.

Juliette Gordon Low (1860–1927), the founder of the American Girl Scouts, was born on October 31, 1860, the daughter of an officer in the Confederate army. She grew up and married a wealthy Scotsman, but yearned to be devoted to a single cause. After meeting Robert Baden-Powell, founder of the Boy Scouts, she discovered her calling: the founding and development of the American Girl Scouts. Juliette Low, who once wore expensive gowns from Paris, now loved wearing the khaki uniform of the group she founded. She was buried in her full dress uniform, with a tin cup and a knife on the belt.

Ida Wells Barnett (1862–1931). Born in Holly Springs, Mississippi, the child of a former slave, Barnett became a journalist who championed fair trials for African-Americans and who spoke out to end lynchings. She was the first African-American woman to sue a railroad and win. Her name is included on the list of twenty-five outstanding women in Chicago's history.

When Barnett was sixteen, her parents and youngest brother died of yellow fever, so she took over the responsibility of rearing her five remaining siblings. By claiming that she was eighteen, she was able to get a job as a teacher in Memphis, where she began to edit and publish a newspaper for a local church. Soon, she began to write articles herself, one of which caught the attention of the minister of another church. He asked her to write an article for his paper, which had a circulation of several hundred. Her first article described an incident where she was asked to leave the women's car in a train and to ride in the smoking car because she was black. She successfully sued the railroad for discriminatory practices and humiliation. Later she lost on appeal to the Supreme Court of Tennessee. Because of her clear and vivid writing about this experience, the article was picked up by other newspapers. Soon she was asked to write for a number of papers. She wrote under the name of Iola, Princess of the Negro Press.

After writing an article about the shabby condition of the buildings and lack of materials in schools for African-American children, Barnett was fired from her teaching position. She then became a part owner of a popular African-American weekly newspaper, *Memphis Free Speech and Headlight*. After saving enough money to buy out her two partners, she changed the name to *Free Speech* and began printing the newspaper on pink paper. Under her sole ownership, circulation more than doubled.

When three young African-American men were lynched, Barnett researched and wrote about the incident. In her article, she quoted one of the lynching victims, who had yelled, "Tell my people to go West. There is no justice for them here [in Memphis]." Soon she was writing articles urging African-Americans to leave the city. Those who did not leave boycotted stores and businesses that had white owners or bosses. When Barnett left for a convention in Philadelphia, she prepared an article to be published during her absence; it caused so much anger that a mob stormed her newspaper office. An article written by her about this incident was published on the front page of *New York Age*. As threats against her became more vicious, she never returned to Memphis. She continued to write numerous investigative pieces about lynchings. She also wrote a book about lynchings, *The Red Record*, published in 1895, the same year that she married widower Ferdinand Barnett. A prominent Illinois lawyer and newspaperman, he also was a leader in the struggle for equal rights.

In 1896, Ida Barnett went to Washington to help form the National Association of Colored Women. Although overlooked for leadership roles in this organization and in the National Association for the Advancement of Colored People, which formed a few years later, she continued to work on behalf of African-Americans. In 1930, she ran on the Independent ticket for state senator in Illinois but was defeated.

Throughout her years of work against injustice, Barnett met with seven presidents of the United States. When she died on March 31, 1931, newspapers across the country paid tribute.

Eleanor Roosevelt (1884–1962). During her lifetime, Eleanor Roosevelt was called the "First Lady of the World" because of her work on behalf of others and her commitment to world peace. Although born in New York to a family in the upper ranks of society, she was always interested in the welfare of others. Even as a young women with social obligations, she volunteered to work in a slum neighborhood as a part-time teacher.

She married a distant cousin, Franklin Roosevelt, in 1905. During his tenure as governor of New York and later as president of the United States, Eleanor was a tireless worker on projects for him and on those which met her own interests. She organized get-out-the-vote drives, took a leading part in women's groups, inspected government projects, and made speeches to minority groups. After her husband died, President Truman appointed her the American delegate to the United Nations. In that role, she demonstrated her skill in negotiation. She is credited by some for the United Nations' adoption of the international charter on human rights. She traveled extensively, working for world peace.

Louise Nevelson (1900–1988) was a Russian immigrant to the United States who became a sculptor. She is best known for her assemblages, usually large, complex wooden constructions. At the age of nine, she knew that she wanted to be an artist. She had to persevere against seemingly insurmountable odds to reach this goal. Not until she was fifty-eight did the art world accept her work.

Margaret Mead (1901–1978), an anthropologist known for her work on the influence of culture on the development of personality, was born in Philadelphia. As a young girl, Mead was schooled by her grandmother, and it was under her supervision that she began observing and recording the behavior of others—even keeping notebooks on the growth and development of her younger sisters. This was the beginning of the skills she would need later in life. However, it was not until her last year at Barnard, when she enrolled in a

class taught by Franz Boas, that she discovered the emerging field of anthropology—a discovery that was to take her life in a new direction.

In 1925, having earned her doctoral degree in anthropology, Mead sailed to Samoa. She lived with an American seaman and his family in the naval dispensary on Tau, one of the smaller Polynesian islands. To gather information about the native people living on this island, she became, as much as possible, one of the women she was studying. She dressed in native clothes, wove mats and baskets with them, danced, chanted, and worked in the sugarcane fields. Her careful research into the relationship between adolescent behavior and culture was reported in her book *Coming of Age in Samoa.*

In 1926 Mead returned to New York and began working for the American Museum of Natural History. However, afraid that the cultures in the South Pacific would disappear because of increasing contact with visitors from the western world, she traveled to the Admiralty Islands north of New Guinea, where she worked with Reo Fortune to study children and adolescents. In another New Guinea study, she and Fortune observed three different groups of aboriginal people. In 1934, as a result of this study, she wrote *Sex and Temperament in Three Primitive Societies.*

Although Mead's studies were later challenged as anthropologists became aware that field research into the behavior of groups of people can be interpreted in more than one way, her books did help people understand how children learn to become part of the culture in which they live. Mead showed us that we can learn about our own culture by studying others, that the upheavals during adolescent years are largely due to culture, and that people in all cultures share common interests and needs.

Annie Dodge Wauneka (1910–) was the first Navajo woman to be elected to the tribal council. She made significant gains in improving the health conditions of Navajo living on the reservation. Her father, Henry Tee Dodge, was a wealthy and great Navajo leader. The family was raised with both Anglo and Navajo customs, eating most meals Navajo-style from a single bowl, but using good china and silver flatware to entertain guests.

Annie's interest in medicine began at the age of eight when she was sent to a government school. During the first year, there was an influenza epidemic. She helped the school nurse by filling kerosene lanterns and by feeding and bathing the sick. Several years later a serious eye infection spread throughout the school and Annie was sent to another school.

As a member of the tribal council, she waged a campaign against tuberculosis, encouraging and arranging for her people to visit a hospital for treatment and explaining their illness to them in their native language. She wrote a Navajo/English medical dictionary, produced two movies on health topics, and hosted her own radio program. In addition, she worked to build a coalition between medical doctors and native medicine men. Annie Wauneka received many honors and awards from health and civic organizations. She was named Woman of the Year by the Arizona Press Women in 1959 and received the Indian Achievement Award that same year. In 1963, President Johnson presented her with the Freedom Award.

Maria Montoya Martinez (1886?–1987), a famous pottery maker, lived most of her life in the pueblo San Ildefonso, where she was born. She and her husband, Julian, helped at an archaeological dig where a buried city was discovered, complete with building structures and artifacts such as pottery. During the winter they returned to the pueblo, where Maria set about restoring fragments of a bowl that had been found at the dig. She also began to make new pots that Julian decorated with designs found on the ancient pots.

The next year Julian returned to the dig, but Maria remained at San Ildefonso and made pottery for Julian to paint when he returned. When Julian was offered the job of janitor in a museum in Santa Fe, the family moved. Maria began studying the pottery in the museum's collection. One day, the museum director showed her bits of a highly polished black pottery that had been found in Pueblo ruins. None of the modern Pueblo people knew anything about making pottery similar to this, so Maria experimented until she could duplicate it. She decorated the pots with a fluid that appeared like a dull etching after being fired in a kiln. Many people wanted to buy these pots. As a result, Maria taught the other women of the pueblo how to make them, and Julian taught the men how to decorate them. Thus San Ildefonso developed a new industry that brought the population a higher income than farming. In 1934, Maria was presented with the Indian Achievement Award. She was the first woman to receive it.

After Julian died, Maria continued to make pottery with her son, who took the name Popovi Da. She also developed a new glaze that gave the ebony pottery a silvery overlay. She continued to create pots until she was in her mid-eighties. She was called the "Mother of the Pueblo," a title of great respect, because she had preserved and upheld tradition, living in the Pueblo way, and because she had raised the prosperity of all.

Rosa Parks (1913–). By refusing to give up her seat to a white passenger on a Montgomery, Alabama, bus in 1955, Rosa Parks helped bring about the civil rights movement. During that time, it took great courage to say "no," because in the 1950s the bus was only one part of an entire system of segregation—a system maintained by police beatings and Ku Klux Klan burnings of homes and churches. Parks' refusal to move from her seat threatened a way of life. The bus driver called the police, and Parks was placed in a patrol car and charged with breaking the law.

Leaders within the African-American community of Montgomery saw her case as an opportunity to make a stand for civil rights. They called for a bus boycott on the following Monday. This action united the African-American community and brought forward one of the great leaders of the movement, Dr. Martin Luther King, Jr. Rosa Parks's defiance of a white bus driver's order to give up her seat was a pivotal moment that united the community against unfair and unjust practices.

Babe Didriksen Zaharias (1914–1956), born in Port Arthur, Texas, as Mildred Didriksen, was one of the greatest woman athletes in history. Although she may be best known as a golfer, she set records in the 1932 Olympic Games in two field events, was named to the All-American woman's basketball team in 1930 and 1931, and played baseball, football, pocket billiards, and tennis.

The sixth of seven children of Norwegian immigrants Ole and Hannah Didriksen, Mildred was an outstanding athlete in any sport she tried. She was so good at playing sandlot baseball that the boys nicknamed her "Babe," after home-run king Babe Ruth. This became the nickname she used for the rest of her life. She could punt a football seventy-five yards, easily won tennis tournaments, and bowled a 170-point average. Her greatest interest, however, was in basketball. During 1930, Babe was recruited for an industrial team in Dallas. She dropped out of high school during her senior year to become a high-scoring basketball player for the Employers Casualty Company. One of the few options open to women who wanted to become athletes at that time was to join an industrial team.

During an off-season, Babe became interested in women's track and field events. In July 1932, the Amateur Athletic Union met in Evanston, Illinois, to determine the national championships and to qualify Americans for the Los Angeles Olympic Games. Babe was the only person on her team. She entered eight events against some of the country's best female athletes and placed first in six of those events. She earned thirty points, beating her next closest competitor by eight points. In the Tenth Olympiad in Los Angeles, Babe won two gold medals and two silver medals.

For the next few years she performed in many sporting events, even playing on men's baseball and basketball teams. In 1934, after seeing an exhibition golf match, she traveled to Los Angeles to learn golf.

She entered her first golf tournament that year and made a first-round score of 77. The following year she won the Texas Women's State Championship. During her professional golf career, she won more than eighty tournaments, was named Woman Athlete of the Year six times by the Associated Press, and won three U.S. Women's Open golf tournaments. Babe Zaharis died of cancer on September 27, 1956.

Maria Tallchief (1925–) is often considered to be America's greatest ballerina because of her superb technical discipline and style. Born in Fairfax, Oklahoma, the granddaughter of a former chief of the Osage, she began playing the piano and dancing at a young age. Her mother wanted Maria to become a concert pianist, so her family moved to California in order to provide her with better instruction. While in high school, Maria began studying ballet with the famous Russian teacher, Madame Bronislava Nijinska.

After high school she went to New York and began dancing with the international Ballet Russe de Monte Carlo. George Balanchine, later a famous choreographer, joined the company and created parts for Maria. Maria and Balanchine married when she was twenty-one. Balanchine began his own ballet company (later to become the New York City Ballet), and Maria became its principal ballerina.

Several years later she divorced Balanchine and married Henry D. Pasche, Jr., an engineer who worked in Chicago. Maria Tallchief danced with several ballet companies after her second marriage. By the time she retired at forty-one, she had danced major roles with ballet companies all over the United States and Europe to great acclaim. She later became the artistic co-director of the Chicago Ballet.

Althea Gibson (1927–). This world-famous athlete, born in Silver, South Carolina, was one of the leading women tennis players from 1950 to 1958, both as an amateur and as a professional. When Gibson was two years old, she went to live with an aunt in Harlem, New York. As a young girl she became interested in tennis by playing paddleball on the streets of Harlem during the summer months. Robert Johnson and Hubert Eaton, two doctors who loved tennis and wanted to help African-American players become experts, saw Gibson play and decided that she had the potential to become a great player; they arranged for her to study tennis. After graduating from high school, she earned an athletic scholarship to Florida A & M University. In 1950, Gibson broke the "color barrier" and was allowed to play in a tournament at the famous Forest Hills Courts. In 1957, she won the women's singles tournament at Wimbledon and, with a partner, also took home the winning trophy for women's doubles. She was named Female Athlete of the Year in 1957 and 1958.

Maya Angelou (1928–). Born Marguerite Johnson in St. Louis, Maya Angelou moved to Stamps, Arkansas, in 1931 to live with her grandmother. Since then, she has lived in various places in the United States, in Egypt, and in Ghana, Africa. She has been a singer, a dancer, an actress, and a producer, but she is best known for her poetry and for her autobiographical books. In 1993, she was chosen by President Clinton to deliver an original poem at his inauguration.

Dolores Huerta (1930–), a political activist, was born in New Mexico and was raised in New Mexico and California. Because of experiences as a teenager, she fought against discrimination. Once she received a "C" in her English class, even though her grades on papers and tests were "A." When she confronted the teacher, the teacher voiced suspicion that someone else must be writing Dolores's papers because they were "too good." While living in Stockton, California, in the 1950s, Huerta became involved with the Community Service Organization (CSO) to help Mexican-Americans. In 1962, she left the CSO to work with Cesar Chavez to organize farmworkers in their fight for better working conditions and wages. She continued to work for the United Farm Workers of America as a policymaker in charge of political and legislative activity.

Katherine Davalos Ortega (1934–) was born in Tularosa, New Mexico. As a child, she worked in her family's restaurant. After graduating from Eastern New Mexico University with honors in business and economics, she worked as a certified public accountant in California until being named as vice president of the Pan American National Bank of Los Angeles. She became the first woman president of a California bank when she was selected to head the Hispanic-owned Santa Anna State Bank.

Ortega's first presidential appointment was to the Advisory Committee on Small and Minority Business Ownership in 1982. Later, she became commissioner of the Copyright Royalty Tribunal. On October 3, 1983, President Reagan appointed her treasurer of the United States. She became the tenth woman and the second Mexican-American woman to hold the office.

Alice Walker (1944–), the first African-American woman to win a Pulitzer Prize for fiction, (*The Color Purple*), was born in Eatonton, Georgia, the youngest of eight children born to sharecroppers. She grew up to become a poet and a writer of short stories and novels.

Wendy Lee Gramm (1945–), who became chair of the Commodities Futures Trade Commission, was born on the island of Oahu in Hawaii. Her grandparents had emigrated from Korea to work in the Hawaiian sugarcane fields in the early 1900s. She earned a bachelor's degree from Wellesley College and a doctorate in economics from Northwestern University. She met her husband, William Philip Gramm, when both were economics professors at Texas A & M University. When Phil Gramm was elected to the U.S. House of Representatives in 1978, the family moved to Washington, DC, where Wendy worked for several different departments of the government and the Federal Trade Commission. She was selected to chair the Commodities Futures Trading Commission by President Reagan in 1988 and was approved for a second term in August 1990.

Connie Chung (1946–). A broadcast journalist, Connie Chung was born in Washington, DC. Her father, a Chinese diplomat, moved with his wife and other children to Washington to begin working in the Chinese Embassy; he later worked at the United Nations.

During summer vacations from the University of Maryland, Chung worked writing news releases for a New York congressman. She then worked as a copy person for a television station. She became a secretary in the news department and a newswriter, finally moving to on-the-air reporter for a Washington television station after graduation from College. In the early 1970s, she was hired by CBS News.

June Okida Kuramota (1948–). Born in Japan on July 22, 1948, Kuramota immigrated with her family to the United States when she was five. She grew up to become a musician and a composer and to play the koto, an ancient Japanese instrument with thirteen strings and small wooden bridges that sounds similar to a harp.

we hope that the first step will be to surround your students with books about the subject of study. Immersion in texts that provide models of writing in a specific genre is important to students' understanding of the writing process.

Standards for Choosing Biographies

1. The book should be readable and written at a level appropriate for its intended audience.
2. The book should present accurate information. The sources used should separate accurate reports from myths and legends. For example, the Reverend Weems' biography of George Washington included the now-famous story about chopping down the cherry tree. Weems invented the story because he wanted to present an unblemished hero who represented morality as the reverend saw it, a hero worthy of emulation (Arbuthnot & Broderick, 1969).
3. The subject's achievements should be evaluated in terms of the times in which he or she lived rather than in light of present standards. The biography should help characterize the subject as an individual but relate the subject to humanity with enough detail to support these ideas. In addition, the biography must build a background of the social, cultural, and economic forces at work during the period of the subject's life (Garraty, 1957).

Instructional Activities

The sampling of biographical sketches included in this unit is neither inclusive nor exhaustive. Many obvious choices are missing; for example, Florence Nightingale, Madame Curie, Sandra Day O'Connor, Sally Ride, and Toni Morrison. Also not included are women governors and members of Congress, explorers, and authors of children's literature. However, women who have achieved significance in a variety of different fields have been included here. This list includes only women who lived in the United States, but your class may choose to take a broader perspective and include women from all parts of the world. Perhaps someday women will automatically be included in all areas of study, eliminating the need to call attention to their accomplishments during one special time of the year.

This unit provides an opportunity to introduce research and report strategies, especially related to biography or autobiography, and to introduce a variety of ways to present information. As in all units of study,

Activity 7.1: Finding Information Using the K-W-L Strategy (What I Know; What I Want to Find Out; What I Learned)

This reading strategy, developed by Ogle (1986), will help students use their prior knowledge about the person they are to research, direct their background reading, and provide a way to record the information learned. The "Biography Research Chart" is an appropriate means for students to prepare their data.

Activity 7.2: Organizing Information for a Biographical Narrative

Biography is one of the oldest literary forms, and it is also one of the most difficult forms to evaluate. The writer's perspective may influence interpretation of the subject, including the events and the people surrounding the subject.

BIOGRAPHY RESEARCH CHART

My biography is about _____

She is best known for _____

What I know	What I want to find out	What I learned

Source:

When an author chooses to write about someone, he or she must be "intrigued" by that individual because of the amount of time and effort it takes to research a subject adequately. Arbuthnot and Broderick (1969) use "intrigue" to mean that the would-be writer may not necessarily like the subject but has enough interest in that individual to take the time necessary to conduct the research and to write fairly about the subject.

The author must decide on the intended audience. This will help determine which aspects of the subject's life will be emphasized and which incidents and events may best be used to illustrate a point but still keep the narrative moving at a lively rate. The "Biography Data Sheet" can be used by students to organize biographical information in a meaningful manner.

Activity 7.3: Presenting Information

For this activity, use Margaret Wise Brown's *The Important Book* (1990) as a writing model. The students can develop their own "Important Books" about the women they choose to research. The first page contains the most important item about the person and should show her major contribution. The subsequent pages could include significant events, birth date, place of birth, education, other events or contributions, and then repeat the text used on the first page.

Example (use one page for each line):

Emily Dickinson is a great American poet.
She was born in Massachusetts in 1830.
She rarely left her home state.
She published only seven poems before she died.
She spent her time in Massachusetts writing.
Her poems help us understand loneliness. But
The most important thing about *Emily Dickinson* is—
Emily Dickinson is a great American poet.

Students can then illustrate their books and place them in the library, or they may be retained in the room as a "room set" of *Important Books about American Women*.

Timeline. If the class has developed a timeline as part of its continuing study for the year, women can be positioned on the line. You may want to have the students color-code the various areas of endeavor (i.e., art, entertainment, music, science, literature, etc.).

Other Ideas. The class can develop a yearly calendar or almanac devoted to women of achievement. If the class works with the parent-teacher organization, they might want to print it and sell it as a way of making money, or at least of promoting student accomplishment.

BIOGRAPHY DATA SHEET

My biography is about _____

Birth information (date and place) _____

_____

_____

Information about parents (if important)_____

_____

Area(s) of achievement: _____

_____

Focus idea about the subject: _____

Organization Chart for Subjects in the Arts

Type of work	Date	Theme
Example: *Name of Poem*	*1845*	*People are part of nature, not above it.*

Your class may also write plays, present performances, conduct interviews, and produce videotapes related to women of achievement for various instructional purposes.

References and Bibliography

Aaseng, N. (1981). *Winning women of tennis*. Minneapolis Lerner Publications. Brief biographies of eight women who played international tennis. Includes Americans Helen Willis, Althea Gibson, Billy Jean King, Chris Evert Lloyd, and Martina Navratilova.

Arbuthnot, M., & Broderick, D. M. (1969). *Time for biography*. Glenview, IL: Scott, Foresman. Representative collection of biographies for children, with special section for teachers on biography in the classroom. The theme of the biographies is that to achieve greatness, people must persevere even in the face of obstacles. Biographies of very few women are included, although many of the authors are women.

Blacknall, C. (1984). *Sally Ride: America's first woman in space*. Minneapolis: Dillon Press. Photographs.

Block, I. (1973). *The lives of Pearl Buck: A tale of China and America*. New York: Thomas Y. Crowell.

Bober, N. (1984). *Breaking tradition: The story of Louise Nevelson*. New York: Atheneum.

Broewn, M. (1988). *Sacagawea: Indian interpreter to Lewis and Clark*. Chicago: Childrens Press. Based on documented history. Journal entries by members of the Lewis and Clark expedition indicate that the title is the correct spelling of her name.

Brown, M. W. (1990). *The important book*. New York: Harper Trophy. Reissue of an old classic.

Browne, A. (1986). *Piggybook*. New York: Alfred A. Knopf. When Mrs. Piggy leaves her family, the father and sons realize how much they relied on her to do the work around the house. Presents humorous solution to role stereotyping.

Burt, O. (1974). *Black women of valor*. New York: Julian Messner.

Crawford, A. F. (1990). *Jane Long: Frontier woman*. Austin: W. S. Benson. Biography of the woman who became known as the "Mother of Texas."

Crawford, A. F. (1990). *Lizzie: Queen of the cattle trails*. Austin: W. S. Benson. Biography of Lizzie Williams, a pioneer Texas cattle woman who rode the trail from Texas to Abilene, Kansas.

DePauw, L. (1982). *Seafaring women*. Boston: Houghton Mifflin.

Faber, D., & Faber, H. (1988). *Great lives: American government.* New York: Charles Scribner's Sons. One of a series of books on great lives. Contains information about three women: Jeanette Rankin (first U.S. congresswoman), Eleanor Roosevelt, and Margaret Chase Smith.

Falkof, L. (1992). *Helen Gurley Brown: The queen of Cosmopolitan.* Ada, OK: Garrett Educational Corp. Biography of the woman from Green Forest, Arkansas, who grew up to write several books and become the editor-in-chief of *Cosmopolitan* magazine. One in a series of Wizards of Business published by Garrett.

Ferris, J. (1988). *Walking the road to freedom: A story about Sojourner Truth.* Minneapolis: Carolrhoda Books.

Ferris, J. (1991). *Native American doctor: the story of Susan LaFlesche Picotte.* Minneapolis: Carolrhoda Books.

Fisher, M. (1973). *Jacqueline Cochran: First lady of flight.* Champaign, IL: Garrard Publishing. Biography of the woman who organized and commanded the Women's Air Force service pilots during World War II.

Garraty, J. (1957). *The nature of biography.* New York: Alfred A. Knopf.

Gonzalez, C. (1982). *Jane Long: The mother of Texas.* Austin: Eakin Press.

Greenfield, E. (1977). *Mary McLeod Bethune.* New York: Thomas Y. Crowell. Easy-to-read biography of a famous African-American educator.

Grant, M. (1974). *Harriet Tubman: black liberator.* Monkato, MN: Creative Education. The life of a woman born a slave but who later became the "Moses" of her people.

Gridley, M. (1974). *American Indian women.* New York: Hawthorn Books.

Hodgman, A. & Djabbaroff, R. (1981). *Skystars: The history of women in aviation.* New York: Atheneum.

Hume, R. F. (1964). *Great women of medicine.* New York: Random House.

Jacobs, W. (1983). *Eleanor Roosevelt: a life of happiness and tears.* New York: Coward-McCann. Despite her shyness, this First Lady devoted her life to helping others and seeking world peace.

Jacobs, W. (1990). *Great lives: human rights.* New York: Charles Scribner's Sons. Part of Scribner's Great Lives series. Contains short biographies of Ann Hutchinson, Harriet Beecher Stowe, Sojourner Truth, Clara Barton, Dorothy Day, Eleanor Roosevelt, and others.

Huber, P. (1990). *Sandra Day O'Connor.* New York: Chelsea House. Part of a series, this book relates the life of the first woman Supreme Court justice.

Kittredge, M. (1988). *Jane Addams.* New York: Chelsea House. One in this publisher's series on American Women of Achievement.

Levenson, D. (1973). *Women of the west.* New York: Franklin Watts. Explains the lives of African-American, white, and Native American women in the western United States since 1818.

Lewis, S. (Adapt.). (1990). *One-minute stories of great Americans.* New York: Doubleday. Twenty biographical anecdotes about important people in American history. Designed to be read aloud in one minute or less. Includes information about Clara Barton, Susan B. Anthony, Helen Keller, and Anne Sullivan.

McKissack, P. & McKissack, F. (1992). *Sojourner Truth. Ain't I a woman?* New York: Scholastic.

Meltzer, M. (1985). *Dorothea Lange: life through the camera.* New York: Viking Kestrel. Short biography of the early life of a woman whose photographs of migrant workers helped bring about social change.

Modell, J. (1986). Margaret Mead. In *The world book encyclopedia* (Vol. 13, p. 278). Chicago: World Book.

Morey, J., & Dunn, W. (1989). *Famous Mexican Americans.* New York: Cobblehill Books.

Morey, J., & Dunn, W. (1992). *Famous Asian Americans.* New York: Cobblehill Books.

Ogle, D. (1986). The K-W-L: a teaching model that develops active reading of expository text. *Reading Teacher,* pp. 364–370.

O'Connor, K. (1984). *Contributions of women: Literature.* Minneapolis: Dillon Press. Biographical information about five women who made outstanding contributions to American literature. Part of a series entitled *Contributions of Women,* which includes books about women in art, aviation, business, dance, education, labor, literature, medicine, music, politics and government, religion, science, social reform, sports, theater, and "The First Women Who Spoke Out."

Paradis, A. (1985). *Ida M. Tarbell: Pioneer woman, journalist, and biographer.* Chicago: Childrens Press. Biography of the woman who in 1902 exposed the dishonesty of the Standard Oil Company.

Peavy, L., & Smith, U. (1985). *Dreams into deeds: nine women who dared.* New York: Charles Scribner's Sons. Tells of women who, from 1930 through 1990, changed the lives of others and opened up opportunities for those who followed.

Penner, L. R. (1986). *The Thanksgiving book.* New York: Hastings House.

Rollins, C. H. (1964). *They showed the way: Forty American Negro leaders.* Binghamton, NY: Vail-Ballou Press. Includes several women, some well known and some lesser known.

Rylant, C. (1989). *But I'll be back again: an album.* New York: Orchard Books. Autobiography of writer of children's books and winner of the 1993 Newbery Award.

Scheader, C. (1985). *Contributions of women: Music.* Minneapolis: Dillon Press.

Schlissel, L. (1982). *Women's diaries of the westward journey.* New York: Schocken Books. Although the women represented in these diaries not famous, they truly are women of achievement.

Shiels, B. (1985). *Winners: women and the Nobel Prize.* Minneapolis: Dillon Press. Includes women from around the world. Extended biographies of American women in this collection are provided for Rosalyn Yalow, Maria Goeppert Mayer, Pearl S. Buck, and Barbara McClintock. Shorter biographies of other American honorees also are included.

Shumate, J. (1991). *Sojourner Truth and the voice of freedom.* Brookfield, CT: Millbrook Press. Account of a former slave who dedicated her life to achieve equal rights for African-Americans and women.

Siegel, B. (1992). *The year they walked: Rosa Parks and the Montgomery bus boycott.* New York: Four Winds Press.

Summarizes the life of Rosa Parks and the role she played in the civil rights movement.

Stoddard, H. (1970) *Famous American women.* New York: Thomas Y. Crowell. Biographies of forty-two American women who lived during the nineteenth and twentieth centuries, representing a variety of fields.

Summers, B., & Lanker, B. (Eds.). (1989). *I dream a world: Portraits of black women who changed America.* New York: Stewart, Tabor & Chang.

Thomas, A. (1981). *Like it is.* New York: E. P. Dutton. Interviews with twelve important African-American leaders, including Maya Angelou.

Tobias, T. (1970). *Maria Tallchief.* New York: Thomas Y. Crowell. Biography of the woman who grew up to become "America's greatest ballerina."

Turner, C. T. (1989). *Take a walk in their shoes.* New York: Cobble Hill Books. Biographical sketches of fourteen famous African-Americans, including Rosa Parks, Leontyne Price, Ida Wells, Mary McLeod Bethune, and Maggie Lena Walker. Includes brief skits that can be performed in nonprofit situations.

Vigil, E. (Ed.). (1987). *Woman of her word: Hispanic women write.* Houston: Arte Publico Press.

Voight, V. F. (1967). *Sacajawea.* New York: G. P. Putnam's Sons. Easy-to-read biography of the life of this Shoshone Indian princess.

Yost, E. (1961). *Famous American pioneering women from the seventeenth century to the present.* New York: Dodd Mead.

March's Potpourri of Teaching Ideas

The purpose of each month's Potpourri of Teaching Ideas is to provide additional resources from which to build your curriculum. Most, but not all, of the activities listed each month relate directly to that month. It is not intended that you use them all, but rather that you choose those which are appropriate for your program. Although the topics are written for a particular month, many of them would be appropriate for use throughout the year. How you use these activities will depend on your curricular goals. You may wish to use some of the activities as they are presented, and you may need to modify some to meet your needs. Perhaps some of them will give you ideas for entirely different potpourris.

Schoolteachers in the American West

In addition to women in history whose names and achievements are well known, there is a group of "unknown" women who were important to the development of this country—the early schoolteachers, particularly those in the Southwest and West. Because not much education was required to teach school in the eighteenth century, girls began teaching at fifteen or sixteen years of age. Salaries were approximately

twelve dollars a month. The teacher was expected to stay with a different family in the community every few weeks so that everyone could share in the cost of her board. She walked from these homes the two or three miles to the schoolhouse, which was usually a sod house or board shanty. The teacher cleaned the floor and built and tended the fire. She taught all the students—from the youngest to the oldest (who probably was her age or older). There were few books, usually only those that the children's families happened to own. The children wrote on pieces of slate and then erased their work. Because the older children were needed to help plant and harvest crops, schools were open only a few months each year.

Many African-American women became teachers in separate schools for black children. In Nicodemus, Kansas, a town whose inhabitants were African-American, forty-five children attend class in a dugout, which was their first school.

Despite poor conditions and low wages, schoolteaching was one of the few careers open to young women, both African-American and white. Many farmers allowed their daughters to remain in school to become teachers so that they could contribute to the family income.

Try These Activities

1. Ask your students to interview their grandparents or other older adults who may have attended a small rural school. They can write a narrative account of the interview or present an oral report to the class.

2. Read aloud accounts found in either adult or children's literature related to early schoolteachers. Laura Ingalls Wilder draws a graphic picture of her first year's teaching experiences in Dakota Territory in the early 1880s in *These Happy Golden Years.* Compare and contrast her account with a schoolteacher's tasks today.

3. Invite a senior member of the community who remembers "the good old days." Encourage him or her to share with the class early school experiences.

4. Local government records and historical information about the early days of a community or county are usually available to students and teachers. Using these records, determine the number of school districts within your county a century ago. How many districts exist today? Ask the students to hypothesize as to the reasons for the change.

Between Love and Hate: The Poetry Debate

March is National Poetry Month, so this is a good time to sample poetry from a variety of cultures. Many teachers have had negative experiences with poetry; consequently, they often ignore the subject. To allow this to happen in your classroom robs your students of an important genre of literature. Poetry offers a rich repertoire of language, rhythm, rhyme, and deep emotional experiences.

Too frequently students are required to read poems that are beyond their maturity levels. This results in feelings of confusion, for they often lack the experience to bring meaning to the works. Many students complain that they are asked to analyze a poem to find the author's "true meaning." They insist this

---

Poets Worth Knowing

Rosemary and Steven Vincent Benet
Gwendolyn Brooks
John Ciardi
Paul Fleischman
Robert Frost
Nikki Giovanni
Eloise Greenfield
Langston Hughes
Karla Kuskin
Edward Lear
Jean Little
Myra Cohn Livingston
Henry Wadsworth Longfellow
Eve Merriam
Ogden Nash
Jack Prelutsky
Carl Sandburg
Robert Service
Shel Silverstein
Robert Louis Stevenson
Judith Viorst
Jane Yolen

Collectors and Compilers of Poems

Arnold Adoff
Byrd Baylor
Edward Blishen
Joanna Cole
William Cole
Stephen Dunning
Scott Elledge
Helen Ferris
Lee Bennett Hopkins
Nancy Larrick

---

becomes a guessing game, for "only the teacher and the author know the hidden or true meaning" (and many times the teacher is the only one who cares!). Other students dread having to memorize long, dull poems that contain obscure messages or difficult word groupings. For students who find memorization easy, this may be acceptable, but for most the lesson learned is "I hate poetry!"

An easy way to work with this assignment is to begin with poems that have meaning for children and young people. Shel Silverstein's works may not be judged by literary critics as great masterpieces, but students almost universally find them meaningful, funny, creative, and occasionally a little naughty. Read some of his poems from *A Light in the Attic* or *Where the Sidewalk Ends* and see how "the boy who hates poems" reacts. Listed in the box are writers of juvenile poetry whose works you may wish to share with your class. Do not forget to include a variety from several cultures, including Japanese writers of haiku and African-American authors.

Purim: A Joyous Holiday

Purim is a Jewish holiday celebrated in spring that commemorates a time when a Jewish woman and her cousin saved the Jews of Persia from being decimated. The story is read in the synagogues during Purim. When the name of Haman, the antagonist in this story, is read aloud, the people in the congregation make noises to drown it out.

The story is that Haman became angry when Mordecai, an advisor to the king, refused to bow down to him. Because Mordecai was Jewish, Haman, a Persian, devised a plan for revenge. Haman went to King Ahasuerus with a story about how the Jews were disrupting the country and convinced him to order the killing of all Jews. Lots were drawn to determine the exact date when the executions would begin. Esther, a beautiful Jewish woman married to the king, was a cousin to Mordecai. When Mordecai heard of Haman's plan, he went to Esther. Esther then risked her life by having an audience with the king without his prior permission. She told King Ahasuerus of Haman's deceit. The King ordered that Haman be hanged.

Purim is celebrated today as a joyous holiday. People dress in costumes, eat Homentashen cookies (shaped like Haman's ears or hat), send gifts of food to friends, and sing and dance. The Hebrew calendar date is the fourteenth of Adar, but the Gregorian date varies between late February and early March.

Try These Activities

1. Use this as a time to talk about women in history who have risked their lives to save others. Fictional heroines could also be discussed.
2. Esther, although she was a queen, was not allowed to see the king unless he called her to him. Some students may be interested in learning about women's roles and behaviors in cultures different from their own.
3. Because there is a custom of giving food as presents on this holiday, this might be another time when the class can collect food items to be donated to local soup kitchens or food banks.
4. Add a recipe for Homentaschen cookies to your international cookbook.

- -

Homentaschen or Asnei Haman

Homentaschen are triangle-shaped cookies with poppyseed or fruit fillings. There are many different recipes for making the dough.

DOUGH	FILLING
4 ½ cups flour	½ cup ground graham
2 tsp. baking powder	crackers mixed with
1 cup granulated sugar	1 cup fruit preserves
2 tsp. vanilla	or pie filling (or use
4 egg yolks	canned poppyseed
1 cup orange juice	filling)

DIRECTIONS:
Combine all ingredients for the dough and form a ball. Chill the dough until firm, about 2 hours. Roll dough out to approximately ¼ inch thick. Use a glass to cut circles from the dough. Place ½ tsp. of filling in the center of each circle. Pinch or fold the dough around the filling into a triangular shape. Place on ungreased baking sheet. Bake in preheated 375°F oven for 15 to 20 minutes, until lightly browned.

- -

What's in a Name: Whose Name?

This activity involves the students in some linguistic detective capers. Using a variety of data sources, your students can inquire about the origin of a particular class of words. They may be acquainted with the origins of some of their own names. In some cases they are derived from the place where one's ancestors originally lived—for example, Erasmus Rotterdamus, a Renaissance humanist of some note. In many cases the family name stems from the occupation or trade of an early family member. Many names such as Smith, Taylor, Miller, and Brewer, or the term representing this word in another language, are derived from a craft or trade.

In some cases, adjectives are applied to individuals that owe their origins to stories or fictional accounts. For example someone who acts in an excessively obsequious manner could be labeled as a Uriah Heep, after a character in one of Dickens's novels. Other adjectives, when applied to humans, describe traits that are attributed to certain animals: "a very bear of a man" (for one who is physically strong) "a foxy individual" (for one whose cunning is a significant attribute).

Names of objects often owe their origins to the original producer or creator of a particular product. For example, people often will ask for a Kleenex rather than a "facial tissue." For many years Kodak was almost synonymous with cameras. More recently, Xerox has come to denote a copying machine, even if the machine has been produced by another company. Such terms are the source of advertisers' delight or despair, depending on who their clients happen to be.

The particular group of words that serves as the basis for this instructional activity is composed of terms that originally were the names of individuals. Because of some action or discovery on the part of each individual, his or her name became a descriptive term in our language. Examples include such words as boycott, gerrymander, watt, voltage and bowdlerize.

Using library resources, students, working either individually or in groups, can develop lists of such words. Are certain fields of endeavor, such as science or politics, more likely to produce these types of words? To display the data, have your students construct a bulletin board with a picture and brief description of the person for whom each word was named.

Special Days to Remember and Celebrate

Each of us has days that hold special meaning and significance. Students, when queried about such days, will likely first include their birthdays. Other examples often may mark some "rite of passage": the day they received their first two-wheeler, the first time they were allowed to do something special or go somewhere on their own, and so forth.

Other days are celebrated and set apart because they have special meaning for a particular group or a whole people. Nations often celebrate their birthdays, the days that they were "born" as independent political entities. Other days are memorialized, or set aside as days to remember, to recall great events or individuals who have made great contributions to the nation or to a particular group. Such occasions often are festive times of feasting and celebration.

Religions also have particular days that hold special meaning, those deemed "holy" days (from which is derived the word "holidays"). These may be occasions for feasts or celebration, but they may also be times of somber and serious reflection.

Investigating these "days of significance" may prove to be a worthwhile beginning to the study of a country or culture. Students can begin by reflecting on special days in their own lives. Each student can develop a poster that indicates particular dates and what makes these days special. The posters might include pictures (perhaps photographs taken when they were born) or drawings that are linked to each of these days.

Students then can make similar posters for a particular nation, culture, or religion, with drawings, photos, or other materials to illustrate significant days. For a country, the data could be displayed as a timeline showing the date it was born (became independent) along with other special days in its life (see the sample chart).

The calendars included in this book can serve as a starting point. Students could begin their research by selecting one of the days noted on the calendar, determining the culture or country with which it is associated. Then, using other resources available in the library, they could discover other dates or occasions that hold special importance for the group or nation.

Your students can also construct their own monthly calendars, concentrating on various types of significant days. One month might be devoted to political units, such as countries or states. They might also attempt to develop a timeline of significant days related to their own community. Other months could be devoted to special days associated with religions or cultures. Each entry should include a brief note as to the importance of day or event from the perspective of the country or group.

Focus on a Country

Every month includes days on which significant events occurred in countries around the world. Your students can select a country they wish to research and write reports similar to the example given here. They can then share their information in oral reports, a group presentation, or on a display chart or bulletin board.

Tunisia

Tunisia's capital, Tunis, sits on the site of ancient Carthage, so its beginnings go back nearly three thousand years. However, this country did not become a republic until 1957, less than forty years ago. It celebrates Independence Day on March 20 and Constitution Day on June 1.

Tunisia extends farther north than any other country on the African continent. Although it borders on the Mediterranean and was controlled by the French from 1881 to 1956, it is part of the Arab world. Its neighbors are Algeria to the west and Libya to the east. The Sahara Desert forms part of the southern end of this country. The Arabic name for the Republic of Tunisia is *Al-Jumhuriyah al Tunusiyah.*

The Carthaginian Empire was founded by the Phoenicians in Tunisia around 1100 B.C. Carthage was supposedly established near present-day Tunis in about 814 B.C. In addition to the Phoenicians, Tunisia

---

TIMELINE OF THE LIFE OF OUR NATION

1776	*1803*	*1861-65*	*1868*
We're born	We grow!	_____	_____

Find the right place in our country's life for these events [samples]:
  Bill of rights ratified
  Women granted right to vote
  Last state admitted
  A "fight with our neighbor"
  We "stretch for the moon"
  Our population exceeds 100 million
  Civil War

---

has been occupied and governed by the Romans, the Vandals, the Byzantines, the Ottoman Empire, and the French before becoming independent. It was declared a republic in 1957. At that time Habib Bourguiba, a leader in the independence movement, was elected president. Constitution Day on June 1 marks the anniversary of President Bourguiba's return from exile.

The national flag is bright red with a white disk; and inside the disk are a red crescent and a star. The white circle signifies the sun, and the crescent and star, emblems of the Muslim religion, retain the history of Turkish influence.

Written by Jallal Eddine Ennakache, Tunisia's national anthem, *A La Khallidi ya dimana-l Ghaouali Jihada-l watan,* translates to "Oh! Our Blood, Immortalize the Dear Ones Who Fight for the Homeland." The anthem begins, "Immortal and precious the blood we have shed for our dear fatherland."

Try These Activities

Map Skills. Using an atlas or another appropriate source, locate Tunisia. Based on your observations, hypothesize as to why this location was desired by so many different groups. Check your answer by consulting an encyclopedia or other book.

History. Reread the first line of Tunisia's national anthem. After reading about the history of Tunisia, decide whether this line accurately reflects the country's history. Support your position with specifics.

Suggested Readings

Brown, L. (1986). Tunisia. In *The world book encyclopedia* (Vol. 19) Chicago: World Book.

Dobler, L. (1968). *National holidays around the world.* New York: Fleet Press.

Chapter 8

The Glory of an April Day

APRIL, the fourth month of the year, probably comes from the Latin word *aperire,* meaning "to open." In the Northern Hemisphere it is the time of year when buds begin to open and plants start to grow after the long winter. The Anglo-Saxon name for April, *Eostre monath,* became the name of the Christian holiday of Easter.

April begins with All Fool's or April Fool's Day, a time to play tricks on people or to try to make them believe tall tales. Many countries of the world share this custom. A person who is successfully tricked in Scotland is called a gowk or cuckoo. Hindus celebrate Holi, a similar type of holiday.

Many major religions have holidays during this month (in some years, these holidays may occur during late March if the event is determined by a lunar calendar). Buddhists honor the birth of Lord Buddha. Buddhists in Japan bathe statues of Buddha with tea made from hydrangea leaves. The Chinese calendar sets aside the holiday of Ching Ming, a time when people must go and visit the graves of their ancestors with offerings of flowers. Christians commemorate Christ's entry into Jerusalem and his death on the cross. Jews celebrate Passover, a holiday that commemorates their escape from Egypt during biblical times. For the Sikhs, a day honors Gurur Govind Singh's baptism of his first five disciples. Amrit is the name of the ceremony during which people are baptized into the Sikh faith.

Reference

Hughes, P. (1989). *The months of the year.* Ada, OK: Garrett Educational Corp.

Sunday	Monday	Tuesday	Wednesday April	Thursday	Friday	Saturday

APRIL

People, Places, and Events of April

What's Happening in April:

Mathematics Education Month
Month of the Young Child
National Garden Month
Prevention of Animal Cruelty Month

Other April Events:

Week that includes April 14: Pan American Week

Events Scheduled According to Non-Gregorian Calendar Usually Occurring in April:

Passover. Commemorating the escape of Jews from Egypt.
Good Friday. Oldest Christian celebration; commemorating the day of crucifixion.
Easter Sunday (usually in April, but sometimes in March). Celebrated by Christians as the day of the resurrection of Christ.
Yom Hashoa (Holocaust Day)
Egypt: Sham El-Nesim. Sporting holiday celebrated since the time of the pharoahs.
Festival of Ridvan. Baha'i celebration in honor of Baha'u'llah, prophet and founder of the Baha'i faith.

April's Daily Calendar

1

April Fool's Day
India: Ramnavami. Commemorating the birth of Lord Rama.
Birth anniversary of:
    Jagjivan Ram (1908–1986). Political leader who worked with Gandhi and Nehru in the fight to gain independence for India. He was the spokesman for one hundred million "untouchables," having overcome most of the handicaps of the caste system.

2

International Children's Book Day. Observed in connection with the birthday of Hans Christian Andersen.
Birth anniversary of:
    Hans Christian Andersen (1805–1875). Danish writer and teller of fairy tales.

Frederic Auguste Bertholdi (1834–1904). French sculptor and creator of the Statue of Liberty in New York Bay.

Emile Zola (1840–1902). French novelist.

Giacomo Girolamo Casanova (1725–1798). Italian writer and librarian, noted for his accounts of his "love life."

3

Pony Express founded (1860)

Birth anniversary of:

John Burroughs (1837–1921). Naturalist and writer.

Washington Irving (1783–1859). Author, best remembered for his stories "Rip Van Winkle" and "The Legend of Sleepy Hollow."

4

Martin Luther King, Jr., assassinated (1968)

NATO founded (1949)

Birth anniversary of:

Dorothea Lynde Dix (1802–1887). Social reformer and activist who worked to improve conditions in asylums for the insane.

Isoroku Yamamoto (1884–1942). Japanese naval officer in World War II; said to be Japan's greatest naval strategist.

5

Singapore: Qing Ming Festival. Honoring family ancestors.

Taiwan: National Tomb-Sweeping Day. Honoring family ancestors by cleaning the tombs.

Birth anniversary of:

Joseph Lister (1827–1912). English physician and founder of aseptic surgery.

Booker T. Washington (1856–1915). African-American educator and leader.

6

China: Ching Ming Festival. Now called All Souls' Day. Families gather at graves of ancestors to honor the dead.

North Pole reached by Robert E. Peary's expedition (1909).

Thailand: Chakri Day. Commemorating King Rama I's founding of present dynasty.

Birth anniversary of:

Raphael (1483–1520). Italian painter and architect.

Lowell Thomas (1892–1981). Reporter and radio news broadcaster.

7

Birth anniversary of:

Walter Winchell (1879–1972). Journalist, actor, broadcaster, and gossip columnist.

William Wordsworth (1770–1850). English poet and philosopher.

8

Birthday of the Buddha (ca. 563–483 B.C.). Commemorating the birth of the founder of Buddhism.

Japan Flower Festival (Hana Matsuri). Celebration of Buddha's birth.

9

United States Civil War ended (1865).

Birth anniversary of:

W. C. Fields (1879–1946). Stage and movie entertainer.

10

Birth anniversary of:

William Booth (1829–1912). English founder of the Salvation Army.

Hugo Grotius (1583–1645). Dutch theologian and scholar.

Frances Perkins (1880–1965). First woman member of U.S. cabinet; appointed secretary of labor by Franklin Roosevelt in 1933.

Joseph Pulitzer (1847–1911). Hungarian-born American journalist, founder of the Pulitzer Prizes given since 1917.

11

Civil Rights Act of 1968 enacted.

Uganda Liberation Day. Commemorating the end of the dictatorial rule of Idi Amin in 1979.

12

Salk vaccine developed by Jonas E. Salk in 1955; vaccine for poliomyelitis was declared safe and effective for prevention of this crippling disease.

13

India: Hindu New Year (Baisakhi) .

Singapore: Songkran Festival. Joyous water festival to welcome the new year.

Birth anniversary of:

Thomas Jefferson (1743–1826). Third president of the United States; born in Virginia. Author of the Declaration of Independence and founder of the University of Virginia; died on July 4, exactly fifty years after the signing of the Declaration of Independence.

14

First U.S. abolition society founded. The Society for the Relief of Free Negroes Unlawfully Held in Bondage was founded in Philadelphia in 1775.

Hong Kong: Tin Hau Festival. Honoring the goddess of fishermen.

Abraham Lincoln assassinated (1865).
Birth anniversary of:
Arnold Joseph Toynbee (1889–1975). English historian and author.

15

Federal income tax filing day.
Anniversary of the sinking of the *Titanic* (1912).
Birth anniversary of:
Thomas Hart Benton (1889–1975). Artist, noted for his murals of southern and midwestern life.
Charles Wilson Peale (1741–1827). Portrait painter.
Bessie Smith (1894–1937). African-American blues singer.

16

Birth anniversary of:
Charles Spencer Chaplin (1889–1977). English-born silent film star, director, and producer.
José de Diego (1867–?) Puerto Rican political leader.
Wilbur Wright (1867–1912). Aviation pioneer.

17

American Samoa: Flag Day
Syrian Arab Republic Independence Day. Gained full independence from France in 1946.
Birth anniversary of:
John Pierpont Morgan (1837–1913). Financier and one of the world's wealthiest men of his time.
Thornton Wilder (1897–1975). Playwright and novelist.

18

Signing of Canadian Constitution Act (1982).
Paul Revere's ride (1775).
San Francisco earthquake (1906).
Zimbabwe Independence Day. Formerly called Southern Rhodesia and controlled by Britain, this southern African country gained independence in 1980.
Birth anniversary of:
Clarence Seward Darrow (1857–1938). Attorney and agnostic.

19

Sierra Leone National Holiday. Celebrating the occasion of becoming a republic in 1971.
Warsaw ghetto revolt (1943).

20

Birth anniversary of:
Daniel Chester French (1850–1931). Sculptor.
Adolf Hitler (1889–1945). Infamous German dictator, leader of the Third Reich, and principal player in World War II.

21

Brazil: Tiradentes Day. Commemorating the death of national hero, José de Silva Xavier.
Indonesia: Kartini Day. Honoring Raden Adjeng Kartini, leader of the emancipation of Indonesian women.
Italy: Founding of Rome (753 B.C.).
Birth anniversary of:
Freidrich Froebel (1782–1852). German educator and author, founder of the first kindergarten.
John Muir (1838–1914). Naturalist and conservationist.

22

Brazil Discovery Day. Pedro Alvares Cabral, a Portuguese navigator, is believed to be the first European to land in Brazil (1500).
Earth Day
Birth anniversary of:
Nikolai Lenin (1870–1924). Russian socialist and leader of the Bolshevik Revolution.

23

Turkey: National Sovereignty and Children's Day
Birth anniversary of:
James Buchanan (1791–1868). Fifteenth president of the United States; born in Pennsylvania.
William Shakespeare (1564–1616). Recognized as England's greatest playwright.

24

Birth anniversary of:
Robert Penn Warren (1905–1989). Poet and novelist.

25

Anzac Day. Memorial day and veterans' observance in Australia, New Zealand, and Western Samoa.
Portugal's Day. New government formed after junta led by General Antonio de Spinola (1974).
Birth anniversary of:
Guglielmo Marconi (1874–1937). Italian inventor noted for the wireless telegraph.
Martin Waldseemuller (ca. 1470–1520). German geographer and mapmaker.

26

Chernobyl (USSR) nuclear reactor disaster (1986).
Maryland became seventh state to ratify the Constitution (1788).
Tanzania Union Day. East African republics of Tanganyika and Zanzibar merged into a single nation in 1964.
Birth anniversary of:
John James Audubon (1785–1851). Naturalist and artist.

27

Afghanistan: Saur Revolution Day. Commemorating the end of Soviet-backed rule in 1992.

Sierra Leone Independence Day. Located on western coast of Africa; gained independence from Britain in 1971.

Togo Independence Day. Located in western Africa; became republic in 1960 following French rule.

Birth anniversary of:

Edward Gibbon (1737–1794). English historian and author of *History of the Decline and Fall of the Roman Empire.*

Ulysses S. Grant (1822–1885). Eighteenth president of the United States; born in Ohio.

Samuel F. Morse (1791–1872). Inventor and creator of Morse code.

28

Canadian National Day of Mourning. Remembering and honoring workers killed or injured on the job in Canada.

Birth anniversary of:

Lionel Barrymore (1878–1954). Actor and member of famous theatrical family.

James Monroe (1758–1831). Fifth president of the United States; born in Virginia.

29

Birth anniversary of:

William Randolph Hearst (1863–1951). Newspaper editor and publisher.

Hirohito (1901–1989). Long-ruling emperor of Japan, in power during World War II.

30

Louisiana Admission Day. Became eighteenth state admitted to the Union (1812).

Netherlands: Dutch National Day. Commemorating the start of the reign of Queen Beatrix in 1980.

Walpurgis Night. Celebrated especially by university students in northern Europe. Also called Witches' Sabbath. In Sweden the holiday is called Feast of Valborg.

Birth anniversary of:

William Lilly (1602–1681). English astrologer and almanac compiler.

The Holocaust, or Yom Hoshoa

Teaching Unit for April

A Word about This Unit. Although the Holocaust can be studied as part of a unit on World War II, its victims were not prisoners of war nor were they necessarily conquered by an invading army. Rather, some were citizens of the aggressor nation. The Holocaust is studied as a separate unit because of what it teaches about the nature of prejudice and the results of its extreme manifestation. From 1933 to 1945, Adolf Hitler, the leader of the highly developed country of Germany, made annihilation of the Jews of Europe one of his goals. Although he never succeeded in completely in achieving this goal, when this terrible time in history was over, six million Jews had been exterminated because of their religious beliefs. The Jewish cultural and communal heritage of almost two thousand years of European history was nearly gone (Gilbert, 1994).

Rationale. Jews set aside a special day, Yom Hoshoa, to remember those who died during the Holocaust. Each year, Yom Hoshoa falls almost immediately after Passover, usually in April. This date was chosen to commemorate the beginning of the Warsaw uprising, when a small group of Jews living in the Warsaw ghetto organized an assault on the occupying Nazi army. Because Jewish holidays follow the lunar calendar, the actual Gregorian calendar date of Yom Hoshoa varies from year to year.

Motivation. In Jane Yolen's novel, *The Devil's Arithmetic* (1988), one of the characters explains that her identity is contained in the numbers on her arm: J18202—the *J* because she is a Jew; the *one* because she is alone; the *eight* a reminder of how many were in her family; the *two* those who are left in her family; and the *zero* for her brother, who considers himself to be a nothing. This scene, in which people have numbers on their arms but no names, sounds as if it is from a novel set in the future; however, this novel deals with actual events of the past. This was part of the lives of the Jews who were sent to Auschwitz and other concentration camps, or "death camps," established by the Nazis.

Why would one group use numbers to identify individuals in a different group? Why do people kill each other? Why would one individual want to order the killing of masses of people? When the nightmare was over, six million Jews and five million non-Jews had been systematically murdered by Nazis under the di-

rect orders of Hitler. The Jews were killed solely because they were Jews. Killed were people of all ages, young and old, people who had not committed any "crime" other than having at least one Jewish parent or grandparent.

How could such events happen during the twentieth century in one of the most cultured countries in the world? Although there is probably no satisfactory answer to that question, to attempt to make sense of it, one needs to understand the nature of prejudice, the social and economic conditions in Europe after World War I, and the rise to power of Adolf Hitler.

Immersion. Information and studies about the Holocaust can be divided into several different areas: (1) the nature of prejudice, (2) the history of the political and social problems in Germany in the period between the two world wars, (3) the rise of Adolf Hitler, (4) World War II, and (5) the events and experiences of the Holocaust itself. Information about these topics is available in both fictional and nonfictional sources.

Whatever the focus, we can never forget that this event represented one of the greatest periods of man's inhumanity to man; for, as the philosopher George Santayana wrote, "Those who cannot remember the past are condemned to repeat it" (Santayana, 1981).

The Nature of Prejudice

Entire societies or separate individuals may exhibit prejudice toward any group or any person who is viewed as being somewhat different. Prejudice occurs when one person forms an adverse opinion about another person without full knowledge or complete examination of the facts. The dictionary continues this definition by adding that prejudice is also "an irrational attitude of hostility directed against . . . a group, a race, or their supposed characteristics" (*Merriam-Webster*, 1993). Dolan (1985) explains that negative actions related to this irrational hatred take three forms: personal prejudice, discrimination, and persecution. Personal prejudice is exhibited when one person makes derogatory statements or tells bigoted jokes about a group of people who are different from that individual. Discrimination is practiced when groups of people are prohibited from participating in activities that other citizens of a country enjoy. Persecution means that deliberate negative acts are directed toward a particular group of people.

Allport (1954) describes a slightly different hierarchy of "negative actions" that are the result of prejudice: (1) derogatory speech, including stereotyping; (2) avoidance of the stereotyped group; (3) discrimination, or a way to separate the target group from the rest of the population; (4) physical attack, which may be caused by individual or mob violence; and (5) extermination, which includes lynchings, massacres, and attempts to kill members of the targeted group. Unfortunately, all of these actions came into play as the Nazis under Adolf Hitler organized a deliberate plan to rid Europe of the Jews. Hitler called this the "final solution" to the Jewish problem.

Anti-Semitism is the special term for prejudice directed against Jews. One result of prejudice is termed "scapegoating." The concept of scapegoating comes from the biblical practice of sacrificing animals. The early Jews would select a goat from their flocks, take it to the Temple, and the priests would announce that all the sins of the past year were placed on the head of the goat as it was turned loose into the wilderness. The people believed that this act would ensure forgiveness and that their lives would be spared for another year (Rossel, 1981). In the study of prejudice, scapegoating means that an individual or group of people is singled out to bear the blame for others. Hitler used the Jews as scapegoats for the troubles in Germany during and after World War I.

Prejudice also leads to stereotyping, which involves assigning to an entire group a single, oversimplified image (Rossel, 1981). Some stereotypes used in Germany against the Jews were statements such as "all Jews are rich" or "the Jews operate like parasites."

Early History. Jews have a long history in Europe (Baner, 1982; Gilbert, 1994) Before 1939, Jews had lived in Poland for 850 years and in Czechoslovakia for a thousand years, as well as in other parts of Europe. Many Jewish communities in Europe had existed for hundreds of years before the founding of individual countries or states. Some of the Jewish communities had been destroyed during the Middle Ages but had been reestablished a second or even a third time. Jewish people lived in what was Germany for more than fifteen hundred years before German unity under Bismarck in 1870 (Gilbert, 1994, p. 2). During the nineteenth century, many Jews achieved civic equality in these European states. Bauer (1982, p. 27) points out that between the Congress of Vienna in 1815 and the Congress of Berlin in 1878, Jewish equality advanced in most countries except for Russia and Turkey.

Unfortunately, there also was a long history of anti-Jewish sentiment in Germany and in Europe even before Hitler began his attempt at the final extermination. During the Middle Ages, Jews were blamed for causing the plague. Untrue rumors were spread that Jews were devil worshipers or poisoned the wells of Christians (Chaikin, 1987). At the time of the Spanish Inquisition, Jews were killed for not converting to Christianity. Between the thirteenth and sixteenth centuries, Jews were expelled from England, France, Portugal, Italy, Spain, and Germany or forced to live in special areas called ghettos. At different times, governments in the countries in which Jews were allowed to live placed limits on what they were allowed to do. In some places they were not permitted to become doctors, lawyers, or teachers or to sell food to non-Jews.

Germany had a long history of religious prejudice and hatred toward the Jews. Thousands of Jews in Germany were murdered by German Christian Crusaders (Rogasky, 1988).

In 1873, Wilhelm Marr wrote *The Triumph of Jewry over Germanism,* in which he claimed that being Jewish meant that a person belonged to a race, the Semites, rather than to a group of people with shared religious beliefs (Rogasky, 1988). According to Marr, this meant that the Jews were deeply different from everyone else. His idea was that race determines human abilities and qualities. Thus, some racial groups were inferior and others superior. There is no evidence to support Marr's suppositions. After Marr's book, other anti-Jewish books and pamphlets appeared and anti-Semitic politicians were elected to the government. This laid the foundation for what was to follow.

Europe between the Wars. After the end of World War I, Europe was in turmoil. In Germany, unemployment was high, people fought in the streets, and the government seemed unable to govern. Many new political organizations began to appear, each offering solutions to the problems.

By 1923, inflation was the worst that the world had ever seen. In Germany, the country's money was almost worthless.

The Architect of the Holocaust. In 1889, Adolf Hitler was born in Braunau, an Austrian village across the border from Bavaria. His father, a minor customs official, died in 1903, leaving his widow with only a small pension to support Adolf and his sister. Because of this, Hitler dropped out of school. Unable to find a job, he spent several years roaming the countryside. After he was rejected by an art school in 1907, he spent four years in Vienna living in flophouses and eating from soup kitchens. He spent his time reading German history and mythology. In 1913, he left Vienna for Germany, where he joined the army in Bavaria. While fighting on the western front, he was wounded and received a military decoration.

In Munich during 1919, Hitler joined the National Socialist German Workers' party (NSDAP), or Nazis. This small group of men talked about politics and listened to speeches about rebuilding Germany. They believed that it was the state's responsibility to find work and food for its citizens. They were against the Jews, calling them "vermin." They wanted Jews removed from all government jobs, from newspapers, and from the production of motion pictures (Adler, 1989). The Nazi party claimed that Germany must be allowed to take its rightful place among the nations of the world.

Because of his magnetic personality and his speaking ability, Hitler became the leader of the Nazis in 1920. He claimed that Germany lost World War I because its own government had aligned itself with Jews, who weakened its determination to fight. The party also claimed that only a racial comrade, a person of German blood, could be a citizen. Therefore, no Jew could be a citizen (Rogasky, 1988, p. 15). The Nazis promised food, jobs, and education to all Germans.

In 1923, during the period of the worst inflation in Germany, the NSDAP attempted to take control of the government by force. When this failed, Hitler was sent to prison for thirteen months. It was there that he wrote his book, *Mein Kampf (My Struggle),* in which he explicated Nazi beliefs. His anti-Jewish feelings permeated this work. *Mein Kampf* stated that Germany was the greatest nation on earth and was destined to be the leader of all others. This book developed and expanded the idea of a master people or race. Hitler, building on Marr's thesis, claimed that each race had its own particular blood and warned against mixing the blood strains. According to Hitler, the most superior type of blood was that of the Aryan race of the Germans. Rogasky (1988, p. 16) refutes Hitler's ideas about the Aryans, stating, "There is no such thing as an Aryan race, but that made no difference to Hitler or his followers."

According to Hitler's book, this "master race" had been betrayed by greedy capitalists and deluded revolutionaries during World War I. Hitler claimed that the Jews were the leaders of these traitors. He further stated that the Jews were a wicked race who hated and wished to destroy Germany. He continued with statements that the Jews' true purpose was to dominate and to replace the best in the nation with members of their own race. Jews were not a religious group, but a people with definite racial qualities. Because of this, they and other inferior races had to be driven out and destroyed. He called for the expansion of Germany by taking control of the land to the east that belonged to the Slavs, whom he classified as another inferior race.

Hitler, using existing prejudice and despair, offered scapegoating and stereotyping as easy solutions to complex problems. In May of 1928, the Nazi party secured twelve seats in the Reichstag and Hitler became a member of the Weimar assembly (Gilbert, 1994). By January 30, 1933, the Nazis were the majority party in the Reichstag and the government, thinking that the Nazis could be controlled, had to offer Hitler the chancellorship. In the meantime, inflation had begun to rise again and unemployment grew to new levels. Businesses closed and economic distress grew. The Nazis blamed these conditions on Jewish "wealth" and "conspiracy" (Gilbert, 1994). The Weimar ideal of democracy was replaced by extremism.

Events Leading to the Holocaust. For Hitler to achieve his aims, including extermination of the Jews, he had to gain complete control of the country. Therefore, the Nazi party began to change Germany's laws. Two months after Hitler was made chancellor, the Reichstag passed an emergency decree suspending all civil rights: free speech, freedom of the press, and the right to assembly. One month later, the Enabling Act allowed the government to pass any law and to write decrees even if they violated the constitution. This act granted Hitler dictatorial powers.

After the Enabling Act, opponents to the regime were locked up without charges filed against them or warrants for their arrests. Gilbert (1994) reports that throughout Germany critics of the regime, Jews as well as non-Jewish, were attacked and beaten. All non-Nazi voices in Germany were silenced (Chaikin, 1987, p. 31). The first concentration camp, Dachau, was opened to detain political prisoners. During March 1933, Dachau was enlarged to hold as many as five thousand prisoners. People were tortured or disappeared, never to be seen again. Other camps were built. Within a year, fifty such camps were located all over Germany.

The Jews were called opponents of the Germans and enemies of the state. Throughout Germany, Jews were attacked, beaten, and killed, and Jewish shops and stores were vandalized. Although the Jews constituted less than 1 percent of the entire German population, Hitler claimed that the Jews dominated the country.

In protest of the lawlessness in Germany, some people in the United States started an unofficial boycott of German products. In retaliation Hitler called for a boycott of all Jewish businesses in Germany (Rogasky, 1988). This boycott lasted one day—April 1, 1933. German storm troopers and members of the SS (an elite police group) stood in front of each Jewish store, and "Jude," the German word for Jew, was painted on the windows.

On April 7, the Law for the Restoration of the Civil Service expelled all non-Aryans from civil-service jobs. Anyone who had Jewish parents or two or more Jewish grandparents was considered to be a non-Aryan. During the next year, more anti-Jewish laws were enacted, prohibiting Jews from working in the movies, theater, arts, literature, universities, courts, hospitals, and newspapers and magazines. On May 1, Berlin University students burned seventy thousand tons of books that they claimed were written by "undesirable authors." Joseph Goebbels, Hitler's propaganda director who was at the scene, proclaimed, "The age of extreme Jewish intellectualism is now ended" (Rogasky, 1988).

The Jews were not the only members of the German population who lost their rights. In July 1933, the Law for the Prevention of Offspring with Hereditary Defects was passed, requiring sterilization of any person who had hereditary limiting conditions (Friedman, 1990). A health tribunal was established to determine who would be sterilized. The victims were not permitted to examine any of the documents used against them, nor did most have lawyers for their defense. During the years from 1934 to 1939, approximately 375,000 people were sterilized.

As Chaikin (1987, p. 35) points out, "In 1935, Hitler made anti-Semitism law." On September 15, 1935, the Nuremberg laws were passed, limiting even more the freedom and civil rights of the Jews. These laws stated that only full citizens of the Reich could enjoy full political rights. A citizen of the Reich was a subject of Germany who proved by his actions that he was ready and able to serve the German people and the Reich faithfully. In addition, "race defilement" was prohibited, so Christians were forbidden to marry Jews. Property owned by Jews had to be registered with the government. The government published a list of recognizable Jewish names. To make them conspicuous, Jews without a recognizable Jewish name were required to take Sarah or Israel as middle names. Jewish passports were stamped with a "J" or the word "Jude."

When seventeen thousand Jews originally from Poland were expelled from Germany and forced to live in stables because Poland would not repatriate them, a seventeen-year-old student whose parents were part of that group shot and killed a minor official, Ernest vom Rath, at the German Embassy in Paris. In retaliation, the Nazis used this as an excuse to destroy Jewish property. The result of this order was *Kristallnacht*, or "The Night of Broken Glass," which occurred on November 9 and 10, 1938 (see Chapter 3). Because the government wanted this event to appear to be spontaneous, the orders given to the police ended with the admonition that they were to carry out these actions wearing civilian clothes. Throughout Germany, Jewish offices, shops, businesses, and private homes were ransacked, looted, and burned while the police stood by. Fires were allowed to burn while uniformed firefighters watched (Resnick, 1991). At the end of Kristallnacht, 91 Jews had been killed, more than 30,000 Jewish males had been sent to concentration camps, 815 shops had been destroyed, and 191 synagogues had been burned and six more completely demolished. Jews were then ordered to repair and pay for all damages. They had to pay one billion reichsmarks for the death of vom Rath and another 250 million reichsmarks for insurance benefits for destroyed property.

Although the Nazis used the shooting of vom Rath as a way to justify the mass action against the Jews as revenge for his death, mass arrests actually had been planned long before the shooting in Paris. Barracks to accommodate tens of thousands of Jews had been built in concentration camps (Bauer, 1982, p. 108).

Half a million Jews lived in Germany when Hitler came to power in 1933, 20 percent of whom were recent immigrants from eastern Europe. The remaining 80 percent were German citizens, descendants of those who had settled there over the past two thousand years (Bauer, 1982). These Jews had participated in the German economic, cultural, and political life. These German Jews were loyal to Germany and did not understand the extent of anti-Semitism. After Kristallnacht, thousands of Jews emigrated. To ensure migration, the Nazis established a Central Office for Jewish Emigration. However, it was often difficult for Jews either to raise the money needed to emigrate or to find a country willing to take them. By 1941, 164,000 Jews remained in Germany (Rogasky, 1988).

In 1939, Hitler directed that a program of "mercy killing" be initiated to eliminate mentally ill and retarded individuals, regardless of their race or ethnicity. This was also the year when he began expansion to the east. Hitler and Joseph Stalin, the dictator of Russia, made a pact that Russia and Germany would not fight each other. Instead, Germany would attack Poland and the land would be divided between the two dictators. On September 1, 1939, Germany attacked and destroyed the Polish air force, and within three weeks Hitler had conquered Poland. During April 1940, the German army marched into Norway and continued through Denmark, Holland, and Belgium, heading toward France. By 1942, Germany occupied all of Europe, except for Switzerland, the Iberian Peninsula, and Sweden.

In September 1941, all Jews in Germany were ordered to wear a Jewish star when they appeared in public. By October, they were not allowed to leave their homes without permission, nor were they allowed to leave the country. Hitler ordered Jews to be concentrated in smaller areas, arrested, herded into freight cars, and sent to concentration or death camps. In some locations, people were forced to dig a large mass grave site. They were then lined up along the edge and shot. In others, special trucks were built that gassed the people inside as they were being transported to the burial site. In still others, special showers and ovens were built at the camps in which to gas the Jews and burn their bodies.

In each of the conquered countries, Hitler attacked the Jews. Operation Barbarossa began on June 22, 1941, with the German invasion of Russia. Horror stories abound about the treatment of the Jews at this time. As Hitler's troops advanced into Russia, entire Jewish villages were massacred. For example, the thirty-four hundred Jews of the village of Ejszyszki (nearly three-fourths of which were women and children) were led to the Jewish cemetery and shot at specially prepared pits (Gilbert, 1994). Entire Jewish-Polish communities were deported and gassed during 1942.

The Warsaw Ghetto. After Hitler invaded Poland, he annexed sections of the country and kept up his assault of the Jews. The Germans set up ghettos, committed mass murders, and established concentration camps and death camps in Poland and eastern Europe. These ghettoes provided slave labor for the Nazi war machine, placing people in German offices, installations, and workshops. In some places wages were not paid; in others, a minimal sum per day was offered.

Jews had lived in Poland since the 1300s. Although many lived in the large cities, by 1939 four hundred thousand Jews were living in Warsaw, the largest Jewish population of any European city. A large number also were living in thousands of small towns and villages in Poland and Russia. In these areas, the Jews formed separate and identifiable communities. Many cities and towns to the west had Jewish quarters, while some small villages were entirely Jewish.

An official announcement on September 20, 1939, ordered all Jews into special places created for them in the major cities of occupied Poland. The first ghetto, a little over 1.5 miles square in area, was in Lodz. More than 150,000 Jews lived in this ghetto under extremely crowded conditions.

In Warsaw, the ghetto was one hundred square blocks or 1.6 square miles and was contained by walls. Jews moving into the ghetto could bring only bedding, clothing, pots and pans, and a few basic items. The Poles who left the area of the ghetto, however, could take whatever they wanted. After the Jews moved in, they discovered that it was to be a closed ghetto. This meant that they would need Nazi permission to go in or out. Living in this ghetto were more than half a million Jews, including more than one hundred thousand children under the age of fifteen.

People within the ghetto had to depend on the Germans for food, which usually consisted of only bread and potatoes. The Nazis would often reduce and restrict these food rations, using the threat of starvation to control the people. The daily ration was 220 calories, approximately 15 percent of the normal requirement. In 1940, ninety people were dead of starvation. By the second year, eleven thousand had died of starvation (Rogasky, 1988). In addition to lack of food, people suffered the effects of the weather. The first winter was one of the coldest on record, but fuel was not allowed to be shipped into the ghetto. An epidemic of typhus soon spread, killing many. Life in the ghetto became even more restrictive when the Nazis forbid the people from holding worship services or from sending their children to school.

Because life in the ghetto offered very little choice—if you steal, you die quickly by a bullet; if you don't, you die slowly of hunger—the Jews built underground tunnels to the other side of the walls. These connected to sewer lines. Each day people would leave the ghetto through these secret tunnels to search for food. Because they were small, many children became successful at smuggling food.

By 1942, several of the resistance groups within the ghetto had banded together under the leadership of Pinya Kartin. On "Bloody Friday," April 17, 1942, the SS rounded up and shot fifty Jews whom they suspected to be anti-German activists. During July 1942, the SS announced that "unproductive" Jews would be moving to the east. They rounded up those in jails and orphanages, and some of the homeless. Six thousand people were moved to railroad cars and taken away. The next day, another six thousand were packed into railroad cars. The daily quotas increased and often included children. By September, three hundred thousand people had been taken from the ghetto and sent to their deaths at the camp in Treblinka.

On April 18, 1943, the remaining Polish Jews who had been incarcerated in the Warsaw ghetto organized themselves to fight back against the Nazi oppressors. While the Germans were preparing eight hundred soldiers to destroy the ghetto, a small group of armed resistance fighters prepared to meet them. At six the next morning, when the German troops came through the gates, the Jews were ready and fired the first shots. When darkness fell, the Germans withdrew. On April 20, the second day, General Jürgen Stroop led thirteen hundred German soldiers into the ghetto. The fighting continued block by block. Over the next month, the German troops razed the ghetto and the resistance was broken.

The Camps. In each of the conquered countries, Hitler attacked the Jews. They were arrested, herded into freight cars, and sent to concentration or death camps. By late 1941, the "final solution" was in effect. Hitler and his staff had built centers and were prepared to exterminate millions. Men, women, and children were sent by trainloads to the camps. Those who were healthy and strong were assigned to slave labor until they were exhausted and weak. Those who were unable to work were sent to scientifically constructed gas chambers where they were gassed and their bodies burned (Friedman, 1990). Scientists and doctors subjected some of the inmates to untested experimental procedures.

Jews were not the only people sent to concentration camps. Christians who resisted Nazism, Gypsies, and homosexuals were also rounded up and incarcerated, and nearly twenty-three hundred priests and pastors from nineteen occupied countries were sent to Dachau (Friedman, 1990). Of the three million non-Jewish Poles killed during World War II, more than one-third were among the most educated and creative people in that country.

Not only did the Nazis want to get rid of the Jews, but they wanted it to be economically profitable to do so. The extermination machinery was to pay for itself using stolen Jewish property and by having the Jews help build and repair the camps. On one of the gates at the entrance to the camp at Auschwitz was a sign reading *Arbeit Macht Frei!* which translates as "Work Means Freedom!" A sign at Buchenwald read *Jedem Das Sein,* meaning "Each Gets What He Deserves."

Once inside the camps, people were herded into huge rooms where all of their clothes, jewelry, and money were taken. They were bullied, their heads were shaved, and they were sent into showers to be disinfected and given clothes taken from others who had been killed or uniforms made of rough cloth. Then each was assigned a number. Auschwitz prisoners had their numbers tattooed in blue ink on their left forearms. Rogasky (1988, p. 89) reports a young survivor recalling a camp leader's words:

From now on you have no identity.
You have no place of origin.
All you have is a number.
Except for the number you have nothing.

Food rations in the camps were below subsistence level. Prisoners starved, died of disease, and were beaten and ridiculed by prison guards. They were forced to work until they had no strength left, and many were selected for the gas chambers.

Some did not even make it into the camps. At Auschwitz, people were marched off the train and quickly sorted into two lines. One line allowed people to live, even though it was under the harsh conditions of the camp. The other line, however, led to a building marked "Wash and Disinfection Room." The building actually was a gas chamber. Women and children were pushed and beaten into the "showers." Once everyone was inside, pellets of poisoned gas were thrown in or gas was dispensed through the showerheads. Within fifteen or twenty minutes, all were dead. As cars carried away the corpses to be burned, the chamber was washed and made ready for the next column. The ashes were buried, spread on roads, or used as fertilizer. The trains that brought the new arrivals carried away those who were left alive to work as slave laborers in Germany or elsewhere.

The Nazi death machine was very efficient. For example, at Terezin, a camp for children, of the approximately fifteen thousand children under the age of fifteen who were sent there, only about a hundred came back. The German army estimated that it had captured more than five million Russian prisoners of war. By 1944, only about two million were still alive. The numbers killed at each death camp are incomprehensible. For example, at Chelmo there were 360,000 victims and three survivors, and at Belzec there were 600,000 victims and two survivors. Inmates at other camps fared only slightly better. At Sobibor there were 250,000 victims and sixty-four survivors; at Maidanek, with 500,000 victims, fewer than six hundred survived. At Auschwitz, which was both a concentration camp and a death camp, one and a half to two million people died and only several thousand survived (Rogasky, 1988).

Those who survived the camps did so by learning to steal to buy or exchange what little they could find for food. Survivors tell about the close attachments they formed. One prisoner would help hide another inmate

North
Sea

Baltic Sea

Klooga
Vaivara
ESTONIA

LATVIA

LITHUANIA

USSR

Stutthof

Neuengamme
Ravensbrück
Bergen-Belsen
Sachsenhausen
Chelmno
Trablinka
POLAND
Mittelbau Dora
Gross Rosen
Buchenwald
Sobibor
Auschwitz
Maidanek
GERMANY
Flossenberg
Plaszow
Belzec
Natzweiler
CZECHOSLOVAKIA
FRANCE
Dachau
Mauthausen
AUSTRIA
HUNGARY
ROMANIA

Gospic
Jasenovac
YUGOSLAVIA
Sajmiste
ITALY
Adriatic Sea

Auschwitz Concentration camp in which more than 2 million people were murdered between 1941 and 1944, including Jews, Gypsies, and Soviet prisoners-of-war.

Camps set up solely for the murder of Jews.

Other camps in which Jews and non-Jews were put to forced labor, starved, tortured, and murdered in conditions of the worst imagineable cruelty. Most of these camps had "satellite" labour camps nearby.

who was sick during selection for the gas chambers; rations would be shared with weaker prisoners. Despite the harshness of the physical conditions, some wrote poetry or music and the children played games.

Righteous Gentiles or Non-Jews. Not all people in Europe supported Hitler or the Nazis. Many helped the Jews and others to avoid being captured, sometimes at the risk of their own lives. These people were called "Righteous Gentiles" by the Jews. Spain, which had friendly relations with Germany during the war, saved

forty thousand Jews by allowing them to enter the country. Italian officials gave Jewish refugees false identity papers so that they could pass as Catholics. Japan offered Jewish refugees sanctuary in Shanghai. In Warsaw, approximately eighteen thousand Jews were hidden and fed by the Poles who lived there.

Sweden, a neutral country, provided haven for many Jews from Norway and offered to restore citizenship to all Norwegian Jews who had once been citizens of Sweden. Sweden also invited arrested Jews to become citizens.

Denmark, because its citizens were considered to be Aryans, was allowed by the Nazis to keep its own government and was not subject to anti-Jewish legislation until late 1942, when it was occupied for the first time. Hearing rumors of an action to deport the Jews, the citizens contributed money, food, shelter, and boats to ferry them to Sweden and safety. More than half of Norway's Jews made it to safety in Sweden with the help of Norwegian resistance. Although four hundred Danish Jews were caught and sent to a concentration camp, where fifty-one died of natural causes, all eight thousand Danish Jews survived the war (Meltzer, 1988; Rogasky, 1988).

Raoul Wallenberg is credited with saving thousands of Jews. He was a Swedish aristocrat who worked in the embassy in Budapest, Hungary. In this position, he designed and printed thousands of Swedish citizenship papers, which he then gave to Jews. He bought houses and apartments where these new "Swedish citizens" lived. He flew the flag of neutral Sweden to protect his Hungarian ghetto, which may have housed as many as thirty-three thousand Jews. He also was able to get food and clothing to Jews on deportation trains and sometimes removed them from death marches.

Bauer (1982) lists others who are included on the Avenue of the Righteous at Yad Vashem, the memorial to the Holocaust in Jerusalem. Otto Busse, a director of a German factory in Bialystok, smuggled food into the ghetto and helped the resistance fighters. Paul Grinninger, a Swiss border police officer near St. Gallen, allowed many Jews to cross illegally into Switzerland. Anna Shimaite, a Lithuanian, hid Jewish cultural treasures.

Survivors. On April 30, 1945, Hitler committed suicide in Berlin and Germany surrendered on May 7. The war was over and the camps opened. When the Allies liberated the camps, they found thousands of unburied bodies, as well as many people so sick, starved, and weak that they were barely alive. Having lost from 50 to 60 percent of their normal body weight, many died when they were fed by the Allies because their bodies could not handle the rich food.

The survivors had no homes. Their communities were destroyed, and frequently they were the only survivors left from large families or even entire communities. Many were sent to displaced person's camps, where they were cared for by organizations such as the United Nations, the Quakers, the Red Cross, and Jewish relief agencies. For a long time, many survivors did not have any other place to go. They did not want to return to the bitter memories associated with their homelands, nor would the United States or many European countries allow them to immigrate. Many of the survivors finally went to Palestine, the country that is now Israel.

Memories still linger for survivors and those who are the children of these survivors. The poem "Speaking for Others" was written in their honor.

Speaking for Others

There's a part of my life you don't know about
Asleep under my father's coffin, far from the Mount of Olives.
In darkness it mingles with broken glass and bones
That still ache from untimely separations.
This life you know nothing about
Owns an old violin that sang Beethoven
And a prosthesis that kept time to old drinking songs;
It keeps pictures of distant European cousins in a pocket:
Folded over and over and over, one upon the other,
Their faces have worn away.
The life hidden from you
Wanders empty streets like a blind tourist
Groping for a family scattered to the winds
In a land that turns strangers to dust.
That life of secrets carries old books to unlock mysteries of space and self:
A Berlin Telephone Directory, 1937, numbers long since disconnected.
A World Atlas, 1930, with many obscure, mourning dots,
Their names lost to darkened memories and large erasers
A Who's Who, 1935, of authors later burned beside their books.
The part of my life of which you know nothing
Sings Lamentations and Tehilim,
Shredding page after page with gnarled, twisted hands,
Shedding tear after tear of salted poisons
That mingle with the earth,
Sowing gravestones, the dried leaves of a family tree.
    —Rabbi Keith Stern

Reprinted with permission of Rabbi Stern; written for Yom Hoshoa, 1993, Fort Worth, Texas

Instructional Activities

A portfolio is a systematic collection of artifacts that demonstrate learning or achievement. In addition to the collection of artifacts or projects, one item should be the learner's evaluation of the products within this portfolio and a reflection about the learning that took place.

For this unit, the student will produce a portfolio containing demonstrations of learning activities as well as an evaluation about the value of the projects in an attempt to understand the lessons of the Holocaust. After completing a variety of activities, the student will write or in some way demonstrate his or her understanding of the lesson to be learned by studying the Holocaust.

There will be three types of activities: (1) activities that focus on the historical facts related to this period of time, (2) activities that help students to develop empathy or an understanding of the human aspect, and (3) social action and critical thinking activities.

Activity 8.1: Historical Background

After consulting several factual sources of information about the Holocaust, the student will choose two of the following: (1) make a map of the territories controlled by the Allied and Axis powers; (2) make a map of the locations of concentration camps and explain why they were located at these places; (3) complete a chart that lists the number of people killed at each of the concentration camps, including the various categories of non-Jews; or (4) construct a timeline of the events that led to the Holocaust. An example of a time line is shown here.

Activity 8.2: Understanding the Human Element

The student will have at least one type of vicarious experience which will help him or her understand the feelings of people who were living through the Holocaust. Two activities are suggested here.

1. The student will read a book of fiction, poetry, historical recounts, or oral histories, or view films related to the Holocaust, and then respond in some way. The response may be written, artistic, or media centered.
2. The student will take part in a role-playing drama to learn what it would be like to live in an occupied country. O'Neill (1985) has designed a learning activity which she used with a group of fourteen-year-old students in London. The role-playing drama within this report may be employed.

Activity 8.3: Synthesis, Evaluation, or Social Action

The student will choose at least one of the activities described here.

TIMELINE

1939:   Germany invades Poland.

War declared on Germany by Great Britain, France, Australia, and New Zealand.

1940:   Germany invades Denmark, Norway, Belgium, Luxembourg, and the Netherlands.

Italy declares war on Britain and France.

France surrenders to Germany.

1941:   Germany invades Russia, captures Kiev.

Etc: _____

Charting the "Negative Actions" That Led to the Holocaust. Rossel (1981) compares the stages of prejudice from the book by Allport (1954), *The Nature of Prejudice,* to the events of the Holocaust. In this book, Allport examines the "negative actions" that result from prejudice: speech, avoidance, discrimination, physical attack, and extermination. Rossel compares the stages in the Holocaust to these steps. For example, stereotyped drawings of Jews date from the end of the 1600s, and Nazis often spoke about Jews as a "disease" or as "lice." Using this example, the students will construct a diagram showing examples of events within the Holocaust which support the theory of Allport on the "negative actions" resulting from prejudice. The student will then add a column that recounts similar negative actions toward a current minority somewhere in the world.

Recommending Social Action. At the time of the Holocaust, many people had heard rumors of what was happening to the Jews in Germany and in the occupied countries, yet very little was done to stop this annihilation. Martin Numoller, a Protestant minister, is given credit for the following:

> The Nazis came first for the communists. But I wasn't a communist, so I didn't speak up. Then they came for the Jews, but I wasn't a Jew so I didn't speak up. Then they came for the trade unionists, but I wasn't a trade unionist so I didn't speak up. Then they came for the Catholics, but I was a Protestant so I didn't speak up. Then they came for me. By that time there was no one left to speak up.

CHARTING THE ACTIONS OF PREJUDICE

Negative Action	Holocaust	(Other)
Speech	"lice," "disease"	slant eyes
Avoidance	_____	_____
Discrimination	_____	_____
Physical attack	_____	_____
Extermination	_____	_____

WHAT COULD/SHOULD HAVE BEEN THE WORLD'S RESPONSE?

Action	Probable Consequence	Positive/Negative Results
Offer to ransom the Jews.	Jews would be bought and sent to other countries.	The price might escalate. Money used to fight the Allies.
_____	_____	_____
_____	_____	_____
_____	_____	_____

Activity suggested by work in Swartz & Black (1991).

Brainstorm possible actions that individuals, countries, or international organizations could have done to prevent or stop the Holocaust. Determine what the consequences of such action might have been. Decide whether the probable or possible results would be worth the risk. When you have completed this analysis, present a position paper requesting immediate social action. The students also will write an essay that explains which of the calls to action they would support and why they would support such action.

What Makes a Hero? At the time of the Holocaust, there were people who were willing to risk their own freedom and lives to hide or save Jews or political refugees. The student will read first-, or third-person accounts of "Righteous Gentiles" who saved Jews. While reading these accounts, the student will focus on the psychological aspects of the hero. For each account,

a reader could summarize what made that person risk his or her life for others. Several readers can form a group to determine whether there are generalizable characteristics that can be used to predict what type of person would be willing to sacrifice all for social justice or so that others might survive.

For the More Mature Student. The mature student should begin to understand the type of data used by social scientists to interpret events. This activity is intended to give these students the opportunity to locate the types of evidence that are used for historical research and determine its limitations.

The Fort Worth *Star-Telegram* on Saturday, July 17, 1993, carried a wire report that stated that France for the first time would commemorate the round-up of thirteen thousand Jews who were jammed into a Paris stadium and then shipped to Auschwitz fifty-one years before. The article stated that approximately seventy-six thousand French Jews were deported during World War II, but only about twenty-five hundred survived.

Some people claim that the Holocaust did not happen. Starting with the news article above, what evidence could you collect to determine whether the facts are correct? What is the reliability of this evidence? Based on the evidence, what is your position on whether the Holocaust took place? What is the type of evidence you accepted to support your position? How have you verified this evidence?

References and Bibliography

Adler, D. (1989). *We remember the Holocaust.* New York: Henry Holt. Discusses the Holocaust, including personal accounts of survivors of the concentration camps.

Allport, G. (1954). *The nature of prejudice.* Cambridge, MA: Addison-Wesley.

Bauer, Y. (1982). *A history of the Holocaust.* New York: Franklin Watts.

Bernbaum, I. (1985). *My brother's keeper. The Holocaust through the eyes of an artist.* New York: G. P. Putnam's Sons.

Chaikin, M. (1987). *A nightmare in history: The Holocaust 1933–1945.* New York: Clarion Books.

Dolan, E. (1985). *Anti-Semitism.* New York: Franklin Watts.

Eisen, G. (1988). *Children and play in the Holocaust: Games among the shadows.* Amherst: University of Massachusetts Press.

Emmerich, E., with Hull, R. (1991). *My childhood in Nazi Germany.* New York: Bookwright Press.

Gairns, T. (1983). *The twentieth century. The Cambridge introduction to history.* Minneapolis: Lerner Publications and Cambridge University Press.

Gilbert, M. (1994). *The Holocaust. A record of the destruction of Jewish life in Europe during the dark years of Nazi rule.* (3rd Ed.) New York: Anti-Defamation League.

Gilbert, M. (1985). *The Holocaust: A history of the Jews of Europe during the second world war.* New York: Holt, Rinehart and Winston.

Goodrich, F. (Ed.). (1956). *The diary of Anne Frank.* New York: Random House.

Graff, S. (1978). *The story of World War II.* New York: E. P. Dutton.

Gurdus, L. (1978). *The death train: A personal account of a Holocaust survivor.* New York: Holocaust Library.

Finkelstein, N. (1985). *Remember not to forget. A memory of the Holocaust.* New York: Franklin Watts.

Flaim, R., Reynolds, E., et al., (Eds.). (1986). *The Holocaust and genocide: A search for conscience.* New York: Anti-Defamation League of B'nai Brith.

Friedman, I. (1990). *The other victims. First person stories of non-Jews persecuted by the Nazis.* Boston: Houghton Mifflin.

Klein, G. (1957). *All but my life.* New York: Hill and Wang.

Klinger, R., & Mann, P. (1978). *The secret ship.* Garden City, NJ: Doubleday.

Lowrie, D. (1963). *The hunted children.* New York: W. W. Norton. Story of Jewish refugees to France and the relief agencies that developed, saving tens of thousands of lives.

Meltzer, M. (1976). *Never to forget: the Jews of the Holocaust.* New York: Harper & Row.

Meltzer, M. (1988). *Rescue: The story of how Gentiles saved Jews in the Holocaust.* New York: Harper & Row. Record of the many individual acts of heroism committed by non-Jews to rescue Jews from the Holocaust.

Merriam-Webster's Collegiate Dictionary. (1993). 10th ed. Springfield, MA: Merriam-Webster.

Muffs, J., & Klein, D. (Eds.). (1986). *The Holocaust in books and films: A selected and annotated list.* New York: Hippocrene Books.

Nomberg-Przytyk, S. (1985). In Pfefferkorn, E., & Hirsch, D. H. (Eds.). *Auschwitz: True tales from a grotesque land.* Chapel Hill: University of North Carolina Press.

O'Neill, C. (1985). Imagined worlds in theatre and drama. *Theory into Practice,* 24(3), pp. 161–164.

Rabinsky, L., & Mann, G. (1979). *Journey of conscience: Young people respond to the Holocaust.* Cleveland: William Collins.

Rogasky, B. (1988). *Smoke and ashes: the story of the Holocaust.* New York: Holiday House.

Rosenfield, A. (Ed.). (1992). *Fifty years ago: Revolt amid the darkness.* Washington, DC: United States Holocaust Memorial Museum.

Rossel, S. (1981). *The Holocaust.* New York: Franklin Watts. Details the rise of Hitler and the history and mechanisms of prejudice.

Santayana, G. (1981). *Life of reason.* New York: Macmillan.

Siegal, A. (1981). *Upon the head of the goat: A childhood in Hungary, 1939–1944.* New York: Farrar, Straus & Giroux. In this Newbery Honor Book, the author tells how she and her family were able to survive during World War II.

Stein, R. C. (1985). *World at war. Warsaw ghetto.* Chicago: Childrens Press.

Swartz, R., & Black, S. (1991). *Infusing critical and creative thinking into content instruction.* Paper presented at Conference on Critical Thinking and Educational Reform, Sonoma, CA.

Szonyi, D. (Ed.). (1985). *The Holocaust: An annotated bibliography and resource guide.* New York: KTAV.

Unsdorfer, S. (1983). *The yellow stars.* New York: Feldheim. Account of the author's experiences in Nazi concentration camps and factories during the Holocaust.

Vegh, C. (Trans.). (1984). *I didn't say goodbye: Interviews with children of the Holocaust.* New York: E. P. Dutton. Accounts by twenty-eight French men and women about their experiences of losing one or both parents as children during the Holocaust.

Yolen, J. (1988). *The devil's arithmetic.* New York: Viking Kestrel.

Yolen, J. (1992). *Briar rose.* New York: Tom Doherty Associates. Part of the Tor Fairy Tale series; the tale of Sleeping Beauty superimposed on a story of the Holocaust.

Zar, R. (1983). *In the mouth of the wolf.* Philadelphia: Jewish Publication Society of America. Author's story of how she lived using false papers as a housekeeper for an SS officer during World War II. Following her father's advice that the best place to hide is in the mouth of the wolf, she was able to escape being murdered during the Holocaust.

Zeinert, K. (1993). *The Warsaw ghetto uprising.* Brookfield, CT: Millbrook Press. Describes life in the Warsaw ghetto where Polish Jews were confined by the Nazis. Discusses the activities of the Jewish resistance there before its complete destruction by the Nazis in 1943.

I never saw another butterfly: Children's drawings and poems from Teretzin concentration camp, 1942–1944. (1978). New York: Schocken Books.

Guidelines for teaching about the Holocaust. (1993). Washington, DC: United States Holocaust Memorial Museum.

An Afterword: The Jews as a Race

Although we use the term "anti-Semitism" to discuss prejudice against the Jews, the authors know that Jews do not consider themselves to be a separate race, nor has there ever been any evidence that they belong to a separate race. Jews are a religious, ethnic, and cultural group that originated in the area that is presently Israel. Jews come in all descriptions: some are dark haired and dark eyed; others are blond or have blue eyes. Judaism is a religion. Jewish rabbis consider anyone born from a Jewish mother or who has gone through the process of conversion to be a Jew.

Those who follow the traditional practices of Judaism adhere to dietary restrictions, worship, and hold holiday and Sabbath practices that set them apart from their non-Jewish neighbors. Some Jews in eastern Europe dress in a style that further sets them apart from their neighbors. For these reasons, Jews have been identified as a group and have frequently tended to live together in communities. Therefore, they were a visible target.

April's Potpourri of Teaching Ideas

The purpose of each month's Potpourri of Teaching Ideas is to provide additional resources from which to build your curriculum. Most, but not all, of the activities listed each month relate directly to that month. It is not intended that you use them all, but rather that you choose those which are appropriate for your program. Although the topics are written for a particular month, many of them would be appropriate for use throughout the year. How you use these activities will depend on your curricular goals. You may wish to use some of the activities as they are presented, and you may need to modify some to meet your needs. Perhaps some of them will give you ideas for entirely different potpourris.

Children of the Holocaust: They Kept Their Spirit

During the Holocaust of World War II, many Jewish children were killed outright or sent to various concentration or death camps. Even under these extreme conditions, children continued to play many of the same games they knew when they lived under less harsh conditions. They drew pictures, composed poetry and prose, sang songs, and played games devised using their limited resources.

Even in the ghettos without parks or open areas to play, parents encouraged children play in empty lots or streets where the rubble of destroyed buildings had been cleared away. During this infamous time, the Nazis built special children's homes with playgrounds, even while planning the execution of the inhabitants. In some of the camps and ghettos, there was debate as to whether the children should be allowed to play, dance, or sing in the presence of the constant death that surrounded them.

In the ghettos, children had to invent their own toys and games. Some have reported inventing toys and games in their imaginations and playing with these. Others have told of regarding cigarette boxes as prized toys, using the colorful tops as playing cards. In one ghetto, children used small pieces of wood that they could hold in their hands to play like castanets.

Many of the games mimicked scenes the children saw inside the ghettos. For example, in the game "Coming Through the Gate," they would act out the procedures followed by workers leaving and returning to the ghetto. Girls would pretend to be mothers standing in line for food rations.

Try This: Invent a game that can be played in a small space and which uses only natural materials found in the schoolyard or another area. Hop scotch is a good example, because this game can be played by making a diagram in dirt and using stones as markers. Singing games, riddles, and games using pebbles or stones might be developed. Write out the equipment necessary and the rules for your game, then demonstrate how to play it.

Suggested Readings

Eisen, G. (1988). *Children and play in the Holocaust.* Amherst: University of Massachusetts Press.

April: A Month for Fools, Jesters, and Tricksters

Most of your students will be especially cautious and leery on the first day of April. Some, however, may have a sly, cunning look on their face, revealing unwittingly that they are about to play a trick on someone. Perhaps the ones to really look out for are those with an innocent, even angelic, visage. These individuals are likely to be the most devious tricksters of all.

April Fool's Day has been celebrated for generations, and playing tricks on this day is a customary practice in many countries. While the particulars of inflicting or avoiding such pranks may vary, the label for those who fall prey to the tricks is not complimentary. In the United States, one who falls for a trick is labeled an "April Fool"; in England the title of "noddy" is applied; and in France one is ridiculed as an "April fish," possibly because one who is so gullible is as easily caught as a newly hatched fish.

Playing tricks or pranks on someone else, and even laughing at another's expense, has long been a human characteristic. Indeed, humor and laughter have always been part of the human scene, and we have always appreciated (unless we happened to be the one on the receiving end of such a trick) the prankster or "practical joker."

In earlier times, there were those who became court jesters as a means of earning their keep when times were difficult. Some of these individuals may have suffered from physical handicaps, which at the time was thought to make them appear all the more ludicrous. This type of humor was often gained at the expense or embarrassment of the one who was the brunt of the joke.

Try This: Involve your students in the study of humor and noted tricksters, both actual and fictional, who have gained notoriety through the ages. It is equally appropriate to use this activity during this time of year to discuss the undesirable side effects of such tricks and jokes. Frequently, tricks are played on those who are different, for example, those with some physical or emotional handicap that makes them an easy target. Jokes about them often elicit laughter and ridicule. Unfortunately, ethnic humor is almost endemic throughout the world. The same joke or story appears in many garbs and in many languages. Such jokes are almost generic in their nature, and one group merely plugs in the name of another group that is held in low regard.

This activity would involve "sharing" such humor and expressing the feelings that one has when subjected to such ridicule. You could lead your students by helping them recognize cruel and hurtful jokes and have them suggest ways that they, as a class or as individual

students, could reduce the incidence of such jokes, not only in the school, but in the community as a whole.

The Ugly Duckling: Hans Christian Andersen

Hans Christian Andersen was born the son of a poor shoemaker in Denmark on April 2, 1805. His father often read to him in the evenings from *The Arabian Nights* and other works of literature. Hans had a small puppet theater and would often entertain his friends and family with plays he had written.

Shortly after his father's death, when Hans was fourteen, he went to Copenhagen to become an actor and poet. He was a awkward lad, lanky, big-nosed, and with a voice that was high and thin—not the qualities usually found in great actors. He met with disappointment and failure again and again. He was eventually awarded a scholarship from the king to study writing. In 1835, in need of money, he wrote four fairy tales, not really his first love in literature, but they brought him fame and fortune.

Some of his best-known works include "The Emperor's New Clothes," "The Little Mermaid," "The Red Shoes," and, of course, "The Ugly Duckling." Andersen said that his life was a beautiful fairy tale, rich and happy. However, "The Ugly Duckling" more accurately describes his own life. He was often ill and unhappy and had an obsessive fear of accidents, murder, and robbery. On display in the Hans Christian Andersen Museum in his hometown of Odense is the rope that he carried with him at all times in case he needed to escape a hotel fire.

The "ugly duckling" finally grew up to be a "swan," except for one major disappointment. He had hoped to marry the Swedish singer, Jenny Lind, but that never happened. Consequently, he never married, and the only children he had were those who loved his stories. Before he died at age seventy, despite a life filled with much unhappiness, he was recognized as a great teller of tales and was given the honor due him by his countrymen and the children of the world. He asked a friend once to compose a march to be used at his funeral. He told the friend that most of the people who would walk after him would be children. He said to his friend, "Make the beat keep time with little steps." Children around the world are still marching to the beat of Andersen's works, perhaps some of the best-loved literature of all time.

Try These Activities

1. Have a Hans Christian Andersen Day. The students may select their favorite Andersen tale to share with the class. If you have an older group of students, they could share their stories with a group of

younger children. Many teachers report positive results when older students (fifth grade and above) are paired with younger ones (second grade and below) for a time of reading and sharing.

2. What happened to the *son?* Ask your students to explore why Hans's family spelled their name *Andersen* rather than *Anderson.* What does the spelling tell one about the origin of his name?

3. Read and discuss "The Emperor's New Clothes." Ask your students to give examples they have encountered of people who have been involved in gullible situations. What is meant when someone says, "He doesn't have any clothes on," or "The Emperor is naked?"

Suggested Reading

Fadiman, C. (Ed.). (1984). *The world treasury of children's literature, book two.* Boston: Little, Brown.

Unsung Heroes with "Social Courage"

When we think of the heroes associated with a group of people or a nation, they are frequently those who have accomplished great feats of strength, valor, or courage in the military arena. Examples of heroes include Washington, Grant, and General Patton. Other nations and cultures have similar individuals who are honored in this regard. These heroes are heralded because their exploits resulted in benefit to their native lands.

Other individuals are esteemed because of a successful series of adventures in which they overcame great odds, either in terms of other human foes, or in the case of certain mythological heroes such as Hercules, against creatures ferocious to behold or obstacles seemingly insurmountable. In this case, the hero is admired for the sake of his heroic efforts alone. Increasingly, such heroes may be athletes whose feats of physical ability seem to rival those of ancient legendary figures.

While any of these heroes may be held up as a model to be emulated, other types of heroes are less likely to be esteemed and valued. If, however, a hero is one whose actions are courageous (and someone who stands for an unpopular, but just, cause surely is courageous), then there are many individuals who qualify as heroes. In many cases, the benefits that resulted from their actions were more significant, as well as longer lasting, than the accomplishments of military conquerors or sports legends.

These individuals are those who engaged in activities aimed at improving the social conditions of groups of people or who were concerned with assisting people who had less than full status within the society. Often these individuals stood against the intellectual currents of their times and took unpopular and perhaps dangerous positions on issues of significance. Many of these figures are not contained in lists of important people included in texts, although many eventually received the recognition that they deserved. Among those that we honor are Martin Luther King, Jr., a giant in the area of civil rights, and Dorothea Dix, who worked so diligently to improve the conditions and the care given to the mentally ill.

Many of these heroes have risked ridicule and, in some cases, even physical threats to ameliorate the conditions under which their contemporaries lived. For example, Cesar Chávez endangered his health in his attempts throughout his life to bring the nation's attention to the plight of migrant workers, who were not only underpaid but were forced to live under atrocious conditions. It takes a hero to stand against injustice.

While Americans have their heroes, other nations are able to point to those who have been active in their societies as well. Born during this month was Jagjivan Ram, perhaps less known than his associates, Ghandi and Nehru, but who served the interest of the vast class of "untouchables" in India.

After students have conducted their inquiries, the results can be shared with the class in many ways, either as charts, as messages over the school public address system, or as short biographical vignettes.

This particular activity could serve as an introduction to a more general discussion of heroes: which members of society ought to be held in high esteem. There are two possible criteria to use in determining who are the heroes of a group. First, an individual's actions should result in some marked benefit to that person's culture or group. Second, the individual should demonstrate a significant degree of courage despite great odds. Other factors might be taken into account as well—for example, the significance of the "odds" or barriers that would impede one's efforts and performance. These barriers or handicaps may be physical, social, or political. Who should be held in higher esteem: one with great talent and ability who accomplished a high level of performance, but through greater effort, could have accomplished much more, or the person of lesser talent and ability who had to fight against intolerance and prejudice to accomplish gains for his cause?

The Enlightened One

Buddhism was founded in India by a Hindu prince, Siddhartha Gautama, about twenty-five hundred years ago. When he was a young man, he thought that life was filled with suffering and unhappiness. He left his wife and son and lived the life of a wandering monk, seeking religious enlightenment. While traveling through northern India, he became "enlightened" as to how people could escape from the life of suffering and unhappiness. Buddhists believe in reincarnation, hoping to reach Nirvana, the state of being free from pain and suffering.

Buddha, as Siddhartha Gautama became known, preached that each person's position in this life is determined by his or her behavior during a previous life. If one was evil in a previous life, in this life one would be a poor and sickly person. People can achieve perfect peace and happiness, or Nirvana, by ridding themselves of attachment to worldly things. To do this, one must follow the path of the Middle Way and the Noble Eightfold Path. This Noble Eightfold Path consists of knowing the truth, intending to resist evil, saying nothing to hurt others, respecting life, holding a job that does not hurt others, freeing one's mind of evil, controlling one's own thoughts, and practicing forms of meditation.

Buddhists celebrate two spring festivals: Songkran, the Buddhist new year; and Visakha Puja, the celebration of the birth, enlightenment, and passing into Nirvana of Buddha.

In Japan and Sri Lanka (Ceylon), the holiday commemorating the birth, enlightenment, and death of Buddha is called Wesak. In Japan, Buddhists observe the birth of Buddha by visiting shrines dedicated to Buddha and decorating them with fresh flowers. They also hold parades. Children wear flowers in their hair and have their faces painted or powdered white to show they are pure before Buddha. This holiday is also called Hana Matsuri, or flower festival. In Sri Lanka, public buildings and houses are decorated with lights.

During the summer, there is the Feast of Lanterns for the Dead, called O-Bon. Originally a Buddhist service, in Japan its purpose is to keep alive the memory of ancestors. Older family members may follow the custom of placing food and water in front of pictures of deceased relatives. At night, there is a dance to mark the end of the festival. The dance is held at the shrine or temple and lasts until dawn.

In Hawaii, the O-Bon Festival is celebrated in July or August. There, dances and lanterns are used to express joy and fellowship. Lantern ceremonies close the O-Bon celebration.

In the United States, Buddhists at the Todaiji temple hold a short mass and then the congregants launch several hundred small wooden boats decorated with colored lanterns and filled with food, incense, and memorial tables with the names of ancestors written on them.

Try This: Determine the ways in which the major religions of the world are the same and the ways in which they differ.

Suggested Readings

Burnett, B. (1983). *The first book of holidays.* (rev. ed.). New York: Franklin Watts.
Reynolds, F. (1986). Buddhism. In *The World Book Encyclopedia* (Vol. 2). Chicago: World Book.
Spier, P. (1980). *People.* Garden City, NJ: Doubleday.

RELIGIONS: ALIKE OR DIFFERENT?

Religion	Founder	Year	Major Beliefs	Important Holy Days
Buddhism				
Christianity				
Confucianism				
Hinduism				
Judaism				
Mohammedanism or Muslim				
Shintoism				
Sikhism				
Taoism				

Chapter 9
Welcome Faire, Fresshe May

A S DID CHAUCER in *The Canterbury Tales*, we "welcome faire, fresshe May." For it is after the showers of April that we can enjoy the flowers that "bloom in May," at least in the more temperate regions of the Northern Hemisphere. In earlier times, the beginning of this month often included festive occasions in which young people decorated with garlands of flowers would dance around a "may pole" that had been erected. Many of the parents or grandparents of your students likely participated in such events, and some even may have been selected as the "queen" of such festivities. May Day was a holiday of sorts in many countries. As the May Day-type activities that occurred in communist-dominated countries became more marked, however, there was more hesitancy in the West to celebrate this traditional festival.

Indeed, the very term "Mayday" came to be used as a signal of distress or danger. For example, if an aircraft or vessel was stricken with some sort of emergency, the message "Mayday" was sent as an indication of the immediacy and extent of the situation: "We are in trouble—lots of it!" was the message intended.

May is a month in which countries such as Japan, Norway, and Poland commemorate the establishment of their constitutions. Many countries, including Paraguay, Norway, Chad, Zambia, Argentina, and Jordan, celebrate their independence during this month.

Other countries celebrate military victories. Cinco de Mayo (May 5) is a day when all of Mexico recalls the Battle of Puebla. The countries that fought on the Allied side during World War II recall the eighth of May as V-E Day, the day on which hostilities ended in Europe. The last Monday in May is when the United States remembers all of those who have given their lives in the defense of our country.

Sunday	Monday	Tuesday	Wednesday	Thursday	Friday	Saturday

May

MAY

SELECTED EVENTS

1   May Day
    Mary Harris Jones (1830–1930)
2   Mary Cassatt (1844–1926)
    "Bing" Crosby (1904–1977)
3   Japanese Constitution Memorial Day
    Poland Constitution Day
4   Horace Mann (1796–1859)
5   Mexican Cinco de Mayo
    Karl Marx (1818–1883)
6   Robert E. Peary (1856–1920)
7   Johannes Brahms (1833–1897)
    Robert Browning (1812–1889)
8   V-E Day (Victory in Europe Day)
    Jean Henri Dunant (1828–1910)
9   European Common Market created (1950)
    John Brown (1800–1859)
10 Driving of the "Golden Spike"
11 Salvador Dali (1904–1989)
    Martha Graham (1894–1990)
12 Edward Lear (1812–1888)
    Florence Nightingale (1820–1910)
13 Joe Louis (1914–1981)
    Arthur Sullivan (1842–1900)
14 Founding of Jamestown
    Gabriel Daniel Fahrenheit (1686–1736)
15 L. Frank Baum (1856–1919)
16 Henry Fonda (1905–1982)
17 Norway Constitution Day
18 Mount St. Helens eruption (1980)
    Margot Fonteyn (1919–1991)
19 Ho Chi Minh (ca. 1890–1969)
    Malcolm X (1925–1965)
20 Atlantic crossing by Amelia Earhart (1932)
    Henri Rousseau (1844–1910)
21 Founding of Red Cross
    Albrecht Durer (1471–1528)
22 Arthur Conan Doyle (1859–1930)
23 Margaret Fuller (1810–1850)
24 Emanuel Leutze (1816–1868)
25 African Freedom Day
    Ralph Waldo Emerson (1803–1882)
26 Sally Kristen Ride (1951–)
    John Wayne (1907–1979)
27 Rachel Carson (1907–1964)
    Isadora Duncan (1878–1927)
28 Joseph Ignace Guillotin (1738–1814)
    James Francis ("Jim") Thorpe (1888–1953)
29 Patrick Henry (1736–1799)
    John Fitzgerald Kennedy (1917–1963)
30 Memorial Day
    St. Joan of Arc Feast Day
31 Walt Whitman (1819–1892)

People, Places, and Events of May

What's Happening in May:

Mental Health Month
Older Americans Month

Other May Events:

First week: PTA Teacher Appreciation Week
Second Sunday: Mother's Day
Week that includes May 15: Police Week
Third Saturday: Armed Forces Day
Third week: World Trade Week

Events Scheduled According to Non-Gregorian Calendar Usually Occurring in May:

Shavuot: Feast of Weeks (Jewish Pentecost)
Hong Kong: Birthday of Lord Buddha
Pentecost (Christian feast)

May's Daily Calendar

1

Lei Day. Hawaiian version of May Day.
May Day. Ancient celebration that may involve festivals and maypoles. Widely observed in socialist countries as a holiday for workers.
Philippines: Santacruzan. May Day celebration and pageant.
Birth anniversary of:
    Mary Harris Jones (1830–1930). Irish-American activist and labor leader known as "Mother Jones." Gave her last speech when she was one hundred years old.
    Kate Smith (1909–1986). Popular singer, especially noted for her performance of "God Bless America."

2

Birth anniversary of:
    Mary Cassatt (1844–1926). Impressionist painter.
    Harry "Bing" Crosby (1904–1977). Popular singer and actor.

3

Japan Constitution Memorial Day. Commemorating the date when Japan renounced the right to wage war and the emperor's claims to divinity in 1947.
Mexican Day of the Holy Cross. Festive day for construction workers and miners.

Poland Constitution Day. Commemorating the signing of first constitution in 1794, called Swieto Trzeciego Majo in the Polish language.

4

Birth anniversary of:

Horace Mann (1796–1859). Educator, called the "Father of American Education."

5

Mexico: Cinco de Mayo. National Mexican holiday commemorating the Battle of Puebla in 1862. Also widely observed in Mexican communities in the United States.

Birth anniversary of:

Nelly Bly (1867–1922). Journalist and activist for women's rights; real name was Elizabeth Cochrane Seaman.

Karl Marx (1818–1883). German socialist and founder of the communist movement.

6

Hindenburg blimp disaster (1937)

India: Buddha Purnima. Celebrating the birth of Buddha.

Birth anniversary of:

Robert E. Peary (1856–1920). Explorer and leader of expedition to the North Pole.

Rabindranath Tagore (1861–1941). Hindu poet and composer.

Rudolph Valentino (1895–1926). Italian-born actor and star of silent films.

7

Birth anniversary of:

Johannes Brahms (1833–1897). German composer, regarded as one of the greatest composers of the nineteenth century.

Robert Browning (1812–1889). English poet, husband of Elizabeth Barrett Browning.

Gary Cooper (1901–1961). Film star, famous for portrayal of western heroes.

Archibald MacLeish (1892–1982). Poet and playwright.

8

V-E Day (Victory in Europe Day). Commemorating the surrender of Germany to Allied forces in 1945.

Birth anniversary of:

Jean Henri Dunant (1828–1910). Swiss author and founder of the Red Cross Society.

Antoine Laurent Lavoisier (1743–1794). French chemist, called the "Father of Modern Chemistry."

Harry S. Truman (1884–1972). Thirty-third president of the United States; born in Missouri.

9

European Common Market created (1950)

Birth anniversary of:

John Brown (1800–1859). Abolitionist leader of attack on Harper's Ferry in 1859.

10

Driving of the "Golden Spike." The Union Pacific and Central Pacific railways met in Utah in 1869.

11

Minnesota Admission Day. Became thirty-second state admitted to the Union (1858).

Birth anniversary of:

Irvin Berlin (1888–1989). Russian-born American songwriter, especially noted for composing "God Bless America."

Salvador Dali (1904–1989). Spanish painter and leader in the Surrealist movement.

Martha Graham (1894–1990). Dancer and choreographer, credited with incorporating rituals of Native Americans in her works.

12

Birth anniversary of:

Edward Lear (1812–1888). English painter and poet, noted for his nonsense verse.

Florence Nightingale (1820–1910). English nurse and activist for health care.

13

Birth anniversary of:

Joe Louis (1914–1981). African-American world heavyweight boxing champion from 1937 to 1949.

Arthur Sullivan (1842–1900). English composer of light operas, and partner with William Gilbert.

14

Founding of Jamestown (1607). First permanent English settlement in America.

Paraguay Independence Day. Gained independence from Spain in 1811.

Women's Auxilary Army Corps (WAAC) established (1942).

Birth anniversary of:

Gabriel Daniel Fahrenheit (1686–1736). German physicist; temperature measurements bear his name.

Thomas Gainsborough (1727–1788). English artist noted for his landscapes and portraits, including *The Blue Boy.*

15

Birth anniversary of:

L. Frank Baum (1856–1919). Creator of the "Wizard of Oz" stories.

16

Birth anniversary of:

Henry Fonda (1905–1982). Stage and movie actor.

17

Norway: Constitution Day and 17th of May Festival. Commemorating Norway's separation from Denmark in 1814.

18

Mount St. Helens volcanic eruption (1980)

Birth anniversary of:

Margot Fonteyn (1919–1991). English ballerina.

19

Birth anniversary of:

Ho Chi Minh (ca. 1890–1969). Vietnamese leader and president of the Democratic Republic of Vietnam (North Vietnam).

Malcolm X (1925–1965). African-American nationalist and civil rights leader.

Sarah Miriam Peale (1800–1885). Portrait painter.

20

Atlantic crossing by Amelia Earhart (1932). First woman to fly solo across the Atlantic Ocean.

Birth anniversary of:

Henri Rousseau (1844–1910). French painter.

Honore de Balzac (1799–1850). French writer.

21

Red Cross founded by Clara Barton (1881).

Birth anniversary of:

Albrecht Durer (1471–1528). German painter and engraver.

Elizabeth Fry (1780–1845). English social reformer who worked to improve conditions in women's prisons.

Sister Maria Innocentia Hummel (1909–1946). German artist; her paintings of children were first made into figurines by Franz Goebel and marketed under the M. I. Hummel trademark in 1935.

Alexander Pope (1727–1744). English writer and poet.

Andrei Sakharov (1921–1989). Soviet scientist and human rights activist.

22

French West Indies: Slavery Abolition Day

Birth anniversary of:

Arthur Conan Doyle (1859–1930). English writer, best known as the creator of Sherlock Holmes stories.

23

South Carolina became eighth state to ratify the Constitution (1788).

Birth anniversary of:

Margaret Fuller (1810–1850). Feminist writer and activist, author of first American book on feminism.

24

Birth anniversary of:

Emanuel Leutze (1816–1868). German-American painter, remembered for works such as *Washington Crossing the Delaware*.

25

African Freedom Day. Holiday in Chad, Zambia, and other African countries to commemorate independence from foreign rule.

Argentina Independence Day. Gained independence from Spain in 1916.

Birth anniversary of:

Ralph Waldo Emerson (1803–1882). Writer and philosopher.

Bill "Bojangles" Robinson (1878–1949). Dancer and movie actor, called the "King of Tap Dancers."

Igor Sikorsky (1889–1972). Russian-born engineer, remembered as developer of first successful helicopter in 1939.

Tito (1892–1980). Yugoslavian political leader.

26

Birth anniversary of:

Sally Kristen Ride (1951–) First American woman in space.

John Wayne (1907–1979). Movie actor noted for his roles in westerns.

27

Birth anniversary of:

Amelia Jenks Bloomer (1818–1894). Women's rights leader and popularizer of a costume in 1849 that became known as "bloomers."

Rachel Carson (1907–1964). Scientist and author of *Silent Spring*.

Isadora Duncan (1878–1927). Dancer, responsible for bringing new concepts of freedom and liberation into dance.

28

Birth anniversary of:

Joseph Ignace Guillotin (1738–1814). French physician and creator the guillotine.

James Francis ("Jim") Thorpe (1888–1953). Native American athlete and winner of pentathlon and decathlon Olympic events in 1912.

29

Rhode Island became thirteenth state to ratify the Constitution (1790).

Wisconsin Admission Day. Became thirtieth state admitted to the Union (1848).

Birth anniversary of:

Patrick Henry (1736–1799). Revolutionary leader and orator, remembered for "Give me liberty or give me death" speech.

John Fitzgerald Kennedy (1917–1963). Thirty-fifth president of the United States; born in Massachusetts. Assassinated in office while riding in motorcade in Dallas, November 22, 1963.

30

Memorial Day. American holiday commemorating those who died in battle. Now observed as legal holiday on the last Monday in May.

St. Joan of Arc Feast Day. Honoring French martyr known as the "Maid of Orléans."

31

South Africa Republic Day. Became republic in 1961, withdrawing from British Commonwealth.

Birth anniversary of:

Walt Whitman (1819–1892). Writer and poet, noted for *Leaves of Grass.*

The Ultimate Stories—Accounts of Creation around the World

Teaching Unit for May

A Word about This Unit. An explanation is in order about our selection of the term creation "accounts" rather than creation "myths." The latter usage is the one that will likely be encountered more often in the literature by you and your students as they pursue further inquiries in this area. The former term, however, may help you avoid conflicts that might occur in conjunction with the notion of myth.

Myth is a more accurate term to use in regard to these discussions, for the word, derived from the Greek, originally meant the "last word" on a topic, an authority with unquestionable epistemological status. That connotation fits much better with regard to accounts of the beginnings of things that were offered to the listener. It was expected that they would be accepted without question, and that they were not to be subjected to critical scrutiny by the audience.

However, the difficulty that you may encounter in your teaching is that the word "myth," as it is used in ordinary language contexts today, quite ironically, has a connotation almost opposite to its original literal meaning. That is, many people will assess something termed a myth to be akin to a fairy tale, or "make believe." In class, discussions may arise about the creation account, or rather the two accounts that are contained in the Bible. Some parents of students in your class may consider these not as "myths" in this sense, but as factually true accounts of how the cosmos was created. Similar situations might occur with individuals who hold other beliefs.

Thus, we have chosen to use a term that is accurate in its descriptive sense, while having the advantage of possessing a less potent emotive charge. It may be that in your situation, you may choose to use the term "myth" and use the opportunity to examine the connotations that become associated with a particular term. With a group of mature students, this should prove to be a worthwhile exercise in itself, and particularly so in the context of this unit.

This unit will serve as an instructional means for encouraging students to become more familiar with the varying accounts of the creation of the cosmos as a whole, or specific aspects of creation. Several of the units and other instructional activities have been concerned with folk literature of particular cultural groups. The study of the folk literature of a group is a valid and valuable means for discovering the way that the group seeks to explain or account for various things that they encounter in their environment.

In the accounts that these folk traditions give for the beginnings or creation of their surroundings, the intellectual creativity of the cultural group is displayed, as are the fascinating and perceptive insights into the nature of the things that constitute the cosmos from the perspective of the group. Thus, the study of these accounts is a fruitful way to discover what a culture considers to be important, as well as many other aspects of that culture. Among these are (1) how the culture views itself (as a particular group of people); (2) how it conceives of the cosmos as a whole; (3) how it perceives of the relationships that should exist (i.e., as the creator "intended") among the various members of the group; and (4) the group's relationships with other realms of the whole creation, such as animals and other life forms within the cosmos. For example, Native Americans' view of their relationships to the animals that they hunt and to the land and the trees and other plants on the earth is markedly different from the cultural perspective of the European groups that settled the land.

In general, this unit will provide you and your students with an additional opportunity to attain a better understanding of the thoughts and beliefs of cultures throughout the world. These accounts are among the most revealing sources of "basic" information about these groups.

Motivation. You may begin this unit by encouraging students to pursue an activity for which most young people have a talent, namely, asking questions. Many times these queries seek information to account for the "whys" of certain situations or events, or they may be directed at discovering where various things come from. Encourage your students to reflect on the types of such questions that have been discussed in science and history classes, as well as in conversations in less formal settings. One of the students may mention the old question, "Which came first, the chicken or the egg?" What makes this question so puzzling is that, on the one hand, chickens have to come from eggs, but on the other, mature chickens lay these same eggs from which chicks are hatched. Thus, we are left with what seems to be an unresolvable and dismaying query.

Students will note that similar questions may be raised about the origins of other animal species and plants as well. If there is no spontaneous generation of the "young" form of a living thing, then how was it possible for the first of the living beings of a given type to come to be? We humans enjoy scratching our heads over such puzzles, but we do like ultimately have an explanation that accounts for such intellectual conundrums. Cultural groups in their own unique ways have offered different explanations that account for the beginnings of not only humans, but in some cases for the creation of all that is.

To get students starting to think along these lines, you may wish to tie this unit in with previous activities that engaged them in a search for their family's roots, their own genealogical investigations. They would then gain some perspective on the attempts by whole groups of humans to discover the first roots of the entire creation, the world in its beginnings.

Immersion. As has been mentioned, creation accounts, like many of the other stories that are created by a people or group, are likely to reveal as much about the people who have composed them as the plot and the events that are described in the story itself. They indicate how the people perceive themselves in relation to the world of creation—for example, what is their special place within it? These stories of creation express the relationships of a group with other humans and other living things. They may contain an implicit set of ethical guidelines for governing their actions and intentions toward others. A group's view of its significance may be heavily influenced by what the creation account reveals about their place in the scheme of the whole creation.

Information. Creation accounts might be said to represent the culmination of folk literature that seeks to explain aspects of the world in which human cultures live. The particular conditions and environments in which humans exist differ significantly around the world, and folk literature, including creation accounts, reflects these differences. However, despite these varied environments, similarities are found in the literature as well. Common themes, similar predicaments, and situations in which humans find themselves that are recounted in the stories are easily discerned. Thus, it should not be surprising to your students when they discover that similarities exist among creation accounts from all over the world.

These accounts require extremely creative insights and far-reaching visions and are the most fundamental stories of all that are composed by humans. These stories are foundational in the sense that they serve to determine our place in the world and also to give us a connection, a sense of belonging to that period when there was *no time*. They also serve to demonstrate our significance, for we were important enough in the creator's scheme to be worthy of being. By most accounts, our place and status in relation to the creator and the rest of the created world seems closer to the creator than to the other objects in it.

Making Sense of the World

One of the peculiar traits of our species is the human propensity to want to make sense of the world and the particular circumstances of the environment in which we live. This disposition accounts for much of the folk literature that has been created. These creation accounts, however, are unique when compared with other stories that humans have recounted and shared among themselves through untold generations. They are accounts of events that took place when no humans were around to witness them. As Hamilton (1988) notes, these accounts "take place before the 'once upon a time' " that marks the beginning of the fairy tale, for these acts of creation take place before or outside time in a human sense. They signal the beginning of the very phenomenon of time when viewed from the perspective of human beings.

Creation accounts are existential in that they attempt in different ways to address the particular situation and condition of humans, not solely as members of the animal kingdom, but as beings who are conscious of life and death, of good and bad. Thus, we are conscious of not only what *is* the case, but of the possibility of there being something else, and in some situations that something else *ought* to be the case. Many of these stories seek to serve as a means of articulating or trying to delineate our place in the great scheme of things. These accounts recognize that, on the one hand, humans are not truly gods, yet, on the other, they are different from the other things in the created world.

Among that which is revealed by the particular accounts of different groups are the terms given to themselves. For example, the self-referring name of many groups translates into English as simply "the people," a seeming indication of their centrality, if not primacy, in the scheme of creation. It also serves to indicate that ethnocentrism is not a particularly recent phenomenon. In other instances, however, later cultures recognize that they did have predecessors and assign some status to this fact. For example, the Navajo call the culture that had existed in the lands that ultimately served as their home, the Anazazi, or the "old ones." This serves as a tie between their group and an earlier one in the tribal histories, a sense of rootedness to cultures with which they can share something in common.

These accounts recognize that humans do not have the power of gods, and that another being is responsible for the creative process. These accounts typically ascribe two different characteristics to these god-creators. The first is that the entity responsible possesses an enormous amount of power, the power to create the world and the various entities within it, often out of nothing or out of the limited materials that are available. This creator is so potent that things with unexpected characteristics will be developed from these inert materials—for example, humans and other animals and living things out of inanimate dust. Along with this power, these creators have the ability to establish the variety of relationships that exist in the realm of created things. One group of living things, for example, may be given power over other classes of living things. The relation between the light and darkness is revealed, although different accounts will give alternative explanations of what has caused these associations among observable classes of objects, as well as other aspects of natural phenomena.

A second characteristic identified with these creative agents is the ability to make intelligent choices in this creative process. In a few accounts, the creator does not have either absolute dominion or power in this process. In other cases, the creator lacks the wisdom or judgment needed to create the perfect world. The creative agent may either leave out something in the creation, especially something of ultimate importance or significance to humans, or may even be tricked by the cunning of someone who seemingly has

less control over things but is able to interfere with the creation efforts of the gods. To the extent that this occurs, a flaw results in the world because of that lack of wisdom or judgment. These creation accounts articulate the answers to some of the ultimate questions that confront humans: Who are we, and from whence did we come? Why are we here? How did things come to be the way they are? They comprise, among other things, a description of the events that occurred that resulted in the creation of us all.

Other stories dealing with the creation not only describe the origin of the world itself, but also include components that serve to explain the established relations or interactions among human beings. They serve as helpful devices for tracing the roots of some human emotions that can lead to certain actions.

A study of these accounts reveals an awareness of human potency, that we as humans are ourselves capable of creative acts—for example, artists and those skilled in a variety of other crafts. As groups sought for an explanation of the things that they encountered in the world, they recognized that they could account for or even bring about certain kinds of events that occurred in the world. Humans also recognized their own limitations. There were events occurring and things existing in the world that they could not control, and that could not come into being through any express act or will of their own. When they looked for beings who might be responsible for such things beyond their own limited power, it was natural to look for agents of such activity by extrapolating from their own experiences. Thus, although humans were strong and possessed some power to cause events, by this extrapolative process, they might come to conceive of a being who was stronger by far than any man, one who was wiser than the wisest of any known human. They could follow a similar trend with regard to the animals that they encountered. An animal that was ferocious would become extensively more so in their speculations; an animal that seemed intelligent could become a being that possessed far greater amounts of ability and power.

When human speculated and contemplated the very earliest of beginnings, they likely would think that the creator would possess similar skills to those recognized in the artists and practitioners of crafts that they knew from their own experience. The carver could fashion a figure out of wood, the sculptor could create one out of clay. In both instances, the talented artist could create an image that was lifelike. However, it was recognized that although these creations looked almost as if they were alive, they were not. Envisioning an artist whose talents were infinitely greater, one could believe that such a god could create things that actually were alive.

Many of these stories reveal much about how people see the world and themselves in this creation, and their status and relationships among themselves and between themselves and other peoples. Some accounts give reasons as to why there are different races, and some account for the difference between genders.

In approaching this field of study, it may prove helpful to have some schema for analyzing the myriad accounts. A few of the organizing questions that can be used for such purposes follow.

Who is or are the agents of creation? Most often it is a figure denoted as a god. In some cases, however, an animal is the entity that creates the world. An example of the latter type is the role of the Raven in the Inuit account of the origins of the world.

Is the creation a complete or ultimate one, or rather what would be termed a partial one? In the former, nothing exists except perhaps a void and the creator must start at the very beginning. Other creation accounts are quite anthropocentric, for while something exists, the important event occurs when human beings are created and come to play their role in the world.

What are the materials used by the creator? In many cases, man is fashioned from common dirt or clay. In some instances a vast expanse of ocean exists, but there is no place stable enough to support man or the animals of the land. Something must their dive down (a turtle in one account) beneath the water and bring sufficient material to the surface so that *terra firma*, in the literal sense, may come to be.

What types of relations are established among the creatures that are formed? In many accounts, including one of those included in the Bible, man is created first. Then the creator forms woman, almost as an afterthought, often so that the man will not be lonely. Given this situation, it is more understandable that the subservient position of women in such societies is seen as a fixed characteristic of the universe, since it could be claimed that this power relationship was established in the very act of creation.

In other cases, some undesirable aspects of human existence were caused by the acts of folly committed by women. The biblical Eve has many sisters in this regard. Pandora, according to Greek mythic accounts, in order to satisfy her curiosity, opened a box and unleashed the tribulations that plague humans. Less attention is paid to the fact that Zeus was the being who presented the box to her. In an account associated with the Blackfoot nation, an act of a woman resulted in the fact that all must die. Interestingly, an account within

the Tahitian culture places the blame for loss of eternal life on men rather than on women. This tends to be the exception, however.

Human dominance over other creatures is a feature of many creation accounts, although in one account, when men seemed to be devouring the animals that the creator had formed, the creator developed animals that were more ferocious than man, thus ensuring that a least a few could instill fear in mankind.

What interactions occur between the creator and the world after the creative act? In some cases, the "clockmaker" metaphor seems an appropriate one to denote the relationship, for the creator, once having brought things into being, leaves the created world largely alone. In other instances, the creator fashions man, but then proceeds to provide for various human needs with items such as water and food that were not present as components of the original creative act.

Some accounts describe a process in which aspects of the creator are "used" in the process of meeting the necessities of humans. A sacrificial dimension is present since the creator, in the very act of creation, has given of himself to provide his created beings with the necessities required for survival. An instance of this phenomenon is the creator Phan Ku, as expressed in an account from China.

Are the agents of creation omnipotent and omniscient? Certain accounts include the presence of creators who possess less than desirable levels of potency or judgment. In some cases, a well-intentioned creator is tricked into committing an unwise act, and humans are the ones that ultimately suffer.

These queries represent a sample of the types of questions that you may address to your students to help give direction and provide some orientation for their investigation of these accounts. The study of creation accounts is both fascinating and stimulating. Students will undoubtedly soon frame their own questions as they pursue their inquiries.

Instructional Activities

Activity 9.1: Mapping the Creation Accounts

Societies representing all the major geographic regions of the world have developed accounts of how the world came to be. This activity can be used to reinforce students' knowledge of the countries and regions of the globe. Using some of the accounts mentioned above, or by studying books such as those included in the References and Bibliography section of this unit, students could identify the particular culture or group to which the account is attributed. They could locate the area on a modern map, indicating where these tribes or groups lived or still live.

In some cases, this will require some astute detective work on the part of the students, since some cultures may have migrated or have been forced to relocate. For example, some of the Native American cultures have been placed on reservations quite distant from their original homes (see Chapter 2).

In others, the particular culture may no longer be closely related to a modern group. An example of this case would be the creation accounts attributed to civilizations associated with Babylonia or ancient Egypt. There are certainly groups inhabiting these lands today, and these groups are proud of the achievements of these earlier civilizations, but their culture has changed markedly.

Activity 9.2: A Chronological Listing of Creation Accounts

Many of these accounts may be difficult to date with any accuracy. In some cases, however, students may be able through research to give an estimate of the time when the account was developed. It should provide them with a good exercise in the process that historians use in attempting to test various hypotheses or surmises with regard to dates and events. Students could attempt to discover whether there seemed to be similarities among accounts of a particular time period. For example, were those accounts that "began" with an egg as the vessel in which the matter of creation was contained likely to occur during a particular era?

A variation of these suggested activities is to encourage students to display or report the results of their inquiries in the form of a data chart, such as the sample "Accounts of Creation" chart shown here.

Activity 9.3: Further Inquiry about Individual Accounts of Creation

Students can use the reference works cited at the end of this unit, as well as others available in the library, to delve more deeply into the creation accounts merely summarized here. Discussion groups can be formed, and as the students share the results of their inquiries, similarities in themes and story lines may be discovered among seemingly different accounts. Students should be encouraged to suggest reasons that might explain such similarities. Such inquiries can serve as a natural impetus for further study of a culture, since these accounts likely have some influence on other institutional practices of the group. In time, students themselves may serve as "authorities" on a particular cultural group.

ACCOUNTS OF CREATION

Agent	Material	Location
Raven (and wife)	Pea Vine (first man); pebbles (humans and animals)	Inuits (Bering Strait to Greenland)
Lizard (Pupula)	Added eyes, ears, etc., to material "already there" and taught man how to make fire	Australia
Sun	Created world, stars, and then humans from clay	Inca (several different versions)
Bumba	Vomited up sun, moon, living creatures, and at last humans	Zaire
Earthmaker	After creating earth, formed man from a piece of earth shaped like himself	Winnebago (Native American)
Phan Ku (Great Creator)	Created earth and man from his own substance	China

---

Activity 9.4: Composing Creation Accounts

In one sense, many of the stories constituting the literature of a culture might be called "creation" accounts. Many of the stories recounted within folk literature are limited in that they seek to explain how a specific kind of thing came into being, or even how certain animals that had already existed underwent some change. For example, several different Native American tales offer explanations of how the loon, a bird with which they were quite familiar, came to have its strange cry or call, and how it got the stripe around its neck.

There are a variety of explanations for the formation of the stars, and particularly how some constellations came into being. There are accounts given for the existence of the different seasons of the year and how they came to be. What makes creation accounts unique and fundamentally different from these other causal explanations is that they deal with creation in an "ultimate" sense. They describe, or account for, the existence of *any* thing, not necessarily the very first things that existed.

You may wish to engage your students in an activity of developing accounts that a people might have composed. To give some structure and orientation to this activity, first describe the physical environment and living conditions in which the group lived. Students then should be given the task of developing an account of creation that would constitute a "reasonable" explanation for this culture. Actual creation accounts can used from cultures that are described in the reference works cited at the end of this unit. Students conducting independent investigations can also provide data for their classmates. The use of actual accounts will serve as a check of validity for the accounts developed by students. In each case, the composers should be asked to give reasons why they included the particular ingredients in their stories. When the student groups have completed their accounts, they may choose to present their creation to the class in a variety of ways. It can be presented as a poem, a dramatic production, or by other means. They could be encouraged to develop suitable costumes and present their production to other classes in the school with appropriate introductory material so that the audience will have sufficient background to more fully appreciate the production.

Activity 9.5: "Obverse" of Activity 9.4

As an alternative to having students compose a creation account after being given a description of the physical and geographical environment and additional information about social life and other significant conditions, they might instead be given an actual creation account. They would then have to determine where the group that created the account lived, as well as describe as much as they could about the social conditions, possible customs of the group, and so on. Several different teams of students might work on the same account. They should support their views with facts. Afterward, the teams should be given the location and a description of the culture with which the creation account is associated.

Activity 9.6: Composing Limited Creation Accounts

If you believe that there might be serious objections from parents or others in the community if students were asked to develop, "ultimate" creation accounts, you could ask students to create explanations of the more limited variety. After becoming familiar with such accounts from several folk traditions, students could be asked to create stories that describe the reasons why certain animals possess characteristic traits.

These may be physical in nature, such as why the robin has a red breast or how the raccoon came to acquire its "mask." They might also involve stories explaining why animals have come to acquire certain attributes of character, such as the slyness of the fox or the ponderous slowness of the turtle. One such story might begin, "Did you know that at one time the turtle was one of the fastest animals alive? Well, it was, but then something happened . . ." The students would then be asked to finish the story. This also would be an appropriate activity for cooperative writing, with different groups of students offering alternative accounts of why the turtle became so slow.

Activity 9.7: Developing Attitudes of Tolerance and Respect

This unit also provides an excellent opportunity to develop and reinforce attitudes of tolerance and respect for the viewpoints of others. This is an appropriate objective for this unit, because students will be exposed to accounts from societies seemingly more "primitive" than our own. Some of the accounts may strike young people as strange or even weird. Some students might be tempted to make fun of or ridicule stories that seem silly.

You could lead the students to consider why they feel these stories are so weird or strange. After the reasons given are listed on the chalkboard, point out that not too long ago some of the "explanations" given by our culture (in the West) might seem equally odd to modern minds. Only a few centuries ago, scientists believed that the earth was the center of the entire universe and that the sun and all of the stars in all of the myriad of galaxies revolved around our planet. Less than two hundred years ago, many reputable physicians believed that the night air was unhealthy, and that exposure to it might result in one getting a variety of diseases. Others believed that mentally ill people were being tormented by evil spirits that might have invaded their bodies when they sneezed and exposed their souls. In retrospect, the accounts of other cultures may not seem too weird when compared with some of our earlier explanations of various phenomena.

Upon examination, many of these accounts contain insights that display a marked level of sophistication. For example, the "egg" theories of creation that are found in China and other areas indicate an understanding of the development of individual animals and a reasonable inference that, just as the origin of living individuals stems from an egg, so one might hypothesize that all living things may have once come from an egg (although it would have to have been a large one to contain all the entities of which the world is comprised).

Discussions centered in a study of so-called "strange" accounts of creation could serve as a basis for examining the practices and aspects of contemporary cultural groups that are markedly different from our own. By studying these in the context of the culture with which they are associated, a similar understanding and appreciation can be developed.

References and Bibliography

Arnott, D. (1962). *African myths and legends retold*. London: Oxford University Press.

Beier, U. (1966). *The origin of life and death: African creation myths*. London: Heineman Educational Books.

Bullfinch, T. (1962). *The age of fable*. New York: NAL.

Bullfinch, T. (1985). *The golden age of myth and legend*. London: Bracken Books.

Campbell, J. (1976). *Oriental mythology*. New York: Penguin Books.

Campbell, J. (1976). *Primitive mythology*. New York: Penguin Books.

Campbell, J. (1976). *The masks of god: Occidental mythology*. New York: Penguin Books.

Christie, A. (1968). *Chinese mythology*. New York: Hamlyn Publishing Group.

Crossley-Holland, K. (1980). *The Norse myths*. New York: Pantheon Books.

Doria, C., & Lenowitz, H. (1976). *Origins: Creation texts from the ancient Mediterranean*. New York: Penguin Books.

Eliade, M. (1974). *Gods, goddesses and myths of creation*. New York: Harper & Row.

Feldman, S. (Ed.). (1963). *African myths and tales*. New York: Dell Publishing.

Ford, D. (Ed.). (1964). *African worlds*. London: Oxford University Press.

Freund, P. (1964). *Myths of creation*. London: W. H. Allen.

Goodrich, N. L. (1960). *Ancient myths*. New York: NAL.

Grant, M. (1986). *Myths of the Greeks and Romans*. New York: NAL.

Grinnel, G. B. (1916). *Blackfoot lodge tales*. New York: Charles Scribner's Sons.

Hamilton, E. (1969). *Mythology: Timeless tales of gods and heroes*. New York: NAL.

Hamilton, V. (1988). *In the beginning: Creation stories from around the world*. New York: Harcourt Brace Jovanovich.

Heidel, A. (1951). *The Babylonian genesis*. Chicago: University of Chicago Press.

Leach, M. (1956). *The beginning: Creation myths around the world*. New York: Funk & Wagnalls.

Nivedita, S., & Coomaraaswamy, A. K. (1985). *Hindus and Buddhists: myths and legends*. London: Bracken Books.

O'Brien, J., & Major, W. (1982). *In the beginning: Creation myths from ancient Mesopotamia, Israel, and Greece*. Chicago: American Academy of Religion, Scholars Press.

Tedlock, D. (Trans.). (1986). *The Popol Vuh: The Mayan book of the dawn of life and the glories of gods and kings*. New York: Simon & Schuster.

Radin, P. (Ed.). (1952). *African folktales*. Princeton, NJ: Princeton University Press.

Sproul, B. (1979). *Primal myths*. New York: Harper & Row.

Verrier, E. (1958). *Myths of the north east frontier of India*. Calcutta: Sree Saraswatty Press.

May's Potpourri of Teaching Ideas

The purpose of each month's Potpourri of Teaching Ideas is to provide additional resources from which to build your curriculum. Most, but not all, of the activities listed each month relate directly to that month. It is not intended that you use them all, but rather that you choose those which are appropriate for your program. Although the topics are written for a particular month, many of them would be appropriate for use throughout the year. How you use these activities will depend on your curricular goals. You may wish to use some of the activities as they are presented, and you may need to modify some to meet your needs. Perhaps some of them will give you ideas for entirely different potpourris.

A Day for All Mothers

If you speak English, you may call her Mother, Mama, Mommy, Mom, Ma, or another favorite name. In another language, she may be Mater (Latin), Mère (French), Madre (Spanish), Mutter (German), or Meter (Greek). Whatever the term, mothers are special people in the hearts of their offspring. That is why they are so universally honored.

The second Sunday in May has been designated as Mother's Day, a day when Americans honor their mothers. Americans are not alone in choosing this day, for many other countries, including Australia, Belgium, Denmark, Finland, Italy, and Turkey, have also set this day as special for mothers. People in other countries honor their mothers on different days, but regardless of her name, there is almost no place in the world that does not have some special occasion for mothers.

It is unclear just who was the first to honor mothers, but it is known that in ancient Phrygia, people worshiped the goddess Cybele, the daughter of Heaven and Earth and the mother of all gods. Each year a special celebration was held in her honor. The Greeks also honored this goddess, but called her Rhea. Later, when the Romans paid tribute to the goddess, they named her Magna Mater, or Great Mother. During the centuries that followed, Christians did not worship or honor Cybele, Rhea, or Magna Mater. Instead, they held celebrations to honor the "Mother Church."

Perhaps the first occasion to honor mothers occurred during the Middle Ages. Many young people had to leave home to earn money or learn a trade. They were allowed one holiday each year. On the fourth Sunday in Lent, the young people went home to visit their mothers. This was called going "a-mothering." The custom eventually became known as Mothering Sunday.

The holiday as it is observed today began much later. More than a hundred years ago, two women campaigned to begin a movement to honor mothers. Julia Ward Howe, author of "The Battle Hymn of the Republic," first made the suggestion, but nothing came of it. Mary Towles Sasseen, a schoolteacher in Kentucky, helped her pupils present a special musical program for their mothers. This became an annual event, and many other groups followed her lead. However, this, too, did not bring about a national movement.

Credit is given to Anna Jarvis as the real founder of Mother's Day in America. Through an extensive letter-writing campaign, she began to get results. The first Mother's Day service was held on May 12, 1907, in Grafton, West Virginia. The next year, Jarvis organized a special Mother's service in Philadelphia. Her theme was to "honor the best mother who ever lived—*your* mother." She continued to write to influential men and women, and in 1914 a joint resolution was introduced in Congress asking President Woodrow Wilson to proclaim the second Sunday in May as Mother's Day in every state. Wilson signed the proclamation, and sons and daughters have been honoring their mothers on the second Sunday of May ever since.

Try These Activities

1. If your class population includes diverse cultures, it may be interesting to talk about the different terms used for "mother." Even among children whose first language is English, there will likely be several different words for mother used within the group. Sometimes children use several names for their mother, depending on the location and situation. Make a list of the different terms used. Encourage children who speak different languages to share the spelling and pronunciation of words they use for their mothers.

2. Students may research the significance of wearing different colored flowers on Mother's Day. Where did the custom begin? What is used to honor a mother who was living? To honor one who is deceased?

3. The students can research Mother's Day in other countries by completing the chart "Mothers Around the World."

Suggested Reading

Phelan, M. K. (1965). *Mother's day*. New York: Thomas Y. Crowell.

MOTHERS AROUND THE WORLD

Country	Name for Mother	Date of Mother's Day
United States	Mother, Mom, Mama, etc.	Second Sunday in May
Mexico	Madre, Mi Madre, Mama, Mamasita, etc.	
France		Last Sunday in May
Germany		

Celebrating Cinco de Mayo

Cinco de Mayo is an important holiday in the Hispanic communities of Mexico and the Southwest. Mexican students are as knowledgeable about this celebration as most Americans are about the Fourth of July. The following program was written by a group of seventh- and eighth-grade students in an "English as a Second Language" class in Fort Worth, Texas. With the assistance of their teacher, students were given an opportunity to research the meaning of Cinco de Mayo in encyclopedias, reference books, and trade books. They worked in teams to prepare the speaking parts which tell the background and story of the celebration. Their teacher arranged for the group to present an assembly program to the entire student body, using this script as the basis for the program. Songs, dances, and other presentations completed the assembly. You may use this script with your students or adapt it for a presentation to other classes or for a special program for visitors and parents.

Cinco de Mayo: The Fifth of May

Speaker 1: Cinco de Mayo is Spanish for the Fifth of May. It is a very important date in Mexican history, and is celebrated in Mexico with parades, rodeos, dancing, and merrymaking. But Cinco de Mayo is much more than just a reason for partying. Today we are going to tell you what happened on that date and explain why it has meaning for freedom-loving people everywhere. To remember Cinco de Mayo is to honor courage and valor and justice. Let us tell you the story of what happened that day long ago—so that its meaning may remain with us always.

Speaker 2: The year was 1862. Benito Juarez was president of Mexico. The country had made huge debts all over Europe and was unable to pay them. Napoleon III of France saw this as a time that he could use his army to conquer Mexico and thus extend his power and control. He knew the United States was busy with its own Civil War and would not come to Mexico's aid. Napoleon felt nothing stood in the way of his taking over rule of Mexico. So he sent his army to invade.

Speaker 3: Six thousand of Napoleon's finest soldiers were dressed in fancy uniforms and given the finest weapons to fight with. They were loaded onto ships and sent to Mexico. They landed at Vera Cruz and easily defeated the Mexican army which defended that city. The French then began a march to Mexico City to take over the capital. There they would take down the Mexican flag and raise the French flag. If they succeeded, Mexico would then belong to Napoleon and to France.

Speaker 4: It appeared it was going to be an easy task to conquer the Mexican army. They were very poor and struggling, with little training and no money to buy weapons. In fact, their weapons consisted mainly of machetes and knives they had brought from home. Napoleon could only laugh at this pitiful, ragtag Mexican army. He thought there was no way he could lose—but then enters Ignacio Zaragoza, the hero of Cinco de Mayo!

Speaker 5: Ignacio Zaragoza was a Texan by birth but had adopted Mexico for his country. Now, in this terrible hour when Mexico's freedom was being challenged, he vowed to defend her at all costs. Zaragoza was put in charge of the Mexican army and told to try to stop Napoleon's march toward Mexico City. He knew his soldiers were inexperienced in battle with almost nothing to fight with except the machetes and knives they had brought from home. But they had something more important than guns—they had a fierce pride in their country, and they had courage and valor and bravery. But would these be enough to stop the mighty French army?

Speaker 6: Zaragoza determined to make his stand at Puebla. On the night before the battle, he called his men together and passionately told them, "Your enemies are the first soldiers of the world, but you are the First Sons of Mexico. They have come to take your country from you!" The Mexican army rose to Zaragoza's challenge. The next day, May 5, 1862, their badly outnumbered forces fought with zeal and determination and pride—and when the smoke had cleared and the battle was over—they had done the impossible—they had defeated the mighty French army! It was a victory for freedom and truth and justice.

Speaker 7: The patriots at Puebla had consecrated Cinco de Mayo with their blood, their courage, their zeal. But for us—whether we be Hispanic or otherwise—it is important that we remember the lesson of Puebla: that right can triumph—even when it seems hopeless and impossible. We can, if we are determined, win the battle against prejudice, injustice, and hatred. We can come to realize that more important than our ethnic differences is the knowledge that we all are *amigos*. That is the real challenge of Cinco de Mayo—to prove there is room for us all!

Famous Educators: Worthy of Admiration and Acclaim

As the school year is nearing its end, it is a suitable time for students to study some noted educators of the past and the significance that these individuals have for students of the present. On the fourth of May in 1996, for example, educators will observe the one hundredth anniversary of the birth of Horace Mann, often called the father of the common schools, the institutions that were the forerunners to our public school system. Mann was an individual who gave up a promising political career that might have taken him to the highest ranks of the nation's leadership. Instead, he remained in Massachusetts, his native state, and served as the secretary of the state education board. Yet his influence went far beyond the boundaries of Massachusetts, and the series of annual reports that were published during his tenure as secretary became textbooks for those interested in the nation's educational system. He later served as president of Antioch College, an innovative institution.

Horace Mann has been singled out because he was born during this month, but the pantheon of educators is replete with others who, in their own way, made significant contributions to the development of education in the United States. These individuals were not all males and were not all white. Often, the most dedicated and important of these figures labored in much less supportive environments. Among the figures that stand out as examples are the noted African-American educators, Mary McLeod Bethune and Booker T. Washington. A study of both of their lives reveals heroic efforts to overcome the challenges of a less than favorable environment, and overcome them they did. Washington founded Tuskegee Institute, and Mary Bethune established several schools, among them Bethune-Cookman College (by merging her Daytona Normal and Industrial School with Spellman). Bethune also served as advisor to several presidents during a time in which it was unusual for a woman to do so.

Other women worthy of study are Emma Willard, Catherine Beecher, and Mary Lyon. You may wish to consult the Suggested Reading list to gain further information about Bethune, Mann, and Washington. Your students should consult with the school librarian to determine which of the biographies written for younger readers are available.

In addition to the study of these nationally known figures, this activity can provide an opportunity for students to become familiar with teachers who have made a contribution to schools in the local area. A good starting point is an area school that was named for an educator. There will undoubtedly be schools named after Mann, Washington, and others, but the conscience of some communities may lead them to name a school for a local educator. Your students can consult local records or interview individuals who may have been familiar with the person who received this honor.

How to Make a Cat's Cradle

1. Cut a piece of string about six feet long and tie the ends together with a knot.
2. Place the loop of string around your hands, keeping your thumbs outside the loop.
3. Pull the loop tight by moving your hands apart.
4. With the back of one hand, pick up the near string on that hand by going over and then under it. This should give you a loop of string around your palm.
5. Draw your hands apart and do the same with the other hand.
6. With the middle finger of one hand, go underneath the palm string of the other hand. Do the same with the other hand.
7. Draw your hands apart.
   You have constructed a figure called the cat's cradle.

Suggested Readings

Mary McLeod Bethune:

Anderson, L. (1976). *Mary McLeod Bethune, teacher with a dream.* Champaign, IL: Garrard Publishing.

Greenfield, E. (1977). *Mary McLeod Bethune.* New York: Thomas Y. Crowell.

McKissack, E. (1985). *Mary McLeod Bethune.* Chicago: Childrens Press.

Sterne, E. (1957). *Mary McLeod Bethune.* New York: Alfred A. Knopf.

In addition, the *Journal of Negro Education* has published several articles either authored by or about Mary Bethune.

Horace Mann:

Downs, R. (1974). *Horace Mann, champion of public schools.* New York: Twayne Publishers.

Messerli, J. (1972). *Horace Mann: A biography.* New York: Alfred A. Knopf.

Peabody, M. (1969). *Life of Horace Mann.* Boston: Willard Small.

Tharp, L. H. (1953). *Until victory.* Boston: Little, Brown.

Booker T. Washington:

Drinker, F. E. (1970). *Booker T. Washington, the master mind of a child of slavery.* New York: Negro Universities Press.

Harlan, L. R. (1972). *Booker T. Washington, the making of a black leader.* New York: Oxford University Press.

Washington, B. T. (1969). *Black-belt diamonds: Gems from the speeches, addresses, and talks to students of Booker T. Washington.* New York: Negro Universities Press.

Washington, B. T. (1963). *Up from slavery.* Garden City, NY: Doubleday.

Creating with String: The Universal Game

String games are played all over the world and may be one of the oldest amusements ever created. People in different countries often construct games of the same design but with different names and meanings.

In the United States, the most popular string game is cat's cradle (Gryski, 1983). The object of the game is for one player to pick the loops of string off of another player's hands by making different loops and carefully transferring these to her own hands.

String figures in some parts of the world are made by one person. These figures represent something that is important within that culture. By changing the loops in the original figure, stories can be told using the string as action pictures.

Some early cultures viewed string figures as magic. Some Inuit made a magic string design in late autumn as the days became shorter. The string figure was to catch the sun and to keep it from going away too soon. In New Guinea, people used string figures to help the new shoots of the yam plant to climb around sticks placed in the ground. As the yams sprouted and the green shoots appeared, everyone made string figures while watching the yams grow.

Anthropologists have collected string figures. When entering territories where they did not know the people, they found that the sharing of string figures was a way of getting acquainted. The U.S. Army advised soldiers and airmen stationed in the South Pacific during World War II to carry a loop of string with them. If they were downed in the jungle and a native approached, they were to get out the string and play "cat's cradle." The native would be less afraid of the soldier and then might share some of his own string figures.

Suggested Readings

Gryski, C. (1983). *Cat's cradle, owl's eyes: A book of string games.* New York: William Morrow.

Helfman, H. & Helfman, E. (1965). *Strings on your fingers. How to make string figures.* New York: William Morrow.

Jayne, C. (1962). *String figures and how to make them.* New York: Dover Publications.

Section Four: Summer

Summertime and the Livin' Is Easy

JUNE, JULY, AND AUGUST, those months in the Northern Hemisphere called summer, are special to many people. They are associated with warm days and cool nights in some parts of the United States and Canada, but for most of the nation and other parts of the hemisphere, these months bring hot days, days meant for playing, swimming, and sunbathing. This time is often referred to as the hot, lazy days of summer. The words "summertime, and the livin' is easy," from the musical *Porgy and Bess*, echo this sentiment. Of course, south of the equator, June, July, and August bring the cold days of winter.

Several special days occur during the summer. In the United States, June marks the celebration of Father's Day and Flag Day. July holds significance for citizens in both the United States and Canada. July 1, formerly called Dominion Day, is a national holiday for Canadians. Canada Day, as it presently is named, commemorates the confederation of upper and lower Canada and some of the maritime provinces into the Dominion of Canada. In the United States, the Fourth of July is marked by picnics, family gatherings, and fireworks to celebrate the signing of the Declaration of Independence in 1776.

The summer is usually thought of as "vacation time" for, traditionally, schools are not in session and children and young people are free to pursue interests other than homework. It is also the time when many families schedule trips to visit relatives and to see national and historic sites.

Chapter 10

June Is Bustin' Out All Over

June was the fourth month in the early Roman calendar and had twenty-nine days. It was changed to the sixth month and given an extra day when calendar reform was instituted by Julius Caesar. How June received its name is open to question. Some authorities believe it was named for Juno, the Roman goddess of love and marriage. Others think that the name is derived from *juniores,* a Latin word for "young men," because in early Rome the month of June was dedicated to young men.

June 22 is called the summer solstice. That is the time when the vertical rays of the sun strike the earth at their northernmost point. It also marks the longest period of daylight in the Northern Hemisphere. In contrast, this is the shortest period of daylight in the Southern Hemisphere. North of the equator, June brings long hours of sunshine and increasingly high temperatures to most locales. Crops are beginning to grow, many trees are heavy with developing fruits, and flowers are blooming in profusion. This is the time when, in the words of Oscar Hammerstein II, June is bustin' out all over!

The American holidays celebrated in June on the national level are Father's Day and Flag Day. Several other events in this month also are noteworthy. For example, a number of well-known people were born during June, including economist Adam Smith, artists Paul Gauguin and Peter Paul Rubens, actress Judy Garland, and writers Harriet Beecher Stowe and Pearl Buck. Historic events that occurred in June include the massacre at Tiananmen Square, the assassination of Robert F. Kennedy, the signing of the United Nations charter, and the first American woman in space.

Sunday	Monday	Tuesday	Wednesday	Thursday	Friday	Saturday
June						

JUNE

SELECTED EVENTS

1   Brigham Young (1801–1877)
2   Italy: Republic Day
3   Jefferson Davis (1808–1889)
4   Tiananmen Square massacre (1989)
5   Robert F. Kennedy assassinated (1968)
      Adam Smith (1723–1790)
6   Korea Memorial Day
      Nathan Hale (1755–1776)
7   Paul Gauguin (1848–1903)
8   Frank Lloyd Wright (1867–1959)
9   Hong Kong lease (1898)
      Cole Porter (1893–1964)
10   Jordan: Great Arab Revolt and Army Day
      Judy Garland (1922–1969)
11   King Kamehameha I Day
12   Philippines Independence Day
13   William Butler Yeats (1865–1939)
14   Flag Day
      Harriet Beecher Stowe (1811–1896)
15   Magna Carta Day
      Edvard Grieg (1843–1907)
16
17   Igor Stravinsky (1882–1971)
18   First American woman in space (1983)
19   Juneteenth
      Lou Gehrig (1903–1941)
20
21   Summer solstice
      India: Ratha Yatra
22   Malta: Mnarja
23   Midsummer celebration
24   Henry Ward Beecher (1813–1887)
25   Battle of Little Big Horn (1876)
26   United Nations charter signed (1945)
      Pearl Buck (1892–1973)
27   Helen Keller (1880–1968)
28   Jean Rousseau (1712–1778)
      Peter Paul Rubens (1577–1640)
29   William James Mayo (1861–1939)
30

People, Places, and Events of June

What's Happening in June:

First Sunday: Japan: Day of the Rice God
Week including June 14: National Flag Week
Third Sunday: Father's Day

Events Scheduled According to Non-Gregorian Calendar Usually Occurring in June:

Muslim New Year
Muslim holiday: Ashura
Korea: Tano Day
China: Dragon Boat Festival

June's Daily Calendar

1

Tennessee Admission Day. Became the sixteenth state admitted to the Union (1796).
Birth anniversary of:
     Brigham Young (1801–1877). Early leader of the Mormon Church.

2

Italy: Republic Day. Became a republic when Victor Emmanuel III abdicated the throne in 1946.
Birth anniversary of:
     Marquis de Sade (1740–1814). French author and military man noted for acts of cruelty. "Sadist" and "sadism" are derived from his name.

3

First woman rabbi ordained in the United States (1972).
Birth anniversary of:
     Jefferson Davis (1808–1889). Leader and president of the Confederacy during the Civil War.

4

Tiananmen Square massacre (1989). The Chinese People's Army open fire on demonstrators, killing an unknown number of students and protesters.

5

Robert F. Kennedy assassinated (1968).
Birth anniversary of:
     Adam Smith (1723–1790). Scottish economist and author of *An Enquiry into the Nature and Causes of the Wealth of Nations*.

6

Korea Memorial Day.
Birth anniversary of:
> Nathan Hale (1755–1776). Patriot and revolutionary war soldier. Captured and hanged by British as a spy. His last statement is purported to have been, "I only regret that I have but one life to lose for my country."

7

Birth anniversary of:
> Paul Gauguin (1848–1903). French artist noted for works painted in Tahiti.
> Gwendolyn Brooks (1917–) African-American poet.

8

Birth anniversary of:
> Frank Lloyd Wright (1867–1959). Architect.

9

Anniversary of Hong Kong lease (1898). The ninety-nine-year British lease will expire in 1997, at which time Hong Kong will revert to Chinese rule.
Birth anniversary of:
> Cole Porter (1893–1964). Composer.
> George Stephenson (1781–1848). English inventor and developer of the steam locomotive.

10

Jordan: Great Arab Revolt and Army Day.
Birth anniversary of:
> Judy Garland (1922–1969). Actress and singer; best known as Dorothy in *The Wizard of Oz*.
> Hattie McDaniel (1889–1952). First African-American to win an Academy Award.
> Maurice Sendak (1928–). Illustrator and author of *Where the Wild Things Are*.

11

King Kamehameha I Day. Observed in Hawaii to honor the memory of the Hawaiian monarch.
Birth anniversary of:
> Ben Jonson (1572–1637). English playwright and poet.
> Jeannette Rankin (1880–1973). First woman member of the U.S. Congress.

12

Philippines Independence Day. Declared independence from Spain in 1898.
Birth anniversary of:
> George Bush (1924–). Forty-third president of the United States; born in Massachusetts.

13

Birth anniversary of:
> William Butler Yeats (1865–1939). Irish poet and dramatist.

14

Flag Day. Commemorating the anniversary of the Stars and Stripes.
Birth anniversary of:
> Harriet Beecher Stowe (1811–1896). Writer and author of *Uncle Tom's Cabin*.

15

Arkansas Admission Day. Became twenty-fifth state admitted to the Union (1836).
Magna Carta Day. Commemorating the signing of the Magna Carta by King John in 1215.
Birth anniversary of:
> Edvard Grieg (1843–1907). Norwegian pianist and composer.

16

Birth anniversary of:
> John Howard Griffin (1920–1980). Writer and photographer; author of *Black Like Me*.

17

Birth anniversary of:
> Igor Stravinsky (1882–1971). Russian composer.

18

Anniversary of Battle of Waterloo. Commemorating Napoleon's defeat in 1815.
Egypt Evacuation Day. Commemorating the withdrawal of British troops from the Suez Canal in 1954.
First American woman in space. In 1983, Sally Ride became the first American woman to orbit the earth in space.

19

Juneteenth. Celebrated especially in Texas and southern states to commemorate the freeing of slaves in Texas in 1865.
Birth anniversary of:
> Lou Gehrig (1903–1941). Baseball player; died from the degenerative muscle disease alateral sclerosis, often called Lou Gehrig's Disease.
> Blaise Pascal (1623–1662). French philosopher and mathematician.

20

Caroline Baldwin became first woman to earn doctorate in science (1895).

West Virginia Admission Day. Became thirty-fifth state admitted to the Union (1863).

21

Summer solstice. On or about this day each year, the sun shines directly from the northernmost point of its journey.

India: Ratha Yatra. Festival to honor Lord Jagannath, lord of the universe.

New Hampshire became ninth state to ratify the Constitution (1788).

Birth anniversary of:

>Henry Ossawa Tanner (1859–?) First African-American artist allowed to exhibit his works in U.S. galleries.

>Martha Custis Washington (1731–1802). Wife of the first president of the United States.

22

Malta: Mnarja. Folk harvest festival celebrated with music and dancing.

23

Luxembourg National Independence holiday.

Sweden Midsummer celebration. Scandinavian countries celebrate the holiday with games, dancing, and folk music.

24

Margaret Brent became first woman to demand the vote in colonial America (1647).

Birth anniversary of:

>Henry Ward Beecher (1813–1887). Church leader and orator.

25

Battle of Little Big Horn (1876). George Custer and his soldiers killed by Sioux warriors led by Chiefs Sitting Bull and Crazy Horse.

Mozambique National Day. Gained independence from Portugal in 1975.

Virginia became tenth state to ratify the constitution (1788).

26

Madagascar Independence Day. Gained independence from France in 1960.

United Nations charter signed (1945).

Birth anniversary of:

>Pearl Buck (1892–1973). Author known for *The Good Earth.*

27

Djibouti National Holiday. Located in eastern Africa; became independent of foreign rule in 1977.

Birth anniversary of:

>Helen Keller (1880–1968). Advocate for persons who are blind and deaf.

28

Birth anniversary of:

>Clara Maass (1876–1901). Nurse who died during experiments involving the study of yellow fever.

>Jean Rousseau (1712–1778). French philosopher.

>Peter Paul Rubens (1577–1640). Flemish artist.

29

Birth anniversary of:

>William James Mayo (1861–1939). Surgeon and co-founder of the Mayo Clinic in Minnesota.

30

Zaire Independence Day. Became independent of foreign rule in 1960.

Using Oral History
in the Classroom

Teaching Unit for June

A Word about This Unit. Oral histories have been collected for generations. In a sense, an oral history technique was used when, in early civilizations, elders told stories and related past events to the younger members of their group. For the purpose of this unit, oral histories are spoken accounts by an individual about her life or an event in which she was a participant or observed first hand. This oral account, given by one person, the *interviewee,* is then documented or recorded, either in writing or on magnetic tape, by another person, the *interviewer.*

The basis for any historical inquiry is the data that will be used by an investigator to reconstruct and interpret the past. Traditionally, historians have used a variety of written sources for such studies, including books, letters, deeds, diaries, baptismal records, and tax receipts. Particularly in American culture, the historian largely has been a student of written history. However, valid resources other than written works can be used to interpret the past. Indeed, societies without a written language have often transmitted a detailed account of their prior experiences through an oral tradition. Historic and prehistoric periods of human existence have been distinguished between on the basis of the use of an alphabet and written records. Oral, rather than written, transmission need not imply a lack of concern for accuracy. Where they have been validated, oral accounts are often quite accurate when checked against written sources. Thus, oral history has an honorable place within the formal academic discipline.

Although some oral histories were collected during the first part of the twentieth century, it was not until the 1970s that this historical method of gathering data became popular. Prior to that time, oral histories consisted mostly of interviews with famous historical figures or prominent local individuals (Banks, 1990). However, during the last twenty-five years, much has been done to preserve the stories of ordinary people. The Foxfire project, initiated by Eliot Wigginton in Rabun Gap, Georgia, has popularized this approach, especially in middle and high schools across the nation (Sitton et al., 1983).

Rationale. This unit is designed to help motivate students to participate in projects that will bring a better

understanding and a greater appreciation of past events and of people who experienced those events. Too often, historians and recorders of social institutions report only on the lives and events of individuals of the dominant culture. This project will give students an opportunity to learn about and preserve the accounts of people who typically have been excluded from historical tomes in the past. These groups might include, but need not be limited to, members of a minority, women, elderly citizens, children, and similar individuals who have contributions to offer, but whose voices often are not heard in a formal sense.

One important direction that this project can take relates to interviewing and collecting stories from older people. Almost all students have accessibility to older people either in their families or their neighborhoods. For many students, the notion of an extended family that includes grandparents or older aunts and uncles living in the same household is beyond their experience. In today's society, for a student to talk to someone of retirement age or older, in a meaningful context—family member or otherwise—may be an unusual occurrence. However, there is an important lesson to be learned if young people can be brought together with older citizens for meaningful discussion. The value of such an assignment is evident in an account given by one of Wigginton's students during the early years of the Foxfire project (Wigginton; 1972, p. 20). The student, Paul Gillespie, states, "It wasn't until I worked on *Foxfire* for five months that an inexplicable void between myself and the old people of our region disappeared. The void was mysterious, but it still existed." Gillespie speculates, "maybe it was instilled hostilities toward older generations. Maybe it was the fact that I just couldn't see their importance or the relevance of what they had to say to the way I live today." He continues, "then I met Aunt Arie. . . . Everything she had—from the stern-looking pictures of her grandparents to the fireplace that was her only source of heat—made me stop and look deeply for the first time."

Motivation. The value of collecting oral histories, whether as an assignment related to preserving an aspect of local history or to collecting personal histories of family members, should be discussed with the students. This activity should provide a springboard to appropriate topics, as well as ways of "making the connection" between younger and older generations. You should have a variety of possible oral history topics available, but first the class should brainstorm, listing as many potential projects as they can.

Information. A successful oral history project does not happen without teaching students how to plan their projects and instructing them about the techniques which will help create a successful product. The remainder of this unit will outline procedures you can use to help your students undertake a variety of projects related to collecting oral histories.

Continuing the Oral History Tradition

Preparing for an Oral History Project. From a teacher's perspective, an oral history project can be a potent means of introducing students to historical inquiry. It is a stimulating and effective method to enable young people to "do history," that is, to practice the methods of inquiry associated with the discipline. An additional instructional benefit is that at the same time the student also is engaged in reflective, creative, and critical thought processes.

However, it is common for teachers interested in using oral history to fall prey to the common misconception that collecting and recording oral history is easy. Often people believe that all one has to do is ask the subject questions and tape-record the answers. Those who have had experience with collecting oral histories know that this is not the case. Numerous mistakes may result if the teacher does not help the student carefully and deliberately plan for the project. As is the case with many endeavors, the quality of the planning will largely determine the success of the actual interview.

Selecting a Topic for the Project. Students must be clear on at least two interrelated questions before beginning an oral history project: Whom shall I interview, and what shall I ask? You have several options for directing the course of the project. Determining the topic of inquiry may be developed from the district's established curricula or from discussions within the classroom related to local events or persons. For example, if the social science curriculum includes study of the Great Depression, a logical oral history topic would be to interview people who lived during that historic period. Or, if classroom discussion and interest

has turned to war and its effects on people and their attitudes related to it, then interviewing people who lived during one of the wars (World War I, World War II, Korea, or Vietnam) would be appropriate. Another timely subject, but one in which the interviewer must exercise caution, is the topic of integration. Interesting accounts could be obtained from parents of your students relating their experiences and emotions during the time their schools were first integrated. Obviously, this assignment could become a delicate issue and should be handled with sensitivity. The Foxfire concept is a model for interviewing local people who may have a story to tell, either about themselves or some aspect of local history.

Conducting Background Research. Students who are preparing to do an oral history project should conduct background research about the selected topic. Perhaps the most significant reason for this is so that the student can gain the necessary familiarity with, and understanding of, the particular topic that forms the intellectual core of the project. Background research provides particular benefits:

1. It allows the student to make efficient use of time involved in the interview process by limiting the number of questions asked to those that are most appropriate for the aims or the purposes of the study.
2. It enables the student as the interviewer to ask the subject more meaningful questions. This will have the added benefit not only of improving the quality of the oral history project, but will also make a more favorable impression on the interviewee.
3. It assists the interviewer in asking questions or making remarks during the course of the interview and may serve to stimulate the memory of the subject. The more the interviewer knows about the background, the easier it is to check the accuracy of the testimony of the interviewee. That is, either deliberately or unconsciously, the subject of the interview may tend to color his or her responses in favorable or even flattering terms. If the person being interviewed believes that the interviewer knows about the state of affairs or the particular situation that is being discussed, he or she will be less likely to add material that may be of doubtful validity or accuracy.
4. It commits the student to the interview.

Constructing Questions for the Interview. After researching background information about the topic, the class may begin to generate questions which could be answered through interviewing people who were witnesses to or who knew about an event. The quality and relevance of these questions would determine the significance of the outcome of the interview. Thus, it is appropriate to sketch out some guidelines that might be used by students during their interviews. In preparing the set of questions the students should include only those that are most significant and relevant to the project itself.

Two basic strategies can be used in preparing to conduct an interview. One approach is to carefully prepare a list of detailed questions related to the topic to be researched. This could be anything from a set of structured questions for discussion to a questionnaire based on a checklist or short-answer responses. The interview would consist of asking the subject these questions and recording the responses. A second strategy would be to select some general question areas that would be covered; the specific questions and ordering of these questions would depend on the dynamics of the interview as it unfolds. The second strategy probably works better with students who have had some experience as interviewers. An inexperienced interviewer will likely need the structure of prepared questions in order to stay within the confines of the topic.

After the students have formulated an initial set of questions that they feel are significant and relevant to the project, they should determine the proper sequence in which the questions should be asked. Very frequently, a logical relationship will exist among the set of questions. For example, a general question may be posed initially, and then followed with other questions that seek examples or more particular instances.

In the early phase of the interview, questions that are likely to evoke merely yes or no responses, should be avoided. Rather, the interview should begin with a question that will be both easy to answer and is likely to evoke a significant or lengthy response by the subject. This approach gets things going. The idea is to communicate to the subject that the student, as the interviewer, will be primarily a listener and that the purpose of the interview is to allow the subject ample time to respond at length and in detail about the event.

Arranging the Interview. It is important to establish contact with the subject as early as possible. Early contact has benefits to the subject and the interviewer, for it enables the interviewer the opportunity to make necessary modifications in scheduling. This early contact also gives the students a definite orientation and direction on their research efforts and time to prepare further questions.

During the initial contact with the subject, the interviewer will be more likely to get a favorable response if some kind of background or rationale for the requested interview is given. Usually a telephone call is all that is necessary to set up the interview. This initial contact should make clear:

1. The objective of the research study
2. The reason for desiring an interview with that particular person and the importance of the study and this individual's contribution
3. Some details of the projected interview, that is, the particular kinds of questions that will be discussed
4. Whether the subject is able to contribute significantly to the project
5. Whether the subject knows about or owns material that might be relevant to the project and whether the subject knows of other individuals who should be consulted

Practicality dictates that the subject be called a short time before the interview is scheduled, as a reminder, recounting the time and place. This will eliminate surprise visits or "no-shows" when a subject has absent-mindedly forgotten the interview.

Conducting the Interview. Logistical concerns are involved in preparing for the interview. If students use materials such as a tape recorder or, in some cases, even video recorders, then they must ensure that the equipment is working properly. This often can be done within the context of the interview itself. This may serve as one way for helping the interviewer to begin by including the subject without seeming to be too abrupt. For example, while doing an equipment check, one should begin by identifying the individual and noting pertinent information about the interviewee—the answers to the traditional who, when, where, and by whom questions. This allows the interviewer to begin the discussion and check the working condition of the equipment while helping to orient the subject in the process. Such a beginning enables the interviewer to explain the purpose of the interview, to set the general tone, and to document the signing of any releases that are required by law or to comply with various rules and regulations that may be stipulated by the school district. The interviewer could, while identifying the individual being interviewed, indicate (as an initial question) that the subject understands that the content of this interview may be used in documents that may emanate from this oral history project. It is desirable to frame this as a question to get the affirmative response of the subject recorded on the tape. Then a written release should be signed by the subject. It might be appropriate, as well, to communicate to the subject that the interviewer sees the subject as a valuable source of information and, indeed, as a kind of a mentor or teacher during the interview. This may prove to be helpful in gaining the active participation of the subject in the process.

It also is appropriate to use photos or other artifacts to stimulate the memory of the subject during the

course of the interview. For example, if there were others present in the situation in which the subject was a participant, pictures of those individuals would be appropriate. The visual images might serve to stimulate the memory of the subject. Of course, the main crux of the interview would be questions by the interviewer about the topic or event.

Among the other things with which the student should be concerned as the interview progresses is how she is being projected to the subject. The interviewer must be a very attentive participant in this process and communicate that she is listening carefully to the responses. Body language, as well as the kind of overt questions and responses that are made to the subject's remarks, is important. If the student is taking notes, in addition to recording the responses, she must make sure that these activities are done discreetly. In no case should the notetaking interfere with, or retard, the course of the interview.

The focus should be on the subject and not on the interviewer during this process. As a historian, concerned with the accuracy of data, the student should keep several caveats in mind during discussions with the subject. She should also be careful not to ask leading or "loaded" questions. If the words spoken by the subject contain any kind of emotive shadings of meanings or connotations, they should stem from his feelings, rather than from being stimulated or encouraged by the particular phrasing of the questions posed by the interviewer. Periodically during the process, various reinforcers might be used by the interviewer to let the subject know that his responses to the questions are informative and valuable. Such reinforcement serves to give the subject the notion that he is playing an important part in the project.

It is also good to spend some time with the interviewee after the interview is over and to thank him again. The interviewer should try to leave the individual with a good feeling about participation in the project. This will make it easier if an additional interview is necessary. The interviewer should also check to ensure that the spelling of names, dates, and locations mentioned during the interview are accurate.

Following the Interview. After the interviews have been conducted and the data recorded, you should be involved in the process of helping the students transcribe their notes. This should be done as soon after the interviews as possible, so that impressions of the interviews will be fresh in the students' minds and can be verified by referring to the tapes. Transcribing an interview is much more time consuming than might be expected, often taking three or four times longer than the interview itself. However, it is this exercise that will enable students to create a meaningful document from the interview, for without the transcription, the interview remains nothing more than magnetic configurations on a strip of tape.

There is a significant assessment stage in the oral history project itself, namely that of addressing "meta-questions" about those asked during the interview. Examples of these would be how effective or how successful the interview was in accomplishing its purpose, the subject's cooperativeness, and the reliability and validity of the responses. Indeed, one of the most difficult skills for the historian to acquire is that of assessing and evaluating the accuracy and the reliability of subjects' statements.

An issue to be discussed with the students is ways in which the interview could have been improved. If the interview were to be done again, what changes might be incorporated to make it more effective? The final question confronting the interviewer is one of interpretation: What do these data mean? How do they fit with other known information? Do they validate or refute earlier information?

Instructional Activities

Activity 10.1: Family History Project

For this activity, students can interview parents, grandparents, aunts, and uncles to learn as much as possible about their family. They can seek to answer such questions as: Who were our ancestors? Where did they come from? What were they like? How did they live? Family records, Bibles, notebooks, letters, wills, deeds, photographs, and other primary sources may be helpful. Some questions may relate to the disciplines of the social sciences, as discussed in the following paragraphs.

History. Who are/were my parents, grandparents, great-grandparents, and so on? What do you know about my family origin? Nationality? Language? What is our "story" or history? What are the family names in my lineage? What are some interesting stories told in our family about significant events and family members?

Sociology. What values do/did our family hold? How are they alike or different from those held by the majority of our community? Were our family background and experiences similar to or different from those of most other families in our community?

Anthropology. What were/are some important customs practiced in our family? What are some important beliefs we hold? What are/were some family traditions related to weddings, births, deaths, holidays, family folklore, and so on?

Political Science. What are some rules that are/were important in our family? How are/were they enforced and by whom?

Economics. What occupations do/did our family members engage in? Who is/was the principal wage-earner in our family? Were there periods of time in our family when money was especially plentiful or scarce?

Geography. Historically, where were our family's roots? In what cities, states, or countries have the members of our family lived? In what places have I lived since birth?

For the Student. The above are just a few examples of questions which may help you record "Who am I?" and how your heritage has contributed to make you the person you are. In an interview, it is often desirable to record on audio or videotape the conversation between you and the interviewee. This is especially so for older persons or someone who will not be readily available when you need to clarify information from your notes. It is also helpful to have a series of specific questions from which to conduct the process. For example, the statement, "Tell me about our family," doesn't give the interviewee proper focus. Along with general questions about your family, you should ask such things as: Tell me about your very best holiday experience. Were you ever punished at school for something you did not do? What was my father/mother like when he/she was a small child? Why did you move to the place we are living now? Of course, the direction and questions of each interview will depend on who is being interviewed and what information you already know.

A Word of Caution. Some parents may not wish to participate in a project of the type suggested here. There may be a number of reasons given, but regardless of the objections, it would be a good idea to make this assignment optional. A letter to the parents indicating the objectives and mechanics of the assignment should be sent before students are asked to participate in the project. After parental (or guardian) consent is given, the students can proceed.

Activity 10.2: Favorite Family Stories

Students may have heard a particular family story told many times by various family members. It could be about the student, his father, or someone else in the family; if the student considers the story to be very interesting, he may wish to preserve it or transcribe it for future reference. For this activity, the student should identify the best person to give the most accurate and interesting account, and then record it on audio or videotape. After the interview, it should be transcribed into text. If necessary, the interview should be followed with additional questions to help clarify confusing statements or to obtain information that would make the story more complete. Then the account should be revised and edited to include the elements of a good story: who, what, when, where, and how. Bibliographical information about who told the story and when should be included. Students can share these family stories with the class.

Activity 10.3: Where Have We Been? Where Are We Going?

This activity is related to geography. Like all people, the students' ancestors probably have lived in many different places. They should ask their parents and grandparents to list the places they have lived and when, and then complete the chart "The Movers of My Family" with as many facts as they can. On an outline map (state, regional, national, or international) students can trace the movement of their families, placing the dates they lived, if known, by each location.

Activity 10.4: Collecting Oral Histories Among Peers

This activity could be done as an individual or group project. Begin with an appropriate topic for students in your class. Suggestions for such topics include: my favorite stories about me as a child, what I was most afraid of when I was a child, stories about my favorite/least favorite teachers, etc. With an older group,

THE MOVERS OF MY FAMILY

Who	*Time*	*Place Lived*	*Occupation*
_____	_____	_____	_____
_____	_____	_____	_____
_____	_____	_____	_____
_____	_____	_____	_____

you may included topics of a more mature nature: how I overcame my fear of people who are different; how I came to understand what it's like to be handicapped; how I came to a better understanding of people with different religious beliefs. Once the topic or topics have been chosen, students who are willing to tell their story may be interviewed. The interviews can then be transcribed, edited, and compiled into a booklet for distribution.

Activity 10.5: Using Oral Histories for Readers Theater Projects

A good way to share oral histories with your students is to present some of the more interesting accounts in a Readers Theater format. One approach is to use some of the research collected by the students. They would need to select material around an appropriate theme and then edit and organize for it an oral presentation.

A second approach is to take material from published oral history sources and create a Readers Theater program around a desired theme. Several books are available that contain appropriate material. Most of the references available are generally suited for mature audiences. You will need to examine these references carefully to select those appropriate for your students. Sample references are included in the Suggested Reading list.

Suggested Readings

Atkin, S. B. (1993). *Voices from the fields: Children of migrant farmworkers tell their stories.* Boston: Little, Brown.

Cooper, P., & Bradley Buferd, N. (1978). *The quilters: Women and domestic art, an oral history.* Garden City, NY, Doubleday.

Cusick, P. A. (1974). *Inside high school: The student's world.* Nashville: American Association for State and Local History.

Gallagher, D. (1976). *Hannah's daughters: Six generations of an American family, 1876–1976.* New York: Thomas Y. Crowell.

Gluck, S. (1976). *From parlor to prison: Five American suffragists talk about their lives.* New York: Vintage Press.

Jellison, C. A. (1977). *Tomatoes were cheaper: Tales from the thirties.* Syracuse, NY: Syracuse University Press.

Joseph, P. (1974). *Good times: An oral history of America in the nineteen sixties.* New York: William Morrow.

Kahn, K. (1972). *Hillbilly women.* New York: Doubleday.

Lewis, O. (1961). *The children of Sanchez: Autobiography of a Mexican family.* New York: Random House.

Lifton, R. J. (1967). *Death in life: Survivors of Hiroshima.* New York: Random House.

Namias, J. (1978). *First generation: Oral histories of twentieth-century American immigrants.* Boston: Beacon Press.

Robinson, J. L. (1981). *Living hard: Southern Americans in the Great Depression.* Washington, DC: University Press of America.

Terrill, T. E. & Hirsch, J. (Eds.). (1978). *Such as us: Southern voices of the thirties.* Chapel Hill: University of North Carolina Press.

Wigginton, E. (Ed.). (1972). *The foxfire book.* Garden City, NY: Doubleday.

Wigginton, E. (Ed.). (1976). *I wish I could give my son a wild raccoon.* Garden City, NY: Anchor Books.

References and Bibliography

Banks, J. A. (1990). *Teaching strategies for the social studies: Inquiry, valuing, and decision-making* (4th ed.). New York: Longman.

Baum, W. K. (1969). *Oral history for the local historical society.* Stockton: Conference of California Historical Societies.

Baum, W. K. (1977). *Transcribing and editing oral history.* Nashville: American Association for State and Local History.

Harris, R. I. (1975). *The practice of oral history: A handbook.* Glen Rock, NJ: Microfilming Corporation of America.

Hoopes, J. (1979). *Oral history: An introduction for students.* Chapel Hill: University of North Carolina Press.

Ives, E. D. (1980). *The tape-recorded interview: A manual for field workers in folklore and oral history.* Knoxville: University of Tennessee Press.

Neuenschwander, J. A. (1976). *Oral history as a teaching approach.* Washington, DC: National Educational Association.

Schoemaker, G. H. (Ed.). (1990). *The emergence of folklore in everyday life: A fieldguide and sourcebook.* Bloomington: Trickster Press, Indiana University.

Shumway, G. L. (Compiler). (1971). *Oral history in the United States: A directory.* New York: Oral History Association.

Sitton, T., et al. (1983). *Oral history: A guide for teachers (and others)*. Austin: University of Texas Press.

Wigginton, E. (Ed.). (1972). *The foxfire book.* Garden City, NY: Anchor Books.

June's Potpourri of Teaching Ideas

The purpose of each month's Potpourri of Teaching Ideas is to provide additional resources from which to build your curriculum. Most, but not all, of the activities listed each month relate directly to that month. It is not intended that you use them all, but rather that you choose those which are appropriate for your program. Although the topics are written for a particular month, many of them would be appropriate for use throughout the year. How you use these activities will depend on your curricular goals. You may wish to use some of the activities as they are presented, and you may need to modify some to meet your needs. Perhaps some of them will give you ideas for entirely different potpourris.

English: Gifts from Many Languages

Ask your students the following questions and have them write their responses either individually or in groups. As they struggle with the answers, follow with questions such as "How do we know?" and "Why do you think this is true?"

Why do we use the word *senator* for the person who represents us in our government?

When do we *gerrymander?*

Bailiff is a French word, but we use the same word in English. Why?

Information. English, a member of the Indo-European family of languages, is sometimes described as having three main periods representing different stages in its development. The language spoken in England from the end of 700 to 1100 is called Old English or Anglo-Saxon; the language spoken between 1100 and 1500 is known as Middle English; and modern English dates rom 1500. *Beowulf* is written in Old English, *The Canterbury Tales* is written in Middle English, and Shakespeare wrote using early modern English.

Before A.D. 43, when the Romans conquered Britain, the British Isles were inhabited by Celtic-speaking peoples. After the Romans left in A.D. 410, the king of the Romanized Celts in Britain, feeling threatened by the Picts and Scots from the north, asked for aid from three Germanic tribes living in what is today northern Germany and sourthern Denmark. When that aid came, the soldiers decided to settle, leaving the Celts only Scotland, Wales, and Cornwall. This group of invaders spoke closely related dialects of West Germanic. The old English language spoken by these early Germanic invaders of England and their offspring is often called Anglo-Saxon.

Once more, in approximately A.D. 850, the Anglo-Saxon peoples were invaded, this time by other Germanic groups—Danes, Vikings, and Norwegians. After treaties, the Danes agreed to become Christian and to remain in a large section of land in eastern and northern England. By 1400, many English place names were of Scandinavian origin (Finegan & Besnier, 1989). Example are those ending in *-by* (farm, town), *-thorp* (village), *-thwaite* (isolated piece of land), and *-toft* (piece of ground). Like the development of many languages, the mix of Germanic dialects spoken by the Anglo-Saxon invaders and those spoken by the Scandinavian settlers created a distinct language.

The speaking of Old English (700 to 100) resulted from the invasion of England by the Anglos, Saxons, and Jutes. King Alfred was a very powerful leader and his dialect in West Saxon achieved status. This dialect is the language we see in the Old English literature that survives even today. Old English was highly inflected, with suffixes on nouns, pronouns, verbs, adjectives, and even determiners.

Middle English dates from the Norman Invasion in 1066. The French language spoken by the Norman invaders quickly became the language of the ruling class. The vocabulary of Middle English contained thousands of French words. Many of today's words related to religion, government, the courts, and armed forces reflect this period of time. Legal words that became part of English at this time include judgment, plea, evidence, proof, prison, and jail.

During the late 1400s, there was a major shift in English. All the long vowels in Middle English underwent a systematic shift. The inflections at the ends of words had been simplified and word order had become fixed. In modern English, nouns are inflected only for possessive and number, word order signals grammatical relationships. Since that time, words have been added to the language either through invention or through borrowing, but there have been no major changes in the syntax. Probably the most significant reason that English has developed and enlarged is the influence of people from many countries living together and interacting with one another.

Try This: Borrowed or Invented? Many words in English are borrowed from other languages or are created to fit a situation or a recent development or invention. Have your students investiagte the origins of words

BORROWED OR INVENTED?

Word or phrase _____

Meaning _____

Etymology (how the word or phrase came into English) _____

_____

_____

used in social studies. Many of them came directly from the French during the period of Middle English; others, however, are more recent additions.

The class can begin with these words: assassin, attorney, bailiff, capital, caucus, cold war, conquistador, court, decade, felony, glasnost, gerrymander, iron curtain, justice, law larceny, paparazzi, pentagon, plaintiff, senator, witness.

English words have been incorporated into other languages of the world as well. If your students speak a language other than English, or if they know someone who does, have them make a list of English words that have become a part of that language.

Suggested Readings

Bloomfield, M. W. (1972). A brief history of the English language. In Shores, D. L. (Ed.). *Contemporary English: Change and variation.* Philadelphia: J. B. Lippincott.

Brook, G. L. (1958). *A history of the English language.* New York: W. W. Norton.

Finegan, E. & Besnier, N. (1989). *Language: Its structure and use.* San Diego: Harcourt Brace Jovanovich.

Roberts, P. (1985). A brief history of English. In Clark, V. P., et al. (Eds.). *Language: Introductory readings* (4th ed) New York: St. Martin's Press.

Numerals: Gifts from Many Cultures

Ask your students the following questions and have them write their responses either individually or in groups. As they struggle with the answers, follow with questions such as "How do we know?" and "Why do you think this is true?"

Why do we have a number system that is based on ten? Why do we use the terms "arabic" and "roman" numerals?

The history of the beginning of a method for counting and systematic use of numbers demonstrates how great ideas have evolved over time and across various cultures. In the earliest times, there were no numbers nor did there appear to be a need for them because people were hunters and gatherers. Later, as they needed to keep track of the animals they spotted while hunting or of their own animal herd, a way of recording and representing that information was necessary. This first system was probably a one-to-one correspondence using pebbles or twigs to represent the objects being counted.

Once people found the one-to-one correspondence, they probably began to use the idea of more or less. That is, they may have had more or fewer pebbles left than sheep they herded. In addition, it became possible to have a pebble represent more than one. For example, the herder could use one pebble for the same number of animals as there were fingers on one hand or one stick for five pebbles. People then may have moved to the next symbolic representation, the use of language to describe the number of objects. Once people gave quantities names, counting became important.

Today, we use ten as the base for our number system. We group objects in tens; in ten tens, or hundreds, in ten hundreds, or thousands; and so on. At one time, different cultures in the world used different bases for their number systems: the Chinese used two as a base, the people living on the banks of the Euphrates used three, and the people of the Nile region used five. The Babylonian system used sixty as a base, one of the largest. This is the system we employ today when we measure time (sixty minutes are equal to one hour) and angles, which are recorded in degrees.

The Egyptians, Mesopotamians, and Chinese used number signs as they came to understand the idea of numbers. The people in India created nine different numerals to record numbers of objects. They first used a dot to stand in the place where there were no elements. For example, to write *two hundred and two*, a dot was placed in the tens' position. This later became the zero. Because the Indian Hindus were traders, when they traveled they took this idea with them and shared

ONES AROUND THE WORLD

Symbol	Arabic	Country	Name	Pronunciation
1	one	United States	one	wun
___	___	China	ee	ee
___	___	France	un	uhng
___	___	Germany	ein	eyn
___	___	Spain	uno	oo no
___	___	Israel	achoid	ach oid

it with the Arabs, who carried these ideas farther west. The people living in Spain began to use the base ten number signs. These numerals were eventually called arabic numerals and came into use all over Europe. The shape of numerals changed many times until printing was invented. Then, the standard shape we know today was maintained.

Drawing Generalizations. After completing the chart "Ones around the World," students can write in their journals, complete reports, create charts, or engage in discussions related to the following questions:

Why do we have a number system that is a based on ten?

In the modern world, what are examples of other bases?

Suggested Readings

Carona, P. (1964). *The true book of numbers.* Chicago: Childrens Press.

Childcraft: The how and why library: Vol. 13. Mathemagic. (1986). Chicago: World Book.

Dunham, M. (1987). *Numbers: How do you say it?* New York: Lothrop, Lee & Shepard.

Hogben, L. (1968). *The wonderful world of mathematics.* Garden City, NY: Doubleday.

Shaw, A., & Fuge, K. (1963). *The story of mathematics.* London: Edward Arnold Publishers.

More Than a Place to Hang Your Hat and to Rest Your Head: Architecture and Human Culture

Architecture is the "art and science of building," involving both the design and construction of buildings. *Art* and *science* in the definition infer that there are aesthetic as well as practical concerns. Many of those in the field are not only competent in terms of the basic requirements of a structure's safety and utility, but highly creative in their design and conceptualization of the structural plans.

Frank Lloyd Wright, one of America's most notable architects, was born in June 1867 and lived well into this century. As is the case with most innovative minds in any area, his life and architectural work were not without controversy. Others have done much to design and oversee the construction of buildings that all would recognize. A small sampling of more recent figures would include R. Buckminster Fuller (geodesic dome), Walter Gropius, Louis Kahn, Ludwig Mies van der Rohe, Eero Saarinen, Louis Sullivan, and Minoru Yamasaki. Other architects have designed buildings that we would recognize immediately, but their names are much less familiar: James Hoban, Henry Bacon, Benjamin Latrobe, and Frederick Olmsted.

The structure that we think of immediately in this context is our home, although what constitutes the place where we live varies markedly from culture to culture. Many early humans were organized in social groups that tended to be nomadic and did not have permanent habitats. Some of these groups' movements were influenced by seasonal changes as they accompanied their herds to different grazing locales during the year. Others, such as certain Native American groups, followed the herds of bison. These groups, along with all humans, required shelter from the elements, but their way of living necessitated a more portable structure than those constructed by groups that were more pastoral. The tents of the Berbers and Bedouins, the teepees of the Plains Indians and similar structures (in construction though not in shape) of the Chuckchees who live on the tundra regions near the Bering and East Siberian seas, and the wagons of the Gypsy peoples throughout Europe are among the variety of such portable habitats.

It is immediately obvious that our homes fulfill our need for shelter. They provide us with a place in which we are protected from the less desirable features of our physical environment, such as the extremes of temperature and inclement weather, as well as from the physical harm or danger that animals or other humans represent.

In time, the structures that housed the individual members of the society often were perceived as insufficient in size or not appropriate for holding other culturally necessary activities. Other buildings were designed and constructed that were more suited to these economic, political, or religious activities. In climates that were relatively mild, many of these functions could be conducted outdoors, and structures were not as necessary as they were in harsher regions. These structures were often sited in natural settings that fit the purpose for which they were constructed. For example, temples were often located in elevated spots (the temples located on the acropolis in Athens and those of the Mayas in Central America were shaped in such a way that they were directed to the heavens), and amphitheaters took advantage of natural formations such as hillsides. The body of archaeological study seems to support the view that the orientation of many structures held astronomical significance. For example, light shining through some aperture in a structure might fall at a particular place at the time of the equinox or another important time in the life of a group, such as those denoting when crops should be planted or marking other significant events.

Although the practical or scientific aspect of human structures is immediately obvious, the other aspect of the definition should not be neglected. A trait of human beings, whenever and wherever they may be found, is the urge to exhibit creativity in the artifacts used in daily living and in meeting the basic needs of the group. Examples of such creativity, even in the most utilitarian of objects, are abundant. As some people became less nomadic, planted seeds, and remained at least long enough to harvest a crop, structures would be needed to store any surplus that might result, and those responsible for the welfare of the group would recognize that at least some of the crop had to be preserved as seeds for another planting. From a utilitarian perspective, such buildings needed only to be functional. However, many of these structures were not merely aesthetically pleasing, but of exquisite shape and exhibiting complex and intricate designs, each an original work of the hand of its creator. Similar creativity was demonstrated in the design of buildings used as dwellings and for other purposes. These creative touches might include an innovative use of the materials used to construct the building, designs on the exterior or interior of the structure, and even the arrangement of the building with regard to the natural features of the physical environment or its relationship to other buildings in the area.

First, good use would be made of the physical materials at hand, whether it be stone that was easily shaped, wood, bricks of local clays, mud and straw hardened by the sun, skins of animals, bark, even fibrous materials woven together. Long before there were formal schools of architecture, craftsmen worked with materials and designed and built in such a way that the integrity of the structure was maintained, the social functions of the building were met, and the "architect" and those who used it could be proud of its existence.

Certain structures reflect not only the materials at hand, but also the lifestyles of the groups that construct them. Mention has already been made of nomadic peoples. The architects living in these groups must consider many things in the design and construction of structures for their group members, including ease of construction and disassembly, durability, ease of transport, and weight. If one were an Inuit trekking across the polar region, one would certainly want a structure that would make use of materials at hand, be easily and quickly constructed, prove durable, and protect one from the harshness of the weather. It is highly unlikely that even the most sophisticated of architectural designs could meet all of these criteria as well as does the igloo.

Try These Activities

The Need for Shelter. Occasionally a natural disaster strikes a community—a tornado, hurricane, catastrophic fire, or flood. Encourage students to discuss among themselves how they and their families would begin to meet the need for shelter. They should consider not only what constitutes a "roof over their heads" (a shelter that offers a place to sleep and relax, eat, and store one's belongings), but also the extended social function of a home, a place used to entertain company and for other special occasions of family and social life.

As groups of students offer their suggestions to classmates and reflect on the difficulties that would ensue from such a state of affairs, you might point out to the class that for the thousands of homeless individuals in our nation and other nations of the world, this is a fact of their current existence, not merely a temporary problem resulting from some *disastrous* act of Mother Nature.

The "Nomadic" Life. The following scenario could be sketched out for the class. Due to circumstances, your family life requires frequent and extensive travel. It is likely that you will not be living in a space as large as your present home. You will have to strictly limit the amount of personal possessions that you can carry with you during your family's travels.

Students should be encouraged to share their thoughts with their classmates regarding questions such as the following. Which possessions, such as clothes, toys, and electronic devices, would you choose to take along, and why would you make this selection? Who are your friends now? Would you be able to maintain these friendships? How? How would you make new friends? What problems might you face making friends under such conditions?

With the assistance of the librarian, students might read stories of children living in nomadic cultures. Using the skills acquired during the unit on oral history, they might also interview students or individuals who have lived in similar conditions, for example, children of military personnel or workers involved in occupations that required residence in other countries for extended periods.

The Work of the Architect. Invite an architect to visit with the class so that the students can determine what such a person does in his or her work and how he or she sets about developing a design for a particular structure. A sampling of the types of questions that might be asked include: What is involved in your work? For whom do you work? What kinds of information and skills do you provide to your clients, and what kinds of information do you seek from them? What sorts of cultural and environmental factors might you take into account during your work, and what type of impact do they have on your work?

As students have already gleaned from their previous activities in oral history, the list of questions and topics that they wish to pursue with the architect should be formulated well before the session. You may wish to send the list to the architect before the session with the class.

Different groups of students can also develop particular sets of conditions, for example, different physical environments in which a structure is to be sited and various social or cultural activities for which the structure is to be used. They can then work with an architect to learn the process of planning structures appropriate for the site, function, and available materials.

Students can then compare the work of present-day architects with the efforts of artisans and craftspersons from other cultures and periods of history. They should consider whether the same factors that were of importance to earlier architects are still involved in designing and constructing structures.

If a classroom visit is not possible, consider sending a team of students to interview an architect at a more suitable location. Such interviews could be valuable even in addition to the classroom visit, since they would represent a wider sampling of the views and ideas of contemporary architects.

"Cultural Baggage." Those who travel from one part of the world to another bring with them not only their physical belongings or baggage, such as tools, clothing, and other implements of living, but also "baggage" of another kind, often not as easily discerned. Many examples of this have already been mentioned in other parts of this book, but cultural influences also are present in the architectural ideas of such groups. Students can walk through their community to observe the architectural features of various structures that reflect these cultural aspects. Immediately apparent might be the religious structures of different groups, but there may be others as well, such as social halls associated with particular cultural groups.

Students should also be encouraged to look for historical examples. For example, it is not accidental that immigrants from Scandinavia quite naturally used the forests available to construct log cabins. Later groups of these immigrants who settled regions of the country not heavily forested had to find other materials for their houses.

Who Lives Here? To give your students practice in formulating and validating hypotheses about the ideas alluded to in this section, present descriptions of different areas of the world, either graphically or in writing, that offer details of the physical surroundings, including information about the prevailing climatic conditions. Working in groups, students can decide what types of structures might be built in such locations, as well as the materials that might be available for use. Students can sketch out plans for a structure, and justify the particular design that they conceived and the materials proposed for use. They also can include information about the potential uses to which the structure would be put, although this might require additional data. Different groups of students could utilize the same data, and the various plans and designs proposed by different groups could be compared, serving as a basis for further discussion.

If this activity is conducted before the architect's visit, ask him or her to review and comment on the plans of the student groups.

A variation of this activity would be to present pictures of actual structures built by groups in different regions of the world and from different time periods. Ask the students to examine the pictures and formulate hypotheses about who these people might be and the conditions under which they lived. What can be inferred merely from examining the structures that they built and the types of materials that they used?

You might begin this activity with some familiar examples, such as sod houses (plains area of the

United States), long houses (Iroquois nation, New York), or tents (Berbers of North Africa). This way of proceeding would also provide a check on their inferences. Query them as to whether their hypotheses are based only on the data given, or whether they are basing them on other information that they already know about the group.

After the students have become familiar with the task, present graphic images of less familiar structures. You might also include "structures" not typically thought of as such, for example, a canal boat from the nineteenth-century Erie Canal or present-day Europe along the Rhine. Such boats served as "dwellings" for the families that lived on them.

The Golden Lure: Gold and Other Precious Metals

Wherever gold and other precious metals have been found they have played a significant role in human cultures, affecting the lives not only of those seeking out these metals but also of those who happened to be living in the areas where gold was thought to exist. The word "gold" itself has even served as a metaphor indicating worth and exalted status; examples can be seen in everything from the gold medals that are presented to the top performers in the Olympic games to the "Golden Rule." The attraction that gold holds for humans can also be discerned in the efforts by alchemists and "wizards" who were seeking the "philosophers' stone," a substance that would turn base metals into gold.

We also tend to speak of the "golden age" of Greece, Rome, or other civilizations as the period when the culture so named was at its peak in terms of power and achievement. This power typically was best represented in the cultural aspects of that civilization, although there was often a close correlation between the economic and political power of the civilization at this time and its cultural attainments.

Gold itself and the objects fashioned from it have represented many things to humans. First, the metal has served as a vehicle or substance to be worked and fashioned by artisans as a means for expressing their creative talents. It is relatively easy to work and shape, and is not subject to tarnishing and decomposition.

Second, in the economic realm, gold has provided societies with a means of exchange that has many desirable features. Among these are the fact that it is quite scarce. It is also durable and stable, maintaining its value over time regardless of the conditions under which it is stored. Because of its scarcity and value, only relatively small amounts of it are required to represent great wealth.

As a substance, gold has both intrinsic and extrinsic worth. That is, it can be admired and valued because of its beauty, particularly when it has been fashioned into an object that represents the creative efforts of an artist. It also serves as a means to achieve the desired ends of individuals or even nations that possess it in sufficient quantities.

Those in positions of power—the monarchs of distant times, the national governments of more recent ones—have sought to accumulate gold to achieve their political and economic goals. Its possession in large amounts has enabled nations to embark on explorations and expansionist enterprises, not always with desirable consequences for their neighbors. One might claim that this "golden lure" played a significant role as a motivating factor in stimulating explorations by the European nations during the fifteenth and sixteenth centuries. Many of the Spanish explorers sought the gold of the New World; without this lure, it is highly unlikely that there would have been so many European incursions in this hemisphere. Even after the Spanish colonies had attained a foothold in Central and South America, Coronado and others continued the search for El Dorado, the city of gold.

Although we usually do not associate the search for gold with the colonial efforts by Great Britain, France, and the Netherlands in the northern stretches of the hemisphere, investigation reveals that other lures were present that served to motivate them. However, the golden lure that attracted the Spaniards also had an indirect effect on the British and the Dutch. The treasure ships that carried the booty from the Americas to Spain were magnets for pirates and buccaneers of these nations, and these activities were often pursued with the unofficial support of their governments.

The lure of gold continued to attract individuals long after this period of fifteenth- and sixteenth-century interaction between world cultures. The cry of "gold!" heard in some far-off region of the world caused thousands of people in settled areas to trek to the areas that supposedly contained this metal. In the middle of the nineteenth century, people flocked to California after gold was discovered near Sutter's Mill. It is likely that the difficulty of reaching this area from the more populated regions of the nation stimulated efforts to seek a quicker means of travel across the continent, and also a shorter sea route rather than the lengthy one around South America's Cape Horn. In addition, people were less likely to ridicule "Seward's folly" after gold was found in the Klondike regions of this remote territory of the United States. Gold fields in Australia, Siberia, and other regions of the world served as a stimulus for further exploration and development of these areas as well.

The lure of gold was not without its negative social and cultural effects. This was particularly evident when viewed from the perspective of people who already inhabited the regions where gold was sought. The effects on the cultures that existed on this continent before the arrival of Europeans seeking gold are difficult to calculate completely.

In addition, the riches so obtained have not always been put to good use. Over the last century, the wealth that gold represents has supported political regimes that have been noted for their oppressive practices, and this state of affairs has resulted in social and cultural upheaval. An example of this phenomenon would be the gold fields in South Africa; their existence provided economic support for the government's apartheid measures. Students can also find evidence in recent news reports of the catastrophic effects on the indigenous peoples of the efforts by others to exploit the gold fields in Brazil.

Try These Activities

"Lures" to Wealth in the Modern World. After your students have studied the role that precious metals, particularly gold, have played in the drama of human history, ask them to reflect on whether they can think if other "lures" for wealth that play an important role in the contemporary world.

As an example, consider the significance that petroleum (oil and natural gas) has as a lure that has led individuals and groups to explore new regions and eventually to struggle to possess the lands where these riches are to be found. Areas of the world that were once considered to be relatively unknown and insignificant are now highlighted on our maps and constantly of interest in the news.

Another variant of this activity would be to have the students trace on a map the explorations of Coronado and other early explorers who were searching for golden treasures in Mexico and the American Southwest. After investigation and research, students can chart other natural resources that have been found at later periods in these regions, such as copper, coal, uranium, oil, and natural gas. They could also compute the value of these resources when compared to that of the gold and silver sought by earlier explorers.

We still have a tendency, as was often the case in the past, to "value" cultures and groups in terms of the political and economic power that they can muster. That is, the measure that we use is the power that the group or culture wields in the world. A question for students to consider is whether we are as inclined to promote the study and appreciation of another culture if that group is not worthy of note for its present or future power potential. The use of the term "golden age" was pointed out earlier. Related to this topic, students could consider such questions as:

Why do you think that the golden age of a culture tends to occur during the period when it is politically or economically powerful?

What causes or leads to a surge in creativity of expression within a culture?

Creating a Class Museum. Students can attain a better understanding of different cultures by examining objects created by artists using gold as the medium of expression. It is likely that the objects themselves will not be available, but pictures can be used to. Examples from different historical periods and cultures illustrate how gold was fashioned and formed into different objects. It would be worthwhile for students to investigate the uses to which these objects were put, such as cups or other utensils, statues (and the ceremonial purposes that some of these objects may have had), coins, or medals commemorating the lives of famous individuals or events of significance. They can collect pictures, drawings, or even models of these objects and begin a class or school museum to exhibit and maintain them.

Since gold is not found in every region of the world, and since some cultures had no access to it, students could investigate the materials that these groups used for similar purposes, for example, ivory, stones of various kinds, or wood.

In some cases, objects made of valuable metals have been taken because of their potential value and aesthetic interest. Students can investigate instances in which artifacts have been stolen from graves or other sites and removed to museums or possessed by individuals of another nation or culture. A panel discussion could be held, with students articulating and analyzing the arguments that might be presented by both sides of the question, "Should all such artifacts be returned to the country or culture from which they were originally taken?" Related questions include:

Does it make any difference whether the artifacts were removed by archaeologists or others involved in scholarly activities (in contrast to someone appropriating them because they are made of valuable metals)?

Is there any benefit to be obtained through such "cultural dispersion"?

Who "owns" prehistoric artifacts, those possibly representing the creative efforts of early civilizations?

In conjunction with this activity or prior to it, students might visit local museums and, after noting the information given with various exhibits, develop a map of the origins of the materials included in the museum's collections. They can solicit the curators' and director's views on the questions raised in this section.

Chapter 11

Born on the Fourth of July

July, while the seventh month of the year in our present-day calendar, was once the fifth month in the early Roman calendar. Since the Latin word for fifth was *quintilis*, the month was so named. Julius Caesar readjusted the calendar and began the year with January instead of March. He decided to name the month in which he had been born for himself hence the name July.

The most noteworthy time in July is when we celebrate our nation's birthday on the fourth. It was on this date that the Continental Congress adopted the Declaration of Independence. George M. Cohan's song "Yankee Doodle Dandy" celebrates one who was born on the Fourth of July, for when else could a real Yankee be born? Cohan himself only missed by one day, having been born on the third of July in 1878.

It is a time for fireworks, picnics, and, on a more serious note, taking stock of who we Americas are. Several Americans of note were born on the nation's birthday, including Nathaniel Hawthorne, Stephen Foster, and Louis Armstrong, as well as a future American president, Calvin Coolidge. A number of other notable individuals—Thurgood Marshall, P. T. Barnum, John Paul Jones, Beatrix Potter, Elias Howe, James Whistler, John Quincy Adams, Henry David Thoreau, Mary Baker Eddy, Nelson Mandela, Simon Bolivar, Alexandre Dumas, Amelia Earhart, and Henry Ford—were also born during this month.

Several other nations commemorate their independence during July: Canada on the first, the Philippines on the fourth, Venezuela on the fifth, Argentina on the ninth, Belgium on the twenty-first, the Netherlands on the twenty-fifth, and Peru on the twenty-eighth. On the fourteenth of the month the French celebrate Bastille Day, the day on which this infamous prison was stormed in 1789.

Several events of significance to us as a nation occurred during this month. The battles of Gettysburg and Vicksburg were fought early in July of 1863. These two battles are often cited as turning points in our Civil War. Three years after the conclusion of this conflict, one of the more significant amendments to the U.S. Constitution was proclaimed. It stated, among its other provisions, that no state shall "deprive any person of life, liberty, or property, without due process of law, nor deny to any person within its jurisdiction the equal protection of the law." These some two dozen words have had an enormous impact on our society in the last few decades.

The first women's rights convention was held in the United States during July a decade and a half before the Civil War. The atomic age was begun in rather dramatic fashion when scientists set off the first atomic bomb in July 1945.

July

Sunday	Monday	Tuesday	Wednesday	Thursday	Friday	Saturday

JULY

SELECTED EVENTS

1   Canada Day
        Battle of Gettysburg (1863)
2   Civil Rights Act of 1964 passed
        Thurgood Marshall (1908–1993)
3
4   Independence Day
        Louis Armstrong (1900–1971)
5   National Labor Relations Act of 1935
        Phineas T. Barnum (1810–1891)
6   John Paul Jones (1747–1792)
        Beatrix Potter (1866–1943)
7   Japanese Star Festival
8
9   Elias Howe (1819–1867)
10   James Whistler (1834–1903)
11   John Quincy Adams (1767–1848)
12   Henry David Thoreau (1817–1862)
13   France: Night Watch
        Japan: Feast of the Lanterns
14   France: Bastille Day
15   Clement C. Moore (1823–1873)
16   Roald Amundsen (1872–1928)
        Mary Baker Eddy (1821–1910)
17   Puerto Rico: Munoz-Rivera Day
18   Nelson Mandela (1918–)
19   Edgar Degas (1834–1917)
20   Sir Edmund Hillary (1919–)
21   Ernest Hemingway (1899–1961)
22   Pied Piper of Hamelin anniversary
23
24   Simon Bolivar (1783–1830)
        Amelia Earhart (1898–1937)
25
26
27   Korean War Armistice Day
28
29
30   Emily Brontë (1818–1848)
        Henry Ford (1863–1947)
31   Evonne Goolagong (1951–)

People, Places, and Events of July

Events Scheduled According to Non-Gregorian Calendar Usually Occurring in July:

Fast of Tammunz, Jewish holiday commemmorating the Roman siege of Jerusalem during the first century.

July's Daily Calendar

1

Canada Day. Canada's national day; formerly called Dominion Day.

Battle of Gettysburg (1863).

India: Muharram. Muslims observe this day to remember the martyrdom of the grandson of Muhsmmsf, Imam Hassain.

Birth anniversary of:
     Cecil Rhodes (1853–1902). South African politician and the endower of the Rhodes scholarships at Oxford University.

2

Civil Rights Act of 1964 passed. This act forbids discrimination on the basis of race in public facilities and organizations.

Birth anniversary of:
     Thurgood Marshall (1908–1993). First African-American to serve on the Supreme Court.

3

Dog days begin. Hottest days of the year in the Northern Hemisphere, usually from July 3 to August 15.

Idaho Admission Day. Became forty-third state to join the Union (1890).

4

Declaration of Independence approved and signed (1776).

Independence Day; usually called Fourth of July.

Philippines: Fil-American Friendship Day.

Birth anniversary of:
     Louis Armstrong (1900–1971). Noted African-American jazz musician.
     Calvin Coolidge (1872–1933). Thirty-third President of the United States; born in Vermont.
     Stephen Foster (1826–1864). Songwriter; best remembered for his songs about the South.

5

Cape Verde National Day. Gained independence from Portugal in 1975.

National Labor Relations Act of 1935. Allowed workers the right to organize and engage in collective bargaining with their employers.

Birth anniversary of:

Phineas T. Barnum (1810–1891). Showman; one of the partners of Barnum and Bailey Circus.

6

Comoros Independence Day. Island nation located in the Indian Ocean; gained independence from France in 1975.

Malawi Independence Day. Gained independence from Britain in 1964.

Birth anniversary of:

John Paul Jones (1747–1792). Naval officer.

Beatrix Potter (1866–1943). British author of children's stories, including "The Tales of Peter Rabbit."

7

Solomon Islands National Day. Located in the western Pacific Ocean; independence was formally gained from Britain in 1978.

Execution of Mary Surratt (1865). First woman executed in the United States. Controversy still surrounds death of the owner of the boarding house where John Wilkes Booth plotted the assassination of Abraham Lincoln.

Japan: Tanabata, or Star Festival. Children place poems and streamers on bamboo poles as an offering to the stars.

8

India: Naga Panchami. Festival dedicated to the sacred serpent Ananta.

9

Birth anniversary of:

Elias Howe (1819–1867). Inventor of the sewing machine.

10

Bahamas Independence Day. Gained full independence within the British Commonwealth in 1973.

Wyoming Admission Day. Became forty-fourth state admitted to the Union (1890).

Birth anniversary of:

James Whistler (1834–1903). Artist; best known for his painting of his mother.

11

Mongolian People's Republic National Holiday. Mongolian communist regime was established in 1921.

Birth anniversary of:

John Quincy Adams (1767–1848). Sixth president of the United States; born in Massachusetts.

12

Kiribati Independence Day. Located in the mid-Pacific Ocean; independence was attained from Britain in 1979.

Orangemen's Day. Observed in Ireland and Northern Ireland to commemorate the Battle of Boyne.

Sao Tome and Principe National Day. Island nation located off the coast of western Africa in the Atlantic Ocean; gained independence from Portugal in 1975.

Birth anniversary of:

Henry David Thoreau (1817–1862). Author and naturalist.

13

France: Night Watch. Celebrates the eve of the fall of the Bastille.

Japan: Bon Festival or Feast of the Lanterns. Observed in honor of the dead.

14

France: Bastille Day. Commemorating the fall of the Bastille in 1789.

Birth anniversary of:

Gerald R. Ford (1913–) Thirty-eighth president of the United States; born in Nebraska.

15

Birth anniversary of:

Clement C. Moore (1779–1863). Biblical scholar and poet; best remembered for "Visit from St. Nicholas."

16

Atomic Bomb Day. First atomic bomb detonated at Alamogordo, New Mexico, in 1945.

Bolivia: La Paz Day. Commemorating the founding of the city in 1548.

Birth anniversary of:

Roald Amundsen (1872–1928). Norwegian explorer and discoverer of the South Pole.

Mary Baker Eddy (1821–1910). Founder of Christian Science.

17

Puerto Rico: Munoz-Rivera Day. National holiday honoring Luis Munoz-Rivera, patriot, poet, and journalist.

18

Birth anniversary of:

Nelson Mandela (1918–) South African civil rights leader; won the Nobel Peace Prize in 1993; elected to the presidency in 1994.

19

Nicaragua National Liberation Day. Commemorating the ending of civil war in 1979.

Birth anniversary of:

Edgar Degas (1834–1917). French Impressionist painter.

Charles Horace Mayo (1865–1939). Surgeon and one of the founders of the Mayo Clinic.

20

Birth anniversary of:

Sir Edmund Hillary (1919–). Explorer from New Zealand; first person to ascend Mt. Everest.

21

French West Indies: Schoelcher Day. Honoring the campaign to abolish slavery in 1848.

Guam Liberation Day. Located in the Pacific Ocean; was ceded to the United States by Spain in 1898. U.S. armed forces captured Guam from the Japanese on this day in 1944.

World Eskimo-Indian Olympic. Held each year about this date; focuses on traditional competitive games of strength and endurance.

Birth anniversary of:

Ernest Hemingway (1899–1961). Novelist and short story writer.

22

Pied Piper of Hamelin anniversary. Legend holds that in 1376, a piper rid the village of Hamelin, Germany, of rats, but ungrateful town leaders refused to pay his fees. The children followed the piper, never to be seen again.

23

Arab Republic of Egypt National Day. Commemorating the change from a monarchy to a republic after the revolution of July 23, 1952.

24

Birth anniversary of:

Simon Bolivar (1783–1830). Venezuelan political leader; called "The Liberator" by most South Americans.

Alexandre Dumas (1802–1870). French novelist, noted for *The Three Musketeers.*

Amelia Earhart (1898–1937). First woman to fly solo across the Atlantic Ocean. Was lost in the Pacific during a round-the-world flight attempt.

25

Puerto Rico Constitution Day. Commemorating the adoption of a constitution in 1952.

26

Cuba National Holiday. Anniversary of Castro's revolutionary movement in 1953.

Liberia Independence Day. Founded in 1822 by U.S. black freemen; became a republic on July 26, 1847.

Maldives National Day. Located in the Indian Ocean; became independent of British rule in 1965.

New York became the eleventh state to ratify the Constitution (1788).

27

Korean War Armistice Day. Commemorating the end of the war between North and South Korea in 1953.

28

Peru Independence Day. Gained independence from Spain in 1824.

Birth anniversary of:

Rudy Vallee (1901–1986). Singer and movie idol.

29

Norway: Olsok Eve. Honors Viking king St. Olav, who died in battle in 1030.

Zambia: Mutomboko Ceremony. Honoring senior chief of Luuda peoples.

30

Vanuatu Independence Day. Located in the southwestern Pacific Ocean; became an independent republic in 1980.

Birth anniversary of:

Emily Brontë (1818–1848). English novelist (*Wuthering Heights.*)

Henry Ford (1863–1947). Industrialist and builder of automobiles.

31

Birth anniversary of:

Evonne Goolagong (1951–) Australian tennis star.

Striving for Independence—A Continuing Struggle

Teaching Unit for July

A Word About This Unit. One of the major themes evident throughout the world is the continued efforts of groups to become independent of others who control them. This striving for "liberty" takes place in a variety of institutional settings—social, political, economic, and cultural. The empowerment of individuals and groups traditionally underrepresented in the seats of power within a society has emerged as one of the greatest challenges confronting a nation.

Social and political turmoil is likely to result if, as a country, we do not consciously and effectively strive to achieve this goal of equality. The way in which this goal should be accomplished is of primary importance for the political and moral health of our nation. The task of formulating and implementing policies that promote this goal's attainment will require the best efforts of each individual and all groups within our society.

Thus, it seems quite appropriate for our nation's young people to gain some understanding of the variety of historic and contemporary groups who sought a greater say in the decisions that had an impact on their lives, and who wanted a more equitable share of the economic, intellectual, and technological resources that serve as the strongest guarantee of continued autonomy. It is particularly appropriate that students study this topic during the month when we celebrate our own struggles as a nation to gain political independence. We must recognize also that we are still involved in the process of creating a society in which the ideals of democracy are exhibited in both our individual lives and in our political and social institutions.

This unit has Janus-like features. You can look back at previous units and see connections with many of the instructional activities suggested there. The unit also urges one to look forward to the future, since the summer months provide a time for further, albeit less structured, educational opportunities. You will note that some suggestions for such experiences have been included.

This unit is designed to interest students in examining one of the enduring themes of the human drama, namely, the struggle for independence and autonomy. This struggle has exhibited itself in many times and different places, on both individual and group levels. This unit provides some background material that

serves to illustrate the multiple dimensions of the topic.

We hope to encourage you and your students to use the skills and knowledge gained through participating in the activities associated with this unit to move toward the goal desired by proponents of multicultural education: that is, to move beyond a program aimed merely at "adding" incidentals to the curriculum to one in which students benefit from viewing social phenomena from the perspective of other cultures. Ultimately, they may even become committed to social action that will address problems and issues confronting our society.

Another purpose of this unit is to stimulate students to study the meanings of some of the key terms often used in discussions concerning this topic. Such terms are often used without any effort to analyze them; an attempt is made here to engage students in the scrutiny of these concepts, such as "independence," "autonomy," "empowerment," and "responsibility," and to help them see how these terms are illustrated in different historic contexts and in a variety of social and political settings.

Motivation. A significant part of a young person's development (of "growing up" or "standing on one's own feet") is the attempt to gain an increasing degree of independence from parents, teachers, and others in the adult world. Another way to view this process is to see it as one in which an individual is allowed (empowered) to make his or her own decisions about a wider range of affairs that are related to his or her life.

Immersion. You may wish to begin the unit with a discussion of the students' initial and tentative efforts in their own personal searches for autonomy and independence. They then can be led to consider the process through which groups of individuals, both in the past as well as in the contemporary world, are striving to become independent and empowered in order to gain more control over their individual and group lives.

Information. In addition to being the time of year when many students look forward to a rest from the labors of school, July is also the month in which we celebrate our independence as a nation. The traditional story is that this struggle was conducted by noble men (although not all of them were aristocrats in the usual sense of the word) motivated by democratic ideals. What is often left out of the history books are the efforts of other individuals and groups involved in the struggle. In addition, the impression given in many texts is that the goal of independence was fully and completely achieved through the American Revolution, which spanned more than a decade, and that the struggle was concluded when the peace treaty was signed in Paris. A more accurate picture might represent the story in a different manner, emphasizing the fact that although "independence" was achieved, the battle to gain the inalienable rights set forth in the Declaration of Independence for all Americans really only began after the victory had seemingly been won.

Declaring Independence

Our nation's Declaration of Independence, in which we asserted and justified our struggle for independence to the world, contained certain beliefs about humans—namely, that all men are endowed by their creator with certain rights (to life, liberty, and the pursuit of happiness) that should not be infringed upon. This document, along with others, such as those set forth almost two centuries earlier by the Dutch in 1581, shed light on ideas about an individual's right to autonomy. The ideas themselves were present in the minds and hearts of humans in various cultures throughout the world, even if not written.

After we gained our independence from Great Britain, we attempted to establish a political setting and format that would enable humans to live in a manner compatible with the rights that had been enumerated in the Declaration of Independence. However,

when the federal Constitution that was to serve as the foundation for our national government was ratified and in place, the inalienable rights expressed in these noble sentiments were found not to apply to several groups living within the boundaries of our nation. To the extent that these rights were limited, women and certain racial groups were without the fundamental power inherent in the members of a democratic society. They were kept from participating in the selection of those who would represent them in the decision-making process regarding the political affairs of the nation. An optimistic view of our nation's history would hold that one of the enduring themes of our development as a people is this struggle to ensure that those who were denied these rights in the original distribution of political power would eventually be empowered as citizens.

Our own efforts to gain independence served as a stimulus for other groups throughout the world to seek their own. About a decade after our own war for independence, the French endured the same political and associated social upheavals in order to bring forth a more equitable political and social system. In the early decades of the nineteenth century, many areas of Latin American erupted in revolution against Spain, and by mid-century many new nations had emerged on that continent. Again, independence for these nations did not necessarily result in equal political status and an equitable sharing of power and resources among all of their citizens. The struggles in these countries parallel our own as we seek to bring about a more just society.

In time, the locus of these struggles for independence, at least those involving overt conflicts, shifted from the Western to the Eastern Hemisphere. Many such efforts were increasingly successful after World War II. Erstwhile colonies of Great Britain, France, the Netherlands, Portugal, Italy, Spain, and Belgium in Asia and Africa finally became independent countries. Many are still in the throes of these efforts, since the political, social, economic, and cultural impacts of being a subject state for an extended period are such that they create problems that remain long after nominal independence is achieved. Part of the difficulty, of course, stems from the ways in which the European powers divided up the regions among themselves, usually taking little account of the cultural and tribal boundaries prevailing among the indigenous groups.

Many individuals have made contributions to this struggle, the majority of them unheralded and unknown. These ordinary people lived out their lives doing their best to realize their own goals and hoping for better, richer lives for their children.

It is worthy of note that not all of the actors who were involved in these social dramas, these struggles for independence, were members of the groups that were being discriminated against or whose independence of thought and action was being suppressed. In earlier revolutionary struggles, both our own and those taking place in other parts of the world, members of the "privileged" or established strata of a society went against the apparent interests of their own group. These individuals, following the dictates of their consciences, supported movements that sought to empower other groups within the society and to create more equitable political systems. Marquis de Lafayette, a French aristocrat, was one such person who was actively involved both in our struggle to gain independence from Great Britain and later in the revolution in his own country.

During the struggles for the increased empowerment of groups in Great Britain, Robert Owen and Mary Wollstonecraft were but two of those who proposed social and political reforms. Many others, such as Frances Wright, proposed educational reforms that would ultimately lead to the empowerment of those who were not allowed full political rights. It is interesting to note that in several instances, these reformers traveled to our own shores to establish communities where these reforms could be put into practice; Robert Owen was associated with the colony at New Harmony, Indiana, and Frances Wright set up a community at Nashoba, Tennessee, that was planned to educate slaves for eventual freedom. Unfortunately, as was the case with many of the utopian endeavors of nineteenth-century America, neither of these efforts was successful.

The revolutions of the nineteenth century tumbled many royal personages from their thrones and rattled the rafters of many royal houses. In the process it forced these persons of special privilege to accept the rule of law. However, in the course of time, particularly in this century, others have raised the question of whether the laws formulated in earlier "democratic" revolutions adequately protect the rights and liberty of all individuals living within such societies. The debates that have arisen concerning this issue serve to illustrate our own struggles to mature as a nation, and our efforts to live up to the noble precepts contained in the Declaration of Independence and the U.S. Constitution.

An aspect of our continuing struggle involves the attempt to reach the point where we can reap more fully the benefits of a multicultural society. In order to flourish, every society faces the task of ensuring that individuals of talent and ability are recognized, educated, and encouraged to make full use of their gifts, not only to realize their own individual life goals, but also to benefit the society as a whole. This is the formidable challenge that we face. To the extent that we do not take advantage of our multicultural riches, the sources available for enriching all our cultural lives will be underutilized. This is important in terms of not only maintaining supremacy among nations as an economic power, but also creating a just and equitable society in which we can take pride. There is also increasing concern for the "quality of life" that marks our society. However, the quality of our lives is not merely a function of various aspects of our physical environment, but ultimately of our cultural environment as well.

Thus far, we have concentrated almost exclusively on the idea of political independence. Political activity, and the attempt to seek independence in this sphere, is but one dimension of social interaction. There is a sense in which cultural independence is also sought. The political conflicts that have occurred among nations have often had consequences for the cultures of the citizens of those nations as well. A glance at the pages of human history reveals that, when cultures come into contact, mutual understanding and appreciation of one another's culture is not the usual result. This is particularly the case when such interaction occurs within the scope of a political conflict.

The worst consequences of such cultural conflicts are those historical instances in which, for a variety of reasons, cultures have been eradicated. The physical artifacts and the cultural remains, such as literature or evidence of religious practices, of such unfortunate groups are of interest to the cultural anthropologist or to the archaeologist if they existed in the distant past.

In some instances, groups were literally exterminated. Among the examples of these most extreme cases is that of Rome's wars with its Mediterranean rival Carthage. After the completion of the Third Punic War, Rome destroyed all physical remains of Carthage, and killed or enslaved its inhabitants. In time, Rome became more sensible in its treatment of conquered peoples as long as these subject peoples recognized Rome's political supremacy.

In most of these cases of enslavement of an entire group, the unfortunate group would no longer be able to organize their lives in ways compatible with their culture, and usually would have great difficulty in permeating the mainstream culture with elements of their own. In other instances, where members of the cultural group were not forced into slavery, its members sometimes emigrated to a new region with a dominant culture different from their own. For economic reasons or concern for their social status, they deliberately gave up aspects of their culture and attempted to assimilate themselves into the dominant one. This step was often taken so that they, but particularly their children, could enjoy the benefits associated with "belonging" to the mainstream culture.

These sacrifices were traumatic for many, since there was the perception that, in so doing, they were implicitly accepting the view that their particular culture (its language, literature, and range of cultural practices) was "second rate" and not as worthwhile on some broader scale as the culture into which they tried to assimilate themselves.

Before continuing with this discussion of the efforts of various groups to achieve an increased degree of cultural independence and autonomy, it may prove helpful to sketch out what is at stake, that is, the significance that a culture has for human beings, and how it serves as a means of providing humans a sense of being and belonging.

Members of a culture express themselves in many ways, through dance, music, and other art forms. The language that they speak is often a means used to articulate and capture the culture's unique aspects. It also serves as a vehicle for preserving and transmitting those aspects to new generations. The stories and narratives that constitute this cultural heritage may be preserved in either oral or written form.

Other institutions are established over time that have social or cultural utility and significance, and through interaction within these settings, the members of the group learn and practice what "it is" to be a member of that culture. The particular ways in which the young are nurtured and the relations existing among children and adults of different generations are exhibited in a variety of family arrangements.

The religious practices associated with a culture reveal its beliefs about questions of fundamental human concern: How did the world come to be? What is the place of human beings in the scheme of things? The views formulated by a culture influence its particular belief system and its value schema. These beliefs and values serve to guide and govern their behavior, and give meaning to their individual and corporate lives. Thus, we can conceive of the difficulty and of the psychological trauma involved in accepting a state of affairs in which elements of one's culture are judged less worthy or even deemed unacceptable.

Cultures may be suppressed and the practices associated with it may be discouraged in a number of ways. First, they may be forbidden by law, either directly or indirectly. These are overt actions by the dominant powerful elements in a society, the group typically referred to as the "establishment." Any actions by groups in a manner consistent with these forbidden cultural beliefs are thus, by their very nature, illegal activities and subject to the sanctions imposed by law.

Individuals and groups have felt strongly enough to knowingly break such laws and accept the consequences of such actions. Gandhi and Martin Luther King, Jr., were among those who acted in this manner. (Note: This idea of civil disobedience is discussed more fully in Chapter 5, and the instructional activities described there may be used in conjunction with this unit as well.)

However, not all of the attempts to suppress a culture involve the establishment of laws. Stereotypical judgments or views of cultural, ethnic, or gender groups are often of greater impact in forming the perspectives of such groups developed by members of the dominant culture than legal prescriptions. In many cases, these extralegal pejorative views may be the major determiners of the concepts and perspectives that we have of cultural groups other than our own.

Historically, economic and political power have been used as measures or standards to assess cultural power or worth. Political conflicts, and the resultant changes that have occurred in terms of relative political strength, may also have severe consequences for a culture. When we speak of one group conquering another, we tend to think of military actions.

There have been instances in which the conquest was perhaps more of an economic one, but in any event, the results to the institutions of the conquered group may be severe. Ironies in history abound, and the interactions between Rome and Greece illustrate a seeming contradiction to this general phenomenon. It was Horace, a Roman poet, who expressed the irony by remarking that after Rome had conquered Greece (in the military and political sense) it was, in its turn, conquered by Greece (in the cultural sense). The impact of Greek art, literature, philosophy, and science on Roman culture was immense.

Far more frequent, however, are those cases in which the culture of the dominant power tends to overshadow that of the conquered people. This is likely to be the case, even in those instances in which the more powerful group may appear less admirable, from a cultural perspective, than the one displaced. In these instances, the products of the subject people's culture are denigrated, and the practices associated with its social institutions are discouraged or even forbidden by legal edict. Over the course of the last few centuries, the significant effects of European conquests on the cultures of regions in Asia, Africa, and Latin America are evident.

In almost every case, the official language of the colony became that of the European power that controlled it. This was the language that was taught and promoted in educational institutions, and the language used in commerce, the courts, and other civil departments. Postage stamps and currency were also printed in this official language, and the illustrations contained on them often pictured the monarch of the colonial power or commemorated some event in that country's history.

The arts, architecture, and literature of the conquered country would be judged "second rate" or more primitive than the comparable cultural elements of the dominant power, although some aspects of the culture might be found fascinating because of their "exotic" nature. Cultural artifacts might also be removed from the country and shipped to museums in the mother country. The bitter feelings that have marked British and Greek relations in regard to the marble friezes removed from certain Greek temples that now reside in British museums remain as an example of cultural insensitivity. Other examples of cultural insensitivity in this regard are being remedied to some extent. The decision of the Smithsonian Institution to return the remains of Native Americans removed from burial sites by archaeologists is heartening in this respect.

In most cases religious practices, a crucial component of any culture, had to be modified or conducted in secret so that practitioners would not run afoul of the authorities. Instances exist, however, in which the conquering power utilized religion as a means of "pacifying" or assimilating the indigenous peoples.

In many instances, if the group was unable to practice its customs and mores, they would be inclined to act to establish a social or political environment in which they would be free to "live" their culture. This often resulted in social conflict, even revolution, as the group strove to gain political power sufficient to protect their way of thinking and their unique cultural practices.

An examination of historical examples and a reflection on current events offer clear lessons in this regard. To the extent that cultural diversity is not tolerated, the probability of conflict among cultures is likely to increase. This is particularly evident with regard to peoples who perceive themselves as being unable to maintain elements of their culture in the current social and political climate.

One of the key elements of the belief system undergirding our democratic way of life might be expressed as follows: An individual should be allowed the maximum range of freedom with regard to her or his beliefs, the expression of those beliefs, and action motivated by these beliefs, if those actions are commensurate with an equal regard for the freedom of other members of our society. The clearest realization of this postulate is when individuals are empowered with the greatest degree of freedom of opportunity regarding the diversity of cultural manifestations available. We educators can help achieve this by promoting a cultural environment in which all individuals are aware of, comprehend the meaning of, and appreciate the significance of the widest range of cultural attributes. They would also be allowed the freedom to select and live aspects of various cultures, from this rich set of opportunities, and in the process develop their own unique cultural identities.

The dangers to a society characterized by extremes of cultural diversity have often been cited. It is claimed that the lack of a cultural core might result in a "balka-nization" of such a society, and ultimately lead to social and political upheaval. It is perhaps more likely that a society that seeks to suppress or discriminate against its minority cultural groups is acting in a way that will result in such turmoil. Conflicts are more probable in societies composed of a number of intolerant cultural groups, each attempting to gain political power sufficient to establish conditions in which it is able to practice and live its culture. Struggles by groups characterized by a lack of respect for one another's cultures often lead to the long-term hostilities and hatred that we associate with the "hot spots" of our contemporary world. These instances provide us with evidence of the upheaval that can result if we do not develop a society in which tolerance and respect for cultural diversity are key aspects guiding and governing the relationships among individuals and groups living within it.

Many of the global "hot spots" of the present period illustrate the attempts of groups to seek greater political and, in some cases, greater cultural autonomy for themselves. Although the struggles of the black majority in South Africa seem to have borne fruit, other conflicts continue. The struggles of the Serbs and Bosnians, as well as the Croats and Macedonians, in what had been the nation of Yugoslavia, the Azerbaijanians and Armenians in regions of the former Soviet Union, the Tamils' efforts in Sri Lanka, the seemingly eternal quest for autonomy by the Kurds in parts of Turkey, Iraq, and Iran, the conflicting claims of Palestinians and Israelis in the Gaza Strip and in the West Bank areas, the bitter fighting between groups in Northern Ireland, as well as the less publicized efforts of indigenous peoples of Central and Latin America serve to illustrate the fact that people still seek greater autonomy and power for their themselves.

These examples of social disintegration and political conflict serve as clear and powerful examples of what lengths humans will go to in the effort to attain this goal. Terrorist actions that are abhorred by most humans everywhere are judged by those who commit them as appropriate means to achieve this desired end. These acts evoke increasingly repressive measures, and the cycle is maintained. The consequences of ignoring claims for justice and a more equitable distribution of power and resources among groups living together are demonstrated daily.

A study of these examples reveals a variety of specific proximate causes for the conflicts. In many cases, members of one religious group are responding to long-held grievances against members of another religion; when the opportunity to strike at their enemies arises, they do not hesitate. This is particularly evident in cultures in which religion plays a dominant role in the belief system and the social institutions of the group.

In many of these encounters, those struggling are striving not only for greater freedom and power in a political sense, but also implicitly to have their worth as a culture and people more clearly recognized. In some of the examples given here this seems evident, and although the continuing struggles in Africa and Latin America are political in nature, the demand that one's cultural traditions and practices be valued and recognized as significant is a factor of import as well. Indeed, the civil wars that have erupted in a number of former European colonies (for example, Nigeria) years after they have gained their political independence also serve to illustrate this phenomenon.

It appears that some of the turmoil results from a group's perception that it is not being allowed a fair or just measure of independence of belief, expression, and action compatible with its culture. When the worth of diverse cultures is not appreciated and valued, and when their unique perspectives on social issues is not taken into account, these groups may move to demand greater political autonomy, thus increasing the likelihood of political upheaval, even within a customarily tranquil political environment.

This unit and the activities associated with it offer a clear example of an unfinished educational experience. This is true not only from your point of view as a teacher, for we all recognize the ongoing and continuing nature of any educational enterprise. It is also true from the students' perspective, if they are thought of as individuals who are concerned with their own development and maturation, but who, as citizens of our country, must also seek to discover their own rightful place in the world in which they will live. As if this were not a sufficient challenge, they also will be confronted with the more difficult task that awaits them—that of acquiring the measure of wisdom needed to begin to balance seemingly incompatible claims as the various rights or freedoms that we espouse come into conflict.

It is even more clearly the case when we consider the societal stake involved in the education of its younger members. They must be agents within the struggle to understand the significance of, and to bring to fruition in their own lives, the values inherent in the statements that capture the essence of our society: "one nation . . . with liberty and justice for all"; "equal opportunity for all citizens" (and others who seek haven in our midst?); "government of the people, for the people, and by the people"; where we judge the worth of an individual by the "content of his character."

The instructional activities described below are aimed at beginning the process of assisting students in thinking more clearly and intensively about some of the fundamental concepts that underlie the set of beliefs about who we are as a people, and recognizing the individual's responsibility to engage in the formidable task of promoting the development of a culture that not only values the diversity of microcultures of which it is comprised, but also benefits from each of their potential contributions to its fulfillment.

Instructional Activities

Activity 11.1: A Concept Map of "Independence"

You might ask your students, working in groups, to think about the term "independence" and what it means to them. They may wish to have some initial discussions among themselves, formulating questions, and then seek out information that will help them address these questions. After further inquiry, students should construct a graphical map of the concept, including terms or concepts that are similar in meaning, examples of actions that illustrate the concept, terms whose meanings are the opposite of or contradictory to independence, actions or states of affairs that the concept leads to or promotes, and any other elements that you or the students may believe to be appropriate.

The beginning stages of constructing such a map might look like this:

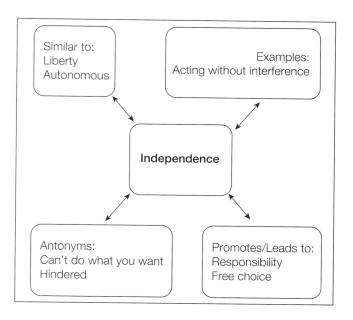

The conceptual maps that are developed by the student group may then be shared and compared. You might stimulate further discussion and reflection by asking them to offer reasons why they included (or excluded) certain items in their maps.

Other questions that can be pursued to assist students in analyzing "independence" and arriving at a better understanding of the concept. (Note: You may wish to introduce the oft-used term "empowered" into these discussions, although you need not do so since an analysis of "being able" should prove equally valuable and insightful to the students.)

What does it mean to be independent?

Is it possible to be partially independent? [seek examples]

Is anyone ever completely independent? [examples, or reasons why this is not possible, given the social nature of human beings]

Is it desirable that we should be/should not be completely independent? [Is it sometimes good that we have to dependent?]

Are there differences in the way in which we use the term if we speak of a "country's independence" versus a "person's independence"?

What is the relationship between "independence" and "being able" to do something?

What does it mean to "be able" to do something?

What kinds of things hinder you from being able to do what you wish to do?

Are there some good/bad or unjustified reasons why you should not be able to do what you wish to do?

What might one do in order to "remove" the unjustified things that keep one from doing what they want to do?

After our discussions thus far, what does the following statement mean to you: "With independence must come responsibility."

These and other questions can enable your students to gain a deeper understanding of the concepts that form the intellectual core of the discourse that should take place with respect to encouraging a tolerance and respect for the many cultures and groups that constitute American society. In such an environment the whole can benefit from the contributions of each individual and ethnic and cultural group within it.

Activity 11.2: Independence and Rights

This activity, similar in approach to Activity 11.1, involves the students in discussions about the nature of our freedoms and rights. We live in a nation that is based on certain beliefs about individuals and their relations with one another. Freedom and independence are closely related concepts.

It is likely that our students will live in a society that will continue to wrestle with the problem of reconciling the various constitutional rights and freedoms that we possess with the boundaries or limits that are sometimes necessarily to place, on these rights because of their potential effects on other members of society.

Students probably will agree and understand that we should have independence or freedom of thought and belief. The difficulty arises when individuals seek to act in a way consistent with those beliefs. In many cases of overt action, the need to place reasonable limits on these free actions may be obvious.

This is a dilemma that historically has challenged moral and political philosophers. You may be wondering why students who are much less mature and sophisticated should deal with the issues involved. The issue of the First Amendment rights of those who express views that have been characterized as "hate speech" is one that confronts us now, and likely will never be completely resolved (at least to all parties' satisfaction) in a democratic society. It is appropriate, however, that students should begin to discuss and confront some of these thorny questions in a setting established by an educator whom they respect and who will lead the discussions with a degree of sensitivity that may be lacking in other arenas.

Some of the topics and questions that might be addressed include:

What do you understand by the terms "independence of belief" and "independence of thought"? Are they identical? Similar?

What is the difference (if any) between "thought," "belief," and "action"?

When does the "expression" of a thought or belief become an action? [This takes account of the fact that difficulties in this area seem to arise when such expressions, which are constitutionally protected rights, become an "action" that can be regulated by law.]

Is it significant when such "expressions" [which may include "hate speech"]

(a) indicate an intention to act;

(b) urge that others as well as the speaker should act;

(c) are likely, by their very utterance, to inflame or incite others.

What are the different ways or channels that are available to individuals to "express" these beliefs or thoughts? [examples of these are "enactive" means such as writing, speech, or graphic expression (illustrations, cartoons)]

Which do you think are more like "actions"?

Which do you think are likely to be more "inflammatory" or evoke a more emotional response?

As in previous activity, you should pursue other questions as they arise. These discussions will prove most effective when the students initiate the questions in the dialogue.

Students should be encouraged to investigate incidents where such activities have been reported. Editorials or letters to the editors of newspapers can provide additional examples. These should be studied to assess whether any fallacious reasoning is evident.

After these issues have been discussed in class, you may wish to invite members of the community to share their views. Your students will be better prepared to listen to and understand these speakers if they have already analyzed some of the questions and issues involved. They may also come to recognize the desirability of pursuing overt actions in their neighborhoods and communities to remedy some of the social problems that may exist there.

Activity 11.3: The Pen May Be Mightier Than the Sword

It has been noted that many participants in independence movements often are less fully represented in texts that students will encounter. Typically, military leaders will receive a disproportionate share of coverage. Thus, students should be encouraged to conduct investigations concerning persons who played roles outside the direct sphere of military conflicts.

Some of these individuals were authors who wielded the pen to seek the goal of freedom. Tom Paine, author of *Common Sense* and *The Rights of Man*, was a significant figure in the American Revolution. A few generations later, Lincoln is reported to have alluded to Harriet Beecher Stowe as the woman who brought on the Civil War. Frederick Douglass was another influential individual during this period who forthrightly and forcefully expressed his views through the written and spoken word. In this regard, you may wish to refer to January's potpourri "Is There a Higher Law That Should Be Obeyed?"

Many of the individuals noted wrote and acted in defense of their beliefs. Henry Thoreau's essay "Civil Disobedience" served to influence others to pursue such courses of action. Although these figures were not involved in an overt struggle for political independence in every case, they certainly were involved in the effort to redress inequities in the political affairs of their nations.

Students should be encouraged to seek out influential figures from all cultures and historic eras that have been overlooked. Biographical reports can be shared with the class, and should specifically address the reasons why students believe their "candidates" deserve further recognition. These reports might be published by the class and distributed to others.

Activity 11.4: They Paid the Price for Us

Periodically, individuals arise who serve as extraordinary examples of those who valued liberty so greatly that they were willing to face social opprobrium or physical punishment, imprisonment, and even death in the struggle to gain freedom and independence for themselves and for others. The human race has been fortunate that so many such individuals have existed. In addition to those already mentioned in other sections of this unit, a small sampling could include Nelson Mandela, the Grimke sisters and others in the North and South who fought slavery in their own unique circumstances, Harriet Tubman, Sojourner Truth, Spartacus, and the inhabitants of Melos in the fifth century B.C.

Ways of reporting these findings include short biographies, dramatic presentations of the significant events in these individuals' lives, news broadcast "reports" covering the impact of these events, debates articulating their positions and those of their opponents, letters or journal entries that they might have written at significant times in their lives, or even letters that they students would now wish to send to these individuals.

Bibliography

Note: Many of the biographies included here can also be used in association with the potpourri titled "'Parents' of Their Country."

Bridgland, F. (1987) *Jonas Savimbi: A key to Africa.* New York: Paragon House.

Brinton, C. (1976). *The anatomy of revolution.* New York: Vintage. Primarily for the teacher, this almost classic work compares the French, English, American, and Russian revolutions.

Cairns, T. (1979). *The old regime and the revolution.* Minneapolis: Lerner Publications.

Cairns, T. (1980). *Power for the people.* Minneapolis: Lerner Publications. Both of the works by Cairns were written for the *Cambridge Introduction to History.* They should be informative to both you and your more able readers.

Carson, S. L. (1988). *Maximilien Robespierre.* New York: Chelsea House.

Cheney, G. A. (1984). *Revolution in Central America.* New York: Franklin Watts.

Cobb, R., & Jones, C. (Eds.). (1988). *Voices of the French revolution.* Topfield, MA: Salem House. Collection of accounts by people living at the time; valuable if you wish to provide primary source material for your students.

DeVarona, F. (1993). *Miguel Hidalgo y Costilla: Father of Mexican independence.* Brookfield, CT: Millbrook Press.

DeVarona, F. (1993). *Simon Bolivar: Latin American liberator.* Brookfield, CT: Millbrook Press.

Dowd, D. L. (1965). *The French revolution.* New York: American Heritage. Well-illustrated account primarily for students.

Hoobler, D. (1987). *Nelson and Winnie Mandela.* New York: Franklin Watts.

Jacobs, J. (1980). *The quest of separatism: Quebec and the struggle over sovereignty.* New York: Random House. Account of the ongoing struggle for autonomy for Quebec just north of our border.

McKown, R. (1973). *Nkrumah.* Garden City, NY: Doubleday. Example of the many biographies available for students recounting the lives of those who led their countries' struggles for independence.

Perlin, D. E. (1991). *Father Miguel Hidalgo: A cry for freedom.* Dallas: Hendrick-Long.

Prago, A. (1970). *The revolution in Spanish America.* New York: Macmillan. Comprehensive treatment of the struggle for independence in Central and South America.

Ragan, J. D. (1989). *Emiliano Zapata.* New York: Chelsea House.

Vail, J. J. (1989). *Nelson and Winnie Mandela.* New York: Chelsea House.

Wake, C. (Trans.) (1988). *Faces of African independence: Three plays.* Charlottesville: University of Virginia. Plays by the African dramatists Guillaume Oyono-Mbia and Seydou Badian.

Whitridge, A. (1954). *Simon Bolivar, the great liberator.* New York: Random House.

Young, B., & Young, J. (1970). *Liberators of Latin America.* New York: Lothrop, Lee and Shephard Books. "Group portrait" of the major figures involved in the efforts to gain independence.

July's Potpourri of Teaching Ideas

The purpose of each month's Potpourri of Teaching Ideas is to provide additional resources from which to build your curriculum. Most, but not all, of the activities listed each month relate directly to that month. It is not intended that you use them all, but rather that you choose those which are appropriate for your program. Although the topics are written for a particular month, many of them would be appropriate for use throughout the year. How you use these activities will depend on your curricular goals. You may wish to use some of the activities as they are presented, and you may need to modify some to meet your needs. Perhaps some of them will give you ideas for entirely different potpourris.

They Took to the Air

Who was the first person to fly? How you answer that question depends on what you mean by "fly" and where and when you lived. In the United States most people would answer the question by saying, "Orville and Wilbur Wright." However, early Greeks would answer that question by referring to the mythical Daedalus and his son Icarus, who flew using wings fashioned of feathers and wax. Scandinavians might tell of Wieland, who escaped captivity by using a flying coat. The Incas had a story of a Peruvian chief who flew all over his kingdom. In the lore of India, Hanouam had a pair of wings and flew.

Later, myths gave way to historical evidence. In Italy, Leonardo da Vinci (1452–1519), designed many unsuccessful flying machines. In 1670, Francesco de Lana (1631–1687), an Italian priest, suggested that pumping air out of a copper ball would make it lighter than the atmosphere, allowing it to float free. This was the first idea based on sound scientific principles and helped people to realize that humans would not be able to fly under their own power. One hundred years later, Joseph and Jacques Montgolfier constructed a paper-bag balloon that flew to the ceiling of their home. On June 5, 1783, the Montgolfier brothers demonstrated that their balloon could travel. In November of that year, two men made the world's first balloon flight, flying for twenty-five minutes to a distance of about five and a half miles.

In England, Sir George Cayley tried to solve the problem of flight. He believed that a fixed wing could function for flying. In 1804, he made a model that flew 390 feet. He developed models of gliders and biplanes and laid down the mathematical principles of lift, thrust, and drag. In 1852, his servant was actually the first man to fly using wing power when he flew twelve hundred feet in a craft made by Cayley. After landing, the coachman resigned as both Cayley's servant and "test pilot."

William Samuel Henson, another Englishman, developed a model airplane with a engine. By 1843, he still had not developed a model able to fly. In 1847, however, he constructed a twenty-foot model of his aerial steam carriage, which he launched from an inclined ramp. The engine was not powerful enough for full flight, but it did manage to hop before it stopped. Its wings were very similar to those on modern airplanes.

John Stringfellow, who began as a partner with Henson, developed an engine-powered model that flew forty yards in 1848. By the beginning of the twentieth century, the glider was a reliable flying machine and the gasoline combustion engine was a source of power.

The Wright brothers combined the glider and the combustion engine. First, they made a glider with controls on the front surfaces of its wings and rudder. Next, they placed a twelve-horsepower engine on a sophisticated airframe. Finally, they connected the engine to a pair of propellers of their own design. Their first flight was on December 17, 1903, when Orville flew 120 feet.

From the first balloon flights to the modern space shuttle, the ability of humans to fly came about because of the work of many people in different parts of the world over long periods of time.

Try These Activities

1. Some of the famous names in the history of flight are listed in the box "What's Their Contribution to Flight?" Interested students can make short pre-

What's Their Contribution to Flight?

Sir John Alcock	Otto Lilienthal
Louis Bleriot	Charles Lindbergh
Richard Byrd	Joseph Montgolfier
Sir George Cayley	Sally Ride
Jacques Charles	Alberto Santos-Dumont
Samuel Cody	Igor Sikorsky
Paul Cornu	Wilbur and Orville
Amy Johnson	Wright

sentations about the life and aeronautical contributions of these or other pioneers in aviation.

2. Students who want to combine science with this unit can make posters of the different types of flying machines available today and explain some of the scientific principles that make them work.

3. Students can make an illustrated timeline showing the progress of flight.

Suggested Readings

Ardley, N. (1984). *Just look at flight*. Vero Beach, FL: Rourke Enterprises.

Cooke, D. (1964). *Who really invented the airplane?* New York: G. P. Putnam's Sons.

Jefferis, D. (1988). *The first flyers*. New York: Franklin Watts.

Maurer, R. (1990). *Airborne: The search for the secret of flight*. New York: Simon & Schuster.

Polley, J. (Ed.). (1980). *Reader's Digest stories behind everyday things*. Pleasantville, NY: Reader's Digest.

Provensen, A., & Provensen, M. (1984). *Leonardo da Vinci*. New York: Viking Press.

"Parents" of Their Country

We citizens of the United States celebrate our independence on the Fourth of July. When people are asked to think of key figures in our struggle for freedom, one individual is likely to come immediately to many minds: George Washington. Generations of American schoolchildren have been taught that Washington was the "Father of Our Country." Although we may be hesitant to think along these more traditional lines, and although we are less willing than in the past to designate him as the sole father of our nation, we might still consider him to be part of the "extended family" of parents who strove to bring it into existence and nurtured it in its rather precarious early years.

We are likely to be less familiar with the fact that other nations also celebrate their own political independence during this month. Several of these nations are our neighbors in the hemisphere. On the first day of July, our northern neighbor, Canada, celebrates the independent status that it gained in 1867. Only a day after our own holiday, Venezuela marks its day of independence, and Colombia celebrates its special day on the twentieth. These nations gained their freedom from Spanish domination only a few decades after we achieved our own.

These nations, as well as others in the region, hold in esteem those individuals largely responsible for leading their struggles for independence. This triumvirate included Simón Bolívar, José de San Martín, and Bernardo O'Higgins. Each was born during our revolutionary war period, San Martín and O'Higgins in 1778, and the younger member of the trio, Bolívar, in 1783.

Simón Bolívar was born into a wealthy Creole family in Venezuela and was well read in the works of the European Enlightenment, including those by Voltaire, Rousseau, and Montesquieu, although they had been banned in his native country. The struggle that he led for Venezuelan independence was similar to our own in that his forces suffered many defeats before their ultimate success. Eventually, stemming in part from his promise to outlaw slavery, he surprised and overcame a Spanish army in Bogotá, Colombia, in 1819. Two years after this victory, Venezuela gained its independence.

Bernardo O'Higgins, son of a former governor of Chile, allied himself with San Martín in the effort to free Latin America from Spanish rule. Their victories in the battles of Chacabuco and Maipu enabled Chile to declare its independence, and a republic was established in 1818. Although his declared aim was to establish democratic institutions in his native land, O'Higgins ruled Chile as a virtual dictator (Director Supremo) for five years until forced to resign in 1823. However, during his term of office, he was able to offer San Martín crucial logistic support.

José San Martín was a native of Argentina, a country located at the other end of South America. When conflicts erupted there, he returned from Europe, where he had been engaged in the struggle against Napoleon. Bolívar and San Martín represented a two-pronged attack against the Spanish forces, with the insurgents led by Bolívar in the north and by San Martín in the south. Although Argentina had declared itself independent in 1816, its precarious state was threatened by the continued presence of Spanish armies in other areas of the continent. After meeting with Bolívar in Guayaquil, Ecuador, San Martín relinquished the command of their united armies to Bolívar and returned home to Argentina. Finally, in December 1824, Bolívar led the forces that defeated the Spanish at Ayacucho in the Andes mountains south and east of Lima, Peru. From a military perspective, this battle ended the conflict. However, the struggle for social and economic equity, as in our own country, continues to the present.

The study of these South American leaders and the roles that they played in the establishment of their countries is a worthwhile one. It provides students with an opportunity to study both the geography and subsequent history of the region from a less traditional perspective, and should serve to encourage independent inquiry and divergent thinking on ideas related to these topics.

Try These Activities

Old and New Boundaries. To gain an additional historical perspective on these South American struggles for independence, students should obtain information about the boundaries drawn in the region as they existed at the beginning of the nineteenth century, shortly before these wars broke out. These data can then be compared with the boundaries at other periods—for example about 1830 or 1840, when the first new boundaries were being established—and finally with current boundaries.

Sample questions that can be raised to direct these inquiries include:

What were the major centers of population during the prerevolutionary periods?
Are these cities still population centers today?
How many of them became capitals of the countries formed from earlier Spanish colonial areas?

City	Former Region	Present Country
Bogotá	Viceroyalty: New Granada	Colombia
Lima	Viceroyalty: Peru	Peru
Buenos Aires	Viceroyalty: La Plata	Argentina
Rio de Janeiro	Viceroyalty: Brazil	Brazil

Colonies of other European powers were located in South America. Why didn't political revolutions occur in these areas during the nineteenth century? What is their political status at the present time?

"What if . . . ?" Numerous struggles occurred among these countries even after they had gained their freedom. Such political frictions continue to the present.

What factors were involved in these subsequent conflicts among the nations that previously had been united in their struggle against Spain?
Can you envision a United States of South America? Why did this not occur?
How might the history of our hemisphere have been different if we had two United States as nations in it? How would this have affected the history of the world?

To begin the inquiry along these lines and to formulate reasonable scenarios, students might draw up a chart comparing data about the two "nations." The potential for a nation known as the United States of South America becomes evident when one compares items such as area, population, and resources. When other data are included, however, such as per capita income, gross national product, and literacy rate, the disparities that currently exist become more pronounced.

Different groups of students could develop a constitution for this hypothetical nation and formulate a tentative map of the individual states that would constitute the United States of South America. This constitution should include; among other items, the relationships that would exist between the "national" and the "state" governments. The maps would establish likely boundaries of the proposed states, offering reasons for the particular way in which they were drawn up. Students could share their proposals, noting differences among them, and stating the reasons for their own particular plans.

National "Parents" around the World. Three individuals who were involved in South American struggles for independence have been discussed. Of course, other

A COMPARISON CHART

	U.S.A. (North)	U.S.A. (South)
Area	_____	_____
Population	_____	_____
Major Resources	_____	_____

figures have played significant roles in the establishment of other nations around the world. In our own hemisphere, François-Dominique Toussaint-Louverture led a revolution in Haiti less than a decade after revolution broke out in France, and years before political upheavals erupted on the continent of South America. Although his rebellion against the French failed, and he was imprisoned and died in France in 1803, Haiti gained its independence shortly thereafter in 1804.

In this century, a number of individuals in Africa have worked to breathe life into independent nations once under the dominance of European countries. Among them are Kwame Nkrumah, who led the struggle for independence in Ghana. After a decades-long struggle, Nelson Mandela, a recipient of the Nobel Peace Prize, and others have successfully gained political freedom for all South Africans.

Direct your students to research the beginnings of other nations in the world and to create biographical sketches of the major figures involved. It might even be possible to draw up a "family tree" of the "parents" of certain countries. Those with artistic ability could create a mural representing significant events in the lives of these individuals or of the nation itself. This would make a good group project involving individuals with artistic talent and other students who could suggest themes and how they might be represented. Variations of this would include portraits (with background scenes) and designs for postage stamps or currency commemorating these individuals and their exploits.

It is obvious that women have not appeared in these citations of "parents" for new political entities. Fruitful discussions could ensue if questions such as the following were posed for the students' consideration:

What was the role of women in the struggles discussed?

Why have they not seemed to play as large a role? [examples: gender roles and status in the cultures, efforts not valued by contemporaries or historians who reported the struggles, an unnecessarily narrow conception of "nation" or "people"]

Were not individuals such as Harriet Tubman "parents" in their people's struggle for "independence"? [other examples might be used to stimulate discussion]

The Beginnings of the Olympic Games

Olympia, a place between the rivers Alpheios and Kladeios, became the setting of the Olympic games in 776 B.C. These games were then held every four years until A.D. 393. The games drew athletes from neighboring areas, with colonies of Athens and Greece along the Aegean Sea taking part. Women and girls were not allowed to compete in the games, and married women were forbidden as spectators. Unmarried women of Greek citizenship, however, were allowed to compete in a different festival honoring the goddess Hera.

In the early days of the Olympics, the winner was given vases filled with wine or olive oil. Later, the prize became a crown of olive branches cut from a sacred grove of trees. The task of cutting the branches, using a golden knife, was given to a youth whose parents were living. Because it had no material value, the crown symbolized the importance of excellence for its own sake. Winners might also be honored in their home states by being exempted from paying taxes or by becoming the subject of a heroic poem or receiving some other special honor.

When the Romans took over Greece, the nature of the competition changed. The Romans enjoyed spectacles and so promoted boxing and chariot racing at the expense of running, jumping, and javelin throwing. In A.D. 393, Theodosius I, the emperor of Constantinople, banned the games.

The modern Olympic games began in 1896 in Athens, Greece. Baron Pierre de Coubertin, a French author and educator, believed that games would be an ideal way to unite students of the world in a peaceful setting.

Try These Activities

1. Research the early Olympic games to find out the type of competitions that took place and compare them to the events of today.
2. Organize mock Olympic games in your school, community center, or local youth group. Substitute modern equipment for the ancient contests. For example, use a frisbee instead of a discus. The contest can stress distance or accuracy or even include tricks such as throwing the frisbee through an old tire hanging from a tree. Instead of a shot put, use a foam ball to hit a target.
3. Participate or help organize and volunteer for the local Special Olympics competition in your community.

Artists: Mirrors, Creators, and Transmitters of Culture

Historically, humans have fashioned the utensils and articles needed for daily living with an eye for beauty as well as utility. These implements for living were but one outlet for the creative expression of the talented artist.

That the world in which we live has an effect on us is a truism that applies to the artist as well. Some talented individuals in a society may have a richer and more vibrant imagination than others, but writers still are best able to write about what they experience, painters to represent or abstract from what they see, musicians to compose works that are stimulated by and perhaps incorporate the folk tunes to which they are exposed. Artists serve as "mirrors" of their cultures, their creative works reflecting the values and significant aspects of the cultures in which they have been raised.

Artists do not play an entirely passive role with regard to their culture, however. As their creations are experienced by other members of society, they may have an impact on the development of that society. Those artists whose work is sufficiently powerful may influence the practices, stories, and symbols that ultimately become an important "defining" element of a culture. Among those cultures that have written traditions, writers may be influential in composing the allegorical and mythic works that help to "create" and form a people. Artists such as sculptors, painters, and architects may create works that play a significant role in the religious rites practiced by a group.

As artists capture significant elements in their works, they also serve to preserve aspects of a culture for transmission from generation to generation. Thus, they also can be viewed as educators. The impact of their efforts may extend beyond the boundaries of their own culture. They are the "texts" and sources used by individuals who wish to study, understand, and appreciate a culture not their own.

Often the creations of artists perform valuable social functions. Stories, pictures, or sculptures may deal with many culturally significant themes. For example, they may relate the history of the people, their origins, their heroes, important events of their past, and perhaps serve as a means to express the group's purpose on earth and its future destiny.

Such art is not limited to literature or graphic art forms. Various religious and political rites may be envisioned almost as "dramas" in which the participants have particular roles, whether in a Christian mass, a political inauguration, or a university commencement ceremony. In some cases, it may be difficult to assign authorship to an individual artist, for the origins of the drama may be lost in the distant past. In any event, the dramatic elements serve to give meaning and worth to the event. One might also claim that the recountings of the oral historian before a group, the sachem's speeches to her people, and the orations of modern political leaders also possess a dramatic dimension.

Dance is another art form that serves additional functions beyond aesthetics. Dance may be used to represent past events or to prepare individuals or groups within the culture for activities that may require extra, intensive, and sustained effort, such as a hunt. Dance can be used for educative purposes, expressing a moral story or lesson, or a means of invoking the aid of some extrahuman influence for the good of the group.

All of these art forms can be used a means of expressing reality as humans experience it, as well as a more idealistic view, one that members of the culture should seek to realize. Indeed, the artists of a culture may serve as agents for change through what they choose to represent in their art and the particular way in which they render or depict their subjects. One might cite the role of artists in the shift from the medieval age to the world of the Renaissance.

One of the added benefits of activities involving the arts is that this is an area of study in which students are less likely to be hindered by language or other factors in understanding and appreciating works of art. Similarities of theme and treatment of artistic subjects enable students to understand how much humans of different cultures share in common.

Try These Activities

Tools and Techniques of Artists around the World. This activity involves students in a search for the different tools and techniques that artists have used throughout different historical periods and in a variety of cultural

ARTISTS' MATERIALS

Material	Art Subject/Theme	Culture	Time Period
Wood	_____	_____	_____
Metal	_____	_____	_____
Stone	_____	_____	_____
Other	_____	_____	_____

contexts throughout the world. For example, they could search for all the art objects made of wood that they can find. The school or local public librarian can suggest books with illustrations of such objects. Talented students can make sketches if the illustrations can not be brought to class. A chart displaying the data collected can be constructed, allowing the class to more readily observe similarities and differences among artists in different cultures and historical periods.

Seek the assistance of art teachers in your school or district, curatorial staff of local museums, or even local artists. They can offer additional suggestions and may be willing to help your students create works that reflect their own cultural backgrounds.

Depicting the Culture through the Arts. Studying the works created by the artists of a particular culture can reveal much about that group and provide answers to questions such as:

Who are they? [How are they depicted by their own artists?]
What is important to them? [What objects and themes are represented most frequently?]
What materials/media do the artists work with?
How do they view the world around them?
What emotions seem to be depicted in the works?

Solicit other questions from your students. To make it intriguing, you may wish to use some works of art from a culture with which your students are unfamiliar. They could then test their speculations about the culture through further reading and research.

Cultural Art Exhibitions. In conjunction with the activity just described, students could assemble their own exhibits of the representative arts of a particular culture and then use the school halls or some other area as their museum's exhibition rooms. The students would have to depend on works of art as the sole means of describing the culture to the "museum" visitors.

Although the emphasis would be on the works of art themselves, students could also prepare a catalog of the exhibit describing what, in their view, these works of art communicate about the particular culture. A set of questions similar to those listed in the previous activity might be a starting point for developing the catalog. The class could be responsible for printing the catalog and sharing it with exhibition visitors. Each of these activities provides an opportunity to invite parents and other members of the community to the school. Their suggestions could also be sought for materials to be included in the exhibit.

Chapter 12

Butterflies Are Yellow with August

August was originally called *sextilis*, the Latin word for sixth, because it used to be the sixth month of the year. During his reign as emperor of Rome, Augustus made several changes in the calendar. One was to name this month in his honor. He also took a day from February and added it to August, giving the month thirty-one days.

In the Northern Hemisphere, August is likely to be the hottest month of the year. Most crops are still in the fields and not yet ready for harvest. However, a hint of the season to come is in the air. Perhaps that is what the American poet Ezra Pound was observing when he wrote, "Butterflies are already yellow with August." In the southern half of the world, August marks the end of winter and the promise of a new spring.

Traditionally, summer has "ended" when schools opened for a new academic year. In some parts of the nation, year-round schools are replacing the nine-month September to June school calendar. However, it may be a long time before this practice is adopted on a wide level. For many students, August will always mean new wardrobes, new teachers, new books, and other changes that often affect families, such as moves to new neighborhoods and adjustments to older siblings leaving home for a career or a college education.

No national American holidays are celebrated in August. Nevertheless, a number of noteworthy events have occurred in this month, including the births of Napoleon Bonaparte, Virginia Dare, Davy Crockett, Annie Oakley, Marjorie Kinnon Rawlings, Alex Haley, and both members of the Lewis and Clark expedition team. Events of historic implication have also occurred in August. Columbus's departure from the port of Palos, Spain, in search of a route to the East Indies, passage of the nineteenth amendment giving women the right to vote, and the tragic bombing of Hiroshima, Japan, all happened during August.

Sunday	Monday	Tuesday	Wednesday	Thursday	Friday	Saturday

August

AUGUST

SELECTED EVENTS

1 William Clark (1770–1838)
   Francis Scott Key (1779–1843)
2 James Baldwin (1924–1987)
3 Columbus sets sail (1492)
4 Coast Guard Day
5 Conrad Aiken (1899–1973)
6 Hiroshima Day
   Lucille Ball (1911–1989)
7 Ralph Bunche (1904–1971)
8 Matthew A. Henson (1866–1955)
   Marjorie Kinnan Rawlings (1896–1953)
9 Singapore Independence Day
10 Herbert Hoover (1874–1964)
11 Alex Haley (1921–1992)
12 Thailand: Birthday of Queen Sirkit
13 Annie Oakley (1860–1926)
   Lucy Stone (1818–1893)
14 V-J Day
15 Napoleon Bonaparte (1769–1821)
16 Klondike Gold Discovery (1896)
17 Davy Crockett (1786–1836)
18 Virginia Dare (1587–1591)
   Meriwether Lewis (1774–1809)
19 Ogden Nash (1902–1971)
   Orville Wright (1871–1948)
20 Turkey: Victory Day
   Bernardo O'Higgins (1778–1842)
21 Aubrey Beardsley (1872–1898)
22 Claude Debussy (1862–1918)
23 Edgar Lee Masters (1869–1950)
24 Destruction of Pompeii
25 Uruguay Independence Day
   Bret Harte (1836–1902)
26 Women's Equality Day
   Lee De Forest (1873–1961)
27 Lyndon B. Johnson (1908–1973)
28 Johann Wolfgang Goethe (1749–1832)
29 Soviet Communist Party Dissolved (1991)
30 Hong Kong Liberation Day
   Roy Wilkins (1901–1981)
31 Founding of Solidarity in Poland (1980)

People, Places, and Events of August

What's Happening in August:

First Monday: Australia: Picnic Day

Events Scheduled According to Non-Gregorian Calendar Usually Occurring in August:

People's Republic of China: Festival of Hungry Ghosts
Muslim festival to honor the birth of the prophet Muhammad

August's Daily Calendar

1

Switzerland National Day. Commemorating the founding of the Swiss Confederation in 1291.
Birth anniversary of:
> William Clark (1770–1838). Explorer who formed half of the famous Lewis and Clark team; noted for the journey to explore the regions of the Louisiana Purchase.
> Francis Scott Key (1779–1843). Writer of the words for "The Star Spangled Banner."
> Herman Melville (1819–1891). Novelist, best known for *Moby Dick*.

2

Birth anniversary of:
> James Baldwin (1924–1987). African-American author of works depicting black life in the United States.

3

Columbus sails west in search of new route to India (1492).

4

Coast Guard Day. Commemorating founding of U.S. Coast Guard in 1790.
Birth anniversary of:
> Glenn Cunningham (1909–1988). Track athlete and world's record holder for the fastest mile during the 1930s.

5

Birth anniversary of:

Conrad Aiken (1899–1973). Poet and Pulitzer Prize winner. Father of Joan Aiken, noted writer of children's books.

6

Bolivia Independence Day. Gained independence from Spain in 1825.

Hiroshima Day. Memorial observance for victims of first atomic bombing of an inhabited area in 1945.

Jamaica Independence Day. Gained independence from British rule in 1962. Celebrated on the first Monday of August.

Birth anniversary of:

Lucille Ball (1911–1989). Actress; best remembered for her role in TV's *I Love Lucy*.

Alfred Tennyson (1809–1892). English poet.

7

Birth anniversary of:

Ralph Bunche (1904–1971). African-American statesman and United Nations official. Winner of the Nobel Peace Prize.

8

Birth anniversary of:

Matthew A. Henson (1866–1955). African-American explorer; accompanied Robert Pearry on seven expeditions, including one to the North Pole.

Marjorie Kinnan Rawlings (1896–1953). Novelist and Pulitzer Prize winner for *The Yearling*.

9

Japan: Moment of Silence. Honoring those who died in Nagasaki during the second atomic bombing of Japan in 1945.

Singapore Independence Day. National day of celebration to commemorate becoming a nation in 1965.

10

Missouri Admission Day. Became twnety-fourth state to join the Union (1821).

Birth anniversary of:

Herbert Hoover (1874–1964). Thirty-first President of the United States; born in Iowa.

11

Chad Independence Day. Gained independence from France in 1960.

Birth anniversary of:

Alex Haley (1921–1992). African-American writer; best remembered for *Roots,* published in 1976 and later made into a TV miniseries.

12

Thailand: National holiday to celebrate the birthday of Queen Sirkit.

Birth anniversary of:

Cecil B. De Mille (1881–1959). Hollywood film producer; best remembered for *The Greatest Show on Earth* and *The Ten Commandments.*

13

Tunisia: Women's Day. General holiday to celebrate the independence of women.

Birth anniversary of:

Alfred Hitchcock (1899–1980). English director of suspense films.

Annie Oakley (1860–1926). Legendary sharpshooter and Wild West show celebrity.

Lucy Stone (1818–1893). Pioneer for the cause of women's rights and the abolition of slavery.

14

Victory Day. Also called V-J Day; commemorating the surrender of Japan to Allied forces in 1945 to end World War II.

15

India Independence Day. Commemorating independence from British rule in 1947.

Korea Liberation Day. Commemorating the freeing of Korea from thirty-six years of Japanese domination.

Birth anniversary of:

Napoleon Bonaparte (1769–1821). French emperor and military leader.

Sir Walter Scott (1771–1832). Scottish poet and novelist.

16

Klondike gold discovery. Anniversary of the discovery of gold in the Yukon Territory in 1896.

Elvis Presley, one of America's most popular singers, died in 1977 at the age of forty-two.

17

Indonesia Independence Day. Commemorating the establishment of a republic after the withdrawal of the Japanese in 1945.

Birth anniversary of:

Davy Crockett (1786–1836). Frontiersman and hero of the Battle of the Alamo.

18

Birth anniversary of:

Virginia Dare (1587–1591). First child born of English parents in what later became the American colonies.

Meriwether Lewis (1774–1809). Explorer who formed half of the famous Lewis and Clark team; noted for the journey to explore the regions of the Louisiana Purchase.

19
Birth anniversary of:
Ogden Nash (1902–1971). Poet and humorist.
Orville Wright (1871–1948). Pioneer in aviation.
Bill Clinton (1946–). Forty-fourth president of the United States; born in Arkansas.

20
Birth anniversary of:
Benjamin Harrison (1833–1901). Twenty-third president of the United States; born in Ohio.
Bernardo O'Higgins (1778–1842). Political leader of Chile; called the "Liberator of Chile."

21
Hawaii Admission Day. Became fiftieth state to join the Union (1959).
Birth anniversary of:
Aubrey Beardsley (1872–1898). English artist and illustrator.

22
Birth anniversary of:
Claude Debussy (1862–1918). French musician and composer.

23
Birth anniversary of:
Edgar Lee Masters (1869–1950). Poet; best remembered for *Spoon River Anthology.*

24
Italy: Vesuvius Day. Anniversary of the eruption in A.D. 79 which destroyed the city of Pompeii.

25
Uruguay Independence Day. Commemorating the declaration of independence from Brazil in 1825.

Birth anniversary of:
Bret Harte (1836–1902). Short story writer; best remembered for stories about California and the West.

26
Women's Equality Day.
Birth anniversary of:
Lee De Forest (1873–1961). Inventor of the electron tube; called the "Father of Radio."
Geraldine Ferraro (1935–) First woman to run for a major national office; nominated for vice president of the United States at the Democratic National Convention in 1984.

27
Birth anniversary of:
Lyndon B. Johnson (1908–1973). Thirty-sixth president of the United States; born in Texas.

28
Birth anniversary of:
Johann Wolfgang Goethe (1749–1832). German author and philosopher.

29
Soviet Communist Party disssolved (1991).

30
Hong Kong Liberation Day.
Peru: Saint Rose of Lima's Day.
Birth anniversary of:
Huey P. Long (1893–1935). Politician and governor of Louisiana.
Roy Wilkins (1901–1981). Grandson of a slave; civil rights leader and executive director of the NAACP (National Association for the Advancement of Colored People).

31
Founding of Solidarity in Poland (1980).
Trinidad and Tobago Independence Day. Located in northeastern regions of South America; became independent of British rule in 1962.

When the World
Comes to Breakfast

Teaching Unit for August

A Word about This Unit. Food is a basic need for all living creatures. This unit will focus on some of the foods eaten for breakfast by various groups around the world. In the United States and other countries where food is plentiful, variety in foods is important. Therefore, breakfast may be quite different from other meals of the day. However, in countries where food is less plentiful, what is eaten at the morning meal may be almost identical to other food eaten throughout the day. Breakfast is an important meal in all parts of the world, and regardless of cultural background, people everywhere and throughout history have been interested in this important meal.

The word "breakfast" is derived from two words, *break* and *fast.* "Break" means to discontinue, as to break or discontinue a habit, and "fast" means to go without food. Breakfast, then, literally means to "break the fast" or to discontinue the long period (throughout the night) of going without food. Hence, the first meal of the day, after a night's sleep, is the "break-fast" meal.

Information. What is a typical American breakfast? Are there certain foods that constitute the typical breakfast meal in our culture? The answer is no. Most American families have some type of first meal each day, but there are dozens of situations and configurations that American people call breakfast. The country breakfast of a farmer and his family may be very different from that of the members of an urban businesswoman's family. Breakfasts eaten in southern California may not be like the breakfasts prepared by many families in Ohio or New York. Hispanic children in Texas will likely eat and enjoy foods that are different from those familiar to the children of Norwegian immigrants. If one could survey the families on a block in any city in America, there would likely be many similarities, but probably no two families would set the table with an identical breakfast.

For many people, breakfast is a quick and simple meal, perhaps a glass of juice, a cup of coffee, and a doughnut or a piece of toast. Others may add eggs, bacon or sausage, and perhaps muffins or other breads. Still others may stop at the fast-food mart for a bagel with cream cheese and a soft drink. In earlier times (especially for people who worked in jobs that required a hard day of physical labor), breakfast was the largest and most important meal of the day. It would not be unusual for a farmer and his family to be served hot biscuits and gravy, a plate of eggs, a platter of meat (usually consisting of one of the following: bacon, sausage, ham, pork chops, fried chicken, fried beef steak, or even fish), plus milk, coffee, or tea. All of this may have been topped off with several more biscuits covered with honey or syrup and a large pat of butter.

Culture influences what people eat for breakfast. The foods that children learn to eat as they grow into adulthood will affect the meals they will provide for their offspring. Foods prepared by parents for their children will usually be considered good and appropriate by the children. Unless children are exposed to a diet with a great deal of variety, they may consider unfamiliar foods not only unusual, but strange, weird, or even bad tasting.

One way to help children appreciate and respect another's cultural heritage and to teach them about the important aspects of that person's background is to provide opportunities for first-hand experiences. The following provides some basic information about breakfasts in other countries and gives some suggestions as to how you can enrich and enhance your students' understanding and appreciation of various cultures by learning what people around the world eat for breakfast.

Breakfast around the World

As in the United States, people in every country eat a variety of items for breakfast. It is impossible to identify the "typical" meal of any locale. However, common items are usually associated with a region, area, or country. Therefore, the following generalizations should be presented as such. In the process of providing information to students, care should be taken to help them avoid stereotyping groups. Stress the similarities within the groups, but remember to note that all members of a group do not think, look, or behave alike. Within each group are a wide range of differences related to all aspects of their lives.

Europe. In **England,** the "traditional full breakfast" may be juice and cereal, followed by sausages, bacon, mushrooms, tomatoes, eggs, and fried bread with toast and tea, coffee, or milk. Eggs are eaten boiled, poached, scrambled, or fried. Different types of fish and fishcakes are also popular. There are many cereals from which to choose, including corn and wheat products with brand names like Weebabix and Rice Krispies. Marmalades are usually eaten on toast or muffins. In some parts of England, a fried black pudding is made from minced pork fat, hog blood, and other ingredients. Many Scottish people eat a porridge from oats served with hot milk.

Breakfast is the most important meal of the day for many families in **Norway.** A table is set with a variety of foods, including fresh, cured, or smoked fish, fishballs, salted herring, and mackerel. This spread is called a *koldtbord,* which means "cold table." Also included are different kinds of bread. Sometimes there are other meats, including reindeer and mutton salamis, as well as cheeses, eggs, and jam. Two types of bread are popular, a whole grain bread and a bread similar to crispbread called *knekklebrod.* The breakfast beverage may be fresh milk, buttermilk, coffee, or hot chocolate. Unlike the English, Norwegians drink very little tea.

A typical breakfast in **the Netherlands** will include a selection of breads—white, brown, black, and rye— as well as spiced or currant rolls, cold meats, cheeses, and eggs. There will be butter, marmalades and jams, and peanut butter for the breads. Thin slices of cheese and cold sausages and ham may also be served. A slice of bread and butter with cheese or jam called *boterham* may be served and is usually eaten with a knife and fork rather than with the fingers as sandwiches are in the United States. Cheeses are important products in the Netherlands. Dutch Edam, Gouda, Limburger, and Leiden are eaten by the Dutch, as well as imported to other parts of the world. The breakfast drink for adults is strong coffee, chocolate with cream, or perhaps tea without milk. Children will drink milk, buttermilk, or "drinking yogurt." Coffeetime occurs around eleven o'clock, when cakes and pastries are served.

The "continental breakfast" is most often served in **France.** This is a light meal of bread with butter and jam and a hot drink, usually "french roast" coffee. The bread may be a *baguette* or a *croissant* bought at the local bakery. The baguette, a long slender roll or loaf with a hard crust, is sliced or broken in chunks and served with butter and jam. The croissant, a sweet, flaky roll shaped like a crescent or half moon, is also eaten with butter and jam. Many western European countries imitate the French continental breakfast. However, each country's meal varies slightly to suit the tastes of the people.

A **Russian** breakfast is often a bowl of *kasha,* or thick porridge. There also may be a tray of cold meats—ham, salami, smoked fish—and different types of cheeses. Fried potatoes may be served as well as a green salad. Yogurt is popular for breakfast, too. Unlike the American breakfast, which is quite different from lunch or dinner, the Russian breakfast is usually very similar to the noon and evening meals. Tea is served as a drink, but is prepared quite differently from the typical English manner. A small bit of tea is poured into a glass with a metal holder designed to keep the drinker from burning his or her fingers. The remainder of the glass is filled with hot water, and sugar or jam is added for sweetening.

Africa/Middle East. In **Turkey,** cheese, olives, honey, jam, and bread are typical items on the breakfast table. In Istanbul, a palamut fish placed between two pieces of bread may be purchased for the morning meal. Strong coffee, dark tea, or *ayran* is served as a beverage. Ayran is a drink made of thin yogurt and is either salted or iced, depending on one's preference. Turkish coffee is brewed in a special manner quite different from American coffee. Coffee beans are finely ground and mixed with water and sugar. This mixture is heated in a pot until it boils to the brim. The boiling is repeated three times. One may drink coffee *sade,* or without sugar; *orta,* which is medium sweet; or very sweet, which is called *sekerli* or *tatli.* The coffee is so strong that only a small cup is served, usually accompanied by a glass of cold water.

Red beans are a staple item of most **Egyptian** breakfast. To prevent food poisoning, the beans must be prepared by boiling for six to eight hours or even overnight. Several items are eaten with the beans, including onions, parsley, and spices, or tomatoes and lentils. Some families create a breakfast dish by adding eggs to minced beans. Cheeses in Egypt are made from cow milk, sheep milk, and even buffalo milk. Bread is also important, but it is made without yeast or other ingredients to help it rise. This "unleavened" bread is round and usually very flat. The preferred breakfast beverage is sweet tea.

Nigeria is Africa's most populated nation and, like most Third World countries, many of its people are very poor. Disease and malnutrition are common and are a result of a diet of starchy foods with little protein. For breakfast, many Nigerians depend on a hot spicy soup and *gari,* a product of the cassava plant, for their nourishment. The soup is made with a few vegetables seasoned with green and red peppers. A fortunate family may have a few small pieces of fish, chicken, or other meat to add to the soup. Salt and spices are used to enhance the taste of the watery mixture.

Asia/Pacific Rim. **Indonesia's** staple food is rice, whether for breakfast or any other meal. The breakfast rice may be fried or boiled and eaten with a hot chili sauce. Coffee is made by pouring boiling water into a glass over coffee grounds and waiting for them to settle to the bottom. When the coffee is almost cold, lots of sugar is added, and the sweet mixture is ready to drink.

In the densely populated country of **China**, one would expect a variety of culinary customs, and such is the case. In this nation of more than a billion people, the menu varies from region to region and city to city. Some people eat steamed breads, either sweet or salty, often stuffed with a variety of meats or vegetables; rice porridge, much like the hot breakfast cereals found in the United States; and/or noodles served with vegetables, eggs, or meat. Baked cakes are typically served in the southern provinces of China. As life in China, particularly in the larger cities such as Shanghai and Beijing, becomes more like urban life in other parts of the world, a breakfast of milk and bread is becoming more popular, because it can be consumed rather hurriedly as one prepares to hasten off to work. Tea with cookies, cakes, or specially made steamed or fried breads is a typical breakfast in Canton and Hong Kong. Often one might receive an invitation to "drink tea" rather than to "have breakfast." This is much like an invitation to afternoon tea in England, where biscuits and sandwiches are served.

A typical breakfast in **Japan** almost always includes soup (usually made from bean flour and fish stock or from soy beans and vegetables), along with rice, grilled fish, pickles, and salad. Rice is eaten at all meals, and for breakfast it may be served with eggs and seaweed. As during other meals of the day, the Japanese eat their breakfast using chopsticks.

Breakfast in **Samoa** may be no more than a sweet potato smeared with coconut cream and wrapped in a banana leaf before it is baked in a hot oven. Coconut trees grow in abundance in Samoa, so there is plenty of fresh coconut for all meals. The beverage of choice is cocoa and is made by placing cocoa beans into a cup and pouring boiling water over them. Sugar is added to taste.

Breakfast in **Australia** and **New Zealand** is similar to that eaten in Great Britain and the United States. There may be toast, cereals, fruits, and coffee. Vegemite, a product made from a yeast extract, is used as a spread for toast. Melons, pawpaws, and kiwi fruit are popular. Some people cook a dish called *offal*, made from the kidneys, livers, and brains of calves, pigs, and lambs. Sausage and bacon are often served, and on special occasions lamb chops may be included on the breakfast menu. Australia and New Zealand are two of the world's leading producers of mutton and wool.

South America. As in many European countries, people in **Argentina** eat a "continental breakfast" of a roll or croissant with butter and jam, served with coffee, milk, or tea. The tea, served with cream and sugar, is made from dried leaves of the yerba mate tree and is called "mate" tea.

While most people of South America are served a continental breakfast, the meal in **Venezuela** will usually be more substantial. It may include juice, eggs, and bread, served with coffee or chocolate. On special days the family may eat *hallacas,* which is created by mixing cornmeal with meat, raisins, and other fruits and vegetables.

Instructional Activities

Activity 12.1: Breakfasts around the World Data Chart

Direct students to construct a chart similar to "Breakfasts around the World" chart shown here. They can use the information given in this unit, plus other sources, to compare what people in various parts of the world eat for breakfast. After the chart is complete, different groups can prepare reports relating to the following topics:

BREAKFASTS AROUND THE WORLD

Country	Protein	Grain/Bread	Other	Beverage
United States	milk, eggs	toast, cereal	fruit	coffee, tea
Turkey	fish	_____	ayran	_____
Nigeria	_____	_____	_____	_____
_____	_____	croissant	_____	_____

JOHN'S [STUDENT'S NAME] FAVORITE BREAKFAST

Location: _____

Time: _____   Date: _____

Menu: _____

Drink: _____

Attire for the Occasion: _____

People around the world eat different things for breakfast. But do they all consume items classified as protein? Grain? Fats? Liquids? Explain.

Is there a "typical" breakfast eaten by members of the class? If so, how does it compare to or differ from meals eaten in other countries?

Research the breads eaten in various cultures around the world. How are they alike? How are they different?

Activity 12.2: "My Favorite Breakfast"

Have students create a menu for their favorite breakfast. If money was of no concern and they could have anything they desired, which items would they choose for breakfast? The menus should be prepared as if for a formal meal during an elegant occasion.

Activity 12.3: Consumer Survey

If breakfast is served in the school cafeteria, assign several students to tally the items students choose to place on their trays. Students may also tally what items are not eaten and are discarded after the meal. This project can be done for one or two days or may be conducted for a week or more. After the data are collected, the class can construct graphs to illustrate items most often selected and eaten, as well as those most likely to be discarded. Discussion could follow about why certain items are so unpopular.

Activity 12.4: What Did You Eat for Breakfast Today?

Without prior notice, survey students to create a profile of what they ate for breakfast. Generally, a more accurate survey will result if an anonymous checklist sheet is used for each child. This will prevent embarrassment for the child who has had little or no breakfast that day and perhaps will encourage more honest responses. Construct a graph showing the different items and how frequently they were eaten by the students for breakfast that day.

Activity 12.5: Sample an Unusual Breakfast Item

Many children have had limited exposure to foods outside their own cultural experience. Have a "Sample the Food Day" where various items are served to give students new experiences. Use items that are simple to prepare and which can be eaten without much fuss. For example, a bagel with cream cheese may be a new experience for many children, or rice (served without sugar as in many countries) may be a food that some have not eaten for breakfast. Parents of students in your class who represent ethnic groups different from the majority of their classmates may be willing to share their heritage. Before attempting this activity, determine whether there is a school policy about serving food in your classroom.

Activity 12.6: What Grandpa Ate for Breakfast

Do children today eat the same types of breakfasts their grandparents ate when they were children? To find out, students can interview their grandparents or other "senior" adults. A sample "Breakfast Survey" is provided in this section and should be modified to meet the needs of your particular class. For example, variations should be made to include items typically eaten by many of the families of the school community. When the interviews are complete, they can be used in several ways:

1. Students could give oral reports about the differences and similarities they discovered. Comments might include the changes that have occurred over the years in the eating habits of children and young people and why they think this has happened.

Students should share those findings they consider to be interesting and unique.

2. A data chart could be completed to tally the breakfast items eaten by the adults interviewed. From the data chart, graphs could be constructed to compare the different types of food eaten.

3. After a class survey of what your students eat for breakfast, construct graphs comparing the eating habits of the older generation with their own.

Suggested Reading

Watson, T., & Watson, J. (1982). *What the world eats: Breakfast.* Chicago: Childrens Press. Chicago Press has two other books in this series: *What the world eats: Midday meal* and *What the world eats: Evening meal.*

August's Potpourri of Teaching Ideas

The purpose of each month's Potpourri of Teaching Ideas is to provide additional resources from which to build your curriculum. Most, but not all, of the activities listed each month relate directly to that month. It is not intended that you use them all, but rather that you choose those which are appropriate for your program. Although the topics are written for a particular month, many of them would be appropriate for use throughout the year. How you use these activities will depend on your curricular goals. You may wish to use some of the activities as they are presented, and you may need to modify some to meet your needs. Perhaps some of them will give you ideas for entirely different potpourris.

The World at Play

With the beginning of the school year nearing (or, in many communities, already begun), August is a good month to look at games that people play around the world. From ancient times to the present, children and young people have created and played all types of games. In early times, games were played for a variety of reasons, using a number of styles and techniques. Some games required little physical activity but were entertaining and mentally challenging. Other games required physical strength, speed, and agility and were highly competitive. The Greek Olympics contests fall in the latter category. This month's potpourri is composed of several games from various parts of the world. Your students may wish to experiment with these games as a part of a class project. You and the physical education instructor may collaborate, providing opportunities for team teaching.

Chase the Dragon: A Game from China (Benarde, 1970). Dragons are very important in Chinese folklore. During the Chinese New Year celebration, the dragon historically goes through the streets bringing good luck to the people. This game is based on that ancient tradition, whereby people form a long line, weaving up and down the village streets, representing the dragon.

To play this game, a group of players line up one behind the other. The person in the lead position is considered to be the head of the dragon; the person at the end, the tail. Players place their hands on the shoulders of the person in front of them. The purpose of the game is for the head to run in such a way as to catch the tail. As the line moves, the dragon twists and turns, making it very difficult for the dragon's head to catch its tail. Chase the Dragon can be played easily on the school grounds or playing field with either a small class or the entire school.

Go Fly a Kite. Kite flying can be an art, a tournament, or just a way to spend the day. The Chinese are given credit for constructing and flying the first kite, perhaps more than three thousand years ago. The ancient Chinese believed that kites could frighten away evil spirits. Today, the kite is regarded as a good-luck symbol in China.

A small Japanese village near Tokyo flies the largest kite in the world each year. It weighs nearly a ton, has two hundred lines from the face to the flying line, and requires fifty or more people to launch it.

The first recorded use of kites to obtain scientific date (Yolen, 1968) was during the eighteenth century when two Scottish scientists fastened thermometers to kites to record the temperature of air at high altitudes.

Make and Fly Your Own Kite (Dolan, E., Jr., 1977). Kites can be very simple or quite complicated to make, depending on the number of parts. The basic parts of the kite are:

Cover: the material that shapes the kite and the surface that catches the wind
Face: the decorated part or side of the cover
Framing sticks: used to support and give the cover shape
Spine: the upright stick in the center of the kite
Spars: the sticks that support the two sides of the face
Flying line: the string or other lines used for flying the kite
Bridle: the line or cord attached from the face that holds the kite at an angle to fly

BREAKFAST SURVEY

Use this survey to interview your grandparents or other adults of a similar age. As you talk to the person, record his or her responses by circling the answer and by making notes in the space provided.

1. When you were a child, what size breakfast did you eat? (large, medium, small, none)

2. When did you eat breakfast?
   - _____ As soon as you got up
   - _____ After your chores were done
   - _____ Later in the morning

3. What did you usually eat for breakfast?

   Eggs?   Yes/No   Type: fried, scrambled, boiled, poached
                                  Other _____

   Meat?   Yes/No   Type: ham, sausage, bacon, fish, beef
                                  Other _____

   Cereal?   Yes/No   Hot: oatmeal, rice, Cream of Wheat
                                  Cold: bran flakes, corn flakes
                                  Other _____

   Juice?   Yes/No   Type: orange, grapefruit, grape, apple
                                  Other _____

   Bread?   Yes/No   Type: toast, biscuits, bagels, muffins
                                  Other _____

   Sweet bread?   Yes/No   Type: pancakes, waffles, rolls, doughnuts
                                  Other _____

   Sweetening?   Yes/No   Type: jam, jelly, honey, syrup
                                  Other _____

   Drink?   Yes/No   Type: milk, hot chocolate, cola, tea, coffee
                                  Other _____

   Other foods? _____

4. What were "special" breakfasts like? How were they different from the ordinary?

   _____

5. How is what you ate for breakfast as a child different from what I usually eat now? (Ask this of the person who prepares your meals.) _____

   _____

6. How is what you eat today for breakfast different from what you ate as a child?

   _____

Other Activities. Kites are used to celebrate many holidays in China, Japan, and other Asian countries. Interested students can research these holidays and make a book in the shape of a kite, with each page explaining a different holiday.

After students have practiced making and flying several kites, they can travel to a local children's home, day-care center, or hospital and help those children make and fly kites or make small kites to hang as decorations on walls or ceilings. Before working with the children on making kites, read aloud *The Emperor and the Kite* by Jane Yolen (1967) or a similar book.

Otedama: A Game from Japan (Robinson, 1983). This game, played in Japan, is similar to the game of jacks

played by schoolchildren across the United States. To play you will need five small beanbags and some practice. (See the boxed instructions for making beanbags.)

To play, scatter all of the bags around a small playing area. The first player chooses one of these and tosses it into the air. The object of the game is to pick up all of the other bags, one at a time with the same hand, catching the bag tossed into the air before it hits the ground. The game continues, with each round requiring the player to pick up one more bag on the succeeding round than on the previous one. So, for round two, the player must pick up two bags from the ground before catching the bag that was thrown in the air. On the last round, all five of the bags are placed in the palm of the player, who tosses them into the air and attempts to catch as many as possible on the back of the hand. If a player is unable to catch all five on the back of his hand, he tosses the remaining bags into the air and tries to catch as many as possible. The first player to complete all five rounds is the winner.

A similar game is played in Korea, but instead of using beanbags, children there use five small flat stones. Sitting on the ground, the player tosses one stone into the air. The object is to catch it on the back of the hand. During the second round, two stones are tossed into the air and caught on the back of the hand. With each round, one more stone is thrown into the air.

Another similar game is a Vietnamese version of "pick-up-sticks." The object of this game is similar to American jacks and to the two games already described. The objective is to bounce a ball, pick up a stick, and then catch the ball in the same hand.

Place ten chopsticks or popsicle sticks in a straight line. Throw a ball into the air, pick up one stick, and catch the ball after it bounces once. On the next round, throw the ball into the air and, keeping the first stick in your hand, pick up another stick and catch the ball after one bounce. Continue until one player has all ten sticks in one hand.

One Foot High Kick: An Inuit Game (Gutelle, 1993). During the spring, boys and girls in elementary and high schools from all over Alaska compete in the

Native Youth Olympics held in Anchorage. Because the events in these Olympics are thought to have been created thousands of years ago by the Inuit, the purpose of this competition is to help people remember the Inuit culture.

To play this game, make a ball by rolling a pair of socks into a sphere. Attach the sock ball to a long piece of string using a safety pin. Hang the ball from a tree branch or doorway so that it is twenty inches above the ground. Stand facing the ball. Jump in the air and kick the ball with one foot and then land on the same foot with which you kicked the ball. You must do this without touching the ground with any other part of your body except your foot. No score or point is allowed if you fall or touch the ground with your other foot or with your hands or body. Each participant is given three chances to kick the sock ball. Then the ball is raised four inches higher. The players are again given three chances to kick the ball. Any player who misses all three times is out. After each round of competition, the ball is raised four inches higher. The player who kicks the ball at the highest height is the winner. In case of a tie, the player with the fewest total misses is the winner.

For two other Inuit events, see Gutelle (1993).

Marbles: A Game from Central America (Benarde, 1970). This game requires two players, each with five marbles or stones. The object of the game is to end up with all of the marbles. To play, determine who will go first by drawing a straight line on the ground and then standing back about six feet. Each player throws a marble or stone toward the line. The player whose marble lands closest to the line goes first.

The winner of the toss stands at attention with heels together and toes spread apart to form a "goal." The other player kneels about five feet away and tries to toss a marble so that it lands between the opponent's toes and heels. The player has three chances to position the marble in the goal. If he is unable to place the marble appropriately, he loses a marble to the other player.

The second player, who is standing, drops one of her marbles to try to hit the opponent's marble. The marble should be dropped from waist height while still standing at attention. If the marble hits the opponent's marble, she wins the marble; if she misses, she must give her own marble to the opponent.

The players then change places and the contest begins again. The game ends when one of the players has all of the marbles.

Marbles: U.S. Style (Sturner & Seltzer, 1973). There are many different games played with marbles. Marbles are small, round glass spheres manufactured in a variety of sizes and colors. Some groups used special names for various types of marbles. The oversized ones were called kabolas. A marble that was of one color but clear enough to see through was called a puree. A pure white puree would be called a milky. Smaller marbles were called peewees or mibbies.

Game One: Marble Toss. Players line up in a straight line, approximately eight feet from a wall or set of stairs. The first player throws a marble underhanded toward the wall or bottom stair. Each player then takes a turn throwing a marble. The game continues with each player taking another turn.

The object of the game is to either hit a marble belonging to another player or to "span" it. Spanning a marble means that one player's marble is within a flat palm's distance from a marble thrown earlier. If one player's marble hits an opponent's marble or spans it, that player gets to keep the marble. The winner is the player who takes the most marbles.

Game Two: Odds or Evens. Player one hides marbles in her closed fist. Player two tries to guess whether the other player is holding an even or odd number of marbles. If the player guesses correctly, she gets to keep the marbles that were hidden. If she guess incorrectly, she must forfeit that number of marbles to the other player. Players alternate turns.

Game Three: True Marbles. Players draw a circle on the ground, approximately twelve to fifteen inches in diameter. Each player places five or six marbles within the circle. Each player takes turn shooting his marble by placing the marble between thumb and forefinger and "shooting" it with a forward motion of the thumb. The object is to use this marble to knock as many of the other players' marbles out of the circle as possible. The player keeps any marbles that were knocked out. The player continues with a turn until he fails to knock a marble from the circle. When all the marbles are out of the circle, the game begins again.

Try This. The game of marbles may serve as a stimulus for an oral history project. Students can interview classmates to see marble games they play and the rules they follow. Those interested can interview older members of their families to record not only the games of marbles but other games played when they were young.

Authors' Note: The rules for playing marbles were usually similar in the games played by the authors when they were young. However, for one author, the social mores of his school were very clear concerning an aspect of this game. In his experience, it was absolutely forbidden to play for keeps—that is, for the winner of the game to keep the marbles that his opponents lost. At the conclusion of each game, it was necessary to return all the marbles to their original owners. Otherwise, the teacher or principal was brought into the act, and the winner lost all his marbles and was no longer allowed to play. Occasionally, a lucky player could get away with keeping his winnings if the loser was not too fond of his property.

Suggested Readings

Benarde, A. (1970). *Games from many lands*. New York: Lion Books.

Dolan, E., Jr. (1977). *The complete beginner's guide to making and flying kites*. Garden City, NY: Doubleday.

Eisen, G. (1988). *Children and play in the Holocaust*. Amherst: University of Massachusetts Press.

Gryski, C. (1983). *Cat's cradle, owl's eyes: A book of string games*. New York: William Morrow.

Gutelle, A. (1993, April). Eskimo games. *Sports Illustrated for Kids*, pp. 52–54.

Helfman, H., & Helfman, E. (1965). *Strings on your fingers: How to make string figures*. New York: William Morrow.

Jayne, C. (1962). *String figures and how to make them*. New York: Dover Publications.

Lyttle, R. B. (1982). *The games they played: Sports in history*. New York: Atheneum.

Marks, B., & Marks, R. (1980). *Kites for kids*. New York: Lothrop, Lee & Shepard.

Robinson, I. (1983). *Activities for anyone, anytime, anywhere: A children's museum activity book*. Boston: Little, Brown.

Sturner, F., & Seltzer, A. (1973). *What did you do when you were a kid?* New York: St. Martin's Press.

Yerian, C., & Yerian, M. (Eds.). (1974). *Fun time: Games for one, two, or more*. Chicago: Childrens Press.

Yolen, J. (1967). *The emperor and the kite*. New York: World Publishing.

Yolen, J. (1968). *World on a string: The story of kites*. New York: World Publishing.

Appendix

Sunday	Monday	Tuesday	Wednesday	Thursday	Friday	Saturday

Selected Bibliography of Multicultural Folk Literature from around the World*

SONG OF THE CHIRIMIA
A Guatemalan Folktale

LA MÚSICA DE LA CHIRIMIA
Folklore Guatemalteco

Retold and illustrated by /
Narrada e ilustrada por
JANE ANNE VOLKMER

---

*This bibliography was first published by the authors in *Storytelling World* (Vol. III, No. 2) as "The World: Our Source and Our Audience: A Bibliography of Multicultural Folk Literature."

General Collections

Brooke, L. L. *The golden goose book: A fairy tale picture book.* Illus. by the author. New York: Clarion Books, 1992.

Clarkson, A., & Cross, G. (Comp.). *World folktales.* New York: Charles Scribner's Sons, 1980.

Cole, J. (Comp.). *Best-loved folktales of the world.* Illus. by J. K. Schwartz. Garden City, NY: Doubleday, 1982.

Crouch, M. *The whole world storybook.* Illus. by W. Stobbs. New York: Oxford University Press, 1983.

dePaola, T. *Tomie dePaola's favorite nursery tales.* New York: G. P. Putnam's Sons, 1986.

Edens, C. (Comp.). *The three princesses: Cinderella, Sleeping Beauty, and Snow White.* New York: Bantam Books, 1991.

Ehrlich, A. (Adapt.). *Random House book of fairy tales.* Illus. by D. Goode. New York: Random House, 1985.

Foreman, M. *Michael Foreman's world of fairy tales.* New York: Arcade Publishing, 1991.

Hamilton, V. *In the beginning.* Illus. by B. Moser. Orlando, FL: Harcourt Brace Jovanovich, 1988.

Hamilton, V. *The dark way: Stories from the spirit world.* Illus. by L. Davis. Orlando, FL: Harcourt Brace Jovanovich, 1990.

Hamilton, V. *The All Jahdu storybook.* Illus. by B. Moser. Orlando, FL: Harcourt Brace Jovanovich, 1991.

Kherdian, D. *Feathers and tales: Animal fables.* Illus. by N. Hogrogian. New York: Philomel Books, 1992.

Lynch, P. J. (Illus.). *East o' the sun and west o' the moon.* Cambridge, MA: Candlewick Press, 1992.

MacDonald, M. R. *Peace tales: World folktales to talk about.* Hambden, CT: Linnet Books, 1992.

Medlicott, M. (Select.). *Tales for telling from around the world.* Illus. by S. Williams. New York: Kingfisher Books, 1992.

Neil, P. *Fairy tales of eastern Europe.* Illus. by L. Wilkes. New York: Clarion Books, 1991.

Opie, I., & Opie, P. *The classic fairy tales.* New York: Oxford University Press, 1974.

Pienkowski, J. *Fairy tale library.* Illus. by the author. New York: Alfred A. Knopf, 1992.

Provensen, A., & Provensen, M. (Comps.). *The Provensen book of fairy tales.* New York: Random House, 1971.

Rackham, A. (Illus.). *Fairy tales from many lands.* New York: Viking, 1974.

Rosen, M. *How the animals got their colors: Animal myths from around the world.* Illus. by J. Clementson. Orlando, FL: Harcourt Brace Jovanovich, 1992.

Rosen, M. (Ed.). *South and north, east and west: The OxFam book of children's stories.* Cambridge, MA: Candlewick Press, 1992.

Schwartz, A. *Ghosts!: Ghostly tales from folklore.* Illus. by V. Chess. New York: HarperCollins, 1991.

Shannon, G. *More stories to solve: Fifteen folktales from around the world.* Illus. by P. Sis. New York: Greenwillow Books, 1991.

Windham, S. *Read me a story: A child's book of favorite tales.* New York: Scholastic, 1991.

African

Aardema, V. *Behind the back of the mountain: Black folktales from southern Africa.* New York: Dial, 1973.

Aardema, V. *Why mosquitoes buzz in people's ears.* New York: Dial, 1975.

Aardema, V. *Who's in rabbit's house? A Masai tale.* New York: Dial, 1977.

Aardema, V. *Half-a-ball-of Kenki.* New York: Warne, Frederick, 1979.

Aardema, V. *Bringing the rain to Kapiti plain: A Nandle tale.* New York: Dial, 1981.

Aardema, V. *Rabbit makes a monkey of lion: A Swahili tale.* Illus. by J. Pinkney. New York: Dial, 1989.

Aardema, V. *Traveling to Tondo: A tale of the Nkundo of Zaire.* New York: Aflred A. Knopf, 1991.

Aardema, V. *Anansi finds a fool: An Ashanti tale.* New York: Dial, 1992.

Appia, P. *Anansi the spider: Tales from an Ashanti village.* New York: Pantheon Books, 1966.

Berry, J. *Spiderman Anancy.* New York: Henry Holt, 1988.

Berger, T. *Black fairy tales.* Illus. by D. O. White. New York: Atheneum, 1975.

Brown, M. *Shadow.* New York: Charles Scribner's Sons, 1982.

Bryan, A. *Lion and ostrich chicks and other African folktales.* Illus. by the author. New York: Atheneum, 1986.

Bryan, A. *Beat the story-drum, pum-pum.* Illus. by the author. New York: Atheneum, 1980.

Bryan, A. *The ox of wonderful horns and other African folk tales.* New York: Atheneum, 1971.

Chocolate, D. *Spider and the sky god: Akan (Ghana) legend.* Mahwah, NJ: Troll Associates, 1992.

Climo, S. *The Egyptian Cinderella.* Illus. by R. Heller. New York: Harper Trophy, 1989.

Courlander, H. *The crest and the hide and other African stories of heroes, chiefs, bards, hunters, sorcerers and common people.* New York: Coward, 1982.

Courlander, H., & Leslau, W. *The fire on the mountain and other Ethiopian stories.* Illus. by R. W. Kane. New York: Henry Holt, 1950.

Dayrell, E. *Why the sun and moon live in the sky: An African folktale.* Boston: Houghton Mifflin, 1968.

Dee, R. *Tower to heaven.* Illus. by J. Bent. New York: Henry Holt, 1991.

De Sauza, J. *Brother Anansi and the cattle ranch.* Illus. by S. von Mason. San Francisco: Children's Book Press, 1989.

Diop, B. *Mother crocodile/Mamancaiman.* Illus. by J. Steptoe. New York: Delacorte Press, 1981.

Diop, B. *Mother crocodile: An Uncle Amadou tale from Senegal.* New York: Delacorte Press, 1982.

Domanska, J. *The tortoise and the tree.* New York: Greenwillow Books, 1978.

Fairman, T. *Bury my bones but keep my words: African tales for retelling.* New York: Henry Holt, 1993.

Gerson, M. J. *Why the sky is far away: A Nigerian folktale.* Illus. by C. Golembe. Boston: Joy Street Books, 1992.

Gleeson, B. *Koi and the kola nuts.* Illus. by R. Ruffins. Saxonville, MA: Rabbit, 1992.

Grifalconi, A. *The village of round and square houses.* Boston: Little, Brown, 1986.

Harris, G. *Gods and pharaohs from Egyptian mythology.* Illus. by D. O'Connor & J. Sibbick. New York: Peter Bedrick Books, 1992.

Kimmel, E. A. *Anansi goes fishing.* Illus. by J. Stevens. New York: Holiday House: 1992.

Knutson, B. *Why the crab has no head.* Illus. by the author. Minneapolis: Carolrhoda Books, 1987.

Knutson, B. *How the guinea fowl got her spots.* Illus. by the author. Minneapolis: Carolrhoda Books, 1990.

McDermott, G. *Anansi the spider.* Orlando, FL: Holt, Rinehart and Winston, 1972.

McDermott, G. *Zomo the rabbit: A trickster tale from west Africa.* Illus. by the author. Orlando, FL: Harcourt Brace Jovanovich, 1992.

Martin, F. *The honey hunters: A traditional African tale.* Illus. by the author. Cambridge, MA: Candlewick Press, 1992.

Mike, J. *Gift of the Nile: An ancient Egyptian legend.* Mahwah, NJ: Troll Associates, 1992.

Mollel, T. *The orphan boy.* Illus. by P. Morin. New York: Clarion Books, 1991.

Mollel, T. *A promise to the sun.* Boston: Little, Brown, 1992.

Mollel, T. *Princess who lost her hair: An Akamba (Africa) legend.* Mahwah, NJ: Troll Associates, 1992.

Prather, R. *The ostrich girl.* New York: Charles Scribner's Sons, 1978.

Serwadda, W. *Songs and stories from Uganda.* Trans. & ed. by H. Pantaleoni. New York: Thomas Y. Crowell, 1974.

Steptoe, J. *Mufaro's beautiful daughters: An African tale.* New York: Lothrop, Lee & Shepard Books, 1987.

Tadjo, V. (Retell.). *Lord of the dance: An African retelling.* Philadelphia: J. B. Lippincott, 1989.

Troughton, J. *How stories came into the world: A folk tale from west Africa.* Illus. by the author. New York: Peter Bedrick Books, 1990.

Asian

Chinese

Bang, M. *Tye May and the magic brush.* New York: Greenwillow Books, 1981.

Bang, M. *The paper crane.* New York: Greenwillow Books, 1985.

Demi. *The magic boat.* New York: Henry Holt, 1990.

Demi. *The artist and the architect.* New York: Henry Holt, 1991.

Demi. *A Chinese zoo: Fables and proverbs.* Illus. by the author. Orlando, FL: Harcourt Brace Jovanovich, 1992.

Hearne, L. *The voice of the great bell.* Adapt. by M. Hodges; illus. by E. Young. Boston: Little, Brown, 1989.

Liyi, H. (Trans.). *The spring of butterflies and other folktales of China's minority peoples.* Ed. by N. Philip; illus. by P. Aiqing & L. Zhoa. New York: Lothrop, Lee & Shepard Books, 1986.

Lattimore, D. N. *The dragon's robe.* Illus. by the author. New York: Harper & Row, 1990.

Leaf, M. *Eyes of the dragon.* Illus. by E. Young. New York: Lothrop, Lee & Shepard Books, 1987.

Louie, A. *Yeh-Shen: A Cinderella story from China.* Illus. by E. Young. New York: Philomel Books, 1982.

Mahy, M. *The seven Chinese brothers.* Illus. by J. & M. Tseng. New York: Scholastic, 1990.

McCunn, R. L. *Pie-Biter.* Illus. by Y. Tang. San Francisco: Design Enterprises of San Francisco, 1983.

Morris, W. *The magic leaf.* Illus. by J.-H. Chen. New York: Atheneum, 1987.

Mosel, A. (Ed.). *Tikki tikki tembo.* Illus. by B. Lent. New York: Henry Holt, 1968.

Otsuka, Y. *Suho and the white horse: A legend of Mongolia.* Illus. by S. Akaba. New York: Viking, 1982.

Rappaport, D. *The journey of Meng.* Illus. by Y. Ming-Yi. New York: Dial, 1991.

Sadler, C. E. (Retell.). *Heaven's reward.* Illus. by C. M. Yun. New York: Atheneum, 1985.

Sadler, C. E. *Treasure mountain: Folktales from southern China.* New York Atheneum, 1982.

Và Leong. *A letter to the king.* Illus. by the author; trans. by J. Anderson. New York: HarperCollins, 1991.

Wang, R. C. *The fourth question: A Chinese tale.* Illus. by J.-H. Chen. New York: Holiday House: 1991.

Yen, C. *Why rat comes first: A story of the Chinese zodiac.* Illus. by H. C. Yoshida. San Francisco: Children's Book Press, 1991.

Yep, L. *The rainbow people.* Illus. by D. Wiesner. New York: Harper & Row, 1989.

Yep, L. *Tongues of jade.* Illus. by D. Wiesner. New York: HarperCollins, 1991.

Young, E. (trans.). *Lon po po: A Red Riding Hood story from China.* Illus. by the author. New York: Philomel Books, 1989.

Indian and Pakistani

Bang, B. *The demons of Rajpur: Five tales from Bengal.* Illus. by M. G. Bang. New York: Greenwillow Books, 1980.

Beach, M. C. *The adventures of Rama* Washington, DC: Smithsonian Institution, 1983.

Brown, M. *Once a mouse.* Illus. by the author. New York: Charles Scribner's Sons, 1961.

Bryan, A. *Sh-ko and his eight wicked brothers.* Illus. by F. Yoshimura. New York: Atheneum, 1988.

Gray, J. E. B. *India's tales and legends.* Illus. by J. Kiddell-Monroe. New York: Walck, 1961.

Jacobs, J. (Ed.). *Indian fairy tales.* Illus. by J. D. Batten. New York: G. P. Putnam's Sons, 1969.

Newton, P. *The stonecutter: An Indian folktale.* Illus. by the author. New York: G. P. Putnam's Sons, 1990.

Reed, G. *The talkative beasts: Myths, fables, and poems of India.* New York: Lothrop, Lee & Shepard Books, 1969.

Japanese

Compton, P. A. *The terrible eek: A Japanese tale.* Illus. by S. Hamanaka. New York: Simon & Schuster, 1991.

Haugaard, E., & Haugaard, M. *The story of Yuriwaka: A Japanese odyssey.* Illus. by B. Saflund. New York: Roberts, Rinehart 1991.

Hedlund, I. *Mighty mountain and the three strong women.* Trans. by J. Elkin. Volcano, CA: Volcano Press, 1990.

Hughes, M. *Little fingerling: A Japanese folktale.* Illus. by B. Clark. Nashville: Ideals Publishing, 1992.

Ikeda, D. *The snow country prince.* Illus. by B. Wildsmith. New York: Alfred A. Knopf, 1991.

Ishii, M. *The tongue-cut sparrow.* Illus. by S. Akaba. New York: Lodestar/E. P. Dutton, 1987.

Kimmel, E. A. *The greatest of all: A Japanese folktale.* Illus. by G. Carmi. New York: Holiday House, 1991.

Mosel, A. (Adapt.). *The funny little woman.* Illus. by B. Lent. New York: E. P. Dutton, 1972.

Newton, P. M. *The five sparrows.* New York: Atheneum, 1982.

Paterson, K. *The tale of the Mandarin ducks.* Illus. by L. & D. Dillon. New York: Lodestar, 1990.

Quayle, E. *The shining princess and other Japanese legends.* Boston: Arcade Publishing, 1989.

San Souci, R. D. *The Samurai's daughter: A Japanese legend.* Illus. by S. T. Johnson. New York: Dial, 1992.

Snyder, D. *The boy of the three-year nap.* Illus. by A. Say. Boston: Houghton Mifflin, 1988.

Stamm, C. *Three strong women: A tall tale from Japan.* Illus. by J. Tseng & M. Tseng. New York: Viking, 1990.

Tejima. *Ho-limlim: A rabbit tale from Japan.* New York: Philomel Books, 1990.

Uchida, Y. *The two foolish cats.* Illus. by M. Zemach. New York: Margaret K. McElderry Books, 1987.

Yagawa, S. *The crane wife.* Trans. by K. Paterson; Illus. by S. Akaba. New York: William Morrow, 1981.

Korean

Ginsburg, M. *The Chinese mirror: A Korean folktale.* Illus. by M. Zemach. Orlando, FL: Harcourt Brace Jovanovich, 1988.

Southeast Asian

Lee, J. M. *Toad is the uncle of heaven: A Vietnamese folk tale.* Orlando, FL: Holt, Rinehart and Winston, 1985.

Robertson, D. L. (Adapt.). *Fairy tales from Viet Nam.* Illus. by W. T. Mars. New York: Dodd, Mead, 1968.

Vuong, L. D. *The brocade slipper and other Vietnamese tales.* Reading, MA: Addison-Wesley, 1982.

Young, E. *The terrible nung gwama.* Cleveland: Collins Publishers, 1978.

Xiong, B. *Nine-in-one, grr! grr!: A folktale from the Hmong people of Laos.* Illus. by N. Hom. Chicago: Childrens Press, 1990.

Australian/New Zealand

Green, M. *The echidna and the shade tree.* Illus. by P. Lofts. San Diego: Mad Hatter Books, 1984.

Kanawa, K. T. *Land of the long white cloud: Maori myths, tales, and legends.* Illus. by M. Foreman. New York: Arcade Publishing, 1990.

Lofts, P. (Retell. and Illus.). *How the birds got their colours.* Sydney, Australia: Ashton Scholastic, 1983.

Lofts, P. (Comp.). *Warnayarra—The rainbow snake.* Sydney, Australia: Ashton Scholastic, 1987.

Lofts, P. (Comp.). *The kangaroo and the porpoise.* Sydney, Australia: Ashton Scholastic, 1987.

Lofts, P. (Comp.), *How the kangaroos got their tails.* Sydney, Australia: Ashton Scholastic, 1987.

Mowaljarlai, D. *When the snake bites the sun.* Illus. by P. Lofts. Sydney, Australia: Ashton Scholastic, 1984.

Parker, K. L. *Australian legendary tales.* Illus. by E. Durack. New York: Viking, 1966.

European

Czechoslovakian

Haviland, V. (Adapt.). *Favorite fairy tales told in Czechoslovakia.* Illus. by T. S. Hyman. Boston: Little, Brown, 1966.

English, Scottish, and Welsh

Cooper, S. *The selkie girl.* Illus. by W. Hutton. New York: Margaret K. McElderry Books, 1986.

Cooper, S. *Tam lin.* Illus. by W. Hutton. New York: Margaret K. McElderry Books, 1991.

Crossley-Holland, K. *British folk tales: New version.* New York: Orchard/Watts, 1987.

Evslin, B. (Retell.). *Drabne of Dole.* New York: Chelsea House, 1990.

Forest, H. *The woman who flummoxed the faries.* Illus. by S. Gaber. Orlando, FL: Harcourt Brace Jovanovich, 1990.

Garner, A. *Alan Garner's book of British fairy tales.* Illus. by D. Collard. Collins/Delacorte, 1985.

Greaves, M. (Retell.). *Tattercoats.* Illus. by M. Chamberlain. New York: Clarkson N. Potter, 1990.

Gross, G. *Knights of the round table.* Illus. by N. Green. New York: Random House, 1991.

Heyer, C. *Excalibur.* Illus. by the author. Nashville: Ideals Publishing, New York: 1991.

Hodges, M. *The kitchen knight: A tale of King Arthur.* Illus. by T. S. Hyman. New York: Holiday House, 1990.

Jacobs, J. (Ed.). *English fairy tales.* Illus. by J. D. Batten. New York: G. P. Putnam's Sons, 1991.

Kerven, R. *The woman who went to fairyland: A Welsh folk tale.* Illus. by H. de Lacey. New York: Peter Bedrick Books, 1992.

Kimmel, E. A. *The old woman and her pig.* Illus. by G. Carmi. New York: Holiday House, 1992.

Marshall, J. *Goldilocks and the three bears.* Illus. by the author. New York: Dial, 1988.

Neodhas, S. N. *Always room for one more.* Illus. by N. Hogrogian. Orlando, FL: Holt, Rinehart and Winston, 1965.

Robertson, J. *Sea witches.* Illus. by L. Gal. New York: Dial, 1991.

Watson, R. J. *Tom thumb.* Illus. by the author. Orlando, FL: Harcourt Brace Jovanovich, 1989.

Wilson, B. K. *Scottish folk tales and legends.* Illus. by J. Kiddell-Monroe. New York: Walck, 1954.

Yolen, J. *Tam lin.* Illus. by C. Mikolaycak. Orlando, FL: Harcourt Brace Jovanovich, 1990.

Zemach, H. *Duffy and the devil: A Cornish tale retold.* Illus. by M. Zemach. New York: Farrar, Straus & Giroux, 1973.

French

Cauley, L. B. *Puss in boots.* Illus. by the author. Orlando, FL: Harcourt Brace Jovanovich.

deChristopher, M. *Greencoat and the swanboy.* Illus. by the author. New York: Philomel Books, 1991.

dePaola, T. *The clown of god.* Illus. by the author. Orlando, FL: Harcourt Brace Jovanovich, 1978.

Gerstein, M. *Beauty and the beast.* Illus. by the author. New York: E. P. Dutton, 1990.

Haley, G. E. *Puss in boots.* Illus. by the author. New York: E. P. Dutton, 1991.

Meyers, O. *The enchanted umbrella.* Illus. by M. Zemach. Orlando, FL: Harcourt Brace Jovanovich, 1988.

Perrault, C. *Cinderella: Or the little glass slipper.* Illus. by M. Brown. New York: Charles Scribner's Sons, 1954.

Perrault, C. *Puss in boots.* Illus. by F. Marcellino. New York: Farrar/di Capua, 1990.

Picard, B. L. *French legends, tales and fairy stories.* Illus. by J. Kiddell-Monroe. New York: Walck, 1955.

Pushkin, A. *The golden cockerel and other fairy tales.* Illus. by B. Zvorykin. Garden City, NY: Doubleday, 1990.

Willard, N. *Beauty and the beast.* Illus. by B. Moser. Orlando, FL: Harcourt Brace Jovanovich, 1992.

German

de la Mare, W. *The turnip.* Illus. by K. Hawkes. Boston: David R. Godine, 1992.

Edens, C. (Select.). *Hansel and Gretel.* La Jolla, CA: Green Tiger Press, 1990.

Esterl, A. *The fine round cake.* Illus. by A. Dugin & O. Dugina. New York: Four Winds Press, 1991.

Grimm, J. & W. *Snow White and the seven dwarfs: A tale from the Brothers Grimm.* Trans. by R. Jarrell; illus. by N. E. Burkert. New York: Farrar, Straus & Giroux, 1972.

Grimm, J. & W. *Grimm's fairy tales: Twenty stories.* Illus. by A. Rackham. New York: Viking, 1973.

Grimm, J. & W. *Grimm's tales for young and old.* Garden City, NY: Doubleday, 1977.

Grimm, J. & W. *The sleeping beauty, from the Brothers Grimm.* Illus. by T. S. Hyman. Boston: Little Brown, 1977.

Grimm, J. & W. *The fisherman and his wife.* Trans. by R. Jarrell; Illus. by M. Zemach. New York: Farrar, Straus & Giroux, 1980.

Grimm, J. & W. *Rapunzel.* Adapt. by B. Rogasky; illus. by T. S. Hyman. New York: Holiday House, 1982.

Grimm, J. & W. *Little Red Riding Hood.* Adapt. & illus. by T. S. Hyman. New York: Holiday House, 1983.

Grimm, J. & W. *Rumplestiltskin.* Adapt. & illus. by P. O. Zelinsky. New York: E. P. Dutton, 1986.

Grimm, J. & W. *The water of life.* Retold by B. Rogasky; illus. by T. S. Hyman. New York: Holiday House, 1986.

Grimm, J. & W. *Red Riding Hood.* Adapt. & illus. by J. Marshall. New York: Dial, 1987.

Grimm, J. & W. *The Bremen town musicians.* Illus. by J. Stevens. New York: Holiday House, 1992.

Grimm, J. & W. *Hansel and Gretel.* Illus. by L. Zwerger. Saxonville, MA: Picture Book Studio, 1992.

Grimm, J. & W. *Snow White and Rose Red.* Illus. by G. Spirin. New York: Philomel Books, 1992.

Poole, J. *Snow White.* Illus. by A. Barett. New York: Alfred A. Knopf, 1991.

Sage, A. *Rumpelstiltskin.* Illus. by G. Sprin. New York: Dial, 1991.

San Souci, R. D. *The white cat.* Illus. by G. Spirin. New York: Orchard Books, 1990.

Zemach, M. (Adapt.). *The three wishes: An old story.* Illus. by the adapter. New York: Farrar, Straus & Giroux, 1986.

Zwerger, L. (Illus.). *The merry pranks of till eulenspiegel.* Saxonville, MA: Picture Book Studio, 1990.

Greek

Ash, R. & Higton, B. (Comp.). *Aesop's fables: A classic illustrated edition.* San Francisco: Chronicle Books, 1990.

Clark, M. *The best of Aesop's fables.* Illus. by C. Voake. Boston: Joy Street Books, 1990.

Connolly, P. *The legend of Odysseus.* Illus. by the author. New York: Oxford University Press, 1986.

d'Aulaire, I., & d'Aulaire, E. *d'Aulaires' book of Greek myths.* Garden City, NY: Doubleday, 1962.

Evslin, B. *The chimaera.* New York: Chelsea House, 1988.

Evslin, B. *The hydra: Monsters of mythology.* New York: Chelsea House, 1989.

Fisher, L. E. *Theseus and the minotaur.* Illus. by the author. New York: Holiday House, 1988.

Fisher, L. E. *Cyclops.* Illus. by the author. New York: Holiday House, 1991.

Gibson, M. *Gods, men and monsters from the Greek myths.* Illus. by G. Caselli. New York: Peter Bedrick Books, 1991.

Hodges, M. *St. Jerome and the lion.* Illus. by B. Moser. New York: Orchard Books, 1991.

Hooks, W. H. *Feed me! An Aesop fable.* Illus. by D. Cushman. New York: Bantam Little Rooster, 1992.

Hutton, W. *The Trojan horse.* Illus. by the author. New York: Margaret K. McElderry Books, 1992.

Low, A. *The Macmillan book of Greek gods and heroes.* Illus. by A. Stewart. New York: Macmillan, 1985.

Marshall, L. *The girl who changed her fate.* Illus. by the author. New York: Atheneum, 1992.

Martin, C. *The race of the golden apples.* Illus. by L. & D. Dillon. New York: Dial, 1991.

McClintock, B. *Animal fables from Aesop.* Boston: David R. Godine, 1991.

Mikolaycak, C. *Orpheus.* Illus. by the author. Orlando, FL: Harcourt Brace Jovanovich, 1992.

Paxton, T. *Belling the cat and other Aesop's fables.* Illus. by R. Rayevsky. New York: William Morrow, 1990.

Paxton, T. *Androcles and the lion and other aesop's fables.* Illus. by R. Rayevsky. New York: William Morrow, 1991.

Simons, J., & Simons, S. *Why dolphins call: A story of Dionysus.* Illus. by D. Winograd. Englewood Cliffs, NJ: Silver Press, 1991.

Simons, J., & Simons, S. *Why spiders spin: a story of Arachne.* Illus. by D. Winograd. Englewood Cliffs, NJ: Silver Press, 1991.

Watts, B. *The wind and the sun: An Aesop fable.* Illus. by the author. New York: North-South Books, 1992.

Williams, M. *Greeks myths for young children.* Cambridge, MA: Candlewick Press, 1992.

Yolen, J. *Wings.* Illus. by D. Nolan. Orlando, FL: Harcourt Brace Jovanovich, 1991.

Irish

Danaher, K. *Folktales of the Irish countryside*. Illus. by H. Berson. Port Washington, NY: White, 1970.

Day, D. *The swan children*. Illus. by R. Evans. Nashville: Ideals Publishing, 1991.

dePaola, T. *Jamie O'Rourke and the big potato*. Illus. by the author. New York: G. P. Putnam's Sons, 1992.

Latimer, J. *The Irish piper*. Illus. by J. O'Brien. New York: Charles Scribner's Sons, 1991.

O'Shea, P. (Adapt.). *Finn MacCool and the small man of Deeds*. Illus. by S. Lavis. New York: Holiday House, 1987.

Shute, L. *Clever Tom and the leprechaun*. Illus. by the author. New York: Lothrop, Lee & Shepard Books, 1988.

Italian

Calvino, I. (Comp.). *Italian folktales*. Trans. by G. Martin. Orlando, FL: Harcourt Brace Jovanovich, 1980.

dePaola, T. (Adapt.). *Strega nona: An old tale retold*. Illus. by the adapter. New York: Prentice Hall, 1975.

dePaola, T. (Adapt.). *The legend of old Befana*. Illus. by the adapter. Orlando, FL: Harcourt Brace Jovanovich, 1980.

dePaola, T. *The prince of the Dolomites*. Illus. by the author. Orlando, FL: Harcourt Brace Jovanovich 1980.

dePaola, T. *The mysterious giant of Barletta*. Illus. by the author. Orlando, FL: Harcourt Brace Jovanovich, 1988.

Manson, C. *The crab prince: An entertainment for children*. Illus. by the author. New York: Henry Holt, 1991.

Plume, I. *The Christmas wish*. Illus. by the author. Westport, CT: Hyperion Press, 1991.

Usher, K. *Heroes, gods, and emperors from Roman mythology*. Illus. by J. Sibbick. New York: Peter Bedrick Books, 1992.

Polish

Haviland, V. (Adapt.). *Favorite fairy tales told in Poland*. Illus. by F. Hoffmann. Boston: Little, Brown, 1963.

Porazinska, J. *The enchanted book: A tale from Krakow*. Illus. by J. Brett. Orlando, FL: Harcourt Brace Jovanovich, 1987.

Russian

Afanasyev, A. N. *Russian folk tales*. Illus. by I. Bilibin; trans. by R. Chandler. New York: Shambhala/Random, 1980.

Afanasyev, A. N. *The fool and the fish*. Illus. by G. Spirin. New York: Dial, 1990.

Afanasyev, A. N. *Salt: A Russian folktale*. Illus. by Plume. Westport, CT: Hyperion Books Press, 1992.

Aksakov, S. *The scarlet flower*. Illus. by B. Diodorov. Orlando, FL: Harcourt Brace Jovanovich, 1992.

Cech, J. *First snow, magic snow*. Illus. by S. McGinley-Nally. New York: Four Winds Press, 1992.

Gal, L. *Prince Ivan and the firebird*. Willowdale, ON, Canada: Firefly Books, 1992.

Ginsburg, M. *Three rolls and one doughnut*. Illus. by A. Lobel. New York: Dial, 1970.

Hogrogian, N. *The cat who loved to sing*. Illus. by the author. New York: Alfred A. Knopf, 1988.

Kimmel, E. A. *Bearhead: A Russian folktale*. Illus. by C. Mikolaycak. New York: Holiday House, 1991.

Kimmel, E. A. *Baba Yaga: A Russian folktale*. Illus. by M. Lloyd. New York: Holiday House, 1991.

Mendelson, S. T. *Stupid Emilien*. Illus. by the author. New York: Stewart, Tabor & Chang, 1991.

Mikolaycak, C. (Adapt.). *Baboushka*. Illus. by the author. New York: Holiday House: 1984.

Ransome, A. (Adapt.). *The fool of the world and the flying ship: A russian tale*. Illus. by U. Shulevitz. New York: Farrar, Straus & Giroux, 1968.

San Souci, R. D. *The tsar's promise: A Russian tale*. Illus. by L. Mills. New York: Philomel Books, 1992.

Sherman, J. *Vassilisa the wise*. Illus. by D. San Souci. Orlando, FL: Harcourt Brace Jovanovich, 1988.

Tripp, W. *The tale of a pig: A Caucasian folktale*. Illus. by the author. New York: McGraw-Hill, 1970.

Winthrop, E. *Vasilissa the beautiful*. Illus. by A. Koshkin. New York: HarperCollins, 1991.

Scandinavian

Arnold, C. *The terrible hodag*. Illus. by L. Davis. Orlando, FL: Harcourt Brace Jovanovich, 1989.

Atwell, D. L. *The day Hans got his way: A Norwegian folktale*. Illus. by D. Atwell. Boston: Houghton Mifflin, 1992.

Barth, E. (Adapt.). *Balder and the mistletoe*. Illus. by R. Cuffari. New York: Clarion Books, 1979.

Bason, L. *Those foolish molboes!* Illus. by M. Tomes. New York: Coward-McCann, 1977.

Daly, K. N. *Norse mythology A to Z: A young reader's companion*. New York: Facts on File, 1991.

Hague, M. & Hague, K. *The man who kept house*. Illus. by M. Hague. Orlando, FL: Harcourt Brace Jovanovich, 1992.

Stevens, J. *The three billy goats gruff*. Illus. by the author. Orlando, FL: Harcourt Brace Jovanovich, 1990.

Willard, N. *East of the sun and west of the moon*. Illus. B. Moser. Orlando, FL: Harcourt Brace Jovanovich, 1991.

Spanish

Duff, M. (Adapt.). *The princess and the pumpkin*. Illus. by C. Stock. New York: Macmillan, 1980.

Haviland, V. (Adapt.). *Favorite fairy tales told in Spain*. Illus. by B. Cooney. Boston: Little, Brown, 1963.

Swiss

Early, M. *William Tell*. New York: Harry N. Abrams, 1991.

Muller-Guggenbuhl, F. *Swiss-Alpine folk-tales*. Trans. by K. Potts; Illus. by J. Kiddell-Monroe. New York: Walck, 1958.

Stone, M. *The singing fir tree: A Swiss folktale*. Illus. by B. Root. New York: Putnam/Whitebird, 1992.

Middle Eastern

Arabian

Al-Saleh, K. *Fabled cities, princes and jinn from Arab myths and legends*. Illus. by R. N. Salim. New York: Schocken Books, 1985.

Colum, P. *The Arabian nights: Tales of wonder and magnificence.* Illus. by L. Ward. New York: Macmillan, 1964.

Lang, A. *Arabian nights.* Illus. by V. Bock. New York: David McKay, 1946.

Lang, A. (Adapt.). *Aladdin and the wonderful lamp.* Illus. by E. Le Cain. New York: Viking, 1981.

Mayer, M. (Adapt.). *Aladdin and the Enchanted lamp.* Illus. by G. McDermott. New York: Macmillan, 1985.

Travers, P. L. *Two pairs of shoes.* Illus. by L. & D. Dillon. New York: Viking, 1980.

Jewish/Yiddish/Israeli

Geras, A. *My grandmother's stories: A collection of Jewish folk tales.* Illus. by J. Jordan. New York: Alfred A. Knopf, 1990.

Hirsh, M. (Adapt.). *Could anything be worse?* Illus. by the author. New York: Holiday House, 1974.

Kimmel, E. A. *The spotted pony: A collection of Hanukkah stories.* Illus. by L. E. Fisher. New York: Holiday House, 1992.

Ludwig, W. *Old Noah's elephants: an Israeli folktale.* Illus. by the author. New York: Putnam/Whitebird, 1991.

Patterson, J. *Angels, prophets, rabbis and kings from the stories of the Jewish people.* Illus. by C. Bushe. New York: Peter Bedrick Books, 1991.

Sanfield, S. *The feather merchants and other tales of the fools of chelm.* Illus. by M. Magaril. New York: Orchard/Jackson, 1991.

Schwartz, H., & Rush, B. *The diamond tree: Jewish tales from around the world.* Illus. by U. Shulevitz. New York: HarperCollins, 1991.

Schwartz, H., & Rush, B. *The sabbath lion: A Jewish folktale from Algeria.* Illus. by S. Fieser. New York: HarperCollins, 1992.

Singer, I. B. *When Shlemiel went to Warsaw: And other stories.* Trans. by the author & E. Shub; Illus. by M. Zemach. New York: Farrar, Straus & Giroux, 1968.

Zemach, H., & Zemach, M. *A penny a look: An old story.* New York: Farrar, Straus & Giroux, Farrar, 1971.

Zemach, M. *It could always be worse.* New York: Farrar, Straus & Giroux, 1976.

The Americas

African-American

Bryan, A. *The dancing granny.* New York: Atheneum, 1977.

Bryan, A. *Turtle knows your name.* New York: Atheneum, 1985.

Hamilton, V. *The people could fly: American black folktales.* Illus. by L. & D. Dillon. New York: Alfred A. Knopf, 1985.

Hamilton, V. *The dark way: Stories from the spirit world.* Illus. by L. Davis. Orlando, FL: Harcourt Brace Jovanovich, 1990.

Harris, J. *Jump! The adventures of Brer Rabbit.* Adapt. by V. D. Parks & M. Jones; Illus. by B. Moser. Orlando, FL: Harcourt Brace Jovanovich, 1986.

Harris, J. C. *Jump again: More adventures of Brer Rabbit.* Adapt. by V. D. Parks; illus. by B. Moser. Orlando, FL: Harcourt Brace Jovanovich, 1987.

Harris, J. C. *Jump on over! The adventures of Brer Rabbit and his family.* Adapt. by V. D. Parks; illus. by B. Moser. Orlando, FL: Harcourt Brace Jovanovich, 1989.

Hooks, W. H. *The ballad of Belle Dorcas.* Illus. by B. Pinkney. New York: Alfred A. Knopf, 1990.

Jaquith, P. *Bo rabbit smart for true: Folktales from the Gullah.* Illus. by E. Young. New York: Philomel Books, 1981.

Joseph, L. *A wave in her pocket: Stories from Trinidad.* Illus. by B. Pinkney. New York: Clarion Books, 1991.

Larungu, R. *Myths and legends from Ghana for African-American cultures.* Mogadore, OH: Telcraft Books, 1992.

Lester, J. (Retell.). *The tales of Uncle Remus: The adventures of Brer Rabbit.* Illus. by Jerry Pinkney. New York: Dial, 1987.

Lester, J. (Retell.). *More tales of Uncle Remus: Further adventures of Brer Rabbit, his friends, enemies, and others.* Illus. by J. Pinkney. New York: Dial, 1988.

Lester, J. (Retell.). *Further tales of Uncle Remus: The misadventures of Brer Rabbit, Brer Fox, Brer Wolf, the Doodang, and other creatures.* Illus. by J. Pinkney. New York: Dial, 1990.

Lyons, M. *Raw head, bloody bones: African-American tales of the supernatural.* New York: Charles Scribner's Sons, 1991.

Michels, B., White, B. *Apples on a stick: The folklore of black children.* Illus. by J. Pinkney. New York: Coward-McCann, 1983.

Sanfield, S. *The adventures of High John: The conqueror.* Illus. by J. Ward. New York: Orchard Books, 1989.

San Souci, R. *The boy and the ghost.* Illus. by J. B. Pinkney, New York: Simon & Schuster, 1989.

San Souci, R. D. *The talking eggs.* Illus. by J. Pinkney. New York: Dial, 1989.

Wahl, J. *Tailyop!* Illus. by W. Clay. New York: Henry Holt, 1991.

Wahl, J. *Little eight John.* Illus. W. Clay. New York: Lodestar, 1992.

Canadian

Bareau, M. *The golden phoenix and other French-Canadian fairy tales.* Retold by M. Hornyansky; Illus. by A. Price. New York: Walck, 1958.

Carlson, N. S. *The talking cat and other stories of French Canada.* Illus. by R. Duvoisin. New York: Harper, 1952.

Martin, E. (Adapt.). *Tales of the far north.* Illus. by L. Gal. New York: Dial, 1986.

Native American and Inuit

Ahenakaw, F. *How the birch tree got its stripes: A Cree story for children.* Illus. by G. Littlechild. Saskatoon, SK, Canada: Fifth House, 1988.

Ahenakaw, F. *How the mouse got brown teeth: A Cree story for children.* Illus. by G. Littlechild. Saskatoon, SK, Canada: Fifth House, 1988.

Ata, T. *Baby rattlesnake.* Illus. by V. Reisberg. Chicago: Childrens Press, 1990.

Baker, B. *And me, coyote!* Illus. by M. Horvath. New York: Macmillan, 1982.

Begay, S. *Ma'ii and cousin horned toad: A traditional Navajo story.* Illus. by the author. New York: Scholastic, 1992.

Belting, N. M. *Moon was tired of walking on air.* Illus. by W. Hillenbrand. Boston: Houghton Mifflin: 1992.

Bierhorst, J. *The mythology of North America.* New York: William Morrow, 1985.

Bierhorst, J. *Doctor coyote: A Native American Aesop's fables.* Illus. by W. Watson. New York: Macmillan, 1987.

Bierhorst, J. *The naked bear: Folktales of the Iroquois.* New York: William Morrow, 1987.

Carey, V. S. *Quail song: A Pueblo Indian folktale.* Illus. by I. Barnett. New York: Putnam-Whitebird, 1990.

Coatsworth, E. & Coatsworth, D. *The adventures on Nanabush: Ojibway Indian stories.* Illus. by F. Kagige. New York: Atheneum, 1980.

Cohen, C. L. *The mud pony: A traditional Skidi Pawnee tale.* Illus. by S. Begay. New York: Scholastic, 1988.

Courlander, H. *People of the short blue corn: Tales and legends of the Hopi Indians.* Illus. by E. Arno. Orlando, FL: Harcourt Brace Jovanovich, 1970.

DeArmond, D. *The boy who found the light.* San Francisco: Sierra Club Books, 1990.

dePaola, T. *The legend of the bluebonnet: An old tale of Texas.* Illus. by the author. New York: G. P. Putnam's Sons, 1983.

deWit, D. *The talking stone: An anthology of Native American tales and legends.* New York: Greenwillow Books, 1979.

Elston, G. (Comp.). *Giving: Ojibwa stories and legends from the children of Curve Lake.* Lakefield, ON, Canada: Waapoone Publishing, 1985.

Grinnell, G. B. *The whistling skeleton: American Indian tales of the supernatural,* Ed. by J. Bierhorst; illus. by R. A. Parker. New York: Four Winds Press, 1982.

Goble, P. *Buffalo woman.* Illus. by the author. New York: Bradbury Press, 1984.

Goble, P. *Iktomi and the berries.* Illus. by the author. New York: Orchard Books, 1989.

Goble, P. *Dream wolf.* New York: Bradbury Press, 1990.

Goble, P. *Iktomi and the ducks: A Plains Indian story.* Illus. by the author. New York: Orchard Books, 1990.

Goble, P. *Iktomi and the buffalo skull.* Illus. by the author. New York: Orchard Books, 1991.

Goble, P. *Love flute.* Illus. by the author: New York: Bradbury Press, 1992.

Harris, C. *The trouble with princesses.* Illus. by D. Tait. New York: Atheneum, 1980.

Hayes, J. (Adapt.). *Coyote and Native American folk tales.* Illus. by L. Jelinek. Santa Fe, NM: Mariposa, 1990.

Highwater, J. *Anpao: An American Indian odyssey.* Philadelphia: J. B. Lippincott, 1977.

Hinton, L. (Trans.). *Ishi's tale of lizard.* Illus. by S. L. Roth. New York: Farrar, Straus & Giroux, 1992.

Kerven, R. *Earth magic, sky magic: North American Indian stories.* New York: Cambridge University Press, 1991.

Lacapa, M. *Antelope woman: An Apache folktale.* Illus. by the author. Flagstaff, AZ: Northland Publishing, 1992.

Mayo, G. W. *Star tales: North American Indian stories about stars.* New York: Walker, 1987.

Mayo, G. W. *Earthmaker's tales: North American Indian stories about earth happenings.* Walker, 1989.

McDermott, G. (Adapt.). *Arrow to the sun: A Pueblo Indian tale.* Illus. by the author. New York: Viking, 1974.

McDermott, G. *Papagayo the mischief maker.* Illus. by the author. Orlando, FL: Harcourt Brace Jovanovich, 1992.

McDermott, G. *Raven: A trickster tale from the Pacific Northwest.* Illus. by the author. Orlando, FL: Harcourt Brace Jovanovich, 1993.

Monroe, J. G., & Williamson, R. A. *They dance in the sky: Native American star myths.* Illus. by E. Stewart Boston: Houghton Mifflin, 1987.

Munsch, R. & Kusugak, M. *A promise is a promise.* Illus. by V. Krykorka. Willowdale, ON, Canada: Annick Press, 1988.

Roth, S. *The story of light.* New York: William Morrow, 1990.

Rucki, A. *Turkey's gift to the people.* Illus. by the author. Flagstaff, AZ: Northland Publishing, 1992.

Schecter, E. *The warrior maiden: A Hopi legend.* Illus. by L. Kelly. New York: Bantam Little Rooster, 1992.

Scheer, G. F. *Cherokee animal tales.* New York: Holiday House, 1966.

Shetterly, S. H. *Raven's light: A myth from the people of the Northwest coast.* Illus. by R. Shetterly. New York: Atheneum, 1991.

Steptoe, J. (Adapt.). *The story of the jumping mouse: A Native American legend.* Illus. by the adapter. New York: Lothrop, Lee & Shepard Books, 1984.

Tanaka, B. *The chase: A Kutenai Indian tale.* Illus. by M. Gay. New York: Crown Publishers, 1991.

Taylor, C. J. *How Two-Feather was saved from loneliness: An Abenaki legend.* Montreal, PQ, Canada: Tundra Books, 1990.

Te A. *Baby rattlesnake.* Adapt. by L. Moroney; Illus. by V. Reisberg. San Francisco: Children's Book Press, 1989.

Troughton, J. *How the seasons came: A North American Indian folk tale.* Illus. by the author. New York: Peter Bedrick Books, 1992.

Van Laan, N. (Retell.). *Rainbow crow.* Illus. by B. Vidal. New York: Alfred A. Knopf, 1989.

Wood, M. *Spirits, heroes, and hunters from North American Indian mythology.* Illus. by J. Sibbick & B. Donohoe. New York: Peter Bedrick Books, 1992.

Yolen, J. *Sky dogs.* Illus. by B. Moser. Orlando, FL: Harcourt Brace Jovanovich, 1990.

Mexican/Latin American/ South American

Aardema, V. *Borreguita and the coyote: A tale from Ayutla, Mexico.* Illus. by P. Mathers. New York: Alfred A. Knopf, 1991.

Aardema, V. *The riddle of the drum: A tale from Tizapan, Mexico.* Illus. by T. Chen, New York: Four Winds Press, 1979.

Aardema, V. *Pedro and the padre: A tale from Jalisco, Mexico.* Illus. by F. Henstra. New York: Dial, 1991.

Alexander, E. *Llama and the great flood.* New York: Thomas Y. Crowell, 1989.

Belpre, P. *Perez and Martina: A Puerto Rican folktale.* Illus. by C. Sanchez. New York: Viking, 1991.

Bierhorst, J. (Ed.). *The hungry woman: Myths and legends of the Aztecs.* Illus. by Aztec artists of the 16th century. New York: William Morrow, 1984.

Bierhorst, J. *The mythology of South America.* New York: William Morrow, 1988.

Bierhorst, J. *The mythology of Mexico and Central America.* New York: William Morrow, 1990.

Brenner, A. *The boy who could do anything and other Mexican folk tales.* Illus. by J. Charlot. Hamden, CT: Linnet Books, 1992.

Ehlert, L. *Moon rope: A Peruvian folktale/Un lazo a la luna: Una leyenda peruana.* Trans. by A. Prince. Orlando, FL: Harcourt Brace Jovanovich, 1992.

Flora, *Feathers like a rainbow: An Amazon Indian tale.* New York: Harper & Row, 1989.

Lattimore, D. *The flame of peace: A tale of the Aztecs.* Illus. by the author. New York: HarperCollins, 1987.

Lattimore, D. *Why there is no arguing in heaven: A Mayan myth.* New York: Harper & Row, 1989.

Lewis, R. *All of you was singing.* Illus. by E. Young. New York: Atheneum, 1991.

Rohmer, H. *The legend of Food Mountain/La montaña de alimento.* Illus. by G. Carrillo. San Francisco: Children's Book Press, 1982.

Rohmer, H. (Ed.). *The invisible hunters/Los cazadores invisbles.* Illus. by J. Sam. San Francisco: Children's Book Press, 1987.

Rohmer, H., & Wilson, D. *Mother scorpion country/La tierra de la madre escorpion: A legend from the Miskito Indians of Nicaragua.* Illus. by V. Stearns. San Francisco: Children's Book Press, 1987.

Rohmer, H. *Uncle Nacho's hat.* Illus. by V. Reisberg. San Francisco: Children's Book Press, 1989.

Stiles, M. B. *James the vine puller: A Brazilian folktale.* Illus. by L. Thomas. Minneapolis: Carolrhoda Books, 1992.

Volkmer, J. A. *Song of the chirimia: A Guatemalan folktale.* Illus. by the author. Minneapolis: Carolrhoda Books, 1990.

Wisniewski, D. *Rain player.* Illus. by the author. New York: Clarion Books, 1991.

Tall Tales

Kellogg, S. (Adapt.). *Paul Bunyan.* Illus. by the adapter. New York: William Morrow, 1984.

Kellogg, S. (Adapt.). *Pecos Bill.* Illus. by the adapter. New York: William Morrow, 1986.

Kellogg, S. *Johnny Appleseed: A tall tale.* Illus. by the author. New York: William Morrow, 1988.

Kellogg, S. *Mike Fink: A tall tale.* Illus. by the author. New York: William Morrow, 1992.

Osborne, M. P. *American tall tales.* Illus. by M. McCurdy. New York: Alfred Knopf, no date.

San Souci, R. D. *Larger than life: The adventures of American legendary heroes.* Illus. by A. Glass. Garden City, NY: Doubleday, no date.

Schwartz, A. (Comp.). *Kickle snifters and other fearsome critters collected from American folklore.* Illus. by G. Rounds. Philadelphia: J. B. Lippincott, 1976.

Shapiro, I. *Heroes in American Folklore.* Illus. by D. McKay & J. Daugherty. Englewood Cliffs, NJ: Messner, 1962.

Variants of European Tales

Chase, R. *The jack tales.* Illus. by B. Williams, Jr. Boston: Houghton Mifflin, 1943.

Chase, R. (Ed.). *Grandfather tales.* Illus. by B. Williams, Jr. Boston: Houghton Mifflin, 1948.

Davis, D. *Jack always seeks his fortune: Authentic Appalachian jack tales.* Little Rock, AK: August House, 1992.

Goode, D. *The Diane Goode book of American folk tales and songs.* Illus. by the author. New York: E. P. Dutton, 1989.

Haley, G. E. *Mountain jack tales.* Illus. by the author. New York: E. P. Dutton, 1992.

Reneaux, J. J. *Cajun folktales.* Little Rock, AK: August House, 1992.

Index

A

Addams, Jane, 17–18, 140
Africa
  harvest holidays of, 54
  history of, 95–99
  map of, 94
  See also Algeria; Benin; Cameroon,
    Chad; Congo; Côte d'Ivoire;
    Egypt; Ghana; Guinea Bissau;
    Kenya; Madagascar; Malawi;
    Mali; Mauritius; Morocco;
    Mozambique; Nigeria; Réu-
    nion, Senegal; Sierra Leone;
    Songhai; South Africa;
    Sudan; Tanzania; Tunisia;
    Uganda; Zaire; Zambia; Zim-
    babwe
African-American history, 122–27
African National Congress (ANC),
  98–99
AIDS, 41
Algeria, 97
All Fool's Day, 157
Almerlia Frances Howard-Gibbon
  Medal, 60
Amrit, 157
Amundsen, Roald Engebreth, 13
ANC
  See African National Congress
Andersen, Hans Christian, 175–76
  See also Hans Christian Andersen
    Prize
Anderson, Marian, 141
Angelou, Maya, 145
Anglo-Saxons, 87, 210
  See also English language
Anthony, Susan B., 139–40
Apartheid, 97–99
April, 157–77
April Fool's Day, 157, 175
Architecture, 212–15
Argentina, 219, 234, 246
  See also San Martín, José
Armstrong, Louis, 219
Artists, 235–37

B

Asia
  See Burma; China; India; Indonesia;
    Iran; Japan; Korea; Myanmar;
    Philippines; Russia; Samoa;
    Turkey; Western Samoa
Assine, 96
Atomic bomb, 219, 239
August, 239–52
Augustus Caesar, 45, 239
Australia
  and creation accounts, 189
  and food, 246
Australian children's books of the year
  awards, 60
Autumn, 1–63
Autumnal equinox, 1
Aztecs, 10, 52
  calendars of, 14
  harvest festivals of, 54

B

Babylonians
  calendars of, 14
Baisakhi, 77
Balboa, Vasco Nuñez de, 11
Barnett, Ida Wells, 142–43
Bastille Day, 219
Belgium
  new year celebrations in, 78, 219
Benin, 96
Bethune, Mary McLeod, 140
Bolívar, Simón, 233
Bonaparte, Napoleon, 239
Bradley, Anne Dudley, 139
Brazil, 234
Bread, 58–59
Breakfast, 244–49
Buck, Pearl S., 141
Buddhism
  history of, 176–77
  holidays of, 77, 157
Burke, Robert, 13
Burma
  new year celebrations in, 78
Burton, Sir Richard, 13

C

Cabot, John 11, 13
Caldecott Medal, 60
Calendars, 13–16
Cameroon, 110
Canada
  holidays of, 54, 197, 219
Canadian Children's Book of the Year
  Award, 60
Carnegie Medal, 60
Carson, Rachael, 142
Cartier, Jacques, 11
Cather, Willa, 141
Catholicism, 65
Cat's cradle, 195
Celts, 210
  harvest festivals of, 54
Chad, 110
Chase the Dragon, 248
Chaucer, Geoffrey, 179
Chávez, Cesar, 176
Children's book awards, 60–61
Children's Book Week, 60–62
China, 1, 15
  calendars of, 14
  and creation accounts, 189
  and exploration of Americas, 10, 11
  and food, 246
  games of, 248, 250
  holidays in, 54, 78, 157
  and number system, 211
  See also Tiananmen Square massacre
Ching Ming, 157
Christkind, 75, 84
Christmas, 65, 67
  international celebrations of, 73–77
Chung, Connie, 146
Cinco de Mayo (Fifth of May), 179, 193
Civil War, U.S., 219
Clark, William, 11, 239
Cohan, George M., 219
Columbus, Christopher, 10–11, 239
  and Columbus Day, 21
  and effects on Native American
    population, 29–30

and games, 248, 250
  harvest holidays of, 55
  new year celebrations in, 78
Jesus of Nazareth, 73–75
Jewish New Year
  See Rosh Hashanah
Joan of Arc, 112–13
Jones, Mary Harris
  See Mother Jones
Judaism, 1, 174
  calendars of, 15
  harvest festivals of, 53
  history of, 164–65
  See also Holocaust; Passover; Rosh
    Hashanah; Yom Kippur
Julius Caesar, 3
  and Julian calendar, 14, 15, 45, 87,
    133, 199, 219
July, 219–37
June, 199–217

K

Karenga, Maulina, 41–42
Kate Greenaway Medal, 60
Kennedy, Robert F., 199
Kenya, 103
Kepler, Johannes, 84
Kickball, 41
Kilwa, 96
King, Corretta Scott, 60, 61
King, Martin Luther, Jr.
  and holiday, 65, 87
  and social courage, 176
Kingsley, Mary, 13
Kites, 248, 250
Korea
  harvest holidays of, 55
Kristallnacht (Crystal Night; Night of
    Broken Glass), 59–60, 166
Kuramota, June Okida, 146
Kwanzaa, 67, 75, 80–81

L

Labor Day, 18
Lana, Francesco de, 232
La Salle, René-Robert Cavelier, 11
Latin, 3
Latin America
  See Haiti; Mexico
Laura Ingalls Wilder Award,
    60, 61
Lazarus, Emma, 111
League of Nations, 111–12
Leap years, 117
LeFlesch, Susan, 140
Lenni Lenape, 32
Lent, 65, 131
Lewis, Meriwether, 11, 239

Libya, 97
Lincoln, Abraham
  and holiday, 65, 117
Low, Juliette Gordon, 142

M

Madagascar
  and new year celebrations in, 78
Magi, 84
Malawi, 97
Mali, 10, 11, 95–96
Mandela, Nelson, 98
Maori, 129
Marbles
  in Central America, 251
  in United States, 251–52
March, 133–54
Mardi Gras, 65
Marshall, Thurgood, 127–28
Martinez, Maria Montoya, 144
Maryland, 133
Masai, 97
Mauritius, 97
May, 179–95
Mayas, 10, 52
  calendars of, 15
  harvest festivals of, 54
May Day, 179
Mayflower, 30
Mead, Margaret, 143
Meir, Golda, 141
Mexico
  New Year celebrations in, 79
  See also Aztecs; Day of the Dead
Mildred Batchleder Award, 60, 61
Monomotapa, 96
Morharram, 77–78
Morocco, 97
Mother Jones, 142
Mother's Day, 191–92
Mozambique, 103
Muhammed, 15
Muslims
  See Islam
Myanmar, 110

N

Names, 152
National Association for the Advance-
    ment of Colored People
    (NAACP), 127
National Dessert Month, 42
National Hispanic Heritage Week, 19
National Rice Month, 17
Native Americans, 1, 28–41, 78
  and stereotyping, 28, 37, 40
  and Thanksgiving, 51–52
  and tribes of California and the
    Pacific Northwest, 35–36

  and tribes of the Great Plains,
    33–34
  and tribes of the Northeast and
    Great Lakes, 30–32
  and tribes of the North Lands of the
    Arctic and Subarctic, 36–37
  and tribes of the Southeast, 32–33
  and tribes of the Southwest, Great
    Basin and Plateau, 34–35
Nauru, 110
Nehru, Jawaharal, 176
Netherlands
  See Holland
Nevelson, Louise, 143
Newbery, John, 81
Newbery Medal, 60, 81
Newton, Sir Isaac, 84
New Year celebrations, 77–80, 87
  in Africa, 78
  in Asia, 78
  in Europe, 78–79
  in Latin America, 79
  in the Middle East, 79–80
New Zealand, 128–29, 246
Nguzo Saba, 81
Nigeria, 21, 103, 245
Niña, 29
Norsemen, 87
  See also Vikings
Northern Europe
  harvest holidays of, 55
Norway, 245
November, 45–63
Numerals, 211–12
Nyassaland
  See Malawi

O

Oakley, Annie, 239
October, 21–43
Olmecs, 10
Olympics, 235
One-foot-high kick, 250–51
Oral history, 204–10
Orellana, Francisco de, 13
Ortega, Katherine Davolos, 145
Otedama, 250

P

Papa Noel, 84
Parents of their countries, 233–35
Parks, Rosa, 122–25, 144
Passover, 131, 133, 157
Pasteur, Louis, 84
Peary, Robert, 13
Père Noel, 84
Perrault, Charles, 127
Peru, 234
Philippines, 219